The Covenant of Grace

by

John Colquhoun, D. D.
Minister of the Gospel, Leith

"I have made a covenant with My chosen." Psalm 89:3

He will ever be mindful of His covenant." Psalm 111:5

The secret of the Lord is with them that fear Him; and He will show them His covenant." Psalm 25:14

Edited by Dr. Don Kistler

The Northampton Press
". . .for instruction in righteousness. . ."

The Northampton Press
A division of Don Kistler Ministries, Inc.
P.O. Box 781135, Orlando, FL 32878-1135
www.northamptonpress.org

*

The Covenant of Grace was published in Edinburgh, Scotland in 1818. This Northampton Press edition, in which spelling, grammar, and formatting changes have been made, is ©2020 by Don Kistler.

*

ISBN 978-1-7321550-4-6

*

Library of Congress Control Number: 2020930291

CONTENTS

Foreword by Dr. Sinclair Ferguson   vi

The Dedication   xi

The Introduction   xiv

Chapter 1   1
The Parties Contracting in the Covenant of Grace

Chapter 2   48
The Making of the Covenant of Grace

Chapter 3   97
The Conditions of the Covenant of Grace

Chapter 4   147
    The Promises of the Covenant of Grace

Chapter 5   253
    The Administration of the Covenant of Grace

Chapter 6   339
    The Dispensations of the Covenant of Grace

Chapter 7   361
    The Way in Which a Sinner Enters Into the Covenant of Grace So as to Become Personally Interested in It

Chapter 8   422
    Evidences of One's Being Personally Instated in the Covenant of Grace

Chapter 9   456
    The Seals of the Covenant of Grace

Contents

Chapter 10   484
    The Properties of the Covenant of Grace

Chapter 11   500
    The Points of Difference Between the Covenant of Grace and the Covenant of Works

Chapter 12   507
    The Conclusion

Foreword
To John Colquhoun's *The Covenant of Grace*
by Sinclair Ferguson

The name of John Colquhoun (1748-1825) is relatively little-known today, even among Christians who can pronounce his surname (-quhoun is pronounced "hoon"). He is never feted as a spiritual guru, or as an authority to whom people appeal either to settle an issue, or to display their own enviable knowledge; indeed, he is rarely quoted. But his spiritual stature and theological insight made him a leader among evangelicals in late eighteenth and early nineteenth century Scotland. And of his theological acumen and pastoral wisdom these pages should leave contemporary Christians in no doubt. But more than that, this particular work on the Covenant of Grace, read carefully, thoughtfully, and not least prayerfully, has the potential to serve as spiritual deep vein therapy for us all. It will help to clear up some of the clots that have developed in our thinking, dissolve obstacles in our minds (as Colquhoun specifically seeks to do) and give us a fresh and refreshing perspective on God, on the gospel, and on the Christian life.

But, first, a word about Colquhoun himself. He was born in Scotland in 1748 into a modest home and family in the village of Luss, halfway up the west side of Loch Lomond, some thirty miles from Glasgow. It was the year that David Hume published his *Enquiry Concerning Human Understanding* (a book whose argument Immanuel Kant said "awoke me from my dogmatic slumber"). Sometime later John Colquhoun would also be awakened from a slumber, but the voice he heard was that of God calling him to faith in Christ. He came to a living faith in his teens under the impact of the Shorter Catechism's answer to the question "What is effectual calling?": "Effectual calling is the work of God's Spirit whereby, convincing us of our sin and misery, enlightening our minds in the knowledge of Christ, and renewing our wills, He doth persuade and enable us to embrace Jesus Christ, freely offered to us in the gospel." In many ways these words became an important substratum in his later ministry and especially in his writings.

Next to his Bible (of which he had a prodigious, Puritan-like knowledge) the greatest influence on Colquhoun's life and ministry was a classic work in Scottish pastoral theology, *Human Nature in its Fourfold State* by the "Marrow Man" Thomas Boston. Whereas Hume's *Enquiry* was a reworking of his little appreciated *Treatise on Human Nature*, Boston's work on the same theme has often been used by the Spirit of God to raise its readers from the slumber of spiritual death. How the young John first encountered it we do not know. But he lived in a time when if a Christian in Scotland had two or three books in addition to the Bible, then Boston's *Fourfold State* was probably one of them. Colquhoun probably heard older Christians speak of it and perhaps had even read their copies. He determined to have his own copy, and some time after his conversion he walked the thirty miles from his home in Luss to Glasgow in order to buy the book for himself.

The fingerprints of Thomas Boston were a present influence in everything John Colquhoun would later write. The emphases that had been expounded and defended by the men who had found *The Marrow of Modern Divinity* so stimulating to their thinking about and preaching of the gospel in the decades preceding his birth—the sufficiency of Christ to save all who come to him, the free offer of the gospel, the difference between legal and evangelical repentance, the blessings of assurance—all feature largely in his works. The result was the presence in his ministry of the special "tincture" that a previous generation had earlier noticed in Boston's. Famously, since *The Marrow of Modern Divinity* had been for all practical purposes banned in the

Church of Scotland (ministers were not to recommend it to their congregations), the wily Colquhoun used to tell theology students "Noo, I daurna advise ye to read The Marrow o' Modern Deeveenity, for ye ken the Assembly condemned it. But they didna condemn Tammas Bowston's notes on The Marrow."

Colquhoun studied at the University of Glasgow from 1768-1778, just missing the instruction of Adam Smith (who had held the chair of Moral Philosophy until 1764). In 1781 he was inducted to a chapel of ease charge, St John's, South Leith, and there he remained in harness until his retirement through illness in 1826. He died on 27th November 1827.

One of the most impressive testimonies to the quality of this long ministry has been left to us by Alexander Moody Stuart. He told of a weekend spent in an inn where he noticed two young workmen arriving late on a Saturday night, leaving on Sunday morning and then returning late on Sunday night before rising again very early on Monday morning in order to be at work in Glasgow. These young men were so enriched by Colquhoun's preaching that they had been willing to walk a round trip of one hundred miles from finishing work on Saturday and beginning again on Monday at 6.00 a.m. in order to sit under his ministry.

Several of Colquhoun's works have been reprinted in the past half-century or so. Those include *Sermons on Important Doctrines* and *Saving Faith* (The Northampton Press), *A Treatise on the Law and the Gospel* and *Spiritual Comfort* (Soli Deo Gloria), and *Repentance* (Banner of Truth). But to the best of my knowledge *The Covenant of Grace* now reappears for the first time in almost two centuries. During that time the significance of its central theme—God's covenantal dealings with us—all but disappeared from evangelical preaching and writing. Within fifty years of its writing, Hugh Martin would lament (in his famous work on *The Atonement*) that there was a famine in the land of preaching either on the covenant or shaped by it. He viewed this as a sign of doctrinal and spiritual enervation. If anything, the century that followed saw that trend continue. Writing and speaking on covenantal themes could be found only by those who knew the nooks and crannies of the evangelical world where it had been sustained.

In the second half of the twentieth century an unprophesied awakening of interest in biblical covenants took place. But this was largely in the academic community stimulated by the discovery of, and research into the significance of, covenants in the ancient near east.

At the same time, in a completely unconnected way, an awakening of interest was also taking place (and still is) in many parts of the world in which the importance of covenant theology was being restored to preaching and teaching in many churches. But, that said, there is still a long way to go before evangelical Christians think about the gospel and the Christian life through lenses crafted to a covenantal prescription. In terms of what our contemporaries like to call "the Bible's big picture" the theme of the kingdom of God seems to dominate, at least in most popular literature and preaching. And perhaps it would not be unfair of a Presbyterian to say that an allergy to covenant thought and language exists in some quarters where "kingdom" is viewed as the only legitimate master principle for reading Scripture. None of us should however lose sight of the fact that the "master principle" of Scripture is the Triune God Himself—Father, Son, and Holy Spirit. And this is why—as becomes clear in these pages— the covenant perspective wonderfully weaves together the person and ministry of each Person of the Trinity without losing sight of the unity they share both in being and in doing.

So the republication of Colquhoun's work should be welcomed as a wonderful instrument to recalibrate our theological and spiritual engines. It is well worthy of a place among the books that we "read, mark, learn, and inwardly digest" because it is so Scripture-concentrated, pastorally sensitive, and full of spiritual wisdom.

Given the sheer amount of preaching that marked Colquhoun's life, and the burden of much pastoral visitation, catechizing, and counseling that were the standard features of his ministry, it is a wonder that he was able to produce a book of this length and depth, as well as a steady stream of other works. Each of his publications marks him out as a man and minister of unusual gifts. And here in *The Covenant of Grace* he has given us a work of substance and significance as well as size. The Northampton Press has done a considerable service to the church by making it once again available to contemporary Christians.

Sinclair B Ferguson

Dedication

To the managers and the other members of the congregation of South Leith Chapel, the following treatise is humbly dedicated by their affectionate pastor, the author

My Dear Friends,
    My heart's desire and prayer to God for you is that you may be saved. Bound as I unquestionably am by the most sacred ties to endeavor, by manifestation of the truth, to commend myself to every man's conscience in the sight of God, and especially to watch for your souls as one who must give account, I have composed the following treatise more immediately for your spiritual benefit. Gratitude for the numerous, and continued tokens of your firm attachment both to my ministry and to myself impels me to dedicate it to you. The substance of it I have, with pleasure, and I trust with profit to my own soul, endeavored from time to time, in various points of view, to set before you. To not a few I have reason to believe that the doctrines, admonitions, and exhortations contained in it have, through the influence of the Holy Spirit, been already useful; and I have now put it into your hands so that, by the blessing of the chief Shepherd, you may have a second benefit, and that thus something of mine may remain with you in your several houses after I myself shall have become no longer capable of ministering the gospel among you. Accept then this humble testimony of my sincere gratitude and cordial regard. This, my beloved hearers, is my real design in sending these sheets to the press.

Thirty-six years have now elapsed since you called me to the honorable and delightful work of ministering the glorious gospel among you; and during that time my cares and studies, my labors and prayers, though with much imperfection, have been employed for your salvation. I trust that they have been graciously approved of by God while of their acceptance with you I have such plain evidence that I cannot entertain a doubt of it, which I desire most thankfully to acknowledge.

In a work that professes to be for the most part a compilation, and that, from its very nature, must in a great measure consist of materials selected from the writings of others, it is scarcely necessary to offer an apology for the use that I have made of the labors of my predecessors, and for omitting to insert their names. From the alterations that have been made, especially in the mode of expression, in order to suit the connection, as well as to adapt these materials to the particular purposes for which they are introduced, names could seldom be inserted with propriety. It is, however, proper to acknowledge that the authors to whom much of the doctrinal part of this treatise is indebted for its materials are: [Johannes] Cloppenburg, [Herman] Witsius, [Francis] Turretin, [John] Moor, [Ralph] Erskine, [John] Brown, [James] Hervey, [Adam] Gib, Muirhead, [John] Gill, and [Thomas] Boston. As to the last judicious writer, I freely acknowledge that, so far as he has proceeded, I have followed him so closely as often to adopt for the most part his method, and even his illustrations and proofs. Indeed, the substance of the greater part of his book on the *Covenant of Grace* is extracted, and will be found in the following pages, though the sentiments are expressed in a different manner.

Various modes of expression are used that may, to some of you as well as to others, appear antiquated and unsuitable to the taste of the present age. But they will, on that very account, bear

Dedication

the greater resemblance to the sentiments that they convey. As no tenet is introduced but what evidently appears to me to be founded on the oracles of truth, and to be conformable to our Confession of Faith, so I studied to speak not in the words that man's wisdom teaches, but that the Holy Ghost teaches. Such forms of expression, indeed, have been abused, and they will still, by men of corrupt minds, continue to be so; but this is no good reason why they should be rejected so long as they appear more adapted than others to convey the sentiments clearly and fully.

That the Lord Jesus Christ, with whom is the residue of the Spirit, may render the following treatise the blessed means of convincing and converting sinners, and of increasing the knowledge, confirming the faith, and promoting the holiness of saints; and especially that He may make it highly useful to you, is the sincere and ardent prayer of your affectionate servant in the gospel,

John Colquhoun
Leith, 12th June, 1818

Introduction

By the breach of the covenant of works, Adam, the head and representative of his posterity, precipitated himself from the height of innocence and happiness on which his bountiful Creator had placed him into a horrible abyss of sin and misery. No sooner had he done this than the most melancholy spectacle that ever the sun beheld presented itself to view. He was a creature, but just now the darling of heaven, whom God had created in His own image, and whom He had delighted to honor, was at once reduced to such a sinful, to such a miserable condition, as might render even annihilation itself desirable. He was now sunk and overwhelmed under the guilt, the pollution, the power of sin, and under the awful curse of the broken law that, by his consenting to the divine covenant proposed to him, he himself had acknowledged to be in all points equitable. God, who had been graciously pleased to connect Himself in covenant with him, was, upon man's breach of that covenant, freed from the obligation that otherwise would have lain on Him to secure the happiness of man, and was thenceforth to be regarded as a righteous Judge, bound to vindicate His honor by ensuring the execution of the threatening of the holy law upon him as a sinner. Fallen man had now, therefore, no ground left him ever to expect deliverance from this deplorable condition in the way of strict justice, or of that violated covenant that was the rule of it.

Introduction

The flaming sword that guarded the way of the tree of life turned every way, so that whatever method of attaining life by the law the sinner might choose to adopt he must run upon the point of it.

It is evident then that the transgressor might as well pretend to be able to wrest salvation by force out of the hands of Omnipotence as to seek it by the works of the law. If the fallen race of Adam ever attains life, it cannot possibly be in virtue of the covenant of works, which can speak nothing to a sinner but terror and death. The condition of that covenant has, in consequence of our violation of it, become infinitely more difficult than it was before the covenant was violated. It comprehends now not merely perfect and personal obedience to the precepts, but infinite satisfaction for our criminal violation of the law of that covenant. This is what no sinful, no finite creature can ever be able to give (Romans 3:20; Psalm 49:7). Besides, the sinner under the dominion of the broken law is also under the dominion of sin, which renders him, in the highest degree, loathsome in the sight of an infinitely holy God, and utterly incapable either of conformity to Him or of communion with Him. No sooner had man subjected himself to sin and to the condemning sentence of the law than he was, by that righteous and awful sentence, deprived of any power that he might otherwise have had to regain his liberty. By the curse of the broken law, condemning him to spiritual death, he is sold under sin; and sin, to secure the continuance of its dominion over him, has rendered him his own greatest enemy. His nature is so depraved, so infatuated by sin, that, as he can relish nothing so much as the pleasures of sin, so he is ready to treat that one as his worst enemy who should attempt to deprive him of those imaginary delights (1 Kings 21:20). Hence it is easy to see that it is utterly impossible for sinners of mankind, by any righteousness or strength of their own, ever to free themselves either from the guilt or from the dominion of sin. And, if it is reasonable to judge the greatness of their sinfulness and misery by the infinite difficulty of removing these, how inconceivably great must they be!

As man's misery was entirely owing to his voluntary apostasy from God, and therefore was wholly from himself, it was impossible that his recovery could proceed from the offended majesty of heaven by any necessity of nature. His condemnation was infinitely just; and therefore, though God is naturally as well as necessarily good and merciful, yet it was not necessary that His goodness and mercy should interpose for the redemption of His inveterate enemy who had sought not only His crown, but His very life, and who, for his heinous transgressions, had justly been sentenced by His law to everlasting punishment. As God has justly condemned, so with equal justice He might have executed the tremendous sentence on every transgressor of His righteous law (Psalm 11:5, 6, 7); and as He is infinitely and unchangeably happy in and from Himself, the eternal misery of the sinner could not, in the least degree, have impaired His blessedness (1 Timothy 6:15-16). Goodness, as well as justice, is always essential, and therefore, always necessary to God; but it is far from being necessary that He should extend His goodness to creatures, especially to sinful creatures. The glory of His good and merciful nature is, and from eternity was, necessary to Him; but it was not necessary that He should show forth that glory in the salvation of sinners who deserved eternally to perish. He was infinitely, eternally, and immutably sufficient within Himself; and therefore He stood in no need of manifested glory outside Himself (Genesis 17:1; Acts 17:25). If sinners of mankind, then, are ever to be recovered from their undone condition, their restoration must be wholly ascribed to sovereign, free, and bound-

Introduction xvii

less grace.

Still, however, it cannot be denied that if all the human race had been lost irrecoverably and eternally, the wisdom and goodness of the Lord in creating and sustaining them would not have been so illustriously displayed. To have been seemingly disappointed of His immediate design respecting the whole of mankind could not, as far as we can discern, have afford such a glorious manifestation of His manifold wisdom to the universe; and to have excluded the whole of them from being objects of His special favor could not have occasioned such a bright display of His infinite goodness and of His boundless compassion. He, accordingly, has elected to eternal life a certain number both of angels and of men.

In accomplishing the recovery of the elect of mankind from sin and misery, Jehovah could not, consistently with the honor of His holiness, justice, and faithfulness, have entered into any covenant with themselves as the immediate party. He could not have renewed the first covenant with them. That was a covenant of friendship, but they were enemies; it was a covenant of innocence, but they were guilty sinners; a covenant of works, but they were without strength and could not of themselves either will or do any work that is spiritually good; and a covenant of life, but they were dead in trespasses and sins and could no more perform acceptable obedience than a dead body can perform the functions of a living man.

In consequence of the curse of the law, which is the strength of sin, lying on their conscience, and of the dominion of sin in their heart, they, as well as the rest of mankind, were as unable, while in their natural state, to cease from doing that which is evil as to do acceptably that which is good (1 Corinthians 15:56). Besides, as the whole plan of the covenant of works was of God, His holiness, justice, and faithfulness, as was already observed, were deeply interested in retrieving the injured honor of that covenant. As a just and holy God, He could not forbear to punish so heinous a sin as that by which it was violated; as a faithful God, a God who keeps covenant, He could not dispense with the infliction of that death which was secured by the threatening. Neither could He recede from His original demand of perfect obedience as the settled condition of life.

As God, therefore, could not have renewed the covenant of works with sinners, so neither could He have entered into any other covenant with them as the immediate party. Their ignominious character as transgressors rendered it dishonorable for Him to have any immediate intercourse with them. Besides, they were prisoners, confined under a sentence of death, and for a debt to divine justice of "ten thousand talents," which it was utterly impossible for them ever to discharge. They therefore were, in their own persons, legally as well as morally, incapable of treating with the high and holy one. There could be no other dealings between Jehovah and them, considered as in themselves, than such as are between a righteous judge or avenger and a convicted criminal. A holy God cannot look on sinners without infinite abhorrence, nor without breaking forth against them as a consuming fire (Hebrews 12:29); and they cannot in such a condition approach Him without inevitable destruction. It was necessary, therefore, that if any covenant was ever to be made for the salvation of sinners of mankind, it should be made primarily and immediately with a divine Person who, in the same nature that had sinned, could afford to pay their boundless debt, as stated according to the broken covenant of works.

While the unutterable misery into which all the children of Adam by transgression fell was the occasion of God's making another covenant for the redemption of elect sinners, His own sovereign, distinguishing grace was the cause or source of it.

Introduction

Hence it is usually called "the covenant of grace." It originated from the boundless grace or sovereign good pleasure of God; and ever thing settled in it is, and ever will be "to the praise of the glory of His grace" (Ephesians 1:6). In and by this covenant God has manifested the unfathomable depths of His manifold wisdom, the unsearchable riches of his glorious grace, and the transcendent greatness of His astonishing love far more clearly than if man himself had performed the condition and had been adjudged to eternal life, according to the tenor of the covenant of works. The eternal Father, in the amazing depth of His infinite wisdom, and according to the predetermination of His sovereign will, devised this method of displaying His glory and of manifesting His mercy, that amiable attribute of the divine nature, which could not have shone forth with such transcendent luster if man had not been permitted to render himself miserable.

The covenant of grace for the redemption of sinners of mankind was concerted and entered into between Jehovah the eternal Father and His co-eternal Son as the last Adam, with the approbation of the Holy Spirit, long before it began to be published and offered to them for their consent and acceptance. This directs us to two different views of this august contract: First, as it is established between God and the Mediator; and next, as it is exhibited in the gospel to sinners for their approbation and consent. In the former view, it was made from eternity; in the latter, it was manifested in time; in that view, it is a federal transaction, or covenant properly so called, between Jehovah the Father and His only begotten Son; in this, it is a testamentary deed or disposition.

That the covenant of grace ought to be taken in this twofold view is evident from the terms in sacred Scripture that the Holy Spirit employs to express that covenant.

In the original language of the Old Testament, the word that we translate "covenant" is, according to some, derived from a root that signifies to cut down, or cut off, because in ancient times it was, in making a solemn covenant, usual for the parties contracting to cut beasts for sacrifice in two, and to pass between the parts of them in order to confirm their agreement (Genesis 15:10; Jeremiah 34:18).

According to others, it is more properly derived from a root that signifies "to choose," and is expressive of the nature of a free compact; for in every such compact a choice is made of the parties between whom, of the objects about which, and of the conditions on which, the agreement is made.

Now that word is, in the Old Testament, employed by the sacred writers to express the covenant of grace, considered as a compact, or covenant properly so called, or as made from all eternity between the Father and the Son as the last Adam. In this sense it is used especially in Psalm 89:3, where the eternal Father said, "I have made a covenant with My chosen One."

The same word is also used, and used most frequently, to signify the covenant of grace considered as a testament or testamentary deed, and as manifested to sinners in time. It is employed to express that glorious covenant as published and offered to sinners (Isaiah 55:3), as accepted by the faith of elect sinners (2 Samuel 23:5), as ratified by the sacraments (Genesis 17:10), and by the internal sealing of the Holy Spirit, by which it is rendered effectual (Jeremiah 31:33). In a word, it is often used to express the covenant in its testamentary form as administered by the Lord Jesus Christ to sinners of mankind.

The term in the original language of the New Testament, by which the inspired penmen of it have translated the one above mentioned from the Old, is in like manner used by them sometimes to express the covenant of grace, considered as a proper compact or federal settlement between the Father and the Son as the Representative of His elect. In this sense the Apostle Paul uses it in Hebrews 7:22 when he says, "By so much was Jesus made a Surety of a better covenant."

It appears to me, as it does to many others, that the original word should, in this passage, be translated "covenant" rather than "testament." While there is ordinarily no place in a testament for a surety, it is proper, and often indispensably requisite, that there should be one in a covenant. The term is better translated "covenant" than "testament" in Luke 1:72, Acts 3:25, and Hebrews 8:6, 9, and perhaps in every other passage where it occurs, except in Galatians 3:15 and Hebrews 9:15-17. In the translation of the seventy scholars, the Septuagint, the Hebrew word is translated as "covenant" in all the places where it is to be found except Deuteronomy 9:15 and I Kings 11:11; and the term occurs in the Old Testament above two hundred times. The Septuagint is, in this, confirmed by the inspired penmen of the New Testament. In our language, no word is found so proper to express the meaning of both these terms as the word "covenant."

The same term is also used by the apostle in the same epistle to signify the same covenant as turned into a testament or testamentary disposition. And for this cause, says he, He is the Mediator of the new testament so that, by means of death for the redemption of the transgressions that were under the first testament, they who are called might receive the promise of eternal inheritance. For where a testament is, there must also of necessity be the death of the testator. For a testament is of force after men are dead; otherwise it is of no strength at all, while the testator lives (Hebrews 9:15-17). The blessings of salvation are, in verse 15, called the eternal inheritance because they are not given to believers on condition of the good works that they perform, but are bequeathed to them, in a testament, ratified by the death of the blessed Testator. As the covenant, considered as administered to sinners of mankind, is of a testamentary form in which the Lord Jesus, who purchased all the benefits of it, and who, as the Trustee of it, has them all committed to Him, actually bequeaths them to poor sinners, so it was necessary that by His death He should render it as a testamentary deed, firm and irreversible.

The same word is likewise employed by the Apostle Paul to express at once the idea both of a covenant properly so called, and of a testament. In his epistle to the Galatians he says, "Brethren, I speak after the manner of men; though it be but a man's covenant, yet if it be confirmed, no man disannulleth, or addeth thereto" (Galatians 3:15). Here the term is used in a mixed sense to signify the covenant of grace, considered both as a covenant and as a testament, or as a testamentary covenant. This glorious covenant was made to assume a testamentary form in every dispensation of it, whether as typically confirmed by the death of typical sacrifices, or as actually ratified by the death of Jesus Christ.

Thus, then, it is manifest, from the original terms that are used in sacred Scripture to express the covenant of grace, that this august contract is to be considered on the one hand as a covenant or compact properly so called, and on the other as a testamentary disposition or deed of conveyance. In respect of Christ it is a proper covenant; in regard to us, it is a testament. Considered as made in eternity, it is a covenant, a covenant of redeeming grace; considered as administered to sinners in time, it is a testament, ratified by the death of the adorable Testator.

This divine covenant, accordingly, is the measure and the rule of all Jehovah's dealings with the elect, whether in this life or in that which is to come. In whatever way He comes forth to

Introduction   xxiii

His people, it is always in a covenant-way. The covenant is the center and the bond of all true religion, of all spiritual intercourse with the blessed and adorable Trinity. No emanations of redeeming love, no streams of saving and sanctifying grace, overflow from God to sinners, or return in spiritual exercises or acceptable performances from believers to God, but in the channel of that wonderful covenant. All the privileges and the duties of them who are heirs of God and joint heirs with Christ are comprised in their knowing, accepting, and cleaving to it. What is the gospel, the glorious gospel of the blessed God, but a revelation and an offer to lost sinners of that glorious covenant that the eternal Father made with his chosen One, the Representative of His elect, and which, from everlasting, lay hidden in the infinite depth of the divine counsel?

Surely, then, if it is allowed to be of the utmost importance spiritually to understand the word of grace, it must at least be of equal importance justly and distinctly to know the covenant of grace. Indeed, if any object in the universe can deserve a sinner's most attentive consideration, it is this divine, this excellent covenant. There is no saving knowledge of Christ, and of Him crucified, whom to know is life eternal, without a spiritual discernment of this everlasting covenant, of which He is the blessed Mediator; and no receiving of Him as a Savior without taking hold of it so as cordially to say, "This everlasting covenant, ordered in all things and sure, is all my salvation, and all my desire" (2 Samuel 23:5).

That I may in some degree assist the humble and devout reader to attain more Scriptural and distinct views of that divine contract, I shall, in dependence on the Spirit of truth, endeavor to point out, first, the parties contracting; second, the making of the covenant; in the third place, the conditions; fourth, the promises of it; next, the administration thereof; then, the dispensations of it. Afterwards, I shall consider the way in which a sinner enters personally into the bond of the covenant; next, the marks or evidences of one's being personally instated in it; then, the seals by which it is confirmed with believers; afterwards, the qualities or properties of it; next, I shall how the difference between it and the covenant of works; and then shall conclude the whole by pointing out the duty incumbent on them who are personally interested in that holy covenant.

1

The Parties Contracting in the Covenant of Grace

Seeing a covenant is a free compact upon certain terms expressed, or a contract in which a condition is prescribed, a promise is made, and both ratified by mutual agreement, there must, in the nature of the thing, be parties contracting. In all covenants, whether they are conditional or whether they are covenants merely of free and absolute promise, there must be at least two distinct parties. One may, indeed, purpose or decree with himself without another party; but he cannot stipulate or so much as promise anything without another. The covenant of redeeming grace, which is an eternal covenant, a covenant that never began to be made, could not be established but between parties; and those parties, before creation began, could exist nowhere but in the eternal, the ever-blessed Godhead. It therefore necessarily supposes a plurality of persons in the adorable Godhead.

As that glorious covenant took its rise from the everlasting and equal love of all the three divine Persons, so they all had an equal part concerning the making of it, and each took His respective part in the economy of it. The ever-blessed Trinity, moved by infinitely free love and transcendent mercy, devised the amazing scheme of man's redemption; and each of the divine Persons was to get himself a glorious name by sustaining a distinct, a peculiar office in the accomplishment of the covenant. The eternal Father was to maintain the rights and to consult the glory of the holiness, justice and truth of the Godhead by demanding perfect obedience to His violated law, and full satisfaction for sin to His offended justice. The eternal Son covenanted to answer these demands, and so to glorify the wisdom, love, mercy, and other perfections of the divine essence. And the Holy Spirit agreed to glorify the grace and power of the Godhead by quickening the elect dead in sin, and by enabling them to walk in newness of life till they should attain the perfection of life eternal. But, though the eternal Spirit was deeply concerned in the making of that divine covenant, yet God the Father entered into it in a peculiar manner with His only begotten Son, the Head and Representative of His elect. Accordingly, in the covenant of grace, three parties present themselves to our consideration: first, the party contracting on the part of heaven; second, the party contracting on the part of man; and last the party contracted for.

SECTION 1. The Party Contracting on the Part of Heaven

In the first place, the high contracting party on behalf of heaven presents Himself to our view. The party contracting on the side of heaven, or the party who, in the covenant, sustains the honor of the infinite majesty and authority of the glorious Godhead, is Jehovah essentially considered in the person of the Father (Titus 1:2; Ephesians 1:3). The whole divine essence, or God essentially considered, in the person of the Father, is the party contracting on the part of heaven. It is hereby freely acknowledged that the Son and the Holy Spirit, as the parties likewise offended by the disobedience of mankind, have their due share in the covenant on the side of heaven, and that, in the meantime, a peculiar agency on that side is and ought to be attributed to the Father as is, on the part of man, to the Son. God Himself, then, or God essentially considered in the person of the Father, and no other, is the party contracting who, in that august treaty, consults the interest and supports the honor of the glorious Godhead.

That we may have just views of the high party contracting on the part of heaven in that divine transaction, it will be proper briefly to observe that from all eternity He purposed to create in time man after His own image, and then to enter into a covenant of works with him. All things produced in time had their being from eternity in the womb of the divine decree before they began to have their existence in time. The decree, therefore, is in Scripture (Zephaniah 2:2) said to bring forth. God all-sufficient could have no need either of angels or of men but, in order to manifest His glory, He from all eternity purposed to create them, and to enter into such a covenant with the first man that therein the man should be the public representative of all his natural posterity. Besides, He resolved to give the man sufficient ability to retain his innocence if he so pleased. Thus, then, the covenant of works that was to be made with the first Adam was from everlasting present to the infinite mind of Jehovah, to whom all His works, from the beginning of the world, were and still are infinitely well known.

Further, let it be remarked too that God from all eternity purposed to permit the first man, as the root and the representative of his natural descendants, to break that covenant, and so to involve himself and them in sin, and in all its dreadful consequences. While on the one hand it is manifest from the infinite and immutable holiness of Jehovah, as well as from the nature of the thing itself, that the divine permission could not possibly be the cause of the fall of man, it is, on the other, no less evident, from the necessary dependence of the creature on the Creator, that without such permission he could not have fallen.

Having, in order to clear the way, merely hinted at these remarks, I now proceed to observe that the glorious party contracting on the part of heaven in the covenant of grace is, in this divine treaty, to be considered in a fourfold point of view.

1. He is to be considered as a God of manifold and infinite wisdom. In planning and proposing that wonderful covenant to His eternal Son, He displayed the most unsearchable, the most astonishing, treasures of wisdom. Hence the Lord Jesus, that great ordinance of Jehovah, for the salvation of lost sinners of mankind is, by the Apostle Paul, called "Christ, the wisdom of God" (1 Corinthians 1:24). In Christ's glorious undertaking, God has abounded toward us in all wisdom and prudence (Ephesians 1:8). In permitting mankind to fall into sin, that only evil in which there is no good, so that, by the redemption of sinners, He might bring the greatest good out of the greatest evil, and might render the deepest misery the occasion of the highest happiness to His elect, and that in subservience to the most astonishing displays of the glory of every divine perfection, He manifested the most unfathomable depths, the most unsearchable treasures, of wisdom and knowledge in having devised a plan according to which sin might be punished and yet the sinner pardoned; justice might be satisfied and yet the offender saved; holiness glorified and yet the believing sinner admitted to intimate communion with the High and Holy One; truth magnified, and yet the penalty of the broken law remitted to the transgressor—a plan according to which mercy and truth might meet together, righteousness and peace might kiss each other, truth might spring out of the earth, and righteousness look down from heaven (Psalm 85:10-11). In having devised such an astonishing plan, the manifold wisdom of God is most gloriously displayed. Hence are these words of the holy Apostle Paul: "To the intent that now, unto the principalities and pow-

ers in heavenly places, might be made known by the church the manifold wisdom of God" (Ephesians 3:10); and hence too this ardent exclamation of his: "Oh, the depth of the riches both of the wisdom and knowledge of God! How unsearchable are His judgments, and His ways past finding out" (Romans 11:33).

2. He is also in that divine transaction to be viewed as a God who is infinitely displeased with the sins of mankind. When the Lord looked down from heaven upon the children of men, He saw that they were all gone aside, that they were altogether become filthy, that there was none who did good, no, not one (Psalm 14:2-3). He saw that the wickedness of man was great in the earth, and that every imagination of the thoughts of his heart was only evil continually (Genesis 6:5). All the children of Adam appeared in His view as corrupt and loathsome, the very reverse of that spotless holiness that shines forth with such transcendent luster in His nature and His law. In the covenant of works, Jehovah contracted with man himself as with a friend, but in the covenant of grace He could not do so; for in this covenant man was considered as an enemy to Him, as a sinner against Him. The covenant of grace, therefore, is in Scripture called the covenant of His peace, the covenant in which a Mediator between Him and man is indispensably necessary.

3. He is at the same time to be considered as purposing from eternity to display in the redemption of lost sinners of mankind the exceeding riches of His grace and mercy. "Who hath saved us," says the Apostle Paul, "and called us with a holy calling, not according to our works, but according to His own purpose and grace, which was given us in Christ Jesus before the world began" (2 Timothy 1:9). The covenant of grace that Jehovah the Father made with His chosen One was the consequence of His having formed a purpose of grace toward His elect. This gracious purpose is, in the passage just now cited, called "His own

purpose and grace"; and therefore the divine covenant, which is the result of it, is, in many places of sacred writ called His covenant; but in none is it called man's covenant. If a purpose of grace had not previously been in the heart of God, there could never have been a covenant of grace. It was because He, from eternity, entertained thoughts of love toward sinners of mankind that He purposed in Himself to make them everlasting monuments of His redeeming grace and mercy, and to make a covenant of grace on which mercy should be built up forever in order to accomplish that gracious purpose. He purposed in Himself to do this, and was not moved to do it by any impulsive cause whatever outside Himself. He was not influenced to do it either by the merit or by the misery of man; not by the merit of man, for if an innocent person could merit no good thing at the hand of the Lord, much less could a guilty sinner; nor yet by his misery, for if the misery of fallen angels could not prevail with Him to save them, why should the misery of fallen men who, in the scale of existence, are far inferior to the former be supposed to influence Him to show mercy to them? Jehovah the Father, therefore, in making the everlasting covenant, is to be considered as purposing to display, in the redemption of sinners of mankind, the glory of His transcendently free and sovereign grace. The mere good pleasure of His will, His sovereign, gratuitous love, rising of its own accord in His heart, and not in the least influenced by the consideration of anything outside Himself, determined Him to enter into that well-ordered covenant.

4. Last, the party in behalf of heaven in that divine contract is to be viewed as infinitely and immutably just, as one who cannot but do that which is right, and therefore cannot but give to sin its due recompense; as one who cannot save a sinner but in a way of vindicating His own affronted holiness, of satisfying His offended justice, of appeasing His incensed wrath and of

magnifying His violated law (Genesis 18:25). In that solemn contract He is to be considered as one who cannot so deny Himself as to prove unjust, either to Himself or to the sinner. It would not be consistent, either with the nature of Jehovah or with His faithfulness in the threatening of His violated law, to pardon sin without full satisfaction to His affronted justice. If a throne of grace is to be erected, it must not be on the ruins of the honor of divine justice. Upon the motion, then, for extending mercy to lost sinners of the human race, the offended justice of Jehovah interposed and pled that mercy should not be shown but in a manner consistent with the honor of law and justice; that the law which was violated should be satisfied, and the honor of it repaired, both by suffering unto death and by obeying for life; that such sufferings should be endured as might satisfy the penal sanction and such obedience be performed as might answer the righteous precept. To answer these demands was far beyond the reach of sinful men; and therefore they must have died without mercy unless a sufficient surety could be found who might, as a second Adam, be divinely substituted and accepted in their stead. Those impediments, in the way of mercy to sinners of mankind, were to them quite insuperable; and therefore, to remove them out of the way, the eternal Father proposed the covenant of grace to His eternal Son, and intended that it should be the glorious channel in which the streams of redeeming love, grace, and mercy might freely and forever flow for the everlasting salvation of lost sinners of mankind.

Thus, then, the glorious party contracting on the part of heaven in the covenant of grace is, in this august transaction, to be viewed as a God of unsearchable wisdom, as infinitely displeased with the sins of mankind, as purposing from eternity to display, in the redemption of sinners of mankind, the exceeding riches of His grace and mercy, and as infinitely and immutably just.

SECTION 2. The Party Contracting on the Part of Man

The glorious party contracting on the side of man in that divine treaty is now, as was proposed, to present Himself to our view. This illustrious party is no other than the Lord Jesus Christ, the eternal Son of the Father, with His spiritual seed. "Behold I, and the children which God hath given me" (Hebrews 2:13). It is as if the Son had said, "Behold I, the glorious party contracting in the everlasting covenant, and they, the children whom God the Father has given Me, and for whom I have contracted." Accordingly, in Matthew 1:23 we read that His name was to be called "Immanuel," which, being interpreted, is "God with us." We have already seen that the party contracting on the part of heaven is God in the first Person of the eternal Trinity. The party, then, contracting on the side of man, is God in the second Person, or Jehovah the only begotten, the eternal Son. Between these two glorious Persons the covenant was made and established; and they entered into it, the one as the first and the other as the second Person, or, as the Father and the Son in the ever-blessed Trinity. For before they entered into that covenant they did not have any other distinguishing characters under which they could, as far as we know, have entered into it. Hence are these words of our great Redeemer: "The Father loveth the Son and hath given all things into His hand" (John 3:35). "He that honoreth not the Son honoreth not the Father which hath sent Him" (John 5:23). And these are the words of the Apostle John: "We have seen and do testify that the Father sent the Son to be the savior of the world" (1 John 4:14).

The Parties Contracting

That the covenant of grace was made between the first Person of the adorable Trinity and the second under the distinguishing characters of Father and Son is manifest, for:

1. Jehovah the Father is plainly represented in the Scripture as having made a covenant with Christ, His Son. "I," said God the Father, "have made a covenant with my chosen One...Thy seed will I establish forever. I have laid help upon One that is mighty. I have exalted One chosen out of the people. Also, I will make Him my first-born, higher than the kings of the earth. My mercy will I keep from Him forevermore, and My covenant shall stand fast with Him" (Psalm 89:3-4, 19, 27, 28). In these texts the expressions are too emphatic and glowing to admit of having their full application to the covenant of royalty over Israel made with David. David was an eminent type of Messiah who, for that reason, is sometimes in sacred writ called David (Ezekiel 34:23, 24); and the covenant of royalty made with David was a type of the covenant of grace made with Messiah.

Christ the eternal Son is eminently the chosen of God, as the rulers and people of Israel supposed Messiah to be (Luke 23:35). Jehovah the Father called Him His Elect. "Behold . . . Mine Elect, in whom My soul delighteth" (Isaiah 42:1). In Psalm 40:6-8, Messiah speaks of His covenant with the Father in these endearing expressions: "Sacrifice and offering Thou didst not desire; mine ears hast Thou opened; burnt-offering and sin-offering hast Thou not required. Then said I, 'Lo, I come; in the volume of the book it is written of me: I delight to do Thy will, O my God; yea, Thy law is within my heart.' " And the prophet Zechariah said: "The counsel of peace shall be between them both" (Zechariah 6:13). He does not say that it was, but that it shall be between them; for the covenant is an everlasting covenant, and the execution of the counsel of Jehovah's will, in the redemption of His elect, will continue to all eternity. This counsel shall be between them both, between Jehovah the Father and the man whose name is the Branch, who was to build the temple of the Lord and to bear the glory. It is and shall be, according to the contrivance and direction of infinite wisdom, the mutual will of both the Father and the Son. Our blessed Lord, in the days of His humiliation, said to His disciples, "I appoint unto you a kingdom, as My Father hath appointed to Me" (Luke 22:29). Accordingly we read that our Lord Jesus was made a Surety of a better covenant (Hebrews 7:22), that He is the Mediator of a better covenant (Hebrews 8:6), and the Mediator of the new testament (Hebrews 9:15). We read too that the promises of that covenant were made to Christ the eternal Son (Titus 1:2), and that the covenant itself was confirmed by God in or on Christ (Galatians 3:16-17). God the Father then is plainly represented in the sacred records as having entered into covenant with His Son Jesus Christ.

2. Jehovah the Father is, in Scripture, called the God, the Head, and the Judge or Justifier of Christ His beloved Son. He is called His God, among other passages, in the following: "God thy God hath anointed thee, with the oil of gladness above thy fellows" (Psalm 45:7). "My God, My God, why hast Thou forsaken me?" (Psalm 22:1) "I ascend unto My Father and your Father, and to My God and your God" (John 20:17). "Blessed be the God and Father of our Lord Jesus Christ" (Ephesians 1:3). He is also called the Head or Lord of Christ, to intimate that Christ, in His mediatorial office, is subordinate to Him. The Head of Christ is God (1 Corinthians 11:3). "God so loved the world that He gave His only begotten Son" (John 3:16). "God sent His only begotten Son in the world, that we might live through Him . . . He loved us, and sent His Son to be the propitiation for our sins" (1 John 4:9-10). "And now the Lord God and His Spirit hath sent me" (Isaiah 48:16). "He that spared not

The Parties Contracting 11

His own Son, but delivered Him up for us all" (Romans 8:32). "Wherefore God also hath highly exalted Him, and given Him a name which is above every name" (Philippians 2:9).

The following passages represent the Father as the Judge or Justifier of Christ the Son. "He is near that justifieth Me, who will contend with Me? Behold, the Lord God will help Me; who is he that shall condemn Me?" (Isaiah 50:8-9). "Therefore, will I divide Him a portion with the great, and He shall divide the spoil with the strong because He hath poured out His soul unto death" (Isaiah 53:12). "Who by Him do believe in God that raised Him up from the dead, and gave Him glory" (1 Peter 1:21). "God was manifest in the flesh, justified in the Spirit, . . . received up into glory" (1 Timothy 3:16). Thus, Jehovah the Father is represented in sacred writ as the God, the Head, and the Judge of Christ His blessed Son, which supremacy over the Son as Mediator evidently supposes that the Father entered into a covenant with Him.

3. Things are said of the Lord Jesus Christ in the Scripture that necessarily imply that His eternal Father entered into a covenant with Him. He is called the Servant of the Father. "Behold my Servant whom I uphold" (Isaiah 42:1). "The Lord said unto me, 'Thou art my Servant, O Israel, in whom I will be glorified' " (Isaiah 49:1, 3). He is called His Messenger, and the Messenger of the covenant (Malachi 3:1). "This is the work of God, that ye believe on him whom He hath sent" (John 6:29). "Say ye of him whom the Father hath sanctified and sent into the world, 'Thou blasphemest'; because I said, I am the Son of God?" (John 10:36). "The Lord whom ye seek, shall suddenly come to His temple; even the Messenger of the covenant, whom I delight in" (Malachi 3:1). He is also represented as made under the law (Galatians 4:4) and as made obedient unto death (Philippians 2:8; Hebrews 5:8). It is recorded of Him that He was made sin for us

(2 Corinthians 5:21); that He was made a curse for us (Galatians 3:13); that He was a sufferer for us (Isaiah 53:5; 1 Peter 3:18); and that He received from the Father a reward for His work (Philippians 2:8-9; Hebrews 2:9).

4. Last, a solemn contract between the Father and the Son is in Scripture represented as confirmed by divine oaths and seals. Jehovah the Father, on the one hand, to show the absolute certainty and the necessary belief of that which He had declared concerning Christ the Son, swore it to Him. "I have sworn unto David My Servant. Once have I sworn by My holiness, that I will not lie unto David" (Psalm 89:3, 35). "The Lord hath sworn and will not repent. Thou art a Priest forever after the order of Melchizedeck" (Psalm 110:4). "The law maketh men high-priests which have infirmity; but the word of the oath, which was since the law, maketh the Son, who is consecrated forevermore" (Hebrews 7:28).

On the other hand, Christ the Son engaged His heart, or solemnly contracted, that He would approach, as a sacrificing Priest and an atoning sacrifice, to the offended Majesty of heaven. "Who is this, that engaged his heart to approach unto Me? saith the Lord" (Jeremiah 30:21). Jehovah the Father also granted, and Christ the Son received, the seals both of the old dispensation of the covenant and of the new, as will be afterwards explained more particularly. Christ indeed did this in obedience to the commandment of His eternal Father as a means of confirming the graces of His human nature, and as a solemn acknowledgement both of His communion with the visible Church and of His cheerfulness in the work of our redemption. But, at the same time, He likewise received them as confirmations of the solemn contract between Jehovah the Father and Him, concerning the redemption of lost sinners.

The Parties Contracting

That the covenant of redeeming grace, then, was made between the first and second Persons of the adorable Trinity, under the distinguishing characters of Father and Son, is evident; for Jehovah the Father is represented in Scripture as having made a covenant with Christ the Son. He is in Scripture called the God, the Head, and the Judge or Justifier of Christ His only begotten Son. Things are in sacred writ said of Jehovah the Son that necessarily imply that His eternal Father entered into a covenant with Him. And a solemn contract between the Father and the Son is in the Scripture represented as confirmed by divine oaths and seals.

Thus it is evident that the Son of God is the glorious Party contracting on the part of man, and that the eternal Father, or first Person of the blessed Trinity, made the covenant of grace with Him as the eternal Son, or second Person. And in making it, as shall be more clearly shown in the next chapter, the Son was, with infinite willingness, constituted by the Father as the Mediator between God and men. While He still continues, and must forever continue, in His state of divine equality with the Father, He willingly agreed to enter upon a state of mediatorial inferiority to Him. This inferiority as Mediator is most perfectly consistent with His divine equality and unity with Jehovah the Father. Thus the eternal Son, with infinite condescension, consented to become the blessed Mediator between an offended God and offending men. Accordingly we read that there is one Mediator between God and men, the man Christ Jesus (1 Timothy 2:5). The term Mediator does not, in the Scriptures, appear to be applied to any other except Moses. The law, said the Apostle Paul, was ordained by angels in the hand of a mediator (Galatians 3:19). Of Moses, the typical mediator here mentioned, it may be observed that he was not merely a messenger between God and Israel, but that, when God renewed His covenant of reconciliation with Israel after the breaking of the tables of stone, He condescended to make it with him as their representative. He said, "Behold, I make a covenant; before all thy people I will do marvels. After the tenor of these words, I have made a covenant with thee and with Israel." He wrote upon the tables the words of the covenant, the Ten Commandments (Exodus 34:10, 27-28). Now Moses was alone on the mount with God during all the time of this solemn transaction; and in it, Jehovah spoke of him and the people as of one moral agent or person. As Moses, then, in becoming a mediator between God and Israel was, in the covenant of reconciliation, renewed with them, a representative of Israel. So the Lord Jesus Christ, the antitype of Moses, did, in becoming the Mediator between God and men, become the federal Representative of His spiritual Israel.

In the covenant of grace, then, the Lord Jesus is considered in a threefold point of view:

1. He is to be viewed as the second Person of the ever-blessed Trinity, as a Person of all possible excellence, of all divine perfection, having in and from Himself wisdom, power, holiness, justice, goodness, and faithfulness, sufficient, and more than sufficient, for the infinitely arduous work of the redemption of sinners (Psalm 89:19; Zechariah 13:7; Isaiah 9:6).

2. He is to be considered as our sovereign and rightful Proprietor, who might and could, if He pleased, save us, and who had from everlasting a tender regard to the work of His own hands (Romans 9:23; Psalm 100:3; Job 14:15).

3. He is to be regarded too as the Head and Representative of all the elect of mankind who were, in the covenant, given to Him as His spiritual children (Ephesians 1:3-4; Psalm 89:3-4). In the Father's contracting with Him, He is to be considered not only as the eternal Son, and as the sovereign Proprietor of man-

kind, but as the last Adam, the public Representative of a seed, the party for whom He contracted with the Father.

Now, that the covenant of redeeming grace was made with Christ as the last Adam, the Head and Representative of elect sinners of mankind, His spiritual seed, will be evident from the following arguments:

ARGUMENT 1. The Lord Jesus is, in the Scriptures, expressly called the last Adam (1 Corinthians 15:45). This appellation could not be given Him on account of the human nature that He had in common with the first Adam, for of that every man partakes; but it was given to Him because of the common office of headship and representation in their respective covenants that was peculiar to themselves and to none else. Adam is also called the first man and Christ the second man (1 Corinthians 15:47); but Christ is the second man no otherwise than as He is the second federal Head, or the Representative, in the second covenant, as Adam was the first federal head, or the representative, in the first covenant. Adam, accordingly, is represented as the head of the earthly men and Christ as the Head of the heavenly men. Those bear the image of the first Adam who are of the earth, earthy; these, the image of the second Adam, who is the Lord from heaven (verses 47, 48, 49). Moreover, the Apostle Paul expressly declares that Adam was a type or figure of Christ (Romans 5:14), and then draws a parallel between them both in which he shows that as by Adam's breach of the covenant of works sin and death came upon all his natural descendants, so, by Christ's fulfilling of the covenant of grace, righteousness and life came upon all His spiritual seed (Romans 5:17-19). As therefore the covenant of works was made with Adam as the representative of his natural posterity, so the covenant of grace was made with Christ as the Representative of His spiritual offspring.

The first individual of mankind bore the name of his posterity, and they go under his name. He was denominated "man," which is the meaning of "Adam," to show that he was the natural root and the moral representative of men or mankind, or that God entered into a covenant with him as their head and representative. And, on the other hand, his posterity are, in the language of the Holy Spirit, called "Adam" to show that they all sprang from him, and that they were all represented by him when God made the covenant of works with him. "Verily," said the Psalmist, "every man, at his best state, is altogether vanity." And again, "Surely every man is vanity" (Psalm 39:5, 11). In both places, "every man" is, in the original, "every Adam."

In like manner, Christ bears the name of His spiritual seed, and they His name. Israel is the name of the spiritual seed (Galatians 6:16), and Christ is called by the same name. "Thou," said Jehovah the Father, "art My Servant, O Israel, in whom I will be glorified" (Isaiah 49:3). The whole context shows that it is Messiah who is here meant; and it is as if the Father had said to Him, "Thou art My Servant, O Thou who represents Israel, in and by whom I will afford a most illustrious display of the glory of all My perfections, the honor of which had been obscured by the sins of Israel, Thy spiritual seed."

Thus Christ bears the name of His spiritual offspring; and they, on the other hand, are called by His name. They are called Christ: "He saith not, 'And to seeds,' as of many, but as of one, And to Thy seed, which is Christ" (Galatians 3:16). Now, Christ's being called in the Scripture by their name, and they by His name, is clear evidence that He and they were one in law, and that Jehovah the Father entered into covenant with Him as their public Representative, and with them as represented by Him.

The Parties Contracting

The covenants recorded in the Old Testament that, in one view of them, were typical or figurative of the covenant of grace were made with parents or ancestors as the representatives of their respective offspring. The covenant of the day and night that was made with Noah and his sons was made with them as the representatives of their seed. "Behold," said Jehovah, "I establish My covenant with you, and with your seed after you" (Genesis 9:9). But that this covenant was a type of the covenant of grace is evident from the nature and import of it, namely that there should never be another deluge upon the earth (Genesis 9:11). The substance of it, as figurative of the covenant of grace, is declared in Isaiah 54:9-10: "As I have sworn," said Jehovah, "that the waters of Noah should no more go over the earth, so have I sworn that I would not be wroth with thee, nor rebuke thee."

That it was typical of the covenant of grace is also manifest from its having been made upon a sacrifice (Genesis 8:20-22), and especially from the rainbow that was the token of it, appearing round about the throne of Jehovah, as in Christ, a God of grace (Revelation 4:3). The covenant too, respecting the land of Canaan, into which Jehovah entered with Abraham, was made with him as a representative of his seed (Genesis 15:18); and afterwards, when it was confirmed to him by an oath, it was, as their representative, that it was confirmed to him (Genesis 22:16-17). Now in this Abraham was a type of Messiah, the second Adam, the everlasting Father of the great multitude of true believers who, at the call of Jehovah, came from heaven, His native country, sojourned among the sinful race of Adam, offered up Himself a sacrifice at the commandment of God; and so, becoming the true heir of the world, He received the promises for His spiritual seed.

The promises that He received for them may all be comprehended in the account that Zacharias gives of the covenant made with Abraham (Luke 1:72-75). The covenant of an everlasting priesthood, made with Phinehas, which likewise was a type of the covenant of grace, was made with him as a representative of his descendants. And he shall have it, and his seed after him, even the covenant of an everlasting priesthood (Numbers 25:13). In that covenant he typified Jesus Christ, representing His spiritual seed in the covenant of grace; for it is in Christ, who made full atonement for the sins of His people, that the everlasting priesthood promised to Phinehas has its full accomplishment. The spiritual seed of Christ, in a more exalted degree, partake of the same privilege in Him. "The Lord hath sworn and will not repent, Thou art a priest forever" (Psalm 110:4). "Jesus Christ . . . hath made us kings and priests unto God and His Father" (Revelation 1:5, 6).

Once more, the covenant of royalty made with David, that was an undoubted type of the covenant of grace, was made with him as a representative of his seed. "I have made a covenant with My chosen One, I have sworn unto David My servant, Thy seed will I establish forever, and build up thy throne to all generations" (Psalm 89:3, 4). Now David was an illustrious type of Messiah the Prince who for that reason is sometimes in the Scripture called "David." "I will set up," said Jehovah the Father, "one shepherd over them, and he shall feed them, even my servant David; and I the Lord will be their God, and My servant David, a prince among them" (Ezekiel 34:23-24). "My servant David shall be their prince forever" (Ezekiel 37:25).

The benefits of the covenant of grace made with Him are called "the sure mercies of David" (Isaiah 55:3). Therefore the covenant of grace typified thereby was made with Christ as the Head and Representative of His spiritual children; for whatso-

The Parties Contracting

ever is attributed to any person or thing as a type has its real accomplishment chiefly in the person or thing thereby typified. We read in Hebrews 7:22, as has been observed above, that Jesus was made a Surety of a better covenant. Now it is evident from His office of suretiship in that glorious covenant of redeeming grace that it was established with Him as the public Head and Representative of a spiritual seed. By His becoming a surety or sponsor for them as sinners, who in themselves were utterly insolvent, He took upon Himself the burden of discharging their whole debt, both of penal suffering for sin and of perfect obedience for life. But such a Surety as this is cannot but be a true and proper Representative of those for whom He acts as Surety. By being legally substituted in their stead, to answer for them, He represents or sustains their persons in law. Accordingly we read that God made Christ, who knew no sin, to be sin for us (2 Corinthians 5:21); that Christ died for us (Romans 5:8); that we are crucified with Christ (Galatians 2:20); that we are made alive in Christ, as we die in Adam (1 Corinthians 15:22); and that we are raised up together and made to sit together in heavenly places in Christ Jesus (Ephesians 2:6). All this necessarily requires that He be the Head and Representative of the elect in the covenant of grace. Hence the performing of the proper conditions of the covenant was demanded from Him instead of them (John 14:31 with 10:18; Psalm 40:8); and He finished the work that the Father gave Him to do (John 17:4).

Last, the promises of the covenant that were to be fulfilled to His spiritual seed were made by the Father primarily to Christ Himself as their Head and Representative. "Now to Abraham and his seed were the promises made. He saith not, And to seeds, as of many; but as of one, And to thy seed, which is Christ" (Galatians 3:16). Though it is readily acknowledged that Christ mystical may be intended here, yet the passage itself, as well as the context, shows that Christ personal, or Christ considered as the Representative of His spiritual offspring, is mainly intended. It is indeed to Christ mystical that the promises are here said to be made; but it is primarily to Christ the Head, and secondarily to the members in and under Him; just as the promise of life in the covenant of works was originally or primarily made to Adam as the representative, and secondarily to his natural posterity in him.

In the typical covenant with Abraham, the promises of the earthly inheritance were primarily made to that patriarch himself, and secondarily to his seed according to the flesh. In like manner, the promise of the eternal inheritance is declared to have been made to Christ as the Representative of God's elect in eternity before any of them existed, when there was none but Himself to whom it could be made in person. "Who hath saved us," says an apostle, "not according to our works, but according to His own purpose and grace, which was given us in Christ Jesus before the world began" (2 Timothy 1:9). It is accordingly observable that when it was foretold that a new covenant would be made with the house of Israel, the true Israel of God, the promises of it, notwithstanding, were directed not to themselves, but to another. "They shall (Jehovah does not say, 'Ye shall,' but, 'they shall') be My people, and I will be their God" (Jeremiah 32:38). The reason for this seems to be that the promises of it were primarily made not to themselves, but to another, namely to Christ as their federal Representative. Seeing then that those promise are promises of the covenant of grace, which therefore is denominated the covenants of promise (Ephesians 2:12), it is obvious that if they were primarily made to Christ as the Representative of His spiritual seed, the covenant itself must have been made with Him in that public capacity.

The Parties Contracting

Thus it is manifest that the covenant of grace, that divine contract, was made with Christ as the second Adam, the Representative of all His spiritual seed. It was evidenced above that the covenant was proposed to Him, and accepted by Him, as the eternal Son of the Father. In accepting it under that divine character, He consented to become the last Adam, the public Representative, of a certain number of lost mankind, upon which it was also established with Him as their Head and Representative.

QUESTION. But why was the covenant of grace made with Jehovah the Son as the Representative of His spiritual seed?

ANSWER. Let it be observed that that infinitely glorious compact was made with Him as the last Adam, the public Representative of His elect seed:

1. Because it could not otherwise, as a proper covenant, have been made at all. Unless it had been made with a divine person, as the Head and Representative of a seed, it could never have been so made as to answer the purposes intended by it. They whose salvation was intended in it were considered as lost sinners, as persons so weak and so wicked as to be utterly unable to perform any condition of life (Romans 8:7-8; Jeremiah 17:9). In the meantime the law, having been already broken, had raised its terms of obtaining eternal life to perfect obedience under the curse, and to infinite satisfaction for sin, neither of which any except a divine person could fulfill (Matthew 19:17; Galatians 3:10; Ezekiel 18:4). Sinners of mankind too were dead in trespasses and sins; and how could a conditional or proper covenant be made with dead sinners otherwise than in a representative? Sinners, legally and morally dead, can perform no condition of life that can be acceptable to the living God. They must have life before they can so much as begin to do anything that will be pleasing to the High and Holy One. A conditional

covenant, therefore, could not be made with such sinners in their own persons. Add to this the great design of the covenant of grace was that dead sinners might have life, and might have it more abundantly; and in order thereto, the righteous Lord stood upon conditions, without the performance of which that life was not to be afforded; which conditions, as was just now observed, were so high that none except a Divine person could fulfill them.

2. It was made with Jehovah the eternal Son as the Representative of His spiritual seed in order that redeeming love and grace might issue forth toward them as early as was possible. It was in and by the covenant of grace that the infinite love of God to sinners of mankind was to begin to vent itself. Seeing that redeeming love was an eternal love, it was requisite that the covenant, in which it was to have as early a vent as possible, should likewise be an eternal covenant. Hence, that love and that covenant are in the Scripture said to be of the same eternal date. "I have loved thee with an everlasting love." The Hebrew is, "with a love of eternity" (Jeremiah 31:3). "Hear and your soul shall live; and I will make an everlasting covenant with you." The Hebrew is, "a covenant of eternity" (Isaiah 55:3). But if the covenant had not been established with the Lord Jesus as the Head and Representative of the objects of that love, it could not have been a covenant of eternity. The promise of eternal life, that all-comprehensive promise of the covenant, could not, surely, have been made to any other so early as before the world began (Titus 1:2). How could a covenant of eternity be primarily made with creatures of time, creatures of a day, creatures but of yesterday, except in such a Representative as existed from eternity? Or how could an eternal covenant be made with them, or be applied to them personally, in time if it had not, before time began, been established with another as their representative? The covenant

of redeeming grace, then, was planned by infinite wisdom, and was established with the only begotten Son of the Father before the world began in order that redeeming love might vent itself toward the objects of it long before any of them began to exist. By this wonderful device of the manifold wisdom of God, His free love had an early vent and did not wait the slow and successive motion of its objects into existence.

3. It was established with Him in that endearing character that to sinners of mankind it might in reality be a covenant of infinitely free grace. It is evident from the sacred records that this august treaty was designed chiefly for the purpose of affording the most transcendent display of the glory of redeeming grace; and, therefore, in regard to sinners themselves, it is and it must be not a covenant of works, but a covenant of immensely rich, of absolutely free grace. "Therefore it is of faith that it might be by grace" (Romans 4:16). "For by grace are ye saved through faith. . .not of works, lest any man should boast" (Ephesians 2:8, 9). It was, indeed, in the strictest sense, a covenant of works to Christ the second Adam; but it is a covenant of the freest, the most unmerited grace to sinners. The Lord Jesus Christ, as the Representative of elect sinners, was Himself the sole Performer of the conditions of the covenant in their stead; and therefore every ground of boasting is removed from them. But if the covenant were made not with Christ as the Representative of the elect sinner, but with the sinner himself as the principal party, undertaking and fulfilling the conditions of it for himself, it could not be to him a covenant of absolutely free grace; but on the contrary it would be a real covenant of works; for however low such conditions undertaken and fulfilled by the sinner himself might be supposed to be, still the promise of life would be understood as made to them; and so, according to the doctrine of Scripture, it would be a proper covenant of works;

and between such a contract and Adam's covenant of works there could be no material difference but in degree; which would leave it still a covenant of the same kind. "For to him that worketh," whether he work perfectly or imperfectly, much or little, "is the reward not reckoned of grace, but of debt" (Romans 4:4).

4. The covenant was established with Him in that public capacity that it might be a sure covenant, or, as the Apostle Paul expresses it, that the promise might be sure to all the seed (Romans 4:16). In order that mercy might be built up forever, and the faithfulness of Jehovah be established in the very heavens, it was requisite that the covenant should be made with such a Representative as could not fail, as could not be either discouraged or seduced by Satan. The old covenant was made with a mere man, as a party contracting; and though he was an upright man, yet he was so mutable that he failed to perform the condition that he had undertaken; and therefore the benefit promised was lost. A fallen creature, then, was wholly unfit to be a principal party in that new covenant, in which the promise was to be sure, and not to fail of being performed to the elect seed. Jehovah the Father, therefore, foreseeing that they were all to become a broken, a ruined company, and that, as such, they were not fit to be trusted in a matter of such unspeakable importance, proposed to His only begotten Son to become the Head of the new covenant, and as such to transact in the name of those who should be given Him for a seed; which proposal being accepted, the covenant, in regard to the accomplishment of the promise was made sure. The eternal Father looked to Him, and to Him alone, for the fulfilling of the conditions. The promises were primarily made to Him, and therefore they are sure to all the seed. This, according to sacred Scripture, is the immovable hinge on which the stability of the covenant turns.

The Parties Contracting   25

"My covenant shall stand fast with Him" (Psalm 89:28). The enemy shall not exact upon Him (verse 22) or, as some translate the passage more agreeably to the original, "The enemy shall not beguile Him." The original verb signifies, "He shall deceive, beguile, or impose upon." It is the same verb, and the same part of it too, that is used in 2 Chronicles 32:15 where in our translation the passage is rendered, "Let not Hezekiah deceive you." The enemy shall not beguile [his soul] (Jeremiah 37:9) in him, as he did, the soul of the first Adam. The covenant, then, was established with Christ as the last Adam that it might be so well ordered in all things as to be sure (2 Samuel 23:5).

5. Finally, it was made with Christ as the Representative of His spiritual offspring to the end that righteousness and life might be conveyed to them in as compendious a way as sin and death were to the natural descendants of the first Adam. For, says the Apostle Paul, "as by one man's disobedience many were made sinners, so by the obedience of One shall many be made righteous" (Romans 5:19). Upon Adam's breach of that covenant of life that had been made with him as the representative of his natural posterity, sin and death from him as a deadly head, as a killing stock, began to be communicated to them. This having been the case, it was not suitable to the Divine procedure with the children of men to treat with those elected to eternal life severally, or with each as a principal party, contracting for himself, but on the contrary to treat for them all with one public person who, by his fulfilling of the contract, should be a quickening Head to them; from whom righteousness and life might be communicated to them in as compendious a manner as sin and death were from the first Adam. This was most agreeable to the manner of Him whose tender mercies are over all His works; while it serves in an eminent degree to justify His perfections in His having entered into a covenant of life for all

mankind with Adam as their head and representative (1 Corinthians 15:45-49).

Thus I have assigned some of the reasons why the everlasting covenant of grace was established with Jehovah the Son as the glorious Representative of His spiritual seed.

While this eternal covenant took its rise from the everlasting and equal love of all the three Persons in the adorable Godhead, they were equally employed in the making of it; and they took, each His respective share, in the execution of it. It is abundantly evident that the Holy Spirit always was, and still is, deeply concerned therein. His will is necessarily the same as that of the Father and the Son. "It is the Spirit that beareth witness, because the Spirit is truth. For there are three that bear record in heaven, the Father, the Word, and the Holy Ghost; and these three are one" (1 John 5:6-7). A peculiar office in the covenant was assigned and proposed to Him and was, with infinite willingness, accepted by Him. He was to be employed, especially, about the accomplishment of the covenant. Though He is infinitely independent, and free in His agency, yet, as the Spirit of the Father and of the Son, He is by them sent to accomplish the covenant, and that by revealing and publishing the glad tidings in it (1 Corinthians 2:10, 12, 13; 2 Peter 1:21), by forming, anointing, and supporting the human nature of Christ, the Representative of men in it (Luke 1:35; Isaiah 11:2, 3), by erecting and governing the Church according to it (John 16:7-15; Romans 8:13-16), and by the effectual application of the blessings of it to elect sinners (Ephesians 1:17, 18). Now this employment of the Holy Spirit in time must be considered as the consequence of the fruit of His having accepted the assignment that was made of it to Him in eternity. What He does, respecting the application of redemption in the ages of time, could not but have been the matter of His engagement as the concurring Party in the covenant before the beginning of time. In the execution of His office He proceeds invariably, and in the strictest conformity, to what was therein settled between the Father and the Son. Our Lord Jesus, therefore, when speaking of this adorable Spirit, said, "He shall not speak of himself; but whatsoever he shall hear, that shall he speak" (John 16:13). Agreeably to His having been an approving and concurring Party in the making of the covenant, He is, in the hearts of believers, an Intercessor for their complete enjoyment of all the benefits of it (Romans 8:26, 27).

The contracting parties, then, of the covenant of grace, were the eternal Father, and the eternal Son, as the Representative of elect sinners, with the infinite approbation and concurrence of the eternal Spirit.

Some have insinuated that, seeing these three Divine persons are one God, or have one individual essence, there can be no place for the formality of a covenant between them. This objection comes rather too late since, from what has been above stated, we are certain that, that formality has already taken place. It is to no purpose to allege that as the essence of the Father, and of the Son, and of the Holy Spirit, is one so their will is one; for it may easily be replied that as the same Divine essence subsists in these three adorable Persons who, notwithstanding, are really distinct from each other, so the same Divine will may be, and really is, applied to distinct and peculiar acts in each of those distinct Persons, though in a manner far above our comprehension.

SECTION 3. Of the Party contracted for, in the Covenant.

It will be proper now to consider briefly the party represented and contracted for in the covenant of grace.

As the Party contracting on the side of man was a Representative, so the party contracted for were represented by Him. Those whom one represents in a covenant, he contracts for in that covenant; and those for whom one contracts in a covenant made with him as a representative, he represents in that covenant. As, in the covenant of works, those whom the first Adam contracted for he represented, and those whom he represented he contracted for, so, in the covenant of grace, those whom the second Adam contracted for He represented, and those whom He represented He contracted for. These two then, the persons represented and the persons contracted for, are the same, and therefore must be of equal latitude.

Now the party whom the Lord Jesus, in the covenant of grace, represented and contracted for are the elect of mankind; a certain number of the posterity of Adam, chosen from eternity, to everlasting life; the children, partakers of flesh and blood, whom God gave to Christ as the second Adam, to be by Him redeemed from sin and wrath (Hebrews 2:13, 14). The human race, throughout their generations, were, when they passed under the eye of Jehovah, all in the same fallen and lost condition; all equally sinful and miserable by nature; all equally worthy of eternal death and equally under an utter impossibility in themselves of escaping it. But, in the absolute and infinite sovereignty of His grace, He, before the world began, distinguished some of them from the rest, and from the beginning chose them to salvation through sanctification of the Spirit and belief of the truth (2 Thessalonians 2:13). These are in Scripture called the elect of God (Colossians 3:12), and the election (Romans 11:7). There is, as was above observed, a certain number of them, a number which cannot, and which from all eternity could not, be either increased or diminished by even so much as one. They were chosen individually, one by one. The Lord knows them that are

The Parties Contracting

His, for their names are written in heaven in the book of life of the Lamb. All the parts and circumstances of their salvation were settled in the eternal purpose of Jehovah; and not so much as one of them can ever fail of obtaining that life of grace and glory to which they all were elected. Their being thus, in the eternal purpose of God, selected from the rest of mankind, was of mere grace; it did not proceed upon any consideration of what they were to be or to do in time. God could not but foresee that they would believe, repent, and walk in newness of life; but He did not foresee that they would do so by any exercise merely of their own natural ability or free will. He foresaw it in His own immutable determination freely to give them faith, repentance, and power to perform such sincere obedience as should be an evidence of their having been quickened together with Christ to newness of life. Their faith, repentance, and sincere obedience, therefore, were not the reasons why they were elected, but are parts only of that salvation to which they were chosen.

That the elect of mankind, and they only, were the party represented and contracted for in the covenant of grace, will be evident from the following arguments:

1. The party with whom Jehovah the Father made that covenant is in Scripture called "His chosen One," as representing and contracting for all His elect or chosen. "I have made a covenant," said he, "with my chosen one" (Psalm 89:3). "Behold, mine elect, or chosen one, in whom my soul delighteth" (Isaiah 42:1). As the first of the human race was called Adam, or man, considered as representing and contracting for man, or mankind, in the covenant of works, so Christ was called the elect, the chosen of God, considered as representing and contracting for the elect in the covenant of grace. For, as the apostle Paul says, "both He that sanctifieth, and they who are sanctified, are

all of one" (Hebrews 2:11); they are not merely of one heavenly Father, and of one human nature, but of one body, namely the election. Christ is the head elect (Isaiah 42:1), and they are the body elect (Ephesians 5:23). He and they, therefore, go under one and the same name, a name that principally belongs to Him, and belongs to them only by participation with Him. He is likewise called Abraham's seed (Galatians 3:16) because He represented all the spiritual seed of Abraham; and the seed of the woman (Genesis 3:15), not merely because, according to the flesh, He was to descend from the woman, but because He represented that seed of the woman who are opposed to the seed of the serpent, and between whom, and the serpent with his seed, God, according to His promise, puts enmity. Add to this that it is only they who were chosen in Christ before the foundation of the world, who are in time blessed with all spiritual blessings in heavenly places in Him (Ephesians 1:3, 4).

2. Those whom Christ represented, and for whom He undertook in the everlasting covenant, are in the Scriptures called His seed. "I have sworn unto David my servant: Thy seed will I establish forever" (Psalm 89:3, 4). In covenants typical of the covenant of grace, the parties represented by him were his natural seed. In the covenant, therefore, of the second Adam, the party represented by Him are His spiritual seed. Now the spiritual seed of Christ, the second Adam, are the elect, and none else; for they only are the persons whom He begets with the word of truth (James 1:18), and who, in their regeneration, are born again to Him (1 Peter 1:23). They only are the persons whom He sees as His seed, created again after His own image (Isaiah 53:10). They only are the travail of His soul (verse 11); and they are the seed who shall serve Him (Psalm 22:30), who shall be established in a state of perfect blessedness, and who shall endure forever (Psalm 89:4, 36).

The Parties Contracting 31

3. They whom Christ represented, and for whom in the covenant of grace He contracted, are in Scripture called Israel, and the seed of Abraham. "They are not all Israel, which are of Israel" (Romans 9:6). Now the spiritual Israel, the collective body, are the elect of God. The elect then were the party whom Christ in the covenant represented; and because He therein represented them, and no other, He is, by Jehovah the Father, called Israel. "Thou art My Servant, O Israel, in whom I will be glorified" (Isaiah 49:3). His seed are, under that appellation, plainly determined to be the elect. "In the Lord shall all the seed of Israel be justified" (Isaiah 45:25), even as, in the first man, all the seed of Adam were condemned (Romans 5:18). As the first of the human race was called Adam, which signifies man, because in the covenant of works he was a summary of all mankind, they being all represented by him, so the Lord Jesus was called Israel because He was a compendium of all the true Israel, all the elect of God, they being all represented by Him. Hence we learn the true ground of the universality of this declaration: "The Lord hath laid on Him the iniquity of us all" (Isaiah 53:6), that is, of all the true Israel, all the elect of God.

They whom Christ represented are also called the seed of Abraham. Them, and them only, He took with Him into the bond of the covenant. "For, verily, He took not on Him the nature of angels, but He took on Him the seed of Abraham" (Hebrews 2:16); or rather, as it is rendered on the margin, "He taketh not hold of angels, but of the seed of Abraham He taketh hold." The original verb signifies to take to, or to take hold of an object that is running away or falling down; and it is used to express Christ's taking hold of Peter when he was sinking in the water (Matthew 14:31). Fallen angels and men were both running away from God, and were both sinking in the ocean of His overwhelming wrath. Christ Jesus takes hold of fallen men, but not of fallen angels; these He leaves to sink to the bottom. All the seed of Adam were sinking, as well as the seed of Abraham who are but a part of the seed of Adam. But Christ is not said to have taken hold of the seed of Adam, that is, of all mankind, but only of the seed of Abraham, namely of all the elect who are called the house of Jacob (Luke 1:33). Accordingly, it is remarkable that the first time the covenant of grace was published to mankind, the discourse was directed to the serpent (Genesis 3:14, 15) and not to Adam, as the covenant of works had been (Genesis 2:16, 17); in order that Adam might know that he was to come in there as a private individual only, and not as a public person with his seed. For the same reason also, the Lord Jesus is not called Adam, or man simply, but the last Adam, and the second Man; whose seed differs from that of the first man, as the seed of Abraham does from the seed of Adam.

4. Finally, they whom Christ as the last Adam represented, and for whom He contracted, became heavenly men. "The first man is of the earth, earthy; the second man is the Lord from heaven. As is the earthy, such are they also that are earthy and as is the heavenly, such are they also that are heavenly. And as we have borne the image of the earth, we shall also bar the image of the heavenly" (1 Corinthians 15:47-49). Now the heavenly men, who resemble and belong to Christ the second man, are the elect, and none else. They are contradistinguished from the earthly men who belong to the first man, that is, all mankind, taken into the covenant of works, in the first Adam; and therefore they are the elect men who are taken into the covenant of grace in the second Adam. Again, the heavenly men are they who shall bear the image of the heavenly man, Christ Jesus, who were chosen in Him before the foundation of the world, that they should be holy (Ephesians 1:4); who are risen with Him and seek the things which are above; and who shall appear with

Him in glory, when He Himself who is their life shall appear (Colossians 3:1, 4). But such are the elect of God and they only. For "whom He did foreknow, He also did predestinate to be conformed to the image of His Son, that He might be the firstborn among many brethren" (Romans 8:29). In few words, they are those to whom, in respect of heavenly influence and efficacy, Christ the last Adam is a quickening Spirit; for as is the heavenly, such are they also that are heavenly. As the deadly efficacy of Adam spreads itself as wide as his representation in the covenant of works did, extending to all mankind, his natural seed, and to them only, so the quickening efficacy of Christ diffuses itself as wide as His representation in the covenant of grace did, reaching to all the elect, His spiritual seed, and to none else.

Thus, then, it is manifest that the elect of mankind were the party represented and contracted for in the everlasting covenant.

QUESTION. The reader will now ask, "How were the elect viewed or considered in that federal representation of them?"

ANSWER. They were considered:

1. As sinners, who in themselves were lost and undone by their breach of the covenant of works. They were viewed as lost sheep (Matthew 15:24). In the first covenant all mankind as a flock were put under the hand of one Shepherd, the first Adam; but he, in losing himself, lost all the flock and was never able again to recover so much as one of them. Jehovah had from eternity set a secret mark on some of them, by which He distinguished those from the rest. "Having this seal, the Lord knoweth them that are His" (2 Timothy 2:19). He saw that they, as well as the rest of Adam's posterity, had gone far, and that they were going still farther and farther away from their pasture, wandering as poor strays, a prey to every devourer. In order, therefore, that they may be sought out, brought back, and kept forever safe the new covenant was made with another Shepherd,

the Lord Jesus Christ; and they were put under His hand, as the Shepherd of Israel. In Adam's representation in the covenant of works the party represented were considered as upright, and wholly a right seed; whereas in Christ's representation in the covenant of grace the party represented were viewed as a corrupt, a sinful mass, a people laden with iniquity, under the wrath of the almighty Jehovah, and the curse of the broken law. And who would have contracted for such a company? Who would have substituted himself in their stead? Unmerited, unsolicited, almighty love engaged our infinitely dear Immanuel to do so. The Holy One of God represented unholy creatures; the beloved, the blessed Son of the Father, represented hateful and cursed sinners.

2. They were also considered as altogether unable, either in whole or in part, to recover themselves. When we were yet without strength, in due time, Christ died for the ungodly (Romans 5:6). The Apostle does not say, "When we were yet without perfect strength, or much strength, or a certain degree of strength, but when we were yet without strength; without any strength at all, either to convert ourselves, or to prepare ourselves for conversion; without any strength, so much as to think one single thought that is spiritually good." The elect of God were so enfeebled by their fall that they were utterly unable either to fulfill the righteousness of the law or to atone for their transgression of it; either to redeem themselves from their abject slavery or even to perform so much as one good work. They were debtors and were altogether unable to pay one farthing of their boundless debt; they were criminals and were utterly incapable of enduring, to the satisfaction of Divine justice, their eternal punishment. Had it lain on them to have paid the debt or sustained the punishment, they would have forever sunk under the infinite, the intolerable load. Then, said the only begotten Son of

God, "I cannot see them perish. Father, I substitute Myself in their stead and will answer for them every legal demand. I will pay all their debt and bear all their punishment. I will represent the debtors and criminals and, in the estimation of law, will Myself become the debtor and the criminal." The representation is legally sustained; the payment of all is devolved on Him; and the Divine justice looks for it, neither in whole nor in part, from any other hand (Isaiah 53:6; Psalm 69:4).

3. Once more, they were considered withal as the objects of electing, redeeming, and everlasting love, and as such were given by the eternal Father to Christ, to be by Him redeemed. The Father loved them (John 17:23), and gave them to the Son (verse 6); the Son loved them (Ephesians 5:2) and, accepting the gift, represented them in the covenant as a father does his children. "His name shall be called . . .the everlasting Father" (Isaiah 9:6). And again, "Behold I, and the children which God hath given me" (Hebrews 2:13). That absolutely free love and mere good pleasure of the triune Jehovah was the reason why they, rather than others who were in the same condemnation for their breach of the covenant of works, were represented by the second Adam in the covenant of grace, and why their names were written in that eternal contract while the names of others were left out (Luke 10:20). His love of them was the reason why He set down all their names as in a book in order to be answerable for each of them, and why their names were so written in his book of life that they never can be blotted out of it (Revelation 21:27).

From what has now been discoursed concerning the parties of the covenant of grace, we may with warrant infer that Christ died for those whom He represented, and for none else. Though His death is intrinsically sufficient for the salvation of every sinner of mankind, yet He became obedient unto death in the place of His elect seed, and of them only. The account of the covenant, and of the parties contracting, which has here been given from the sacred records, at once refutes the doctrine of universal redemption, and that of the federal conditionality of our good works in that gracious covenant. If the covenant of grace was, from eternity, entered into with Christ as the Representative of the elect and of them only, it follows that the condition of the covenant, His obedience unto death, was performed for them and for no other. When man enters into a bond of suretiship, his payment, according to that bond, can never be accounted a payment of their debt for whom he is not surety and whose names are not in the bond. Reader, give all diligence to make your calling and election sure. Receive Christ Jesus by faith, so that when He is formed in you it may be to your a sure evidence that you are found in Him.

Was the everlasting covenant made with Christ as the public Representative of His elect? It evidently follows that when He as their Representative obeyed and suffered, they all obeyed and suffered in Him. As all men sinned in Adam, the first man, when he as their public representative violated the covenant of works, so all true believers obeyed and suffered in Christ the second Man when He, as their Head and Representative, fulfilled the covenant of grace. This most comfortable doctrine is clearly taught by the holy Apostle Paul in these expressions: "By the obedience of One shall many be made righteous" (Romans 5:19). "For He hath made Him to be sin for us. . .that we might be made the righteousness of God in Him" (2 Corinthians 5:21). "I am crucified with Christ, nevertheless I live" (Galatians 2:20). The representative and the represented are but one person in law. Then therefore Christ, as the Representative of His people, answered all the demands of the law as a covenant of works; they answered them all in Him. ("What challenges Satan

The Parties Contracting

or conscience can make against the believer, hear an answer I was condemned, I was judged, I was crucified, for sin, when my Surety Christ was condemned, judged, and crucified, for my sins . . . I have paid all because my Surety hath paid all" (Samuel Rutherford's *Trial and Triumph of Faith*). Oh, that the proud legalist would seriously consider that it is far from being enough for him to yield even perfect obedience to the law as a covenant. If ever he would be justified, so as to have a title to life, he must, either by himself or by a representative, be a sufferer as well as a doer.

Again, was the covenant of grace made with Christ as the Representative of His elect seed, and with them, considered as in Him? It necessarily follows that it is not two distinct covenants, but only one covenant (in our Larger Catechism, Quest. 31, we read that "the covenant of grace was made with Christ, as the second Adam, and in Him, with all the elect as his seed"; Isaiah 53:10, 11; Romans 5:15 to the end; Galatians 3:16). The covenant of redemption and the covenant of grace are but two appellations of one and the same covenant, under two different views of it. A covenant of redemption, properly so called, is a contact of buying and selling; and such a covenant it was to Christ only because He, and none but He, engaged to pay the price of man's redemption. A covenant of grace, on the other hand, is a contract, according to which all is to be given and received freely; and such a covenant it is to us, only to us; the whole of it is of free, immensely free grace. Accordingly, we find in Scripture that the covenants for life and salvation to mankind are only two in number, of which the covenant of works is the one and, consequently, the covenant of grace of grace must be the other. These, says the Apostle Paul, "are the two covenants; the one, from the Mount Sinai, which gendereth to bondage" (Galatians 4:24). The generating of bond-children, excluded from the inheritance (verse 30), is a distinguishing character of the covenant of works, and cannot agree to the covenant of grace under any of its dispensations. The one covenant is in Scripture called the law, the other, grace (Romans 6:14); the former is the covenant of the law, with Adam representing his natural posterity; the latter is the covenant of redeeming grace made with Christ, representing His spiritual offspring (1 Corinthians 15:47, 48). Moreover, the blood of Jesus Christ, because redemption was purchased by it, and because grace reigns through it unto eternal life, is with the utmost propriety called the blood of the covenant. Now the Spirit, in sacred Scripture, makes mention of the blood of the covenant in the singular number four several times (To wit, in Exodus 24:8, Zechariah 9:11, Hebrews 10:29 and 13:20). In order to explain and establish this important truth more fully, I cannot deny myself the pleasure of extracting the following paragraphs from Mr. Bell's notes on Witsius's *Irenical Animadversions on the Controversies Agitated in Britain*.

The difference among the evangelic, as to this matter, is rather verbal than real. For the covenant, though one, cannot but come under two considerations, viz. as made either from eternity with the Son of God or in time with the saints. It was made with Him as a Surety for us (Hebrews 7:20); it is made with us through Him as Mediator (1 Timothy 2:5; Hebrews 8:6). His obedience has the same place in the covenant as made with Him that Adam's would have had in the covenant made with him. Neither faith, repentance, nor new obedience have that place in the new covenant, which Adam's obedience would have had in the old; but only that which the sinless obedience of Adam's posterity would have had; that is to say, they are the effects of our Representative's righteousness; duties of the covenant incumbent on us, not its condition required of us. A condition must be performed previous to any right to those benefits of which it is the condition; inasmuch as it is that alone which gives a right to them. And, if so, respecting the right to them, then also as to the possession of them. God is said to have made a covenant with His Son (Psalm 89:3; Isaiah 49:1-12), in which grace was given, i.e., promised unto us (2 Timothy 1:9; Titus 1:2). He is also said to make a covenant with us (2 Samuel 23:5; Isaiah 55:3). But as it was not one covenant that was made with the first Adam, and another that was made with his posterity (Romans 5:12); neither was it one covenant that was made with his with the second Adam (1 Corinthians 15:47), and another that is made with his seed (Romans 5:19). For the same sin Adam and his seed were condemned (Romans 5:12-19); and for the same righteousness Christ and His are justified (2 Corinthians 5:21; 1 Timothy 3:16). In the former case, as soon as Adam's posterity come into being his guilt becomes theirs; and in the latter, as soon as the elect are united to Christ His righteousness becomes theirs, and both in virtue of the covenants under which they exist.

In the dispensation of the gospel, God promises to make a covenant with such as come unto Him (Isaiah 55:3), and no man can do so but by the Mediator (John 14:6). Now what kind of covenant is it that He makes with them? Why, just the sure mercies of David, i.e., all the blessings promised to the elect in Christ on condition of His making His soul an offering for sin (Isaiah 53:10). Therefore the covenant made with Christ, and that made with us, differ no more than a promise from its performance, which are in effect but one. The promise ensures the performance; the performance presupposes it. Sure as God is one in His purposes, they cannot be separated. But to investigate the matter a little more closely, how or whence is it that the elect are enabled to come unto Christ, and to God by Him? By nature they are dead in sin and cannot come, enemies, and will not. In consideration of what, or on what condition is it, that they are quickened and thereby made able and willing to come? It is on behalf of Christ, or on account of what He did and suffered (Philippians 1:29; 2 Peter 1:1). Thus their faith, so far from being the condition of the covenant, presupposes its fulfillment. Faith itself is a leading blessing of the covenant, the golden key that unlocks that precious cabinet. In the administration of the covenant, indeed, God says to sinners, "Hear, and your soul shall live" (Isaiah 55:3). But they must have life before they can hear. For how can the dead hear? It was an important question that none but he who put it could answer, "Can these bones live" (Ezekiel 37:3)?

The dead sinner must, in the order of nature, live before he can hear. The life previous to hearing is as much the subject of a promise (John 5:25; Ephesians 2:1-5), as the life subsequent to it. For before the sinner can do what is here required, a gracious God must do as He has promised. He must take away the stony heart and give him a heart of flesh (Ezekiel 36:26). He must give him ears to hear, otherwise he cannot hear (Deuteronomy 29:4). He must restore the sinner's withered hand before he can actively receive the tried, the all-enriching gold (Revelation 3:18). Precious faith is certainly the gift of God (Ephesians 2:8). Now if the covenant of redemption is distinct from that of grace, Christ's surety-righteousness being the condition of the one, and the believer's faith that of the other, the necessary consequence is that, in virtue of the promise of one covenant, we fulfill the condition of another. It seems, however, more like the unity of the covenant to teach that in virtue of its previous promises fulfilled to us, its duties are performed by us. I say its previous or absolute promises, such as the quickening Spirit, the new heart, etc., in distinction from those that are subsequent, or in some sense conditional, as in these instances, "Hear, and your soul shall live. Believe on the Lord Jesus Christ, and thou shalt be saved" (Acts 16:31), where life, viz., in a state of justification and of comfort, is suspended on hearing, and salvation on believing.

Thus I think it evident that as Christ and His people are one, He, their Head, and they, His body, so the condition exacted of Him and the promises made to Him do not constitute one covenant, and the duties required of them, with the promise made to them another, but rather two parts of the same covenant.

But never does he speak of the blood of the covenants in the plural. The covenant, therefore, the blood of which is the price of man's redemption and is that through which grace reigns to eternal life, is but one covenant and not two. If we view it as a covenant of redemption, it is Christ's covenant; for it was through the blood of it that He was brought again from the dead. If we consider it as a covenant of grace, it is His peoples' covenant; for it is expressly so called in Zechariah 9:11: "As for thee also, by the blood of thy covenant, I have sent forth thy prisoners out of the pit, wherein is no water." It is evident from the words in the original that they are addressed not to Messiah, but to the Church. The covenant of grace, then, is the same individual covenant that in eternity was made with Christ. If the reader will but take hold of it as God's covenant (Isaiah 56:4), he shall soon find it to be a covenant of grace, of infinitely free grace, to himself.

Hence also we learn that the covenant of grace is absolute, and not properly conditional, to the spiritual seed of Christ. Being made with Christ as the Representative of the elect, the conditions of it were charged on Him and fulfilled by Him, just as the condition of the covenant of works was to have been fulfilled by Adam as the representative of his posterity. All of it, therefore, which remains to be fulfilled, is the promises to Him and His spiritual seed. Faith, which is freely promised in it, is indeed necessary to receive and rely on the promises; but it gives no title to the blessings promised; the grace of the promise is given to no man on account of his faith. The office of faith is to receive a title, but not to give one. It is through the righteousness of the second Adam received by faith that the grace of that glorious covenant reigns with absolute sway.

Hence likewise the sovereign freeness of redeeming love gloriously appears. The love of God pitched on fallen men and not on fallen angels. The dear and only begotten Son of the Father took hold of and represented sinful men, and not rebellious angels. He, indeed, could easily have represented the latter as well as the former; but in the infinite sovereignty of His love He passed by angels, though creatures in their own nature, far more excellent, and took hold of men, sinful men, despicable worms of the dust. That He loved men and not angels was owing entirely to the good pleasure of His sovereign will. The sovereignty of His love also appears in this, that it was an electing love, a love of some sinners of mankind and not of all. Christ in the covenant represented some only, and not all of the human race. All men were sinners, equally guilty, equally loathsome, in the sight of the High and Holy One; there was nothing in one sinner more than in another to recommend him to Divine favor. And yet, while free love pitched on objects infinitely unlovely, sovereign love pitched on some such objects and passed by others (Matthew 11:25, 26; Romans 9:21; 9:18). Let not the reader imagine that it is any disparagement to the federal representation of the second Adam that He represented some of mankind only whereas the first Adam represented all of mankind; for it was far more arduous and honorable for Christ to contract for

The Parties Contracting

one sinner than it was for Adam to contract for a whole world of innocent persons. It was more to save one than it was to destroy all. O how surpassing, how amazing, is the distinguishing love that gave rise to that representation! The breadth and length, the depth and height thereof, surpass knowledge. Press, O believer, after more spiritual acquaintance with it, more enlarged experience of it. If you would attain a sweet, a refreshing sense of it in your soul, believe it cordially, and with application to yourself. Believe in order to feel. Your dear Savior offers Himself and all the love of His heart to you as a sinner of mankind. Come near then and, upon the warrant of the indefinite offer, trust with all your heart that He loves you and that He rests in His love to you. This unparalleled love, when cordially believed, will captivate and draw your heart, will constrain and secure your love to Him in return. Oh, believe the love that He has for you and you shall see what salvation it will bring you. Your heart will glow with sacred love to Him, and God in Him; and you will so dwell in love as to dwell in God, and God in you.

Moreover, it is evident from what has been discoursed that the covenant of grace must have been the result of infinite wisdom as well as of sovereign love. Here we see that no wisdom but that which is boundless could ever have devised a covenant so infinitely well ordered in all things. It is a covenant for them who were utterly unable to fulfill even the least condition of life; a covenant made, on the highest terms, with them who could not rise to the lowest. Infinite wisdom devised the way; it found out a Representative. The love of the Father moved Him to propose the representation, and the love of the Son engaged Him to accept it. Thus, Jehovah the Father had One with whom He could, with the safety of His honor, contract, and who was infinitely able to fulfill the covenant; and sinners also had One who was perfectly able to answer and act for them, and so to purchase, at the hand even of an infinitely righteous God, eternal redemption for them. Thus a firm foundation was established on which Jehovah laid the weight of His glory, and on which sinners of mankind may with all safety lay the weight of their salvation (Isaiah 28:16; 1 Peter 2:6). Oh, admirable device of a Divine covenant, with persons who were as incapable as they were unworthy to stand for a moment in the presence of the infinitely holy Lord God! Wonderful contrivance of help for those who had destroyed themselves! "Oh, the depth of the riches, both of the wisdom and knowledge of God! How unsearchable are His judgments, and His ways past finding out!"

But further, from what has been stated, it is no less manifest that they whom Christ represented in the covenant of grace shall all be made to enter personally into the bond of that covenant. Others will reject it and perish, but they will take hold of it and live. As all they whom Adam represented in the covenant of works have been, or will be, brought personally into that covenant under the dominion of sin and death (Romans 5:12), so all they whom Christ represented in the covenant of grace have been, or shall be, made to enter personally into this glorious covenant and to receive righteousness and life (verses 18, 19). The Lord Jesus has fulfilled the conditions of the covenant for them whom He represented; and it would not accord, either with the justice of God, or with the wisdom and love of Christ that He should represent, contract, and fulfill the conditions for any who are never to receive the benefit of the contract. Seeing therefore that every one whom Christ represented will certainly enter personally into the covenant, and that every sinner who hears the gospel has a revealed warrant to enter, as well as the means of entering, within His reach, any sinner may come warrantably into the bond of it. Let every sinner, then, be encouraged to accept without delay Christ Jesus the Lord, and so to take hold of God's covenant. Consider, O sinner, that the covenant lies ready in Him complete, and suitable in all things, to your necessities. When He is offered to you, the covenant is offered with Him; when He is received by faith, the covenant is, at the same time, received; nor is anything further necessary to ensure your interest in the covenant, and in all the privileges and provisions of it, than a personal and saving interest in Him.

Accept then the grant of Him and all that is in the covenant shall be yours. Do not say, "I suspect I am not one of those whom Christ represented in the covenant, and therefore I cannot with any warrant attempt to lay hold on it." For, as it is impossible for you to know that Christ has represented you in the covenant till after you have taken hold of it by faith (2 Peter 1:10), so, on the other hand, unless you are certain that you have committed the unpardonable sin it is impossible for you, so long as you are out of hell, to know assuredly that He has not represented you (Deuteronomy 29:29). Neither does your warrant to take hold of the covenant depend in the least on your having been represented therein; for the non-elect have as good a revealed warrant to lay hold on it as the elect have; otherwise, they could not be condemned for refusing to do so (John 3:18). The offer and call of the gospel, together with the command to believe, are all directed to you (John 6:32; Revelation 22:17; 1 John 3:23); and they afford you a full, a sufficient warrant. Oh, that you knew the gift of God, and who it is that speaks to you! Then you would so believe as to enter the bond of the covenant, and should begin to know your election and representation by the effects of them in your heart and life.

But the reader will ask, "Are there no marks by which a convinced sinner may know whether he is one of those who have been represented and contracted for in the everlasting covenant or not?"

Yes, there are; and I propose in another chapter to consider them; but they are all of such a nature that although having them will evidence a man to have been represented in the eternal covenant, yet the want of them will not prove him not to have been represented in it because he may have afterwards what he has not now.

To conclude, are God and Christ the Parties contracting in that wonderful covenant? Then to have fellowship with the Father, and with His Son Jesus Christ, is the life, the blessedness, of the believing soul. But, O believer, do not mistake the nature of this communion. It is not so much a strict profession of religion, or an external performance of duty, or a high degree of knowledge, as a dwelling in God, and God in the soul. Christ so dwells in the heart by faith as to admit the believer to real, to increasing, to transforming intercourse with Him. The holy soul dwells, and is at home in Him, as its hiding place, its only portion, and its ultimate end. The soul that is favored with such communion knows no other object for its supreme love, no other subject for its delightful meditation, no other end for its endless existence, than HIM, and GOD in Him. It knows no higher degree of happiness for its attainment, and no higher employment for its faculties, than intimate communion with Him and perfect resemblance to Him. In fellowship with God in Christ the soul satiates itself with His love, shares in His fullness, contemplates His glory, and in some degree enters into His joy. His love flows out on the soul, and the love of the redeemed soul goes forth upon Him. By communion, the believing soul dwells with its covenant-God as well as in Him. It is with Him at one time in meditation, at another in the confidence of faith, at another in prayer, and at another in praise. It has not a sin but

The Parties Contracting

it mourns over to Him; not a grief, but it makes known to Him; not a complaint but it reveals to Him; not a request but it presents to Him. Oh, that spiritual intimacy which is between such a holy soul and Christ, that liberty of converse that wrestling with him for the blessing! Let me go. . . "I will not let thee go, except thou bless me" (Genesis 32:26).

This is eternal life begun; it is heaven let down to earth. "Thus the secret of the Lord is with them that fear Him; and He will show them His covenant" (Psalm 25:14).

2

The Making of the Covenant of Grace

Having viewed the parties of the covenant of grace, it will be proper now to consider the making of that eternal compact between those high contracting parties. The infinitely glorious plan of man's redemption, projected from everlasting in the secret counsel of the adorable Trinity, is a manifold mystery, a mystery the complicated plies of which we are infinitely far from being able fully to unfold. In the view of Jehovah, however, if I may so say, it is all one piece; for to Him who inhabits eternity, all things appear together and at once; one object is not before, nor another after, as with us, who are only creatures, and creatures of time. Now it was, according to that stupendous plan of redeeming love, that the covenant of grace was entered into between the contracting parties. According to our finite manner of conceiving spiritual objects, we have to think of that covenant as made of old in a period that is long since elapsed, that has passed away, long, infinitely long, before the world began. But to the eternal, the glorious parties themselves, the making of it is ever new and ever present. Nothing to them can be either past or future. The fulfilling of the conditions of that eternal covenant was to man, when it was at first revealed to him a matter of futurity, and that for so long as four thousand years; but to Jehovah, who inhabits eternity, it was always present; so that in saving sinners under the Patriarchal and Jewish economy He proceeded upon them as conditions in a manner already ful-

The Making of the Covenant of Grace

filled; and though it was a matter of futurity likewise to Christ as man, previous to His finishing His work on the cross and in the grave, yet to Him as God it was neither past nor future, but was ever present. Accordingly, speaking of Himself as God-man, He said to the Jews, "Before Abraham was (not, I was, but) I AM" (John 8:58). All that is past to us, as well as all that is future, is necessarily and invariably present to Him.

But although that wonderful covenant was, in the eternal and mysterious counsel of the ever-blessed Trinity, and by one eternal act of the Divine will, made all at once, yet since we, because of the narrowness and darkness of our understanding, cannot form any apprehensions of it but, as it were, in parcels; we are allowed to conceive a certain order in the making of it, and to consider first one part and then another.

SECTION 1. The Order Observed in Making the Covenant of Grace

We have already seen that the Father, the party contracting on the part of heaven, is, in that great transaction, to be considered as one infinitely offended; but yet, as purposing to manifest in the salvation of some sinners of mankind the glory of His mercy; and at the same time, as a holy and righteous God who cannot but award to transgression a just recompense. We have seen too that the Son, the party contracting on the side of man, is therein to be viewed as the last Adam, the Head and Representative of a seed. It will be proper, therefore, I apprehend, to consider the making of that august contract in the following order:

1. The eternal Father willed and proposed that His eternal Son, for accomplishing His design of mercy towards sinners of mankind, should, in the fullness of time, assume their nature and so became man. He from eternity saw that sacrifice and of-

fering could not answer the exigency, that the debt was too great to be discharged so easily, and that the redemption of souls was too precious to be either purchased or conferred by a person of less than infinite dignity. Therefore, having in his infinite sovereignty purposed that the glory of His darling attribute of mercy should, in the salvation of lost sinners of mankind, be illustriously displayed, He proposed that the human nature should, in the fullness of time, be united to the Divine nature in the person of the adorable Son. He willed and proposed that the eternal Word should be made flesh, that He should take to Himself a true body and a reasonable soul; not as a person distinct from His own divine person, but only as a nature, assumed unto a subsistence in His person.

To this gracious proposal, the only begotten Son, the second person of the eternal Trinity, having as yet no nearer relation to man than that of his Creator and sovereign Lord, did with infinite readiness consent. He said to His eternal Father, "Sacrifice and offering Thou wouldst not, but a body hast Thou prepared Me. Then said I, 'Lo, I come (in the volume of the book it is written of Me) to do Thy will, O God' " (Hebrews 10:5, 7). The eternal Word consented to be made flesh that all flesh might not perish. He agreed to become man that he might be as really the Son of man, and one of the family of Adam, as He was already the Son of God, and one of the family of heaven. This, in Him, was an instance of astonishing condescension. By His consenting to assume, as well as by His act of assuming, the human nature, He made Himself of no reputation. He assumed it with all its sinless infirmities in a state of servile subjection to the law as a covenant, under the meanest appearance, the heaviest load of imputed sin and all the infinite weight of the curse of the law. The highest Monarch's consenting to lay aside His royal robes, to clothe Himself with rags and to become the most abject of the sons of men, is not once to be compared to this. Nay, the highest angel's consenting to become a worm is not once to be named in comparison to the eternal Son, the equal of the Father, consenting to become man; for while the distance between the nature of angels and that of worms of the dust is but finite, the distance between the nature of the only begotten of the Father and that of man is infinite.

Now the immediate consequence of the Son of God's consenting to become man was that He was constituted substantial Mediator, or Mediator in respect of nature, between God and men. Upon His consenting to be God-man in one person, He, as partaking in legal estimation of the nature of both parties, was constituted substantial Mediator. From everlasting He was God equal with the Father, and so stood related to heaven; from eternity He consented to become man and so stood related to earth. The two families of heaven and of earth were at war with each other; and no peace between them could ever be restored but through a Mediator. And where could a Mediator, or Day's man, qualified to interpose between such parties, be found who would not either be too high or else too low in respect of one or other of the parties? A mere man, or an angel, would have been too low in respect of the infinitely High and Holy God; and an unveiled God would have been too high in respect of sinful man, unable to bear immediate intercourse with such glorious Majesty. The only begotten Son, therefore, in order that He might be qualified to mediate as being God equal with the Father, He was already high enough, in respect of the Party offended; so, by consenting to become man, He engaged to become low enough, in regard to the party offending. A type of His substantial mediation was Jacob's ladder, which was set upon the earth and whose top reached to heaven (Genesis 28:12), and therefore was a fit emblem of the Divine and human natures in the person of Christ through whom, as the substantial Mediator, a way was opened for peace and intercourse between God and men. Accordingly, our Lord Jesus applies it to Himself. "Verily, verily, I say unto you, Hereafter you shall see heaven open, and the angels of God, ascending and descending upon the Son of man" (John 1:51). By thus becoming substantial Mediator, He was capable of subjecting Himself to that law which was binding upon us, of paying our debt of love to God and to man, and of suffering and satisfying for sin in the same nature that sinned.

2. Upon this, the eternal Father chose Him to be the federal Head and Representative of those whom He should, according to His sovereign pleasure, select to be the objects of redeeming love and the vessels of saving mercy. He proposed to Him to become a public Representative, with whom He might enter into a covenant for the redemption of them upon whom He should pitch, and whom He should enroll in the book of life in order that they might have a Covenant-head who should be both God and man in one person (Ephesians 1:22).

To this proposal also He with infinite willingness agreed. He consented to become the Head and Representative of such as were to be elected that He might sustain their persons and entreat in their name. "Behold," said Jehovah the Father, "Mine elect, in whom My soul delighteth" (Isaiah 42:1). "I have exalted one chosen out of the people" (Psalm 89:19). "I the Lord have called thee in righteousness, and will...give thee for a covenant of the people" (Isaiah 42:6). The breach between God and sinners of mankind was greater than to be made up by a mere envoy or intercessor who, going between parties at variance, reconciles them by bare words. There could be no covenant of peace between Jehovah and sinners without a reparation of damages done by sin to His infinite honor, nor without an honoring of

His holy law with perfect obedience. Both of these were far beyond their power. The eternal Son of God, therefore, beholding the undone condition to which they had been reduced, while at the same time they could do nothing for themselves, and while none in the whole compass of creation could afford them any relief, said, "Lo, I come. I am willing to become their federal Representative, and to substitute myself in their stead."

Now the effect of His acceptance of the Father's proposal to Him to become the federal Head and Representative of them who should be chosen to salvation was that He was constituted the last or second Adam. The first man was called the first Adam not so much because he was the first parent, as because he was the federal representative of his natural posterity. In like manner, Christ is called the last Adam and the second man (1 Corinthians 15:45, 47), not merely because He was the everlasting Father of His spiritual offspring, but chiefly because He is their federal Representative, a public person representing them and transacting in their stead. The main reason, then, why the only begotten Son of the Father was called the last Adam was His having, in the making of the covenant, become the public Head and Representative of the elect of God.

Moreover, the effect of His having been constituted the last Adam was that He was established the official Mediator, or the Mediator in respect of office between God and men (1 Timothy 2:5). Having His Father's call to that high office, and having consented to the call, He was accordingly invested with the office (Proverbs 8:23). He was constituted the great Mediator between God and men to bring God and men, who had been at variance, to meet again amicably; by the price of His blood to bring God to men, and by the power of His Spirit to bring men to God, and so to make up the breach between heaven and earth. First, then, He consented to assume the nature of such as were to be elected to eternal life, and so was constituted substantial Mediator; next He agreed to assume and sustain their persons in law and so was established official Mediator. The office of a Mediator is the general office that He consented in the covenant to execute. Being the Head or Prince of the eternal covenant He is, in sacred Scripture, called the Mediator of the New Covenant (Hebrews 12:24).

3. All the individuals of mankind, the church chosen to eternal life, were, in a manner, becoming the infinite Majesty of Jehovah given by the Father to Christ and were accepted by Him. The eternal Father designed a certain number of lost mankind to be the constituent members of that body chosen to salvation, of which He was the designed Head, and gave them to Him for that purpose. "Thine they were, and Thou gavest them Me" (John 17:6). They were a chosen company whom sovereign grace selected from among the rest of mankind on a purpose of love, and consigned to Christ the last Adam for a seed. They are therefore said to have been chosen in Him (Ephesians 1:4). In the sovereign decree of their election they were given to Him that they might have, first, a legal, and next, a vital union with Him, and that they might, on the ground of His obedience unto death, inherit everlasting life (1 Thessalonians 5:9). That Divine decree, so far as it relates to the members elect, is called the book of life (Philippians 4:3), it being as it were the roll which the Father delivered to the last Adam, the Head elect, containing the names of them who were chosen to be His seed, and to obtain eternal life by Him as their Head of righteousness and of life. It pleased God in His eternal purpose, to choose and ordain the Lord Jesus, His only begotten Son, to be the Mediator between God and man; the Head and Savior of His Church; unto whom He did, from all eternity, give a people to be His seed,

The Making of the Covenant of Grace 55

and to be by Him in time, redeemed, called, justified, sanctified, and glorified (*Westminster Confession of Faith* Chapter viii. Art. I).

Now the Lord Jesus, considered as the last Adam, the Representative of them whom God, in His sovereign pleasure, should select to be the members of His mystical body, did most willingly accept the gift that was made to Him by the particular persons chosen by the Father. "Thine they were, and Thou gavest them Me. . .Thine are Mine; and I am glorified in them" (John 17:6, 10). As in the making of the covenant of works the first Adam stood alone, without actual offspring, and yet had designed for him a numerous progeny to be included with him in that covenant that he virtually, at least, accepted, so in electing a determinate number of lost mankind to life eternal, the Father gave them to Christ, the second Adam, their appointed Head, to be His spiritual seed and to be comprehended with Him in the covenant of grace while as yet none of them had actual existence. The gift He, with infinite readiness, with unparalleled condescension, accepted at the hand of His eternal Father; and in token of that He, as it were, received and kept as His own, the book in which their names were enrolled, which, for that reason, is called the Lamb's book of life (Revelation 21:17).

4. Last, the eternal Father thereupon proposed to Him, as the last Adam, the covenant of grace for their salvation in the whole tenor, conditions, and promises of it; treating in Him, with all the individual persons of mankind who had been elected to salvation, and given to Him; even as, in the covenant of works, He treated with all mankind in the first Adam. And Christ, as the second Adam, in the name and stead of the particular persons who had been chosen to life and given to Him, most willingly accepted the promises proposed to Him and consented to fulfill the conditions upon which they had been proposed. The promises proposed to Him were indeed exceedingly

great and precious; but the conditions withal on which the performance of them was suspended were exceedingly high and difficult. Notwithstanding, as the first Adam, considered as the representative of his natural offspring, entered into a covenant of works with God, accepting the promise of it and engaging to fulfill the condition therein prescribed, so the Lord Jesus, standing as the last Adam, the glorious Representative of those who were by name elected to salvation and given to Him as His spiritual seed, entered into a covenant of grace with His eternal Father, accepting the promises and engaging to fulfill the conditions therein imposed. As a public person, filling their place by a vicarious character, He in their name received the promises and consented to fulfill the conditions; and by so doing, He entered into that eternal covenant for them. Thus the covenant of grace was, from everlasting, made and established between the Father and the Son as last Adam. The terms of that magnificent treaty were on both sides fixed; the compact was closed; the bargain was, by mutual agreement, completed before any of the objects of redeeming mercy began to exist; and the whole, ratified on both sides, passed into a solemn contract. And therefore, though it was the second covenant in respect of manifestation, it was the first in respect of being. Hence are these cheering declarations: "The second Man is the Lord from heaven" (1 Corinthians 15:47). "Sacrifice and offering Thou didst not desire, Mine ears hast Thou opened; . . . Then said I, Lo, I come; . . . I delight to do Thy will, O my God; yea, Thy law is within My heart" (Psalm 40:6, 7, 8). "In hope of eternal life, which God that cannot lie promised before the world began" (Titus 1:2).

When that gracious covenant was thus made, the terms, and indeed everything concerning the salvation of elect sinners, were fully settled, what ransom should be paid, and in what time and

The Making of the Covenant of Grace

form; what furniture for, assistance in, and reward after His work Christ should receive from the Father; and in what circumstances of manner, duration and degree, grace and glory should be conferred on Him in the human nature, and on every one of His mystical members (Isaiah 49:1-10; Psalm 2:6-9; 20:27-31). It was stipulated that, in executing the plan of redemption, the eternal Father should act the part of a sovereign Lord and Judge with respect to the Son and His elect seed (Isaiah 50:4-9; Zechariah 13:7), that the eternal Son should perform the part of a Mediator and federal Head (Isaiah 41:1-3; Psalm 110 throughout), and that the eternal Spirit should act as a publisher of the doctrines and duties of the covenant (1 Peter 1:11, 12; 2 Peter 1:21) as a furnisher, assistance, and rewarder of the man Christ (Isaiah 11:2-4; Psalm 14:7), as a witness of Christ's and of the Father's fulfilling of the covenant, and as an effectual Applier of the benefits of it to elect sinners (John 14:16, 17, 26; 15:26).

Thus the everlasting covenant was made; thus that transcendently glorious contract was drawn up and settled in the counsel of peace between the Father and the Son, with the approbation and concurrence of the Holy Spirit. And though the spiritual seed of Christ were not consulted in the affair, yet they have no reason to complain that any injury has been done to them; for they have nothing on their part to contract. The breach of the covenant of innocence left them worse than nothing; the first Adam left them under a pressure of extreme poverty and misery, under a burden of the curse of the broken law, yea, under a burden of immense debt; and all that they can do, instead of diminishing, is to increase the boundless sum.

It will be proper now to show that the Lord Jesus, the second Adam, in consenting to the conditions of that wonderful contract, took upon Him characters of infinite importance to the glory of Jehovah in the salvation of lost sinners. He took upon Him, and He still sustains, not only the general character of the Mediator of the covenant, but the particular characters of the Father's Servant, of the Redeemer, of the Surety, and of the sacrificing Priest of the covenant.

SECTION 2. Christ the Servant of His Father in the Covenant of Grace

Christ, the last Adam, in consenting to the terms of the eternal covenant, engaged to become the Servant of His Father in that covenant. In agreeing to take upon Himself the obligation of fulfilling the conditions of the contract, He covenanted to take upon Him the form of a Servant (Philippians 2:7). In undertaking to be the Mediator of the covenant, He consented to be a humbled Mediator, to be humbled in the room of His people, to the state and to the obedience of a servant, and that under the commanding and condemning law of the covenant of works. In the unparalleled depth of His condescending love, He engaged to come under all the perceptive obligations of that law for them by having their obligation to perfect obedience for life transferred to Him; and likewise to come under all the penal obligation of the same law by having the iniquities of them all, by imputation, laid on Him. The form of a servant was not imposed on Him against His will but, in stipulating with His eternal Father, He took it upon Himself and became bound when He might have continued free. The Scriptures represent Christ as a humbled Servant, or a Servant in His state of humiliation (Isa. 49:7); and as an honorary Servant, or a Servant in his state of exaltation (Isaiah 42:1, 4). The form of a humbled Servant He submitted to; the form of an exalted Servant was conferred upon Him as a promised reward of that wonderful submission. In this form of a Servant He has an honorary, a glorious minis-

The Making of the Covenant of Grace

try; in that, of which I am here briefly to treat He had a service, or rather a servitude, humble and onerous; and so the form, mentioned in Philippians 2:7, was the form, as the original word signifies, of a bondservant. It is the same word that is invariably used in those places of the New Testament where we find the expressions, "bond or free, free and bond." The greatest inequality that is to be found in any of the external relations subsisting among men is that which subsists between the bond servant and his master; and the greatest leveling among them is that of which mention is made in Isaiah 24:2. "It shall be . . . as with the servant, so with his master."

Our Lord Jesus Christ is, in the Scripture, expressly called the Servant of Jehovah the Father. "Behold My servant whom I uphold" (Isaiah 42:1). These words are cited in Matthew 12:18 and directly applied to Jesus.

But what kind of a Servant to His Father was He? Did He become a bondservant to Him? Yes, verily, in His wonderful condescension He did. Hear His own declaration respecting Himself: "Sacrifice and offering Thou didst not desire; Mine ears hast Thou opened" (Psalm 40:6). The original word here translated "opened" properly signifies "digged," as it is rendered on the margin; and so the words run, "Mine ears hast Thou digged, or bored through." In the phrase there is evidently an allusion to this law concerning the bondservant: "Then his master shall bring him unto the judges; he shall also bring him to the door, or unto the door-post; and his master shall bore his ear through with an awl; and he shall serve him forever" (Exodus 21:6). It is explained and confirmed by these words in Hosea 3:2: "So I bought her to me, for fifteen pieces of silver; which was the half of the settled price of a bond woman." In the sacred original it is, "So I digged her through to me." The original word here is the same that is used in the passage just now cited from the 40th Psalm, and the meaning is, "I bought her, and bored her ear to my door-post; in order that she might, according to the law, be my bond woman" (Deuteronomy 15:17). As a further proof that in making the covenant Christ engaged to be the Father's bondservant, His precious life, which was a ransom of infinite value for the life of the whole elect world, was, by Judas Iscariot, sold for thirty pieces of silver; the fixed price of the life of a bond servant (Exodus 21:32); and the death likewise that He was condemned to suffer, namely that of crucifixion, was a punishment inflicted by the Romans only, which they used to call the servile punishment, or punishment of bond servants, because it was the kind of death to which malefactors among their bond men were usually condemned. As therefore the only begotten Son, the equal, the fellow, of Jehovah the Father, consented to become, so He actually became His bondservant. Amazing condescension! Unparalleled benignity! He graciously consented, for us men and for our salvation, to enter upon a state of servitude to His righteous Father, who thereupon said to Him, "Thou art my Servant, O Israel" (Isaiah 49:3), and who said concerning Him, "Behold, I will bring forth My Servant the BRANCH" (Zechariah 3:8). It was with His eternal Father that He entered into the covenant as a contract of service; it was His Father's business, about which He was to be employed; and it was to Him that He became bound to do all His work. "I must work the works of Him that sent Me while it is day" (John 9:4). When, in the Scripture, He is called a servant of rulers (Isaiah 49:7), it is not to be understood that He is so called in respect of the principal servile relation in which He stood to the Father (for that relation He bore to His Father only), but in regard merely to a secondary relation, as when a master commands his servant to serve another man by doing some particular piece of work to him. Thus was our Lord Jesus, by the appointment of the Father, subjected to rulers among the Jews and Romans.

Now for whom did He engage to become a bondservant to His eternal Father? He engaged for His elect seed. The elect world were utterly unable to make up their service; they had so disabled themselves by their fall in the first Adam that they could no longer, by any strength of their own, perform acceptable service to the Lord. In the making of the covenant, therefore, it was agreed that the Father's only begotten Son should, in their stead, perform the service that was due in virtue of the original contract. To Him, accordingly, the Father said, "Thou art My Servant, O Israel, in whom I will be glorified" (Isaiah 49:3). It is as if He had said, "Thou, as the Representative of My spiritual Israel, art My servant, from whose hand I will expect that service."

Christ's consenting to become a bondservant for the redemption of the elect world was requisite; for, in the first place, the elect, as well as the rest of mankind, were, by the covenant of works, constituted the hired servants of God; and in the first Adam, their federal representative, they entered to their service. The work that they were to do was perfect obedience to the holy law; in its covenant-form the hire, which they were to have for their work, was life. "The man which doeth those things shall live by them" (Romans 10:5). The penalty of breaking off from their master, or deserting their service, was perpetual bondage under the curse (Galatians 3:10).

Second, they did not accomplish their service. No sooner had they entered home to it than, at the instigation of Satan, they broke off from their Lord, and so violated their covenant of service. They therefore lost all plea for the hire and became bond men under the curse of the broken covenant, liable for their crimes, to die the death of slaves. "These," says the Apostle

Paul, "are the two covenants; the one from the mount Sinai, which gendereth to bondage" (Galatians 4:24). Their having fallen under the curse included their loss of liberty and constituted them perpetual bondmen, as is evident from instances of persons or things having fallen under the curse of God in other cases. "Cursed be Canaan; a servant of servants shall he be unto his brethren" (Genesis 9:25). The very ground, when it was cursed, fell under bondage (Romans 8:21).

Third, by their breach of that covenant, they lost all ability for their service so that, as the Apostle Paul expresses it, they were without strength (Romans 5:6). They had no strength to suffer the punishment due to them for deserting their service, but must have perished under it, and that forever. They had no strength remaining to perform their work to any purpose spiritually good; indeed they had no longer either a hand or a heart for their work. "The carnal mind is . . . not subject to the law of God, neither indeed can be. So then, they that are in the flesh cannot please God" (Romans 8:7, 8). "Ye cannot serve the Lord; for He is an holy God" (Joshua 24:19).

Fourth, still however, the punishment due to them for deserting their service must be endured, and the service itself, according to the original contract, the covenant of works, must be completed; otherwise it would be impossible for them ever to attain life eternal. "In the day that thou eatest thou shalt surely die" (Genesis 2:17). "If thou wilt enter into life, keep the commandments" (Matthew 19:17).

Fifth, since therefore it was indispensably requisite that the misery of servitude should be borne while the elect were not able to bear it, and that the service itself should be performed while they were neither able nor willing to perform it. Christ the last Adam, in the exceeding greatness of His love, consented to come under the curse due to them for sin, to take upon Himself

The Making of the Covenant of Grace

their form and their state of servitude, and to enter home to the arduous service and finish it in their stead. "We," says the Apostle Paul, "were in bondage under the elements of the world; but . . . God sent forth His Son . . . made under the law, to redeem them that were under the law" (Galatians 4:3, 4, 5). "Christ hath redeemed us from the curse of the law, being made a curse for us" (Galatians 3:13).

When, therefore, the covenant of grace was made with Christ, representing the elect of God, it is to be considered with regard to Him as a contract of service in the strictest sense of the expression, according to which so much work was to be done, for so much wages. It was a contract of service that was to be begun and completed by Him in the room of His spiritual seed. In this Divine covenant, it was agreed that the second Adam and He only should work for life to perishing sinners; and that they, receiving life through Him in a way of free grace, should work, not for life, but from life already received (Romans 4:4, 5 compared with 6:23). According to the contract of service, then, into which from eternity He entered, the second Adam did, in the fullness of time, by taking to Himself the human nature, take upon Him the form of a bondservant; and being found in fashion as a man humbled Himself and become obedient unto death, even the death of the cross (Philippians 2:8). As it was love to His eternal Father, and to His spiritual seed, that engaged Him to enter into a contract of service for His glory and their salvation, so it was the same infinite love that determined Him to accomplish the service. He accordingly entered to it by His holy incarnation, went on in it by the perfect obedience of His life, and finished it by His death and burial. The term of His continuance, in this form and state of servitude, was, according to the covenant, till death, but no longer. "I must work the works of Him that sent me while it is day; the night (namely of death) cometh when no man can work" (John 9:4). As it is in the grave that the servant is free from his master (Job 3:19), so it was there that the second Adam, having served out His full time, put off the form of a bondservant. When He rose from the grave, He rose and revived that He might be Lord, both of the dead and living (Romans 14:9).

SECTION 3. Christ, the Redeemer in the Covenant

Christ the second Adam, in consenting to fulfill the conditions of the covenant of grace, took upon Himself the all-important character of a Kinsman-redeemer in that magnificent treaty. In respect of Him, as sustaining this endearing character, it may well be styled a covenant of redemption The salvation provided in it for lost sinners is in the Scripture set forth under the notion of eternal redemption, obtained for them by Him (Hebrews 9:12). He is frequently called the Redeemer. Job, when contemplating Him under this amiable character, said, "I know that my Redeemer liveth" (Job 19:25).

Under the Jewish economy, when a man was not able to act for himself, or assert his own right, the one who was next of kin to him or was his nearest blood-relation had a right by law to stand up in his room and to act for him. Such a one was called his "Goel," which signifies a Kinsman-redeemer. The word, accordingly, is sometimes translated a kinsman and, frequently, a redeemer. It is rendered a kinsman in Numbers 5:8: "If the man have no (goel) kinsman to recompense the trespass unto." And in Ruth 3:12, "I am thy (goel) near kinsman; howbeit there is (goel) a kinsman nearer than I." In many passages, it is rendered "a redeemer." "Their (goel) redeemer is mighty; he shall plead their cause with thee" (Proverbs 23:11). "As for our (goel) Redeemer, the Lord of hosts is His name" (Isaiah 47:4). A man's acting for another in that capacity was usually called a doing of the kinsman's part, or a redeeming by right of kin (Ruth 3:13; 4:6). Such a one might, on some occasions, decline to do the part of a kinsman as the kinsman of Ruth did who resigned his right of redeeming to Boaz and, as a token of that, drew off his shoe and gave it to him (Ruth 4:6, 7).

Now Christ, the second Adam, beheld sinners of mankind, His ruined kinsmen, utterly unable to act for themselves. He saw that there was not so much as one of them who could by any means redeem himself, or his brother, or give to God a ransom for him (Psalm 49:7). He saw that if holy angels had dared to meddle in that redemption they neither could have delivered their poor kinsmen nor have missed thereby to mar their own inheritance. He knew that if He Himself had declined to act and had drawn off His shoe to them, or to any others in the whole creation, there was not so much as one who dared have put his foot in it. "I looked," said he, "and there was none to help; and I wondered that there was one to uphold; therefore, mine own arm brought salvation unto me" (Isaiah 63:5). He therefore, in making the covenant, took upon Himself the endearing character of their Kinsman-redeemer. And it is of Him, under that character, that Job speaks in a fore-cited passage (Job 19:25) which, when translated literally, runs thus: "For I know that my Kinsman-redeemer liveth, and that the latter (or last) One, he shall stand upon the dust." Job, by these words, encouraged himself with a view of Messiah as his Kinsman-redeemer, living, in respect of the Divine nature, even in his days; and as the latter, or last One, namely the latter or last Adam, that Redeemer, in opposition to the former or first Adam, that destroyer; firmly persuaded that the One should, in human nature, as certainly stand up upon the dust of the earth and do the kinsman's part for him; as that the other, having the breath of life breathed into his nostrils, stood up upon it, and ruined him.

It is not for naught that the near kinsman among the ancient Jews, and Christ, the last Adam, are, in the original language of the Old Testament, alike denominated. The name "Goel" was common, both to him who acted the kinsman's part among the Israelites and to the God of Israel, doubtless to intimate that there was a great resemblance between the friendly offices of the one and the gracious benefits of the other. What the earthly Goel then was under the law to do for his brother, the heavenly Goel, the great and gracious Redeemer, has, in the most eminent manner, done for sinners of mankind.

Now there were four things that the Goel, or kinsman-redeemer under the law, was enjoined to do for his kinsman, unable to act for himself; which also the second Adam undertook in making the covenant, to do in a spiritual and eminent sense for poor sinners of the human race.

1. If an Israelite died without children, the Goel was to marry his widow in order to raise up seed to his brother, that his name might not perish in Israel. Of this, Boaz was reminded by Ruth when she said to him, "I am Ruth thine handmaid; spread therefore thy skirt over thine handmaid, for thou art a near kinsman" (Ruth 3:9 compared with 4:10). Our nature was in a fruitful and comfortable condition so long as the image of God, impressed upon it in Adam, continued. But now, by the breach of the covenant of innocence, that image in which it was fruitful to God is miserably defaced. Its husband the law too has, in its covenant-form, become weak through the flesh so that it can bring forth no spiritual offspring to God, no thoughts, words, or deeds that bear any real resemblance to Him. Sin and death are the only offspring of corrupted nature; and we may truly say of all the descendants of Adam in their natural state that they conceive mischief, they bring forth falsehood, and their belly prepares deceit. But the loving Kinsman consented to marry this

widowed nature by assuming it to a personal union with Himself and by uniting spiritually to Himself many individual persons of the human race. It was, indeed, a very unequal match for Him, and would have been so even if the family of Adam had continued in its primitive splendor—but much more so now when it was in the lowest depth of poverty and disgrace. Vast difficulties too were to be surmounted before the bride could be prepared for her husband and the marriage be solemnized. But His love was stronger even than death and believers are become dead to the law by the body of Christ that they might be married to another, even to Him who was raised from the dead, that they might bring forth fruit unto God (Romans 7:7); that the barren woman might keep house and be a joyful mother of children. Now that our Maker is our husband, she that was barren has born seven; and it may be truly said of the happy souls who are espoused to the one husband, every one bears twins, the love of God and of our neighbor, and none is barren among them.

2. If through poverty an Israelite had sold away his possession, the goel was to buy back his inheritance. His nearest of kin had a right, and it was incumbent on him to redeem the mortgaged inheritance of his poor kinsman. "If thy brother be waxen poor, and hath sold away some of his possession, and if any of his kin come to redeem it, then shall he redeem that which his brother sold," or, rather, "then shall come in his kinsman-redeemer, who is near to him, and he shall redeem that which is brother sold" (Leviticus 25:25). Our father Adam, having waxen poor through the deceitful dealing of the tempter with him, sold away the whole inheritance of eternal life for one morsel of forbidden fruit. None of his kin was able to pay the price requisite to redeem it. The money of their obedience and sufferings was quite insufficient for the purpose. His children, waxen poorer

still through their own personal fault, could not among them all have raised what would have redeemed so much as one man's part of it; and yet, unless it were redeemed, they never could have access to it. Elect angels, though glorious and perfect creatures, yet needed all their holiness for themselves. But lo! What men and angels could never have done, the Son of God, clothed with flesh and blood, has completely effected. The ransom was paid down in the liquid gold of His precious blood, to the utmost farthing demanded by the law. Now heaven is a "purchased possession." The second Adam, as our Kinsman-redeemer, took the burden of the redemption on Himself and agreed to pay the price of the purchase. He died for us that "we should live together with Him" (1 Thessalonians 5:10).

3. If an Israelite had, through poverty, sold himself for a servant to another man, his goel was to redeem him from his master. "If . . . thy brother . . . wax poor, and sell himself unto the stranger or sojourner by thee . . . after that he is sold, he may be redeemed again; one of his brethren may redeem him" (Leviticus 25:47, 48). Being reduced to the most abject poverty by our loss or of original righteousness, and of communion with God, we, like the prodigal son in the parable, sold ourselves to the most sordid slavery. Having thus sold ourselves we were brought into bondage under the curse of the law; and, being bondmen, under the dominion of the law as a covenant of works, we were consequently the abject slaves of Satan and of sin, never to be released without a sufficient ransom. It was therefore proposed, in making the covenant of grace, that the heavenly Goel should, in due time, give Himself a ransom for His poor enslaved kinsmen in order to redeem them from their cruel bondage. And He, being the only Kinsman of the human family on whom by law the right of redemption fell, the only Kinsman who had both a right and a capacity to redeem them, most readily con-

The Making of the Covenant of Grace 69

sented to the proposal (1 Timothy 2:6). The ransom was great—soul for soul, body for body, life for life—a person of infinite dignity for His poor kinsmen in bondage. Such were the hard conditions of their release. But the near Kinsman, the compassionate Redeemer, in His love and in His pity, undertook to ransom them and entered with His eternal Father into a covenant for that purpose. In that august compact, He engaged to redeem them from the curse of the law, to redeem them from all iniquity, from the power of Satan, from this present evil world, and to redeem them to God. He undertook to redeem them not merely by the infinite power of His arm, but by the inestimable price of His blood.

4. Once more, if an Israelite had been murdered, his goel was enjoyed to avenge his blood on the willful murderer. "The elders of his city shall send and fetch him thence, and deliver him into the hand of (goel) the avenger of blood, that he may die" (Deuteronomy 19:12). Our heavenly Goel saw all His poor kindred as slain men. The devil, the prince of rebellious angels, was the murderer (John 8:44). He had ministered poison to them in the loins of Adam, their great progenitor; yea, and had smitten them dead, as with an arrow shot through the eye. Thus he was a murderer from the beginning not only of their bodies, which were by his means subjected to the first death, but also of their souls, which were by nature dead in trespasses and sins, and were liable to everlasting destruction, which is the second death. The righteous law of Jehovah, if I may so say, was the city of refuge to which he fled. He thus boasted: Shall the prey be taken from the mighty? Shall the lawful captive be delivered? This murderer, moreover, had the power of death (Hebrews 2:14). "Now the sting of death is sin; and the strength of sin is the law" (1 Corinthians 15:56). It was impossible, therefore, to destroy, or even to disarm the murderer, otherwise than by tak-

ing the sting out of death, of which he had the power; and that was not to be achieved but by removing the guilt of sin, by which sinners were bound over to death. Neither was this to be done otherwise than by satisfying the law, the awful sanction of which fastened strongly the guilt of death on the transgressors. These were the iron gates that were to be broken through before the Goel, the avenger of blood, could reach the murderer. But the almighty Redeemer, in making the eternal covenant, undertook to satisfy the law, and by that means to remove the strength of sin, and by so doing to take away the sting of death; and so, by His own death, to disarm and destroy the murderer that had the power of death. Now by accomplishing all this, our near and dear Kinsman avenged the blood of His slain kinsmen upon their murderer who had the power of death. Now by accomplishing all this, our near and dear Kinsman avenged the blood of His slain kinsmen upon their murderer (Hebrews 2:14). Here, then, let the redeemed of the Lord adopt the triumphant language of the evangelical Prophet: The Lord saw it, and it displeased him that there was no judgment. And he saw that there was no man, and wondered that there was no intercessor; therefore his arm brought salvation unto him, and his righteousness, it sustained him. For he put on righteousness as a breastplate, and an helmet of salvation upon his head; and he put on the garments of vengeance for clothing, and was clad with zeal as a cloak (Isaiah 59:15, 16, 17). Or they may adopt the sweet strain of an apostle when discoursing of the same thing: "Forasmuch then, as the children are partakers of flesh and blood, he also himself likewise took part of them same; that through death he might destroy him that had the power of death, that is, the devil" (Hebrews 2:14). Our incarnate Redeemer, according to His covenant-engagement, has died, yea, rather has risen again; and therefore, believers in Him may triumphantly exclaim, "O death, where is thy sting? O grave, where is thy victory? O Satan, where is thy power? For though the sting of death is sin, and though the strength of sin is the law; yet, thanks be to God who giveth us the victory, through our Lord Jesus Christ" (1 Corinthians 15:57). The omnipotent avenger of our blood has not only punished the murderer (which is all that any other goel could do), but has restored life to the murdered. Thus has He redeemed our soul from deceit and violence; and precious has our blood been in His sight (Psalm 72:14). "Blessed be the Lord, who has not left us this day without a Kinsman . . . a restorer of our life (Ruth 4:14, 15).

SECTION 4. Christ, the SURETY of the Covenant

Christ the second Adam consented, in making the eternal covenant, to the proposal of His becoming a Surety. "By so much was Jesus made a Surety of a better covenant" (Hebrews 7:22). The Father was not more willing to propose than the Son was to agree to the terms of that holy covenant. A surety or sponsor is one who undertakes and answers for another man, obliging himself either for the paying of his debt, civil or criminal, or for his performing of a deed. That the reader may understand aright the nature of the suretiship of Christ, it will be proper to inquire first, for whom, and, second, for what He became a Surety, in that Divine compact.

First, it will be necessary to inquire for whom he was made a Surety, in the covenant of grace.

1. He did not become a surety for God to sinners. A surety is admittable only where one of the parties in a contract has failed, or is at least capable of failing. There can be no place for one where the principal, in point of obligation, is immutable and infallible. There could, therefore, be no room for a surety for the all-powerful and unchangeable Jehovah. A god capable of

failing in the performance of his promise is no God. Indeed, it is absolutely impossible to render Jehovah's engagement by promise more sure than it already is (Hebrews 6:17-19). The promises of God are, in respect of His infallible truth, His inviolable faithfulness, and His pledge in them, most certain in themselves so that they cannot fail of being performed. And since we, being guilty creatures, are slow of heart to believe, and therefore stand in need of something to make the promises sure to us, or to make it sure to our minds that they will be performed to us, He has given them to us in the sacred record under His own hand. He has also given to us the outward seals of the holy sacraments (Romans 4:11) and the inward seal of the Holy Spirit in our hearts, who is likewise the earnest of the inheritance promised to us (Ephesians 1:14; 2 Corinthians 1:22); yea, to show unto the heirs of promise, the immutability of his counsel, He has confirmed it by an oath (Hebrews 6:17), and so has given to them all the security for the performance of His promise that could reasonably have been required, even from the most faithless man in the world. Christ's being a surety for God, therefore, appears to be altogether unnecessary, as well as inconsistent with the character of God.

As it is unnecessary and unsuitable, so it has no foundation in the Scriptures of truth. In a fore-cited text, the only one in which Christ is expressly called a Surety, it is plain that His suretiship there declared represents His Priestly office, in the discharge of which He deals not with us for God, but on the contrary with God for us. "Inasmuch as not without an oath, He was made Priest . . . by so much was Jesus made a Surety of a better covenant" (Hebrews 7:20, 22). But His becoming a Surety for God to us (supposing, but not granting, that He did so) could not relate to His priestly office, but only to His kingly office, in respect of which all power in heaven and on earth is given to Him (Matthew 28:18) and, consequently, power to see that the promises of the covenant be fulfilled to His people. His suretiship, therefore, mentioned in that passage, is not for God to us, but for us to God. It is only in two other passages, as far as I have yet been able to learn, that we read of suretiship, respecting the case between God and a sinner, but on the contrary for the sinner to God. They are Psalm 119:122: "Be surety for Thy servant for good," and Job 17:3: "Lay down now, put me in a surety with Thee." The passage in the original may be rendered thus: "Set, I pray, set me a surety with Thee." It is as if Job had said, "Set, or appoint Messiah who is with Thee, to plead, as a surety, my cause; and then, Who will dare to plead any longer against me?" The same original word is employed in Isaiah 38:14 in this prayer of Hezekiah: "I am oppressed, undertake, or, be a surety for me." His meaning appears to be this: "Set thyself between me and my sickness," as a surety sets himself between the creditor and the debtor to secure the latter against being cast into prison. "My disease has violently seized me, and is dragging me as it were by force to the prison of the grave. Interpose, O Lord, as a surety for my rescue." The original phrase is the same in the one text as in the other; and the same in both, as in the passages where Judah's suretiship for Benjamin, to his father, is expressed (Genesis 43:9 and 44:32). We have then no hint given us in the Scripture that Christ ever became a surety for God to sinners. But:

2. He consented in making the covenant to become a Surety for sinners to God. This is evident from the following passages, as well as from those that have already been cited on this subject: "I have laid help upon one that is mighty" (Psalm 89:19). "Who is this that engaged his heart (or, that was surety with his heart) to approach unto Me, saith the Lord?" (Jeremiah 30:21). "Then I restored that which I took not away" (Psalm 69:4). "The

Lord hath laid on Him the iniquity of us all" (Isaiah 53:6). "He was wounded for our transgressions, He was bruised for our iniquities; the chastisement of our peace was upon Him" (Isaiah 53:5). "For He hath made Him to be sin for us, who knew no sin; that we might be made the righteousness of God in Him" (2 Corinthians 5:21). "Christ hath redeemed us from the curse of the law, being made a curse for us" (Galatians 3:13). "Christ also hath once suffered for sins, the just for the unjust, that He might bring us unto God" (1 Peter 3:18).

When the covenant of grace was made with the elect in Christ, it was established with them in Him as their Surety, taking their whole obligation to answer the demands of the law in its covenant-form upon Himself. Without such a Surety, it could not have been made with them; for they were all a company of insolvent debtors, owing each of them to law and justice, a debt of ten thousand talents; so that their word, in a new bargain for eternal life, could not be of any weight. No regard could be paid to it in heaven. After they had broken the covenant of innocence, neither truth, nor integrity, nor ability remained in them. See how their character, in respect of truth and integrity, is, by the pen of inspiration described: "Let God be true, but every man a liar" (Romans 3:4). "There is none righteous, no not one" (Romans 3:10); and, in point of ability, "When we were yet without strength, in due time Christ died for the ungodly" (Romans 5:6). The demands made in making the everlasting covenant were high and altogether above their power to answer; and they themselves too, as was just now evidenced, were false and inconstant. They broke their word in the old covenant when they were able to keep it; and how could they, in this new compact, be trusted again when their moral ability was entirely gone? Since, therefore, a surety for them was indispensably necessary, and since the blessed Son of God consented to become

The Making of the Covenant of Grace

their Surety, the everlasting covenant on which depends all their security for the possession of eternal life was made, and made sure. Christ, the second Adam, then, did not, in the making of the covenant, consent to become a Surety for God to sinners, but only for sinners to God.

It will now be proper, second, to inquire for what He consented in the covenant of grace, to become a Surety. Suretiship, with respect to the nature of it, is of two kinds. There is (1) a suretiship for one's performance of a deed or obligation, and (2) a suretiship for the payment of one's debt.

1. There is a suretiship for one's performing of an obligation. "Take his garment," said Solomon, "that is surety for a stranger, and take a pledge of him for a strange woman" (Proverbs 20:16); that is, take a pledge of him, who is surety for her good behavior. The suretiship of Christ for sinners of mankind to God was not of this sort. He did not become a sponsor or bondsman to His Father for their good conduct. He did not engage or become Surety in a way of caution to Him that they should believe, repent, and perform sincere obedience. Though it is infallibly secured in the covenant that elect sinners shall believe, repent, and sincerely obey— insomuch that every sinner, attaining the years of understanding, who lives and dies without doing so, must inevitably perish—yet Christ's becoming Surety in a way of security to His Father in the covenant, that the elect should perform those obligations, would not be consistent with the account that the Scriptures give us of that glorious contract. For,

First, such a suretiship as that would obscure the grace of the covenant. The grace of the eternal covenant is infinitely sovereign and free. That covenant is purposely so framed as to afford the most illustrious displays possible of the glory of redeeming grace. Every benefit of it is of faith that it might be by grace

(Romans 4:16). Such a suretiship, or such a security given, for the elect's performance of those or any other duties must belong to the conditions of the covenant, properly so called, as being a deed of the Mediator by which He promises something to God, and pledges Himself that it shall be performed by them, must of consequence form a part of the conditions. But that sinners themselves fulfill any article of the conditions properly so called of the covenant cannot be admitted without injuring the grace of it; for so far as they, in their own persons, fulfill any part of the conditions, the reward to them is no longer of grace, but of debt. "To him that worketh is the reward not reckoned of grace, but of debt" (Romans 4:4). But, since the reward is wholly of debt to Christ, it must be wholly of grace to His spiritual seed. "To him that worketh not, but believeth on Him that justifieth the ungodly, his faith is counted for righteousness" (Romans 4:5). "And if by grace, then it is no more of works; otherwise grace is no more grace" (Romans 11:6). Suppose a man becomes surety for his friend for a great sum of money due by him, who is thereupon to have a right to some benefit, engaging to pay the whole sum for him and, at the same time, becomes surety for his good behavior; it is obvious that in such a case the good behavior of the principal is a part of the condition of the bargain as well as the payment of the money since caution for such behavior is required by him who is to bestow the benefit. In such a case the condition is divided between the surety and the principal; the latter performs a part of it as well as the former; and so the benefit promised is, in part at least, of debt to the latter as well as to the former. The application is obvious. If then Christ did in the covenant become a Surety, in way of caution for His people's performance of some obligation, the fulfilling of the conditions, properly so called, of that eternal covenant would be divided between Him and them, however unequal their respective shares might be; and if the fulfilling of the conditions are divided between Christ and them, so far as their part of the performance goes, the reward should be of debt to them, which would obscure, or rather undermine, the grace of the covenant.

Second, the believing, repenting, and sincere obedience of the elect, according to the sacred records, belong to the promissory part of the covenant. If we consider them in their original form and situation they are benefits promised by God to Christ the blessed Surety as the reward of His fulfilling the conditions of the covenant. The following are some of the promises of them: "All the ends of the world shall remember and turn unto the Lord. A seed shall serve Him. They shall come and shall declare His righteousness unto a people that shall be born" (Psalm 22:27, 30, 31). "In His name shall the Gentiles trust" (Matthew 12:21). "Thy people shall be willing in the day of Thy power" (Psalm 110:3).

Faith, repentance, and the ability sincerely to obey the law as a rule of life, then, are, by the faithfulness of Jehovah the Father, promised in the covenant of grace as well as by His justice, ensured to Christ, on behalf of His elect seed. Now to whom were these and all the other promise of the covenant primarily made? Let the apostle Paul answer: "To Abraham and his seed, were the promises made . . . to thy seed which is Christ" (Galatians 3:16). Promises, indeed, are found in the Scriptures in which Christ Himself is the Undertaker, such as this one: "All that the Father giveth Me shall come to Me; and him that cometh to Me I will in no wise cast out" (John 6:37). But such are never to be understood of Christ's engaging to His Father as Surety for a deed to be performed by His elect but, on the contrary, of His speaking to sinners as the Administrator of the covenant, entrusted with dispensing to them all the blessings purchased by His surety-righteousness, and made over to Him by the promise of the Father. "All things," said He, "are delivered unto Me of My Father . . . come unto Me, all ye that labor and are heavy laden, and I will give you rest" (Matthew 11:27, 28). Those blessings are all to be considered as privileges contained in the promises of the covenant for the performance of which, to the Son as last Adam, and in Him, to His elect seed, the Father is engaged.

2. There is also a suretiship for paying one's debt. "Be not thou," said Solomon, "one of them that strike hands, or of them that are sureties for debts" (Proverbs 22:26). Now the suretiship of the second Adam for His people was of this kind. He became Surety for the debt of the seed represented by Him—not a surety bound merely to see their debt discharged or a surety bound together with themselves, it being impossible for them, in their state of condemnation, to do anything else than increase the boundless sum (Romans 8:7, 8). But He became such a Surety for them as undertook by Himself alone to pay their whole debt to the broken law and the offended justice of Jehovah. The full amount of their debt was, by the foreknowledge of God, stated from the violated covenant of works in the whole latitude of its demands on them; and He became Surety for it, engaging to His righteous Father to discharge it to the utmost farthing. His suretiship consisted in His taking on Himself the whole burden of His people's debt, both of obedience and of suffering, with a full resolution to discharge it. He took it in consequence of the Father's laying of it on Him. "The Lord hath laid on Him the in iniquity of us all" (Isaiah 53:6). The bond of suretiship into which He entered was of equal extent with His people's debt-bond, the covenant of works.

First, He consented to become a Surety for their debt of obedience to the law in its covenant-form. In His suretiship He

The Making of the Covenant of Grace

became a debtor to do the whole law (Galatians 5:3). The law, as a covenant of works, though it was violated by them, yet neither lost its right nor ceased for a moment to demand from them that perfect obedience that, as the condition of life, it at first required from man. The elect were bound to perform perfect obedience, and on no lower terms could they have eternal life, as our blessed Lord, in order to humble him, informed the lawyer: "Thou hast answered right; this do, and thou shalt live" (Luke 10:28). Though the paying of the debt of punishment could satisfy as to the penalty of the bond, yet the principal contained in the bond, namely the debt of perfect obedience to the law as a covenant for eternal life, must likewise be paid. The honor of the High and Holy One and of His most righteous law cannot allow the quitting of it, or even of the smallest part of it. And as for them, they were without strength (Romans 5:6); they were dead in trespasses and sins (Ephesians 2:1), and therefore were utterly unable to clear so much as one farthing of it that would have been current in heaven. The second Adam, then, substituting Himself in their place, became Surety for their debt of perfect obedience to the law in its covenant-form, which was, and still is, the only obliging Himself to discharge it by obeying in their stead, and so fulfilling all that the perceptive part of the law required from them as the proper condition of life. Hear how He expresses Himself on the solemn occasion: "Then said I, Lo, I come . . . I delight to do Thy will, O my God; yea, Thy law is within My heart" (Psalm 40:7, 8). And again, "Think not that I am come to destroy the law . . . I am not come to destroy, but to fulfill" (Matthew 5:17). "Thus it becometh us to fulfill all righteousness" (Matthew 3:15).

Now here it is manifest that there was an exchange of persons in law. Christ substituted Himself in the law-room of His people and took their obligation to obey for life upon Himself;

in consequence of that He became, as was observed above, a debtor to the law for that perfect obedience that they owed to it in its covenant-form. In becoming Surety for them, He took upon Himself their state of servitude, or their obligation to obey for a title to life, upon which the law had a right to demand all that debt from Him that they, upon their breach of the covenant of works, were bound to discharge. This He Himself solemnly owned by His submitting to circumcision, according to these words of the Apostle Paul: "I testify again to every man that is circumcised, that he is a debtor to do the whole law" (Galatians 5:3).

Hence it evidently appears how the unsinning obedience of the adorable Surety comes, in virtue of the covenant, to be imputed to believers for righteousness as well as His satisfactory death. The obedience that He in their stead, as their Surety, performed to the law as a covenant of works was no more due by Him antecedently to His contract of suretiship than were His sufferings or death. Indeed, had His human nature been a human person, instead of being only a human nature, it should have been, as a reasonable creature, subject on its own account to the law as an eternal rule of duty; for every human person is naturally, necessarily, and unchangeably bound to observe it as a rule. But since it never was, for one moment, a human person, but was from the first moment of its formation and assumption a human nature, united to the Divine nature in a Divine person, it never was, it never could be, subject to the law as a rule. The law, considered only as a rule, could never have the least claim upon it. Though it always had, and still has, a natural and necessary claim upon a human person, yet it could have none at all upon a human nature in a Divine person. And, as the Man-Christ could not and did not obey the law for Himself as a rule of life, so neither did He obey it in that view of it for His people.

The Making of the Covenant of Grace 81

To assert that Christ was made under, and that He obeyed the law for believers as a rule would be to teach downright Antinomianism. As He could not have been subject to the moral law as a rule, so neither could He, on His own account, have been under it as a covenant. He never committed any sin, and therefore He could not for Himself be under any obligation to endure the penalty of it. Add to this His holy human nature, from the first moment of its existence and union with the Divine nature, in His glorious person had, in consequence of that personal union, not only a complete title to eternal life for itself, but the actual, the sure, possession of it, and therefore could be under no obligation to obey the precept in order to merit life for itself. His obedience, then, to the law in its covenant-form, as it could not be due, nor in the least degree be performed for Himself, was performed wholly for His spiritual seed. It was entirely voluntary. He did not owe it, otherwise than by His entering into a bond of suretiship to perform it for them; nor otherwise than by His own infinitely free and voluntary engagement. Seeing therefore it was performed not to the law as a rule of life, but to the law as a covenant of works, not in the least article for Christ Himself, but wholly for the elect of God, there is good ground for the imputation of it to them, to entitle them, according to the covenant of grace, to eternal life.

Second, Christ the second Adam consented to become a Surety likewise for their debt of punishment due for violating the law. This was the debt that they owed to Divine justice for their original and actual transgression. The punishment due for their sinning against the infinite Jehovah was, and could not in justice be less than, an infinite punishment; and since they, being finite creatures, could not bear an infinite punishment, but in an infinite or, which is the same thing, in an eternal duration, it could not to them be less than everlasting punishment

(Matthew 25:46). They were liable to bear the pains of death in its fullest extent, to endure the force of revenging wrath until full reparation of the injured honor of Jehovah should be made and complete satisfaction to infinite justice be given. This was their criminal debt, their debt of punishment, a debt that they themselves, though paying it to the very utmost of their power, and that through all eternity, could never have discharged. Now for this debt Christ Jesus also became their Surety, engaging Himself to lay down His life for theirs, which was forfeited to Divine justice. Hence are these consoling words of His: "I lay down My life for the sheep. I lay it down of Myself. I have power to lay it down, and have power to take it again. This commandment have I received of My Father" (John 10:15, 18). Here is a suretiship in which sovereign grace and infinite mercy will shine forth with transcendent, with everlasting splendor. Reuben would venture the life of his two sons for Benjamin (Genesis 42:37), and Judah would venture his own for him (Genesis 43:9), while yet they had hope that all would be safe; but our dear Lord Jesus voluntarily pledged His life for that of lost sinners when it was certain that the precious pledge would go in the cause, and that the death He would endure would be ten thousand deaths in one.

The suretiship of the second Adam for the criminal debt of His spiritual offspring did not imply an insuring of the payment of it, one way or another, as in common cases of suretiship among men; but it implied an exchange of persons in law. The only-begotten Son of God substituted Himself in their stead and took upon Himself their whole obligation of suffering death as well as of serving for life. This, the sovereign grace of Jehovah, the glorious Creditor, did, with infinite readiness, admit when He might have persisted in demanding that the soul that sinned should die. On Christ's thus becoming a Sponsor for His people, the guilt of all their iniquities was transferred to Him and was in due time to be, by the law and justice of God, charged upon Him. "The Lord," said the ancient Church, "hath laid on Him the iniquity of us all" (Isaiah 53:6). It was transferred to Him in order that a foundation in law and justice might be laid for exacting their debt of punishment from Him. Thus the iniquities of all the elect seed were, together and at once, imputed to the Divine Surety and so, in legal estimation, became His, as His righteousness becomes theirs; for, in a fore-cited passage, the Apostle Paul says, "He hath made Him to be sin for us, who knew no sin, that we might be made the righteousness of God in Him" (2 Corinthians 5:21). Hence He Himself thus speaks of those iniquities: "Innumerable evils have compassed me about; mine iniquities have taken hold upon me" (Psalm 40:12). An inspired apostle (Hebrews 10: 5, 6, 7) determines Messiah Himself to be the Speaker in that Psalm. The spotless Lamb of God was, indeed, without sin inherent in Him, but not without sin imputed to Him till, having discharged the debt by His suffering of death, He in His resurrection received from the hand of justice a full discharge. Then it was that He was justified in the Spirit (1 Timothy 3:16); and so He shall appear the second time, without sin (Hebrews 9:28), without that sin which, the first time He appeared, was on Him by imputation. This relation of our sin to the adorable Surety resulted from the nature of suretiship for debt. A debt becomes the debt of the surety the moment he becomes responsible for it. How else could the law, in justice, have proceeded against the immaculate Jesus? How otherwise could the punishment due to us have been justly inflicted upon Him? If the law could not, in consequence of His own voluntary undertaking, have charged our sin on Him, it could not have had a just ground to inflict our punishment upon Him.

Thus we have seen that the suretiship of Christ in the covenant for elect sinners, to God, was of the nature of suretiship for discharging one's debt; and also what the debt was for which He became Surety.

SECTION 5. Christ the Sacrificing Priest of the Covenant

As it was requisite to His finishing His bond service that Christ the second Adam should do the part of a Redeemer, delivering His people from bondage, and to His acting the part of a Redeemer, that He should become a Surety in the covenant, so it was necessary to His discharging of the debt for which He became a Surety that He should be a sacrificing Priest. Having as a Surety engaged to endure, for the elect of God, the penalty of the broken law, it became necessary that as a Priest He should offer Himself as a sacrifice to make atonement for their sins. Accordingly, in consenting to the conditions of the covenant, He became the Priest of the covenant, a High Priest of good things to come (Hebrews 9:11).

A priest is a public person who, in the name of the guilty, deals with an offended God for reconciliation by sacrifice, which he offers to Him upon an altar, being thereto called by God that he may be accepted. A priest bears a relation to an altar, an altar to a sacrifice, and a sacrifice to sin. As all they whom the second Adam represented in the eternal covenant were sinners against God, He became their Priest, their High Priest, appearing before God in their name to make reconciliation for their iniquity. This was the glorious object that the whole priesthood under the law prefigured. Their nature that He assumed was the sacerdotal garment, curiously wrought in the lowest parts of the earth, in which He executed His priestly office; and in their nature, holy and undefiled, He, as their great High Priest, sustained their persons, representing them before the Lord. An eminent type of this was Aaron's bearing the names of the twelve tribes of Israel before Jehovah upon his two shoulders for a memorial, engraved on two onyx-stones, set by Divine appointment in the shoulder-pieces of the Ephod; and also his bearing of them, engraved on twelve precious stones, set in the breast-plate of judgment upon his heart when he went into the holy place (Exodus 28:12, 29). Thus Aaron the high priest, representing all Israel before Jehovah in the holy place, was an eminent type of the second Adam, that great High Priest who, in the covenant, represents His spiritual Israel.

That Christ the second Adam should become a sacrificing Priest in the covenant was absolutely necessary. The necessity of it will appear by considering that they whom He represented in the covenant were sinners, that their sin could not be expiated but by a sacrifice of sufficient value, that no sacrifice for sin could be accepted by God but on such an altar as should sanctify the gift, and that such a sacrifice could not be offered on such an altar but by a Priest called by God for that purpose.

1. The necessity of Christ's becoming, in the covenant of grace, a sacrificing Priest will appear evident when we consider that they whom He therein represented were sinners. They were sinners against the High and Holy One; and such a covenant as should be a covenant of grace to them could not be established without provision made for removing their sin, which necessarily implied a Priest. The covenant of works was made without a priest because the persons who were represented in it were without sin; there, there was no sin to take away. But the covenant of grace was a covenant of peace between an offended God and sinners, and therefore could not be made but by the intervention of a Priest who should be able to repair the injury done to the honor of God, and so to take away sin. Hence are these words of the prophet Zechariah: "He shall be a Priest upon his

throne; and the counsel of peace shall be between them both" (Zechariah 6:13). None of the elect angels could be a Priest of that covenant; for they are finite creatures; none of the sons of Adam could be qualified to support that character, for they are not only finite, but sinful creatures; and "such an High Priest became us, as was holy, harmless, undefiled, and separate from sinners" (Hebrews 7:26). Christ Himself, then, was the only one who was qualified to support that high and endearing character. For:

2. The sin of His spiritual seed could not be taken away but by a sacrifice of infinite value that they themselves could not afford to offer. It was necessary that a covenant of grace for guilty sinners should be a covenant by sacrifice (Psalm 50:5), a covenant written with blood; for without shedding of blood there is no remission (Hebrews 9:22). The covenant, therefore, with Abraham of old was made with the solemnity of a typical sacrifice (Genesis 15:9) in order that he might know it to be a covenant of reconciliation in which a righteous God was not to manifest His mercy to sinners but in a manner fully consistent with the honor of His glorious justice. Such a sacrifice as that, however, was infinitely below the requisite value; it could not take away sin. But the Lord Jesus, called to be a Priest, gave Himself an offering and a sacrifice to God for confirming the covenant; and that inestimably precious sacrifice was for a sweet smelling savor or, according to the style of the Old Testament, for a savor of rest (Genesis 8:21, margin). The persons whom He represented, being sinners, were corrupt and abominable in the sight of the holy Lord God who smelled, as it were, a savor of disquiet from them and their performances. They were a smoke in His nose, a fire that burned all the day (Isaiah 65:5). Their disobedience stirred up His avenging justice, His tremendous fury. But the sacrifice of Christ offered in the room of elect sin-

The Making of the Covenant of Grace

ners sent forth such a sweet smelling savor to God as completely overcame the offensive savor arising from their sin and gave His avenging justice and wrath the calmest and profoundest rest.

The necessity of such a sacrifice in the covenant arose from the justice of God demanding the full execution of the curse of the broken law upon the sinner, by which he should have fallen as a sacrifice for his sin according to this awful threatening: "He shall bring upon them their own iniquity, and shall cut them off in their own wickedness; yea, the Lord our God shall cut them off" (Psalm 94:23). It was an ancient practice in making covenants as was observed above to cut a beast in two and then to pass between the parts of it. The passing between the two parts of it denoted the falling of the curse of the covenant upon the party who should presume to break that covenant. Hence is this dreadful threatening of Jehovah: "I will give the men that have transgressed My covenant, which have not performed the words of the covenant, which they had made before Me, when they cut the calf in twain, and passed between the parts thereof" (Jeremiah 34:18); or, more agreeably to the original, "I will make the men who have transgressed my covenant . . . as the calf which they cut in two, and passed between the parts of it." It is as if He had said, "I will execute the curse upon them, cutting them asunder, as covenant-breakers" (Matthew 24:51). Now the covenant of works being broken, the justice of Jehovah required the execution of the curse of it in order that a covenant of grace and peace might be established. But if the curse had been executed upon the sinners themselves, the fire of Divine wrath should have burned eternally on them; and after all, such a sacrifice could never have sent forth a savor smelling so sweetly as to be a savor of rest to vindicative justice because they were not only mere creatures whose most exquisite torments could never have amounted to a sufficient compensation for the injury done to the honor of infinite Majesty, but were sinful creatures too, who would still, even under their eternal sufferings, have continued to sin. The Lord Jesus, therefore, being both equal with God and separate from sinners did in the covenant consent to be in the room of His elect seed, the sacrifice upon whom the curse of the covenant of works might be fully executed.

This was, in a lively manner, foreshown in the covenant made with Abraham in which he was an illustrious type of Messiah (Genesis 15, throughout). In that transaction, Jehovah promised that He would deliver the natural seed of Abraham out of Egyptian bondage, and that He would give them the land of Canaan for a possession. This was typical of the deliverance of Christ's spiritual seed from the bondage of sin, Satan and the world, and of putting them in possession of heaven. The solemnity observed at the making of that covenant was peculiarly awful. A heifer, a she-goat, and a ram were commanded to be taken, each of them three years old, typifying Christ, who was little more than three years employed in His public ministry. Each of these was divided, or hewn asunder in the midst, which prefigured the awful execution of the curse upon the Lamb of God, our atoning sacrifice. Abraham's driving away of the fowls that came down upon the carcasses typified the victory of Christ over our spiritual enemies during all the time of His humiliation, and especially His triumphing over them on the cross.

3. No sacrifice could be accepted by God but on such an altar as could sanctify the gift to its designed effect (Matthew 23:19); and who could supply that but the last Adam Himself? Accordingly, His Divine nature, that eternal Spirit, was the altar, whence the sacrifice of His human nature derived all its infinite value and efficacy. We, says the Apostle Paul, have an altar, whereof they have no right to eat who serve the tabernacle (Hebrews 13:10); and in another place, "How much more shall the

blood of Christ who, through the eternal Spirit, offered Himself without spot to God, purge your conscience from dead works, to serve the living God?" (Hebrews 9:14). His blessed body, suffering and bleeding to death on the cross, and His holy soul melted within Him by the fire of Divine wrath, both being, at the same time, united to His Divine nature, were the sacrifice burning on the altar from which God smelled a sweet smelling savor. By this infinitely perfect sacrifice, the justice of Jehovah was fully satisfied and His wrath completely appeased. Not that Christ was a sacrifice only while He was on the cross. His offering of Himself as a sacrifice, which He began at His incarnation, to do (the sacrifice having been laid on the altar the first moment thereof (Hebrews 10:5), and which He continued for more than thirty-three years to do, He finished on the cross and in the tomb. Hence are these consoling declarations: "He hath made Him to be sin for us" (2 Corinthians 5:21). "When we shall see him there is no beauty that we should desire him. He is . . . a man of sorrows, and acquainted with grief . . . Surely He hath borne our griefs, and carried our sorrows" (Isaiah 53:2, 3, 4). His Divine nature, then, was the altar that so sanctified the sacrifice of His human nature as to render it valuable in an infinite degree.

4. Finally, such a sacrifice could not be offered with acceptance on such an altar but by a Priest, called by God for that purpose. An acceptable sacrifice and a Priest to offer it are inseparable. Without a Priest, therefore, there could be no sacrifice to be accepted (Hebrews 8:3), and so no removal of sin, and by consequence, no establishment of a covenant of grace. Now as Christ Himself was both the sacrifice and the altar, so none but Himself could be the Priest (Hebrews 5:5); and as in His human nature He was the sacrifice, and in His Divine nature the altar, so it behooved Him in His person to be the Priest.

And, seeing the weight of the salvation of sinners lay on His call to that office, He was, according to the covenant, made a Priest by the oath of Jehovah (Hebrews 7:21). As He had full power over His own life to offer Himself a sacrifice, so His Father's solemn investing of Him with that office by an oath afforded Him access to offer Himself effectually, even in such a manner as thereby to fulfill the conditions of the covenant, and so to purchase for sinners of mankind eternal redemption (Hebrews 9:12). His sacrifice, therefore, needed not to be repeated; for as dying once was the penalty of the law, so, in consideration of the infinite dignity of the glorious Sufferer, His suffering unto death once completely satisfied the penal sanction (Hebrews 9:27, 28).

Thus far, concerning the making of the covenant.

From what has been discoursed in this chapter we may learn that the covenant of grace, with regard to its form and establishment, is primarily in God, Father, Son and Holy Spirit. It is not like those Divine works or dispensations that are merely from God, or which His wisdom and power, in the ages of time produce; but it is the mystery of His will, according to His good pleasure, which He has purposed in Himself (Ephesians 1:9). It is therefore of the same eternity as He Himself is. There never was, there never could be, any conceivable point of time in which it was not, or in which it might have been essentially different from what it is. It does not, however, originally lie in any essential attribute of the Divine nature; for in that case, it could not be a covenant of free grace but of natural necessity. It originally lies in the free determination of the Divine will which, though not a necessary result of the perfections of the Divine nature, is yet equal with them in point of eternity. God would have continued the same in His essential attributes, though such a covenant had never been made.

The Making of the Covenant of Grace

We may hence learn too that as there was an immediate and primary making of that Divine covenant with Christ in eternity, so it was then also settled that there should be a mediate and secondary making of it with sinners of mankind in time. Accordingly, it is exhibited in the offers of the gospel to them, and they are graciously invited, and even commanded, to take hold if it by faith, each of them for himself. And when Jehovah, by a supernatural illumination of their mind, shows them His covenant, and enables them so to take hold of it as to enter into the bond of it, He makes it with them. The glorious conditions of it are made theirs by His imputation thereof to them, and by their fiducial application of them, to themselves; and the precious promises of it are made theirs inasmuch as they have a title to the performance of them on the ground of the conditions fulfilled for them and imputed to them. "Hear," said the Lord, "and your souls shall live; and I will make an everlasting covenant with you, even by the sure mercies of David" (Isaiah 55:3). No sooner are you, reader, united by faith to the last Adam, the glorious Head of the covenant, than the covenant is made with you, considered as in Him. You are brought under the bond of Jehovah's gracious engagement to you, and of your own dutiful engagement to Him.

But, further, we may hence also infer that sinners, in order to be personally in covenant with God, are not, as parties contracting, to make a covenant with Him for their salvation, but are only to take hold of His covenant, the covenant that He has already, even from eternity, made with the second Adam, His chosen One (Isaiah 56:4, 6). I have no intention hereby to find any fault either with national or with personal engagements, when they are formed and entered into in a scriptural manner. These are covenants of duties, and are consequents of our having taken hold of God's covenant of grace. Neither would I offer to dissuade any Christian from taking hold anew of God's covenant, with all the solemnity of the most express words, or even of writing and subscribing such words. But at the same time, I would warn every man to take heed that he does not practically corrupt the covenant of grace by making a covenant of his own on terms that he himself engages to fulfill for the salvation of his soul. Many, alas, imagining that eternal life is, in the gospel, proposed to them on condition of their faith, repentance, and sincere obedience solemnly engage to perform these conditions. They bind themselves to perform those duties in order that God may have mercy upon them and save them; and so they make a pact with the Most High, promising Him service for salvation. When they flatter themselves that they have in some degree performed their part of such a covenant, they think themselves, thereby, entitled to grace and glory. By so doing, they corrupt, yea, they subvert the covenant of grace. "For to him that worketh (for life), the reward is not reckoned of grace, but of debt (Romans 4:4). "And if it be of works, then it is no more grace" (Romans 11:6). The evil and the danger of this practice are inconceivably great. The evil of it is great, for it is a setting of Christ aside, who is the high Party contracting by the appointment of the Father, and a thrusting of themselves into His room to work for a title to eternal life. The danger of it is great; for thereby they lay a foundation to support the weight of their salvation that the only wise God saw to be utterly insufficient to bear it (Galatians 5:4). The duty of sinners in this case then is only to apply or take hold of God's covenant of grace as a covenant already made and exhibited to them in the gospel; and this they do by taking hold of Christ who is given for a covenant of the people, cordially believing that He with His righteousness and fullness is offered to them, and humbly trusting in Him for all the salvation of the covenant (Isaiah 42:6; John 1:12).

Thus it is that the saints of God make a covenant with Him by sacrifice. In Psalm 50 He thus speaks: "Gather My saints together unto Me, those that have made a covenant with Me by sacrifice," or, as it is in the sacred original, "those who cut My covenant upon a sacrifice." Now this they do by laying the hand of their faith upon the head of that great Sacrifice who, according to the covenant, was first typically, and afterwards really, cut down in their stead. While they thus transfer their guilt to the Sacrifice, they spiritually approve the plan of salvation by a crucified Redeemer and fall in with it, as in their estimation the only proper method of salvation for them. By this method of covenanting the rich and free grace of the covenant is preserved entire: "For to him that worketh not, but believeth on Him that justifieth the ungodly, his faith is counted for righteousness" (Romans 4:5). Hereby all the glory of being sole undertaker in the covenant is, according to the appointment of the Father, reserved for Christ, upon whom alone He has laid their help (Psalm 89:19). Here the last Adam, the man whose name is "the BRANCH," builds the temple of the Lord without their laying so much as one stone of it, even as the first Adam destroyed it without their throwing down one stone of it in their own persons. Thus it is that the believer, for his own part, does in time solemnly approve the covenant that was made in eternity, and that he personally consents in time to that to which Christ as his Representative consented in eternity. Thus he in effect repeats or makes again the covenant of grace made with Christ, his blessed Representative. He cordially acquiesces in the whole tenor of it. Now this method of covenanting is what no unregenerate man continuing such ever did or ever will adopt; for in falling in with it, the heart consents to abandon all sin. It is well pleased with all the salvation of the covenant, and is carried forth out of all confidence in its own doings and sufferings for eternal life.

Hence likewise we may learn that the faith of God's elect, though it is a receiving of Christ in all His offices, yet, considered as the instrument of their entering personally into the covenant, it views Him especially in His priestly office. It is looking to Him as their sacrificing Priest who, by His service and suffering, has made reconciliation for iniquity; it is relying on Him as their condescending Surety for the payment of their debt, of perfect obedience and infinite suffering; and it is trusting in Him as their Kinsman-redeemer for deliverance from their spiritual bondage. Their faith in Jesus as a Priest is the principle of their obedience to Him as a King. Man's order naturally is to come to obedience that he may come to Christ But God's order is to come to Christ that he may proceed to obedience. The priestly office of Christ is that to which the awakened sinner, trembling before the righteous Judge of the world, lifts up his eyes and has recourse for safety from Divine vengeance. There, and there only, can one see an atonement, a ransom, a righteousness for justification. What Jesus did as a Bondservant, a Redeemer, a Surety and a sacrificing Priest is the great foundation on which the whole weight of the salvation of a sinner lies. These are glad tidings to the sinner, whose conscience is wounded by arrows of conviction. What subjects of sweet meditation, what grounds of strong consolation, are here! Was ever grace, or love, or mercy, among any of the creatures, like to that which is displayed here! Was ever pardon or peace purchased at so costly a rate or granted upon such good security! What blasphemy then is there in unbelief that doubts the infinite merit of the Savior's righteousness or distrusts the boundless riches of His grace! The righteous law can bring no charge against the blessed Surety because, by His consummate righteousness, He answered all its demands; and it can exhibit no charge of guilt against the believer because he is united to Christ the Surety. It cannot exact the same penalty twice. Consider then, O fainting believer, the infinite sufficiency of the sacrifice of Jesus Christ. Be assured that, as the drop of ink that hangs on the point of a pen would be lost in the waters of the ocean, so all your sins, however aggravated they have been, when cast into the unbounded ocean of the Divine Redeemer's blood, will be utterly absorbed and never any more appear (Micah 7:18, 19).

Once more, how illustrious are the displays of the perfections of Jehovah that are made in that covenant! Behold, believer, how infinite love, grace, and mercy excite! How unsearchable wisdom and knowledge form the plan! How infinite Persons mutually stipulate! How infinite perfections work together for your redemption! Contemplate here the transcendent luster of Divine perfections, the unparalleled glory of redeeming grace. Consider that wonderful contract in which Jehovah takes the whole of your salvation upon Himself to make it effectual to you according to the exceeding riches of His grace. Your redemption is not left to chance; what the Lord has undertaken from His boundless love, He will surely accomplish for you by His infinite power. The foundation of God must stand sure, though everything else should fail. He cannot break His covenant or alter the thing that is gone out of His lips. Why did He engage in that covenant? Why stoop so low for a rebellious, a sinful soul? Why promise and impart inestimable blessings of grace to sinners who, unless He also bestowed the gift of thankfulness on them, would never so much as thank Him for one of His gifts? All was the result of free, of sovereign, of unsolicited grace. Sinners stood in extreme need of the mercies of the covenant, but they neither sought nor desired to seek them. Oh, astonishing love! God only could be the fountain, and man only the object of such love. This amazing love was not only stronger than death and mightier than the grave, but (with adoring reverence let it be said) was, in a sense, mightier than the Most High Himself, and brought Him down to flesh and blood, to the likeness of sinful flesh, to the dust of death, and to the chambers of the grave. It is owing to this redeeming love that the covenant of Jehovah is as firm, as immutable, as His very being. It is as well ordered as His unsearchable wisdom can make it, and as sure as His almighty power can keep it. Remember then, O redeemed soul, that it is your privilege to trust for and to seek, not uncovenanted favor, as many do, but covenanted, purchased, promised grace, grace that could never be procured by you, and that can never be taken from you. Oh, love your covenant-God, and your Kinsman-redeemer, with a supreme, an ardent love; so love Him that your constant pleasing of Him will be an increasing pleasure to you. How should your heart burn within you at the mention of a Name that is more delightful to the soul than ointment poured forth can be to the sense of the body! How should your spirit glow with rapturous love, with transporting devotion to your Redeemer and your God! Oh, let your soul cleave to Him. To know Christ is the most excellent knowledge; to win Christ is the greatest gain; to live upon Him is the happiest life below; and to be in the same covenant with Him is the greatest honor, as well as the highest security, for life eternal in the mansions above. "Because I live, ye shall live also" (John 14:19).

3

The Conditions of the Covenant of Grace

The essential parts of a proper covenant are two, the condition and the promise. The condition properly so called of a covenant is that part of it on the performance of which by the one party his right to the benefit promised by the other is founded; and his plea for it, as become due to him for his performance, is, according to their mutual agreement, established. This is a federal condition, and is what all men, in their converse and intercourse with each other, mean by the condition of a bargain or proper covenant. For example: the performance of such and such an action, or piece of work, for a certain reward or hire, agreed on by the parties, is the condition of a covenant of service; and the payment of a particular sum of money for certain wares or goods, according to the agreement between the parties stipulating, is the condition of a bargain of commerce.

There is also what is called a condition of order or connection in a covenant by which, in the order of the covenant, one thing necessarily goes before, and is connected with another without being the ground on which one's right or title to that other thing is founded. Thus, in the instances above mentioned, the servant's receiving of the hire and the buyer's receiving of the wares bargained for necessarily go before their respective possessing of them; but still it is obvious that this receiving is not the ground on which the servant's title to the hire or the buyer's title to the goods is founded. Though, therefore, it may be called a condition of order and connection IN each of those covenants, yet it cannot with any degree of propriety be called the condition OF them; and though it may be called a condition necessary to the possession of the hire and of the goods, yet it is not, like the former, the condition on which that possession is properly suspended.

Now, to apply this reasoning to the covenant of grace, that glorious covenant consists likewise of two essential parts, which were the articles agreed upon between God the Father and Christ the second Adam, namely the conditional part and the promissory part. In the settled order of that august contract, the having of the quickening Spirit goes before faith, faith before justification, justification before sanctification, true repentance for sin before God's fatherly forgiveness of sin (1 John 1:9), and holiness in time before happiness in eternity. These, therefore, may be called conditions in the covenant of grace, that is to say, conditions of order and connection in it; and they belong to the established order of the promises, and of the administration of the covenant that are distinguished from the condition of it. Such conditions, however, can with no propriety be called the conditions of the covenant of grace any more than the hireling's receiving of his hire can be termed the condition of a covenant of service. When the word "condition" is improperly taken and no more meant by it than that particular duties performed must, in the order of the covenant, precede the enjoyment of particular benefits promised, many duties may be called conditions. As faith in particular is, in the public dispensation of the covenant, not only required (Acts 16:31; Mark 16:16), as is repentance too, but is the appointed instrument by which sinners receive the benefits thereof (Isaiah 45:22; Romans 5:1, 2), it often has been, and still might be, called a condition of connection in it. But when the word condition is used in its proper signification—to express that which in itself, or at least by action, is meritorious of the promised benefit, or that which when performed gives a full right to claim the promised reward of that, on the performance of which not only the possession of the promise or benefit promised, but the right to possess it, is founded; nothing but the spotless, the finished righteousness of Jesus Christ, by which all the demands of the broken law are completely answered, can be admitted to be the condition of that Divine, that eternal covenant. That consummate righteousness is justly called the condition of the covenant for, as the reader will soon see, it comprises all the proper conditions of it.

The condition properly so called, then, of the covenant of grace, is, Christ's fulfilling of all righteousness, owing, in virtue of the broken covenant of works, to God, by His spiritual seed, and that, as the second Adam their federal Representative. Faith, it is true, may be called a condition of saving interest in Christ, of justification and salvation by Him, in the covenant. It is in this sense that faith is, in our Larger Catechism, Question 32, called a condition. There it is called the condition to interest sinners in Christ, that is, as it is expressed in Question 73 of the same Catechism, an instrument by which they receive and apply Christ and His righteousness. Hence it is plain that the venerable Assembly at Westminster considered the words "condition" and "instrument," when applied to faith, as conveying the same idea. But, although they call faith the condition to interest sinners in Christ, yet they nowhere call it the condition of the covenant of grace; but it is the surety-righteousness of the second Adam only that can be regarded as the condition of the covenant. It is that, and nothing else, which of itself as well as by pact, is meritorious of eternal life for believers, and is the proper ground of their title thereto in its beginning, progress, and consummation. They cannot, they must not, presume to plead their imperfect faith as the ground of the title; but they can, and they do, plead that transcendently perfect righteousness.

Having premised these things, it will now be requisite, in the first place, to prove that Christ's fulfilling of all righteousness is the condition of the covenant; and second, to unfold the import of the righteousness that, for that important purpose, He is the last Adam fulfilled.

SECTION 1. Proofs that the Surety-righteousness of Jesus Christ Is the Condition of the Covenant of Grace

In the first place, then, I am to essay to prove that Christ the second Adam's fulfilling all righteousness, in the room of His elect seed, is the condition of the covenant of grace. This will appear evident if we consider that:

1. Christ's fulfilling all righteousness in the room of His spiritual offspring is what the Father, in the covenant, proposed to Him as the terms on which He was to perform to bring them His promise of eternal life. As the condition of the first covenant was to have been performed only by the first Adam, representing his natural posterity, so the condition of the second covenant was, in the nature of things, performable only by the second Adam representing His spiritual progeny. It belonged to Him, and to Him only, as the federal Head and Surety of His people, to fulfill for them the condition of that covenant in which He engaged to represent them. Hence He thus spoke: "Ought not Christ to have suffered these things?" (Luke 24:26). That is, "Ought He not to have done so, as one who as bound faithfully to perform the conditions of a contract to which He had agreed?" And again, "Thus it becometh us to fulfill all righteousness" (Matthew 3:15), just as it becomes a person of honesty and credit to fulfill his engagements. It was on condition of His fulfilling for His seed all the righteousness of the law in its cov-

enant-form, and not on the ground of any works of theirs, that the Father proposed and promised to give them eternal life. The performance of the promise of eternal salvation to them was to be suspended not on any deeds of theirs, but on the perfect righteousness to be fulfilled by the second Adam as their Surety. Hence are these cheering declarations: "When thou shalt make his soul an offering for sin, he shall see his seed . . . He shall see of the travail of his soul, and shall be satisfied; by his knowledge shall my righteous servant justify many; for he shall bear their iniquities" (Isaiah 53:10, 11). "By the obedience of one shall many be made righteous" (Romans 5:19). "This cup is the new testament in My blood, which is shed for you" (Luke 22:20).

2. It will also appear evident if we reflect that Christ, in making the covenant, took on Himself the obligation of paying the whole debt of the elect world, all that debt, the payment of which secures them against eternal death. This is manifest from these, among many other passages of Scripture: "The Son of man came not to be ministered unto, but to minister, and to give His life a ransom for many" (Matthew 20:28). "Who died for us, that whether we wake or sleep, we should live together with Him" (1 Thessalonians 5:10). "Christ also hath once suffered for sins, the just for the unjust, that He might bring us unto God" (1 Peter 3:18). He likewise came under the obligation of discharging all that debt of His elect seed, the payment of which should entitle them to eternal life. This is evident from these Scriptures no less than the former ones, for thus it is written: "If thou wilt enter into life, keep the commandments" (Matthew 19:17). "Think not that I am come to destroy the law or the prophets; I am not come to destroy, but to fulfill" (Matthew 5:17). "By the obedience of One shall many be made righteous" (Romans 5:19). "Even so by the righteousness of One the free gift came upon all men unto justification of life" (Ro-

mans 5:18). Moreover is it possible to conceive that Christ should be the Mediator and Surety of the covenant, and yet that He should not undertake the execution thereof? Or is it possible to suppose that the eternal Son of God, who has faithfulness as the girdle of His reins, should undertake to be the Redeemer, the Surety, the Priest of the covenant, and yet leave it to others to fulfill the condition that is the most difficult part of it? Indeed, it was only He who could and who did perform the infinitely arduous condition.

The first Adam brought in sin to the world; but He brought in everlasting righteousness (Daniel 9:24); and therefore, "This is the name whereby He shall be called, Jehovah our Righteousness" (Jeremiah 23:6). Nothing then remains to be performed or endured by them as the proper condition of the covenant.

3. The perfections of Jehovah made it requisite that the condition of the broken covenant of works should form a principal part of the condition of any covenant for the salvation of fallen men that ever He might make. Unless the holy commandment is honored with perfect obedience, one of the children of Adam can never enter into life. "It thou wilt enter into life, keep the commandments" (Matthew 19:17). "The man that doeth them shall live in them" (Galatians 3:12). Unless the righteousness and truth of Jehovah could fail, the awful penalty must be executed, must be endured (Genesis 2:17). Sin must be expiated by such sufferings and such a death as will give full satisfaction to the justice of the holy Majesty of heaven (Exodus 34:7). Now, nothing but the consummate righteousness of the incarnate God could answer those high demands (Romans 8:3, 4). The debt of perfect righteousness was, and could not but be, stated from the violated covenant of works under which the spiritual seed of Christ lay. The law or covenant of works, then, was so far from being overlooked in the covenant of grace that

whatever demands it had to make upon the elect for salvation, they were all summed up, and the complete answering for them was made the condition of that eternal covenant (Psalm 69:4; Isaiah 42:21).

4. It is upon the perfect righteousness of Christ, and that only, that believers can safely found their plea for and their hope of eternal life. To this purpose are these declarations of the holy Apostle Paul: "That I may win Christ, and be found in Him, not having mine own righteousness, which is of the law, but . . . the righteousness which is of God by faith" (Philippians 3:8, 9). "By the deeds of the law, there shall no flesh be justified in His sight; for by the law is the knowledge of sin. But now the righteousness of God without the law is manifested . . . even the righteousness of God, which is by faith of Jesus Christ, unto all, and upon all them that believe" (Romans 3:20, 21, 22). "In whom we have redemption through His blood, the forgiveness of sins, according to the riches of His grace" (Ephesians 1:7).

The condition of a covenant performed is the sole ground of one's having a right to the benefit therein promised; on that ground and no other, can he warrantably found his claim to it. But it is on Christ's fulfilling of all righteousness only, and not on any work done by the sinner himself, no, not even on his faith, that he may safely found his plea for eternal life. He may plead the righteousness of Jesus Christ; but he must never presume to plead his faith as the foundation of his right. It is Christ's fulfilling of all righteousness, then, and neither the works nor the faith of the sinner himself that is the proper condition of the covenant, or the ground of his title to the life therein promised. It is under the covert of that meritorious righteousness only that the converted sinner flees for refuge; and, relinquishing all the other grounds of hope, he dares to present nothing but that, either to the law's demand of perfect obedience for life or of infinite satisfaction for sin. As to believing in Christ, it is indeed a trusting and pleading on the ground of that spotless righteousness fulfilled; but it is not itself either in whole or in part the ground of the believer's plea. If any man will presume to make his faith the foundation of his plea and of his hope, he must product it as a work of the law, as a perfect work, by which he has fulfilled the law.

5. It is by that consummate righteousness, and that only, that the eternal life promised in the covenant becomes a debt. It is not a debt or a thing due to sinners in themselves, but it is a debt solely to Christ the second Adam. It was not they, therefore, but He who fulfilled the condition of the covenant. Whosoever so works as to fulfill the proper condition of a covenant, the reward promised and suspended on that condition is of debt to him. "Now to him that worketh is the reward not reckoned of grace, but of debt" (Romans 4:4). Eternal life is, to the true believer, a reward of grace because he does not work, that is, does not perform the proper condition of it; but to Christ, and to Christ solely, it is a reward of debt because He and He only so worked as to work out that perfect righteousness that was the meritorious condition of that reward.

This argument will be confirmed if we consider the original situation of mankind with respect to eternal life under the covenant of works. According to the tenor of that covenant, if Adam had performed that perfect obedience that was the condition of life in it eternal life would have become due, or would have been a reward of debt to him; and the plea of his posterity for life in that case would not have been founded on their own personal obedience since that obedience, following after the performance of the condition, would have been a fruit of the promise of the covenant. But it would have been founded solely on that performance of the condition by Adam, their federal representative; and so they would have received life, not for any personal obedience yielded by themselves, but of the obedience of the first Adam their representative imputed to them, to which God in that covenant had made the promise. In like manner, it was to the righteousness of the second Adam, and to that solely, that Jehovah, in the covenant of grace, made the promise of life eternal. To that condition of the covenant, therefore, and to that only, all merit in the affair of the justification and salvation of His elect seed belongs. And to attribute any merit, any desert of good from God, to anything that sinners or even saints do is a gross indignity to the Lord Jesus to whom, as the end of the law for righteousness, they must be wholly indebted for all the blessings of the covenant. It is only to Christ, then, that eternal life, promised in the covenant of grace, is a reward of debt. The title of believers to it is founded on His infinitely perfect merit, which is pactional as well as intrinsic.

6. Faith, repentance, and new obedience are blessings promised in the covenant of grace on the ground of the condition of it; and therefore they cannot themselves be the conditions of the same covenant. As they can by no means answer the demands of the broken law, so, instead of being proper conditions of the covenant of grace, they are inestimable benefits freely promised therein on the footing of that spotless righteousness of the second Adam by which those demands were fully answered. Faith in particular is promised in it: "They shall come" (Psalm 22:31). "In Him shall the Gentiles trust" (Romans 15:12). "Unto you it is given in the behalf of Christ . . . to believe on Him" (Philippians 1:29). Repentance likewise is therein promised: "All the ends of the earth shall remember and turn unto the Lord" (Psalm 22:27). "They shall look upon me whom they have pierced, and they shall mourn for him" (Zechariah 12:10). Ability to perform sincere obedience is also promised in it: "I will

put My Spirit within you and cause you to walk in My statutes, and ye shall keep My judgments and do them" (Ezekiel 36:17). These evidence the very person possessed of them to be already within that covenant, and to be already entitled to all the benefits of it, none of them being performable under the condemning sentence of the covenant of works (1 Corinthians 15:56; Galatians 2:19; Romans 6:14). Besides, being duties as well as graces, and duties performed not under the law as a covenant of works but under it as a rule of life, they can have no covenantal merit, but are founded on communion with Christ in His righteousness and on a previous right to eternal life (Luke 1:75, 76; Hebrews 12:28). It is as the performance of the promises, then, that those graces are produced in the elect. They, therefore, cannot be the conditions of the covenant of grace. Elect infants, dying in infancy, are doubtless entitled to eternal life, though they cannot exercise either faith or repentance; but it is manifest that the condition of the covenant must necessarily have been fulfilled either by themselves who have that title, and consequently are saved, or by another in their stead. The righteousness of Jesus Christ, therefore, which is the only obedience performed in their stead, must be to them, as well as to adults, the condition of the covenant.

7. The covenant of grace excludes all boasting on the part of the creature, which the covenant of works did not. "Where is boasting then?" said the apostle Paul, "it is excluded. By what law? Of works? Nay, but by the law of faith" (Romans 3:27). But if any act or work performed by us is either in whole or in part the condition of the covenant of grace, the doctrine of which is the law of faith, our boasting is not excluded, but on the contrary has place therein, as it had in the covenant of works; for, according to the Scripture, it is working or performing the condition of a covenant that affords ground of boasting to the per-

former. So far as eternal life is acquired by any act of work of our own, performed as the condition of that eternal covenant, our boasting is no more excluded by it than it was by the covenant of works. Nay, on the contrary, the lowest act of faith, or of repentance, or of sincere obedience, under the curse of the law and the dominion of sin, would be a greater ground of boasting than Adam's performing in a state of innocence the condition of the covenant of works could be.

Seeing, therefore, that the covenant of grace is so framed as to leave no ground for our boasting, it follows that no work, no act of ours, but Christ's fulfilling all righteousness, and that only, is the proper condition of the covenant of redeeming grace. "Not by works of righteousness which we have done, but according to His mercy He saved us . . . that, being justified by His grace, we should be made heirs according to the hope of eternal life" (Titus 3:5, 7). "Not of works, lest any man should boast" (Ephesians 2:9).

Do not let my meaning here be mistaken. Though faith and obedience are excluded from being the proper conditions of the covenant, they are far, however, from being excluded from the covenant itself. Faith is necessary as the appointed instrument of union with Christ, and of interest in Him as the glorious Head of the covenant; and none who are of adult age can otherwise than by the Spirit of faith and the exercise of faith either be instated in the covenant or attain that life eternal which is therein promised. New obedience is necessary as the great subordinate end of the covenant; and without such obedience begun and persisted in, none who are subjects capable of it can even enter into the celestial mansions. But at the same time, it is no less necessary that each of these be kept in its proper place, in that place which the Father and the Son from everlasting assigned to it. By faith we take hold of Jehovah's covenant, rely with confidence on the condition of it as fulfilled by our glorious Representative, and so enter personally into the bond of it (John 10:9). By evangelical repentance and obedience we evidence the truth of our faith and of our in-being in the covenant; and also we testify our thankfulness to God as our covenant-God, and to Christ as our Covenant-head (1 Peter 2:9).

In this momentous doctrine the ancient Jewish church was instructed, especially by the prophet Micah, in the following passage: "He hath showed thee, O man, what is good; and what doth the Lord require of thee but to do justly, and to love mercy, and to walk humbly with thy God?" (Micah 6:8). In the preceding context a very important question is put concerning the way of a sinner's attaining acceptance in the sight of God: "Wherewith shall I come before the Lord, and bow myself before the high God?" Several very costly oblations for that purpose are proposed by the sinner, upon which the prophet returns the only proper answer to the question: "He hath shown thee, O man, what is good," that is, what is good or acceptable to Jehovah for the purpose of entitling a guilty sinner to pardon and acceptance in His sight, namely Messiah sacrificed in the room of sinners. This was what Jehovah had, from the beginning, by the ceremonial law and by the holy prophets, pointed out to them as "good" for that important purpose in order that they might by faith look unto Him and be saved (Isaiah 45:22). Messiah sacrificed for sinners is elsewhere spoken of under the same character. Hezekiah, on a particular occasion, thus prayed: "The good Lord pardon every one that prepareth his heart to seek God" (2 Chronicles 30:18, 19). In the sacred original it is, "Jehovah the good," or "Jehovah, that is good," "make atonement for [him who] prepareth his heart to seek God." "The Lord shall give thee that which is good" (Psalm 85:12). "If thou knewest the gift of God, and who it is that saith to thee, 'Give me to drink,' " (John 4:10). "Eat ye that which is good. The bread of God is He which cometh down from heaven, and giveth life unto the world" (Isaiah 55:2). The prophet Micah thus proceeds: Being accepted by Jehovah on the ground of that all-perfect atonement, "What doth He require of thee but to do justly," as one who is pardoned and accepted as righteous on the ground of a righteousness that fully answers the demands of law and justice, "to love mercy," as one who, through an infinite atonement, has obtained mercy, "and to walk humbly with thy God," as one who is an everlasting debtor to His free and sovereign grace?

8. Finally, the righteousness that Christ as our condescending Surety fulfilled, and that is fully answerable to the precept and penalty of the broken covenant of works, is plainly represented in Scripture as the proper condition of eternal life to His spiritual seed. The following passages, selected out of many, may suffice to evidence the truth of this: "When thou shalt make his soul," or, "When his soul shall make itself an offering for sin, he shall see his seed . . . by his knowledge shall My righteous Servant justify many; for He shall bear their iniquities" (Isaiah 53:10, 11). "This cup is the New Testament in My blood, which is shed for you" (Luke 22:20). "He humbled Himself, and became obedient unto death, even the death of the cross" (Philippians 2:8). "Thus it becometh us to fulfill all righteousness" (Matthew 3:15). "That I may win Christ, and be found in Him, not having mine own righteousness, which is of the law, but . . . the righteousness which is of God by faith" (Philippians 3:8, 9). "For He hath made Him to be sin for us, who knew no sin; that we might be made the righteousness of God in Him" (2 Corinthians 5:21). "Therefore, as by the offence of one judgment came upon all men to condemnation, even so, by the righteousness of One, the free gift came upon all men unto jus-

tification of life. For as by one man's disobedience many were made sinners, so by the obedience of One shall many be made righteous; that as sin hath reigned unto death, even so might grace reign through righteousness unto eternal life by Jesus Christ our Lord" (Romans 5:18, 19, 21). "In whom we have redemption through His blood, even the forgiveness of sins" (Colossians 1:14). "For Christ also hath once suffered for sins, the just for the unjust, that He might bring us to God" (1 Peter 3:18). "Who gave Himself for us, that He might redeem us from all iniquity" (Titus 2:14). "Thou wast slain, and hast redeemed us to God by Thy blood" (Revelation. 5:9). "This is His name whereby He shall be called THE LORD OUR RIGHTEOUSNESS" (Jeremiah 23:6). "Even the righteousness of God which is by faith of Jesus Christ, unto all, and upon all them that believe" (Romans 3:22).

Since, then, Christ's fulfilling all righteousness in the room of His spiritual seed is what the Father in the covenant proposed to Him as the terms on which He was to perform His promise of eternal life to them; since, in making the covenant He took upon Himself the obligation of discharging the whole debt of the elect world, the payment of which secures them from eternal death; since the perfections of Jehovah required that the condition of the broken covenant of works should form a part of the condition of any covenant for the salvation of fallen men that ever He might enter into; since it is upon the perfect righteousness of Jesus Christ only that believers can safely found their plea for, and their hope of eternal life; since it is by that consummate righteousness, and that only ,that the life eternal promised in the covenant becomes a debt; since faith, repentance and new obedience are blessings promised in the covenant on the ground of the condition of it, and therefore cannot themselves be the proper conditions of the same covenant; since the covenant of grace excludes all boasting on the part of the creature that the covenant of works did not; and since the righteousness that Christ our condescending Surety fulfilled, and that is fully answerable to the precept and penalty of the broken covenant of works is plainly represented in the Scripture as the proper condition of eternal life to his spiritual seed—it is evident that His fulfilling of that surety-righteousness in the room of His elect seed is the condition of the covenant of grace.

SECTION 2. The Constituent Parts of the Righteousness of Christ Considered

I am now as was proposed in the second place to show what is imported or comprised in that consummate righteousness that Christ the second Adam fulfilled as the great condition of the covenant.

The honor of the Divine perfections required that, seeing Christ undertook to fulfill as their Surety that righteousness in the room of sinners, it should be stated from the broken law or covenant of works under the dominion of which they lay. The law or covenant of works was so far from being overlooked in the new contract that whatever it had to demand from elect sinners as their ground of security from eternal death, and of title to eternal life, was summed up and the complete payment of it was made the condition of this covenant (Romans 8:3, 4; Isaiah 42:21). Stating, then, from the violated covenant of works, the whole of the righteousness to be fulfilled by Christ the second Adam, it may thence be summed up in three parts that may be denominated so many conditions, or stipulated articles, namely perfect holiness of nature, perfect righteousness of life, and complete satisfaction for sin.

Article 1. Perfect Holiness of Nature.

The law required perfect holiness or conformity of nature to all its precepts as a condition of eternal life, inasmuch as saying, "Thou shalt not covet." And so, forbidding and condemning original sin or corruption of nature, it concluded all the children of fallen Adam to be by nature children of wrath (Ephesians 2:3). Since God is infinitely and unchangeably holy, and that by necessity of nature, nothing can be so contrary to Him as an unholy nature. His nature and the sinner's nature are not only infinitely distant from, but infinitely opposite to each other. Indeed, to suppose that His law, which is a fair transcript of the holiness of His own nature, did not require perfect holiness of human nature is much the same as to suppose that the want of original righteousness, and even the corruption of the whole nature, are not sinful. "For where no law is, there is no transgression" (Romans 4:15). Nor can the admitting of the holiness of Christ's human nature into His righteousness imputed to believers any more render their holiness of nature unnecessary than His obedience of life can render their obedience unnecessary. The holiness of their nature is a necessary part of that eternal life that was merited for them by the holiness of Christ's nature. Since then the party contracted for in the covenant of grace had their nature wholly corrupted and were utterly unable to make it holy, even in the lowest degree, it is evident that they could by no means answer, in their own persons, this demand of the law. That the law, therefore, in this demand might be answered, it was settled as a stipulated article of the covenant that Christ the second Adam, representing them, should be a man of a perfectly holy and untainted nature, completely answering, as their Surety, the perfect holiness of nature required by the law. This article consists of two clauses.

1. That He as the last Adam should be conceived and born holy, instead of them who were conceived and born in sin and

The Conditions of the Covenant of Grace

consequently unholy. A perfectly holy nature was conferred on the first Adam as the root and representative of mankind to be kept by him and, in the way of ordinary generation, conveyed to his posterity. Upon that ground the holy law requires all the children of Adam to be born holy, pronouncing them children of wrath if they are not. But how can such a demand as this be answered by sinners? They are all born in sin; and they cannot enter into their mother's womb and be a second time born without sin. No, verily they cannot. And yet the righteous law cannot recede from that demand as a condition of life. It was therefore stipulated that Christ as a public person, representing His spiritual seed, should be born with a nature perfectly holy; that seeing they brought a sinful nature into the world with them, He might bring a holy human nature into the world with Him. And so He was the last Adam, the heavenly One (1 Corinthians 15:45); that holy thing born of the virgin (Luke 1:35). His human nature was, in all respects, conformed to the holy law. "Thy law is within my heart" (Psalm 40:8); than which no words could be more expressive of perfect conformity of nature to the law. He was not, as others are, born in sin because, not having been naturally in the loins of Adam, nor represented by him as a covenant-head, He was not concerned in the violation of Adam's covenant. The effect of this, respecting the demand of the law for life, is that all true believers are, in the estimation of law, born holy in Him like they were in the first Adam, created holy. They are expressly said to be circumcised in Him, which plainly presupposes that they were legally born in Him. And it is in virtue of their being legally born holy in Christ when He was born that, legally united to Him, they are each of them in due time actually born again, and at last made perfect in holiness; just as it is in virtue of their having been legally defiled in Adam when he sinned, that they are actually defiled, each in his own person, when born into the world. A holy nature is actually conveyed to them from the last Adam their spiritual Head in whom they were legally born holy, just as a corrupt nature is actually transmitted to them from the first Adam, their natural head, in whom they in legal estimation sinned. Hence are these words of an apostle: "Such an high Priest became us who is holy, harmless, undefiled, separate from sinners, and made higher than the heavens" (Hebrews 7:26). He does not say, "Such it became Him to be," as denoting merely a qualification for the work of sacrificing, but "it became us; it was suitable and requisite for us; it was necessary on our account."

2. The other clause in that article is that Christ as the last Adam, representing elect sinners, should in their stead retain His perfect holiness of human nature, inviolate to the end. God having made man upright, the law or covenant of works required, as a condition of eternal life, that the holiness of nature given to mankind in Adam should be retained in all its purity and perfection. But, alas! It was soon forfeited; it was entirely lost. And suppose it had been restored, none of the family of Adam amidst so many destructive snares as their spiritual enemies would have continued to lay for them could in their own persons have preserved it unstained, even for a moment. To answer, therefore, this demand of the law, it was provided that Christ as the last Adam, the public Representative of His spiritual seed, should keep the human nature perfectly free from the least stain or imperfection to the end of His humbled life. Hence the eternal Father said concerning Him, "He shall not fail" (Hebrews 7:26); or, "He shall not be dull, dim, or wrinkled," as the skin is when the radical juices of the body begin to be exhausted. The first Adam, when he had newly come out of the Creator's hand, shone in perfect holiness of nature; but he failed; he became dim; and the purity of his nature, having been

exhausted by transgression, all his descendants lost in him their spiritual vigor and beauty. But now that the second Adam did not fail, but on the contrary retained the perfect holiness of His human nature, in all its vigor and without the smallest stain, even to the end of His humbled life, the remains of their corruption of nature are not imputed to believers (Romans 4:8); for, though in themselves they are defiled through these remains cleaving to them, yet in Christ their beauty is perfect. "Thou art all fair, my love, there is no spot in thee" (Song of Solomon 4:7).

Thus, Christ as the second Adam, representing His spiritual seed, was conceived and born holy; and He retained the perfect holiness of His human nature inviolate to the end.

Article 2. Perfect Righteousness of Life.

The law required as a condition of eternal life not only perfect conformity of nature to its precepts, but perfect conformity of life; not only full conformity of the faculties of the soul and members of the body, but of the thoughts, words, and actions of the man. The Lord gave to Adam, and to all mankind in him, a law that was in all points to be obeyed, not merely in virtue of the tie of natural obligation, but in virtue also of the bond of a covenant of life; but that law was not fulfilled by them. Adam, indeed, began a course of obedience to it; but he soon fell off from that obedience, with all his natural posterity in him. Now, it being inconsistent with the honor of the righteous law that man should receive the prize of eternal life without having run the race, it still persisted in its original demand of obedience, saying, "If thou wilt enter into life, keep the commandments" (Matthew 19:17). The children of fallen Adam, however, were without strength and quite unable to run that race. It was therefore settled, as another conditional article of the covenant, that Christ Jesus as a public person, representing those for whom He contracted, should begin and finish a course of perfect obedience or righteousness of life, to the law. Accordingly we read that He became obedient unto death (Philippians 2:8), and that He came not to destroy, but to fulfill the law (Matthew 5:17). The law, which required that obedience from him, was, in its covenant-form, the same law of the Ten Commandments that was given to the first Adam; and that sill continues in that form to be binding on his posterity so long as they continue under it; for Christ was made under the law to redeem them that were under the law (Galatians 4:4, 5). It extended to all the Divine institutions that the last Adam found in existence; whether obliging mankind as members of civil society, or as members of the visible church of God; just as, when it was given to the first Adam, it extended to the positive law, concerning the forbidden fruit that he found in force when he began his covenant-obedience.

This momentous article includes the following clauses:

CLAUSE 1. That Christ as last Adam should, in the place of those whom He represented, obey the whole law. This was a debt that they all owed to God, and that the law required of them as a condition of eternal life. "Cursed is everyone that continueth not in all things, which are written in the book of the law, to do them" (Galatians 3:10). "For whosoever shall keep the whole law, and yet offend in one point, he is guilty of all" (James 2:10). But to answer this demand was far, very far, beyond their power. Man having, by the fall, lost much of his knowledge of the law, he of course lost sight of many of the duties that it required of him. His carnal mind being enmity against God was altogether averse from the spirituality and great extent of the Divine law He was also without strength, and therefore was utterly unable to perform acceptably so much as one of the least of the duties that it required of him (Romans 5:6); so that, by reason of his ignorance, aversion, and impotence, obedience to the whole law was not to be expected from him. It was therefore from eternity stipulated that Christ, the Representative and Surety of the elect, should yield obedience for them to the whole law; that both tables of the law, and every commandment of each table, should have due obedience from Him; that the law, in all its spirituality, extent, and perfection being laid before Him, He should completely answer it with external and internal obedience, not only in mind, will, and affections, but also in thought, word and deed; that He should conform His life to all the moral precepts and to all the Divine institutions, whether ceremonial or political; so as to be circumcised, to keep the Passover, to be baptized, to be subject to rulers, to pay tribute, and so on; in few words, that He should perform the whole will of God expressed in His law; so that His spiritual seed might be entitled to eternal life and attain it, consistently with the honor of law and justice. This was what the first Adam failed in, and what the last Adam, as the Representative of His seed, was to do. As the mercy seat, under the law, was exactly commensurate with the dimensions of the ark, so was the obedience of our blessed Surety, with the whole extent of the law.

CLAUSE 2. It likewise includes that every part of his obedience should be raised to the very highest degree. This perfection of obedience the law required from his spiritual offspring as a condition of life. "Thou shalt love the Lord thy God with all thy heart, and with all thy soul, and with all thy strength, and with all thy mind; and thy neighbor as thyself . . . This do, and thou shalt live" (Luke 10:27, 28). But, since the first Adam had squandered away all their fund of ability, and had left them without strength so much as to think one spiritually good thought, this was a demand that it was impossible for them to answer. They might as soon reach with their hand to the sun in the heavens as now attain that perfection of obedience that the righteous law required from them. It was therefore provided that Christ as last Adam, being made under the law as they were (Galatians 4:4, 5), should, in their stead, obey it in that perfection; that every thought, word, and action of His should possess a goodness not only of matter, but of manner, and that in absolute perfection; that love to God and to man should flame in His holy soul to the highest pitch required by the law; that so He might, as their condescending Surety, discharge their debt of perfect obedience that, as a condition of life, they owed to the law and justice of Jehovah.

The terms of life in the first covenant were perfect obedience; and though the terms once fixed remain unalterable yet, in the second covenant, there is a substitution, and thereby a change as to the performer without the least relaxation as to the performance. Hence our Lord Jesus Himself informs us that He came to fulfill the law. He perfectly fulfilled it. He yielded such a high degree of obedience to the perceptive part of it that there was no room for any more, considered as a proper condition of life. By this consummate obedience, flowing from the perfect holiness of His human nature, our righteous Surety fulfilled every jot, every tittle, of the perceptive part of the law in its covenant-form; yea, moreover, by the infinite value derived from His Divine nature to His obedience, He magnified and made it honorable. He gave it, if I may so say, good measure, pressed down, and shaken together, and running over (Luke 6:38). O Divine, O adorable Surety, we who so believe as to have the witness in ourselves are, by Thy spotless obedience imputed to us, made righteousness in the abstract, even the righteousness of God in Thee (2 Corinthians 5:21)!

CLAUSE 3. Finally, it implies that this obedience should be continued to the end without the least failure in point either of parts or of degrees. This also was settled in the covenant of works as a condition of life eternal. "Cursed is every one that continueth not in all things which are written in the book of the law to do them" (Galatians 3:10). But it was a demand that it was utterly impossible for sinners to answer. The nature of man is so corrupted by his fall that, if ten thousand hells were depending on it, the holiest man on earth could not make, nor keep himself perfectly right, even for one moment. It was therefore from everlasting stipulated that the last Adam should, in the room of them whom He represented, continue in all things written in the book of the law to do them, even to the end; that He should not fail in His begun course of perfect obedience, but run on till He finished the race set before Him. This the blessed Jesus accordingly did. He not only became obedient, but obedient unto death (Philippians 2:8); obedient not only in His death, but through His whole life until His death; so that from the womb to the grave His life as well as His nature, shone in absolute perfection of conformity to the holy law.

Thus, Christ as the last Adam, obeyed the whole law in its covenant-form; His obedience rose in perfection to the highest degree; and without the last failure in point of parts or degrees, He continued in it to the end.

His continuing thus to retain perfect holiness of nature, and to perform perfect obedience of life, was arduous in an infinite degree; inasmuch as He in our stead remained, from the womb to the grave, under the infinite curse of the broken law (Galatians 3:13; 1 Corinthians 15:56).

Article 3. Complete Satisfaction for Sin

The two former articles were all that were comprised in the condition of the covenant of works; this one was not and could not be included in it for while there was no sin, there could be no place for a satisfaction for sin. But it was requisite that the covenant of grace should be established upon condition of a satisfaction for iniquity. Immutable justice is essential to God; and it is a righteous thing with Him that every transgression receive a just recompense (2 Thessalonians 1:6; Hebrews 2:2); and if its receiving of a recompense is just, it would be unjust to pardon it without an adequate satisfaction. The broken law or covenant of works too, in virtue of its awful penalty that the elect had incurred, demanded full satisfaction to justice as a necessary condition of life to them ("God's original constitution that connected sin and the curse was just. He abides by it, reverses it not; to have reversed it, was not to have judged the offenders, but Himself," John Howe, second part of his *Living Temple*). They themselves, however, were infinitely far from being able to answer this demand of the law. If, then, the second Adam will have a seed brought back from a state of death to a state of life, He must lay down for every soul of them, a sufficient ransom, and so buy them back from the hand of inflexible justice (1 Corinthians 6:20). Accordingly, all the sins of every one of them, being from eternity foreseen by the omnipresent Jehovah, were summed up as so many transgressions of the law of works; and it was settled as an additional article in the conditions of the covenant of grace, that Christ as their public Representative should give to law and justice complete satisfaction for all those sins. "The Lord hath laid on Him the iniquity of us all" (Isaiah 53:6). "Christ also hath once suffered for sins, the just for the unjust, that He might bring us unto God" (1 Peter 3:18).

Now, in this article the following clauses were settled:

1. Christ the last Adam, as a public person, should satisfy Divine justice for the sins of an elect world by suffering. Ought not Christ to have suffered these things (Luke 24:26)? The sinners deserved to suffer for the satisfaction of vindicative justice; and nothing but suffering could be accepted as a recompense

The Conditions of the Covenant of Grace

for the injury that, by the violation of His righteous law, was done to the honor of Jehovah. That the only begotten Son, who is in the bosom of the Father, should suffer was indeed an amazing proposal; but it was requisite in order to satisfy for the sins of these who were to be redeemed by Him. Thousands of rams, and ten thousands of rivers of oil, were at Christ's disposal; every beast of the forest was His, and the cattle upon a thousand hills (Psalm 50:10). All the silver was His, and the gold was His. His were all the precious things of the earth and of the sea. None of these, however, could, for this purpose, be of the smallest value: "For the redemption of their soul is precious, and it ceaseth forever" (Psalm 49:8; 1 Peter 1:18). It was His own suffering only that could satisfy infinite justice for sin. He could not satisfy it by doing; it was not by doing, but by suffering, that satisfaction was to be given.

2. It was also agreed that He should not only suffer, but suffer the same punishment that they, in virtue of the penalty of the broken covenant of works, were to have borne, which was death in its utmost latitude. This appears evident from the penal sanction of the covenant, from which the debt of satisfaction for sin was stated: "In the day thou east thereof, thou shalt surely die" (Genesis 2:17), compared with what the Scriptures frequently assert respecting the second Adam, that He died for, that is, in the room of sinners (Romans 5:8; 1 Thessalonians 5:10). And the truth of it is confirmed from what the Scriptures also declare, namely that all they for whom He died, died in Him: "If one died for all, then were all dead," or, "then all died" (2 Corinthians 5:14), that is, in Him, even as they sinned and fell under the sentence of death in the first Adam. They died that death in Him by His dying for them, which they deserved in their own persons to die.

In order to elucidate this particular, two things are carefully to be distinguished in that death, which was the penalty of the covenant of works:

First, that which was essential to it, or included in the very nature of it, and which in the style of the covenant is properly called death. This is comprised in the awful curse of the law, and in the infinite execution of that curse; the former, rendering the death legal and virtual, and the latter, making it real and satisfactory.

Second, that which was accidental to it, arising not from the nature of the thing in itself, but from the nature of the party dying. There are some things in it that proceed from the nature of the party dying, considered as a mere creature, namely the eternity of the punishment and the despair of deliverance. There are some things likewise that arise from the party dying, considered as a sinful creature, that is, divesting the soul of the moral image of God and the extinction of the spiritual relation between it and Him, together with the corruption and dissolution of the body.

Now the accidentals of that death that we, in virtue of the penalty of the broken covenant of works, were to have endured formed no part of the conditions of the covenant of grace imposed upon the second Adam. He was neither a mere man nor a subject of inherent sin; and therefore they could have no place in Him. But the essentials of that death, as a part of the conditions of the covenant, were inflicted on Him, and in our stead He suffered them. For we read that He was made a curse for us (Galatians 3:13), that He gave Himself for us, an offering and a sacrifice to God for a sweet smelling savor (Ephesians 5:2), that is, an offering and a sacrifice fully compensating the infinite offence to the High and Holy One that arose from our sins, and that in consequence thereof He has perfected forever them that

The Conditions of the Covenant of Grace

are sanctified (Hebrews 10:14). He suffered, then, the same death for us that we were condemned to endure inasmuch as the essentials of it were the same.

To explain my meaning, let us suppose, in the case of discharging a debt, that though the debtor himself could not pay his debt but in copper money, and that, advanced by little and little for a long time, or perhaps for the whole remainder of his life, which would issue in the complete ruin of his affairs, yet if his rich sponsor should pay it all at once in a little gold this would be sustained in law as the payment of the debt. Again, suppose that two men, equally guilty of the same crime, are laid under the same sentence of death, and that it is equally executed on them both, but that the one is by a miracle raised again to life while the other continues and consumes in the grave under the power of death. It is plain that the death that they both suffered is the same death, corresponding to one and the same estimate that the law made of the crime, and that therefore the death of the former satisfies the law as much as the death of the latter, so that it cannot any more reach his life for that crime. Still, however, it is no less evident that in accidentals, particularly in the duration of it, there is a vast difference between the death of the one and that of the other. I conclude, therefore, that as Christ the last Adam yielded the same active obedience to the moral law that we should have yielded to it in virtue of the condition of the covenant of works, so He suffered the same death that we should have endured in virtue of the penalty of that broken covenant, seeing that, whatever difference there was in the accidentals of it, the essentials were the same.

Thus, then, as I hinted above, two principal points as essentials of that death were established in this conditional article of the covenant.

First, that the curse of the law, due to the elect of God for their sin, should be transferred to Him as the last Adam their Representative, by which He, in their stead, should forthwith become a man dead in law. It was necessary that either they or He should bear the curse: "For it is written, cursed is every one that continueth not in all things which are written in the book of the law to do them." Since Jehovah had annexed the threatening of death to the first covenant, saying, "In the day that thou eatest thereof thou shalt surely die," His truth secured the curse's taking place as soon as sin should begin to be committed. Now it was impossible for them to endure the awful curse otherwise than by being thereby eternally undone. But, that it might be endured, and they withal saved, it was stipulated that Christ as the last Adam should be subjected thereto in their stead; that as He was made sin for them, so He should in consequence be also made a curse for them (Galatians 3:13).

By the curse that was transferred to Him is meant the sentence of the broken law passed upon a man, adjudging Him to be the vindictive wrath of God for the satisfaction of Divine justice. In this, then, the awful mystery of the substitution of the Lord Jesus lies: He, in virtue of His bond of suretiship registered in the records of heaven, must stand before the tribunal of the holy and righteous law as one who was made sin, who was made responsible for all the sin of an elect world; and sentence must pass upon Him, adjudging Him to endure all the revenging wrath which that sin deserved. Thus, the spotless Lamb of God was made a curse for us; and, as a token of it, being arraigned before the Jewish Sanhedrin, He was judged a blasphemer and worthy of death; and having appeared before Pilate the Roman governor, He was by him sentenced to die, and to die the cursed, the ignominious death of the cross.

The Conditions of the Covenant of Grace

The wonderful result of transferring the curse of the law to the second Adam was (1) that He was hereby constituted the separated one of the elect society. By the curse of the covenant that lay upon Him, the Lord separated Him unto evil (Deuteronomy 29:20, 21). He made Him the devoted head, devoted to expiate for all the rest. He appointed Him to be the receptacle of all the overflowing floods of Divine vengeance issuing from vindictive justice toward the whole body of His elect to swallow them up. Hither, the overwhelming current of all these was turned, that they might together rush upon him Hence He cried, "I sink in deep mire, where there is no sanding; I am come into deep waters, where the floods overflow me" (Psalm 69:2). He was set up as the mark against which all the poisoned arrows of revenging wrath should fly. He was consigned into the hands of vindictive justice that it might, without the least pity or abatement, demand full satisfaction from Him for all the iniquities that were imputed to Him (Zechariah 13:7; Romans 8:32). Hence Jehovah the Father is represented as having been legally wroth with Him (Psalm 89:38; 22:1, 2).

(2) The result of it was that He became the resting place of avenging justice, upon whom it was to prey till it should be completely satisfied. "It pleased the Lord to bruise him; He hath put him to grief . . . Thou shalt make His soul an offering for sin" (Isaiah 53:10). "My strength," said He, "is dried up like a potsherd; and my tongue cleaveth to my jaws; and Thou hast brought me into the dust of death" (Psalm 22:15). As a token of this, He said to the officers who came to apprehend Him, "If ye seek Me, let these go their way." Divine justice, quitting the pursuit of the rebellious multitude, goes forth in quest of Him, their condescending Surety, and of Him only. Thus, the second Adam was devoted to be the sacrifice for His spiritual offspring

that the fire of incensed wrath should consume that it might send forth a savor of rest to the revenging justice of Jehovah.

Second, the other main point established in this conditional article was that the curse transferred to Him should be infinitely executed upon Him as the Representative of His seed, by which He should, in their stead, die really, and so make full compensation to justice for all the injury done by their sin to the honor of the infinite Majesty of heaven. Vain is that curse that has no effect. But as the burse of the broken law could not be causeless, so neither could it fail of coming on, in all its infinite weight, for the satisfaction of Divine justice. Had it so come upon them they should have been eternally satisfying, and yet never have been able to give full satisfaction; but having come upon Him, their infinite Surety, He so endured it as to purchase the church with His own blood (Acts 20:28), and by one offering to perfect forever them who are sanctified (Hebrews 10:14). The infinite dignity of His person rendered His enduring the execution of the curse infinitely valuable, so as abundantly to compensate the infinite wrong done to the honor of the Most High, according to the estimate made of it by law and justice. Being an infinite person, His dignity stamped infinite value on His temporary suffering of death, and rendered it even more than equivalent to that infinite duration of suffering or to those eternal torments that they were otherwise to have endured.

Here it was agreed that the tremendous curse, as due to His spiritual children, should be executed upon His whole man; that in consequence of this, He should become poor and not have where to lay His head; that from want of the necessaries of life He should endure hunger and thirst; that His reputation among men should sink, that it should be covered with the foulest slander and be loaded with the vilest reproach; that He should be counted a worm and no man, a reproach of men, and

The Conditions of the Covenant of Grace

despised of the people; that it should be His lot in the world to be, in an unparalleled degree, persecuted, afflicted and abased and that at last, stripped of His garments, He should be hanged up naked before the sun in the presence of a vast concourse of spectators, and between two condemned malefactors, as if the worst of the three.

But more particularly, it was here settled (1) that the awful curse should be executed upon His immaculate body, inasmuch as their bodies were obnoxious to it, being instruments of unrighteousness to sin and of dishonor to God; that His body, accordingly, should be hanged on a tree in order that all might read thereon the indignation of the Lord against the breach of the first covenant by eating of the fruit of a forbidden tree and, at the same time, His having been made a curse for us since it was written, "cursed is every one that hangeth on a tree"; that the curse should go over, and death make its way through, every part of His blessed body; that His head should be ignominiously wounded with a crown of thorns set upon it, His visage marred more than that of any other man, His back given to the smiters, His cheeks to them that plucked off the hair, His face not hidden from shame and spitting; His tongue made to cleave to His jaws; His hands and feet pierced, nailed to the cross; all His bones drawn out of joint; His heart, likewise, melted in the midst of His bowels; His blood, shed; His strength dried up like a potsherd; and that at length, His body should die and, separated from His soul, be pierced with a spear and laid in a tomb under the power of death. [In *Bereschith Rabba, a Rabbinical Commentary*, the following remarkable passage, concerning the sufferings of Messiah, occurs: "The Holy Blessed God began to covenant with Messiah, and said to Him, 'Messiah, my righteous One, the sins of those who are committed to thee, to be reserved, are about to bring thee under the most grievous yoke;

(or, to the deepest sorrows); thine eyes shall not see light; but thine ears shall hear great reproach from the people of the world; thy mouth shall taste gall; and thy tongue shall cleave to the roof of thy mouth; thy body shall be wasted with grief and sighing. Art thou willing to deliver thy people on these conditions? If thou undertakes their recovery, well; if not, behold, I from this moment will cast them off.' Messiah, in His presence, answered, 'Lord of eternity, I am well pleased with the office, and I undertake to endure these tribulations, provided that Thou revive the dead in my days.' Then said the Holy Blessed God to Him, 'Be it so.' Instantly Messiah from love [to His people] undertook to suffer all tribulations, as it is said, (Isaiah 53:7) 'He is afflicted and brought low.' " See in Vitrin. On *Isaiah*, church. 49:6, a footnote.]

(2) It was here also agreed that it should, in a special manner, be executed on His holy soul; that, since the souls of those whom He represented were the chief actors in sin, He should endure the infinite wrath of Jehovah chiefly in His soul so as to be all His lifetime a man of sorrows and acquainted with grief; that toward the end there should be an hour and power of darkness in which the power and malice of men and the cunning and rage of devils should combine and make their utmost efforts upon Him; that then the overflowing floods of Jehovah's revenging wrath should come rolling in upon His soul; that they should so overflow it as to fill Him with trouble, strike Him with sore amazement, load Him with heaviness, and overwhelm Him with exceeding sorrow; that there should then be such deep impressions of divine wrath made on His immaculate soul as would put Him into such an agony that He should sweat great drops of blood, and bring over Him such a total eclipse of comfort as even to lay Him in the lowest pit, in darkness, in the deeps; that so, while He was dying on the cross, a bodily death,

He might, as far as a holy soul could be capable of it, die by the sword of Divine justice, likewise a spiritual death.

Seeing our Divine Surety was infallible, the covenant of grace could have no proper penalty annexed to it; but, as we have now seen, the penalty of the covenant of works was adopted into the covenant of grace in order that it might be executed upon Him as an essential condition of this covenant. As to spiritual death in particular, it should be observed that it partakes both of the nature of sin and of punishment for sin. In its primary meaning, it is of the nature of sin, or contrariety to the precept of the law being a natural and necessary effect of the first transgression; in its secondary acceptation, it is of the nature of punishment for sin, and so takes its rise from the threatening of the law. Its having the nature of punishment is a secondary object, superadded by Divine appointment to its original nature. Now spiritual death considered as sin could not possibly be inflicted on our immaculate Surety; but, considered as a punishment due to us for sin, it was imposed upon His holy soul, substituted in our place.

Whilst in the covenant, it was stipulated that the curse should be executed both on the body and on the soul of our condescending Surety; it was withal settled that for the satisfaction of justice, the death thereby inflicted on Him should be terrible and tormenting in the most exquisite degree; that His sufferings and death should be carried to the very utmost extremity of anguish and horror, far beyond that of any other sufferings in this world, and even of any that can by creatures be endured in the world to come. The execution of the awful curse upon Him was to be carried to the highest possible degree. There was, therefore, no pity, no indulgence, shown Him. No lenity was shown from devils or from wicked men when they were let loose upon Him. No sooner were their hour and the power of darkness come than they pushed at him like bulls, roared against Him like lions, and rended Him like dogs (Psalm 22:12, 13, 14). Not so much as one kind word from those who surrounded Him was spoken to Him in the midst of His unparalleled anguish; but on the contrary, He was, in the cruelest manner, derided and insulted; much less was a good deed done to Him. In His extreme thirst, effected by the arrows of infinite wrath, the poison of which drank up His spirit, not a cup nor even so much as a drop of water was allowed Him; but vinegar was offered Him to drink. No indulgence was shown Him from an offended Jehovah. "He spared not His own Son" (Romans 8:32). The tortures that were, by the Jews and Romans, inflicted on His body were exceedingly great, and yet were by far the least part of His sufferings. These consisted principally in the inconceivable anguish and agony of His soul. All the waves and billows of infinite vengeance went over Him and thoroughly penetrated His inmost soul. The effect of these were infinitely more real and horrible than even the torments of wicked spirits in hell because those effects were, in an infinite degree, complete on His soul but can never, to all eternity, be so on them. While the face of His eternal Father was, when He hung on the cross, hidden from Him, the very face of the heavens lowered on Him. Because the light is sweet, and it is a pleasant thing for the eyes to behold the sun (Ecclesiastes 11:7), the sun wrapped itself up in darkness from Him.

It was also in that solemn contract settled that the death to be inflicted on Him as the execution of the curse of the law should be of long continuance. His sufferings and death were indeed to be temporary. The infinite dignity of His glorious person imparted an infinite value to His temporary sufferings and rendered them even more than equivalent to the eternal sufferings that we were to have endured; so that here were the temporal sufferings of an infinite person in place of the eternal sufferings of finite creatures. But, though His sufferings and death were temporary, they were of long continuance. He was, in the style of the covenant of works, suffering and dying not only while He was on the cross, but during all the time of His state of humiliation; the death that was the penalty of that covenant worked in Him from the womb till it brought Him to the grave. It behooved Him accordingly to be conceived of a woman of low estate; to be born in the stable of an inn, and not in the inn itself; and to be laid in a manger, and not on a couch or cradle. It behooved His infant-blood to be shed in His circumcision, as if He had been a sinner; yea, His infant-life, to be sought by a cruel persecution so that His mother should be obliged to flee with Him from His native country to Egypt, that house of bondage and land of graven images. Upon His return it behooved Him to live an obscure life, and that in an obscure place, whence nothing great or good was expected (John 1:46), and on emerging from His obscurity to be set up as the object of the spite and obloquy of the ill will and ill treatment of the world till, by the hands of both Jews and Gentiles, He should be put to the death of the cross.

Thus then it was, in the covenant of grace, settled that Christ the second Adam should, in the room of His spiritual seed, suffer the same punishment that they, in virtue of the broken covenant of works, were to have endured, which was death in its utmost latitude, in its fullest extent.

(3) Finally, in this conditional article, it was likewise agreed that, as the Representative of His elect seed, He should from regard to the honor of God bear all this punishment with perfect willingness and resignation. This the law demanded of those for whom He suffered, condemning all impatience and murmuring and binding them both to obedience and to suffer-

ing for sin. But how could they, who cannot bear so much as the shortest pang without some degree of impatience in the sight of the Lord, have endured in such a manner that infinite load of vindictive wrath? It was therefore stipulated that Christ their Representative and Surety should bear their punishment for them voluntarily and with perfect resignation; that He should go as a lamb to the slaughter, calmly resigning His human will to the will of His eternal Father, and so make His obedience that He was suffering as conspicuous as were His sufferings themselves; that, in the greatest extremity of His anguish, He should not admit the least unbecoming thought of Jehovah but, on the contrary, acknowledge that in all He is holy (Psalm 22:3); nor yet the least grudge against His murderers (Luke 23:34).

Accordingly during all the time that His soul was penetrated with the keenest anguish, no impatient thought ruffled His mind, no repining word forced its way from His lips. "Father... not My will, but Thine be done" (Luke 22:42) was His language when the sorrows of death compassed Him, and the pains of hell got hold upon Him; when His murderers gaped upon Him with their mouths and smote Him upon the cheek reproachfully; when His face was foul with weeping, and on his eyelids was the shadow of death; yea, when the Almighty set Him up for the mark of His arrows and broke Him with breach upon breach; and when the weapons of His wrath cleft His reins asunder and poured his gall upon the earth. Amidst all His unparalleled torments, He sinned not by the least irregular perturbation of spirit. This indeed was indispensably requisite; for His sufferings and death, considered as merely penal, could not be satisfactory; in order to this, they must at the same time, be obediential.

From what has now been said it will be evident that the law, in so far from being deprived of any part of its honor by the salvation of the spiritual seed of Christ, that it is in the highest degree magnified and made honorable. The Lord would never pardon sin at the expense of the honor of His righteous law, nor declare a man righteous unless the righteousness of the law were fulfilled either by Himself, or in Him, by a sufficient Surety (Romans 8:4). When therefore it was decreed that the elect should have eternal life, the whole accounts of all that the law had to charge on them for life were taken in; and the most infallible method of discharging them was devised. The whole burden of the payment was devolved on Christ their Surety. By this exchange of persons the law, instead of being a loser, was an infinite gainer. It was infinitely more for the honor of the law that the glorious Son of God became subject to it, and that He, in the room of His elect, answered the demands of it more than if they themselves, being but mere creatures, had answered them. This, however, was what they never could have done for, being transgressors, though it had continued throughout eternity to exact payment, it could never have had enough from them; whereas, by Christ's taking the burden of clearing their debt upon Himself, it was paid to the utmost of the legal demand. Should anyone add to this divinely excellent, this infinitely perfect, righteousness of Jesus Christ, all that ever saints have performed and that martyrs have endured, it would be like adding a single grain to the sands of the sea or a moment to the duration of eternity. What is a drop of a bucket to the unfathomable waters of the ocean? What is a grain of sand to the immeasurable extent of the universe? What is a moment to the endless revolutions of eternity? Such are all human performances compared with the righteousness of HIM who is the great God our Savior (Psalm 71:15).

Hence also the reader may learn that, in order to justification before God, it is as necessary that the active as that the passive obedience of Christ be imputed. It is by the obedience of One that many are made righteous (Romans 5:19); and it is the righteousness of One that is imputed to many for justification of life. The satisfactory sufferings and death of Christ are indeed the ground of a believing sinner's deliverance from the penalty or curse of the law, the ground of the pardon of all his past breaches of it. But this alone would leave him still under the law in its covenant-form for the time to come; so that every new breach of it would render him liable anew to eternal death. It is requisite therefore that he have, in addition to the former, a righteousness comprising perfect conformity of nature and of life to the perceptive part of the law, to be the ground of his deliverance from it as a covenant for the time to come. Such a righteousness he needs as is answerable to the law's demand of perfect holiness of nature and perfect obedience of life, the original and unalterable conditions of eternal life. It is by the satisfactory sufferings and death of Christ ("Suffering for punishment gives a right and title to nothing, only satisfies for something; nor doth it deserve any reward; it is nowhere said, Suffer this and live, but, Do this and live, Owen on *Justification*, p. 464). And yet these two are but one undivided righteousness, to be relied on for one undivided salvation, from eternal death to eternal life. Now if this whole righteousness of Christ is not imputed to a believing sinner, how can he, in the sight of God, be made righteous, and that as the thief on the cross was, in a moment? If a man has no perfect righteousness from himself, he must then have it from another; and from whom can he have it but from Jesus Christ, who is Jehovah our RIGHTEOUSNESS. To show that this divinely excellent righteousness of Jehovah the incarnate Son is imputed to believers, and is meritorious of life to them, it is in Scripture called the righteousness of God (Romans 1:17), the righteousness which is of [or, from] God

(Philippians 3:9), the righteousness by faith (Romans 3:22), the righteousness of the faith (Romans 4:11), righteousness without the law (Romans 3:21), righteousness without works (Romans 4:6), righteousness by the obedience of One (Romans 5:19), righteousness not our own (Philippians 3:9), and righteousness imputed by God (Romans 4:6, 10, 22, 24). If it is not a righteousness within the believer, rendering him inherently and absolutely perfect, it must be a righteousness upon him, by being imputed to him. If it is imputed, as the Scripture affirms it to be (Romans 4, throughout), it must be such a righteousness as his case requires, such a righteousness as will not only secure him from eternal death but entitle him to everlasting life.

Let this then comfort you, O believer, amidst all your perplexities and distresses, all your doubts and fears. You have a righteousness imputed to you that is infinitely perfect, infinitely meritorious of life eternal. Arrayed in this spotless robe, interested in this divinely excellent, this transcendently glorious righteousness, you have an undoubted, an unbounded title to all the grace and glory promised in the eternal covenant. Oh, rely on the righteousness of Jesus Christ that can never fail you and in a little while you shall sit down among the blessed above and eternally shout forth the praises of that dear Lord Jesus who not only redeemed you from sin and misery, but exalted you to a throne of glory above the angels in heaven. Then you will be astonished at the languor and coldness of the warmest heart that ever contemplated Jesus here below, and with joy ineffable be surprised to find that not the half, nor the thousandth part respecting Him and His righteousness, could in this world be told to you.

Hence likewise it will be evident that faith has a broad and a firm foundation to support it in its exercise. The second Adam has fulfilled and brought in everlasting righteousness. As by one man sin entered into the world, and death by sin (Romans 5:12), so by one man righteousness entered into the world and life by righteousness, As death passed upon all men, for that all have sinned, so life passes upon all men united to the last Adam, for that they all are righteous. As the disobedience of Adam, without the sins that we afterwards committed, brought us death, so the righteousness of Christ, without the good works that believers afterwards perform, brings them life. True believers, then, have the firmest foundation for their faith and hope of eternal life (Hebrews 10:19-22). The broken boards of the sinner's own righteousness, and of general mercy, on which he presumptuously relies cannot but fail since the righteous law cannot allow that he should have life on these grounds. But inasmuch as a gift of Christ, and of His perfect righteousness, is, by the high authority of heaven, presented in the gospel to sinners, the man who by faith accepts that Divine gift and makes it his only plea before the Lord cannot but attain salvation. "They who receive abundance of grace, and of the gift of righteousness, shall reign in life by one, Jesus Christ" (Romans 5:17). As a man's covenant-relation to the first Adam makes him partaker of his sin, so his covenant-relation by faith to the last Adam makes him partaker of His righteousness. Since the believer, then, has all that Christ did and suffered to rely on and to plead for his salvation, it is impossible that his plea can fail.

Further, the reader may, from what has been advanced, learn that all who are in Christ as their Covenant-head are conformed to Him; they are all inherently righteous or holy. For as, although it was Adam alone, who personally violated the covenant of works by his first sin, yet they to whom that sin is imputed do thereupon by corruption of nature conveyed from him become inherently sinful; even so, although it was Christ alone who personally fulfilled the conditions of the covenant of grace, yet they to whom His righteousness is imputed do thereon, by sanctifying grace, communicated from Him, become inherently righteous (Romans 5:17). Accordingly, answerable to the three conditional articles of the covenant of grace fulfilled by the last Adam—namely holiness of nature, righteousness of life, and satisfaction for sin—three characters are found in all subjects capable of them who, being personally instated in the covenant, have that consummate righteousness imputed to them.

First, they are all made partakers of a holy nature. Therefore, or since He died for all, "if any man be in Christ, he is a new creature" (2 Corinthians 5:17). He is God's workmanship, created in Christ Jesus unto good works (Ephesians 2:10). Christ's having been born holy in His human nature ensures a new birth, a holy nature to them, so that they are all new creatures, renewed in the second Adam as really as they were marred in the first. Indeed, it cannot be otherwise. Can a man be engrafted in Christ and yet not partake of the Spirit of Christ? No. "If any man have not the Spirit of Christ, he is none of His (Romans 8:9). Or, can a man have the Spirit of Christ and yet have no change produced on his nature? It is impossible. If Christ be in you, . . . the Spirit is life because of righteousness (Romans 8:10). Consider this, you who presume to rest on the righteousness of Jesus Christ while you are indifferent whether a holy nature is derived from Him to you or not. Be persuaded that if you do not have a new and holy nature from Christ you have no part in His righteousness. You might as well pretend that although Adam's first sin was imputed to you, yet no depraved nature was derived from him to you as pretend that the righteousness of Christ is imputed to you while yet your nature is not rendered holy by sanctifying grace communicated by Him. Do not deceive yourself; you must be born again, otherwise you shall not see the kingdom of God (John 3:3).

Second, they are all righteous or holy in their life. "Thy people also shall be all righteous" (Isaiah 60:21). "And they shall call them, the holy people" (Isaiah 62:12). How did unrighteousness and ungodliness enter into and overspread the world? Was it not by the first sin of Adam, imputed to all his natural posterity (Romans 5:12)? Then, doubtless, if the righteousness of the last Adam is imputed to us, righteousness of life in resemblance to Him will follow. Sanctification has a necessary connection with, and a necessary dependence on, justification. Did the immaculate Son of God come into this world, and in our nature live a righteous life, that we might live as we please? Nay, verily, but that we, being delivered out of the hands of our enemies, might serve Him without fear, in holiness and righteousness before Him all the days of our life (Luke 1:74, 75). If Christ lived righteously for you who read this, you assuredly will live righteously for Him. An unrighteous life demonstrates a man to be still in an unregenerate state, and far from righteousness imputed.

Last, the old man, the corruption of their nature, is crucified in them all. They who are Christ's have crucified the flesh with the affections and lusts (Galatians 5:24). When the second Adam was crucified, He hung on the cross as the Representative of all that are His, with all their sins on Him by imputation, that the body of sin might, by His suffering of death for it, be destroyed (Romans 6:6, 7). He hung there as the meritorious and the efficient cause of their mortification of the body of sin so that by His death He might destroy in them the power of spiritual death that reveals itself in nothing more than in living lusts preying on their souls; and He hung there, likewise, as the exemplary cause of their mortification of sin so that all who are His, and who have sinned after the similitude of Adam's transgression, are crucified and dead to sin after the similitude of His crucifixion and death. Accordingly, they are said to be crucified with Him (Galatians 2:20); to be planted together [with Him] in the likeness of His death (Romans 6:5); and through fellowship with Him in His sufferings, to be made conformable to His death (Philippians 3:10).

If then a man who still lives after the flesh and fulfills the lusts of it, or who, instead of mortifying the body of sin, lives in the love and practice of sin, pretend, notwithstanding, that the satisfaction of Christ is imputed to him for the pardon of his sins, he makes a hypocritical, yea, and a blasphemous profession. He might as well say that the death of Christ has proved ineffectual, or that Christ has died for him in order that he might, with impunity, live in sin. Be assured, O presumptuous sinner, that your practice is a course of practical blasphemy against the Holy One of God; hereby, you make Him the minister of sin. Be not deceived; if you have a saving interest in the death of Jesus, your old man is crucified with Him and you yourself are dead with Him (Romans 6:8); you are dead with Him to sin, to the law, and to the world.

You are dead with Him to sin. During all the time that the holy Jesus continued in His state of humiliation, the iniquity of all the elect lay on Him (Isaiah 53:6), adhered to Him, and made Him a man of sorrows; and when He was on the cross it wrought on Him most furiously, stinging Him to the very heart, until it killed Him and procured His being laid in the grave. Having then done its utmost against Him, it had no more that it could do. Thus dying for sin, He died to it, He was delivered from it; and in His resurrection He shook it all off, as Paul shook the viper off his hand into the fire and felt no harm; rising out of the grave He will appear the second time without sin.

If therefore you who read this indeed know the fellowship of His sufferings, death will have made its way from Him the Head to you as a member of His body. His death to sin cannot fail to work your death to it also. To this purpose are these expressions of the holy Apostle Paul: "In that He died, He died unto sin once . . . likewise reckon ye also yourselves to be dead indeed unto sin" (Romans 6:10, 11). "How shall we that are dead to sin live any longer therein?" (Romans 6:2). If you, then, are dead with Christ, the bond that knitted your heart and your sin together is loosed; and you, in the daily exercise of mortification, are shaking it off. If on the contrary you are not dead, but still living to sin, it is a sure evidence that you have no part in the death of Christ.

If you are personally interested in the death of Christ, you are also dead with Him to the law as a covenant of works. After our apostle had said (Galatians 2:19, 20), "I through the law am dead to the law that I might live to God," he added, "I am crucified with Christ." The latter was the foundation of the former. Our condescending Surety, in being made of a woman, was made under the law to redeem those who were under the law (Galatians 4:4, 5). He was born to the law, He lived to the law, and He died to the law, in order fully to answer all its demands and with its full consent, to obtain eternal redemption for us. When once the law began to fall upon Him as our Surety, it never ceased to require from Him until it got the utmost that it could demand; and then, by being quite clear with it, He became dead to it in its covenant form. As a token of this, He took up the bond, blotted it out, and rent it in pieces, nailing it to His cross (Colossians 2:14). Now, Christ having become dead to the law by His dying to it on the cross, the holiness of His nature and the obedience of His life thereafter no more ran in the same channel in which they had run before, from His birth to His death; that is, they were no more to be considered as obedience performed to the law for life to His elect; that having been completely merited and secured already by the obedience that He had yielded to it in its covenant-form from the womb to the grave. If then you who read this are personally interested in His righteousness, you also have become dead to the law by that body of Christ that died to it on the cross (Romans 7:4). As you are dead with Christ to sin, and therefore will not be a libertine, so you are also dead with Him to the law as a covenant, and therefore will not be a legalist. Your obedience will, in resemblance of His, run in a new channel. You will no longer obey for life, as you did when you were under the curse of the law. On the contrary, you will, from principles of faith and love, serve in newness of spirit, and walk in newness of life (Romans 7:6). The law is not of faith (Galatians 3:12); and therefore, if by faith you rely on the righteousness of Christ alone for your salvation, you cannot but be dead to the law as a covenant. It has now no power, either to justify or to condemn you (Romans 8:1, 3); and you have no allowed desire or hope of ever being justified or saved by it.

Once more, if you are interested in the death of Christ, you are likewise dead with Him to the world. "If ye then be risen with Christ," said the Apostle Paul, "seek those things which are above . . . For ye are dead, and your life is hid with Christ in God" (Colossians 3:1, 3). When the Lord Jesus was in the world, the world hated Him and used Him very unkindly; and when He died He parted from it to return as an inhabitant of it no more. "And now," said He, "I am no more in the world" (John 17:11). The quietest lodging that ever the world allowed Him was a grave and, having come out thence, He never slept another night in it. And though after His resurrection He stayed forty days in the world, yet still He was dead to it. He sometimes conversed with His own, but no more with the world. If then you have His satisfaction for sin imputed to you, you are also, in conformity to Him, dead to the world. Being crucified with Him, the world is crucified unto you, and you unto the world (Galatians 6:14). Union and communion with Christ in His righteousness have laid you down, dead in His grave, and so have separated forever between you and the world. And they have also raised you up again in resemblance of Him to a new manner of life (Romans 6:4). Though therefore you are in the world, you are no more of it; you are no more an inhabitant of the world as a native, but are only traveling through it as a stranger. Your treasure and your heart are no more there. Your affection is set on things above. Your conversation is in heaven, from whence also you look for the Savior, the Lord Jesus Christ. Thus you are made conformable to His death.

Still further, did Jesus endure for them the whole penalty of the violated law? It follows that no proper punishment can ever be inflicted on believers to whom His righteousness is imputed. The conditions of the covenant being already fulfilled by Christ and placed on their account in law, no proper penalty or punishment can any more be inflicted on them. They already suffered the whole penalty of the broken law in Christ their federal Representative; and were they after all to be condemned to endure the same or any part of it in their own persons, it would be a requiring from them a double payment of the same debt. If true believers were in their own persons to suffer vindictive punishment, even in the least degree, the same debt would in that degree be paid twice. But is this possible? By no means. Infinite justice is, and must continue to be, infinitely incapable of treating them in such a manner. A holy God is, and always must be, highly displeased with the sins of believers; but this displeasure is far from being vindictive wrath; the chastisement that He inflicts on them is fatherly correction, and no part of the penalty or curse of the law (Romans 8:1). It is indeed inflicted on occasion of their sins, but never as a part of satisfaction to Divine justice for them. It proceeds from the love of God, is purchased by the blood of Christ, and therefore is never hurtful, but always beneficial to them (Psalm 89:30-35; Hebrews 12:6-11).

Hence also it may be inferred that the righteousness of the second Adam is not only the meritorious cause, but the very matter of our justification in the sight of God. That consummate righteousness does not merit that our faith or good works should entitle us to justification; but it so merits our justification as to be itself alone the matter or immediate ground of it. Believers are justified immediately for the righteousness of Christ imputed to them, and that without any righteousness of their own intervening in like manner as all mankind were condemned upon the first sin of Adam before they did any evil in their own persons. That righteousness is not imputed to them in its effects merely so that their faith, repentance, and sincere obedience may, on account of it, be accepted as their evangelical righteousness for which they are justified; but it is imputed to them in itself as the sole and immediate ground of their justification (Psalm 71:16). To make their own works, or even their faith, the immediate ground of their title to justification would be to make Christ's glorious righteousness subordinate to their own. It is not therefore enough to say that the righteousness of Jesus Christ is the meritorious cause; we must also affirm that it is the matter of our justification. What a precious gift, then, is the righteousness of Jesus Christ! Blessed be the Lord for all the innumerable benefits of creation; blessed be the Lord for all the indulgent dispensations of providence; but above all blessed be the Lord our gracious God for the unspeakable gift of Christ—for His transcendently glorious, His divinely excellent RIGHTEOUSNESS!

From what has been advanced, we learn what the concern of faith is in the affair of justification. It is no federal ground of right; it affords no contractual title to justification before God; it entitles to nothing in the covenant; but it is the appointed, and therefore the necessary, instrument of receiving that meritorious righteousness that gives a title to everything in the promise of it. A sinner is justified by faith as the instrument of his justification. Hence the righteousness imputed for justification is in Scripture called the righteousness revealed to faith (Romans 1:17), the righteousness of faith (Romans 4:11), and the righteousness that is by faith of Jesus Christ unto all, and upon all them that believe (Romans 3:22). Faith gives no right to apply to oneself the righteousness of Christ; it is only the instrument, or instrumental means of applying it. Faith in its exercise unites a man to Christ as Jehovah his Righteousness; it also applies the righteousness of Christ and applies justification itself as offered to him in the gospel. In each of these three respects it is the instrument of his justification. As therefore a man cannot be justified without imputed righteousness as the ground, so neither can he be justified without faith as the instrument of justification.

Once more, is it not obvious from what has been discoursed that the redemption of the soul is precious (Psalm 49:8)? Look, reader, to the ransom of souls, the holy birth, the righteous life, and the satisfactory death of the only begotten of the Father, and you must admit that it is a costly redemption. You, who value your soul as a thing of naught, turn your eyes to this object. Learn here the value of that soul which you sell for a thing of no value, for the gratification of a base lust, of a corrupt passion. Costly was the purchase of that which you thus throw away. You let it go indeed at a very low price; but the Redeemer could not have it from the hand of justice but at the price of His own precious blood. You cannot forego the vanities of this present world for it, nor afford so much as one hour to think seriously about it; but He, after a life of sorrows, endured an inconceivably bitter death for the redemption of it. What do you think? Was He inconsiderate? Was He lavish in covenanting to give such a ransom for souls? He was infinitely just who proposed the arduous conditions of the contract. And He was infinitely wise who engaged to fulfill them. He was a Father who demanded this ransom for souls; and He was His only begotten, His infinitely dear Son, who paid it. Be ashamed and blush, then, that you have made such a low estimate of that soul on which the Lord has set such a high price.

You also, who entertain low thoughts of the pardon of sin and of the salvation of the soul, see here your dangerous mistake. You go on securely in sin, thinking that all may be easily set right by saying, "God have mercy on me, God forgive me." Ah, dreadful infatuation! The low birth, the sorrowful life, and the agonizing death of the only begotten Son of God, are not these sufficient to give you just sentiments of the pardon of sin? Consider the unparalleled sufferings and death of the Lamb of God in the room of sinners, and learn what estimate He makes of His pardon of sin. Observe, O secure sinner, that it is not words, but deeds; that it is not promises of amendment, but perfection of obedience; that it is not shedding of tears, but shedding of blood, yea, of blood of infinite value, that can purchase the forgiveness of sin. And if you do not have upon you by faith all that righteousness that the second Adam fulfilled to be the ground of your title to pardon, you cannot attain it. You are disposed especially to overlook the sin that dwells in you, the corruption that cleaves to your nature; but know that the Lord does not pass it by. It was a necessary article of the eternal covenant that Christ should be born holy and retain the perfect holiness of His human nature to the end; otherwise our unholy nature, that was derived to us from Adam, would have fixed every one of us, irrecoverably and eternally, under the wrath and curse of God. You too, who has unworthy thoughts of the law of God, see here your pernicious mistake. You do not hesitate to transgress its righteous commands; you despise its dreadful curse. As it is a law, you show not so much regard to it as even to the laws of men; and as it is a covenant, you are as far from being solicitous how its claims upon you may be satisfied, as if you had no concern in them. And shall the honor of the Divine law, do you think, be laid in the dust in your case rather than it should be so laid in the case of Sodom and Gomorrah? They themselves by brimstone and fire, from the Lord out of heaven, must be laid in ashes; rather than it should in the case of sinners finally impenitent; the earth with all its works must be burnt up, and all the wicked must be cast into the lake that burns with fire and brimstone forevermore; yea, rather, than it should in the case of them who are saved. The penalty of the law must be fully endured, and the precept perfectly obeyed, even by the Father's only begotten Son, in their stead. Surely, O sinner, if ever you are interested in His glorious righteousness, the holy law will be high and honorable in your estimation, as it is in that of God.

4

The Promises of the Covenant of Grace

By a divine promise is meant a divine declaration of some benefit to be graciously conferred, or an act of free grace in God whereby He has engaged in His Word to bestow on believers all the benefits that were, by the surety-righteousness of Jesus Christ, merited for them.

In every federal transaction, whether it is a covenant strictly speaking or not, there must be a promise. In a proper covenant, the promissory part corresponds to the conditional, being an obligation that the contracting party to whom the conditions are performed comes under, for some benefit to be conferred, on account of their performance. That is the promise of a covenant, strictly so called, and is binding on the party who makes it provided the other contracting party performs his part. If the conditions performed are not equivalent to the benefit promised, the promise binds, in point of faithfulness, according to the agreement; if they are equivalent to the benefit promised, the promise binds in point of remunerative justice as well as of faithfulness.

The covenant of grace that the Father made with the Son as the Representative of His elect is a proper covenant; the promissory part of it corresponds to the conditional part already illustrated. The conditional was Christ's part; the promissory was God the Father's. The Father hereby bound Himself to bestow all the benefits therein specified in consideration of the conditions to be fulfilled. And, inasmuch as the conditions fulfilled by the Son of God as last Adam were, in the strictest sense, meritorious of the blessings promised, the promise is binding, not only in respect of the faithfulness but also of the justice of God.

All the promises of the covenant of grace originated immediately from the sovereign, self-influenced grace, or mere good pleasure, of the adorable Godhead in the person of the Father. The performing of them, indeed, was wholly to depend on the second Adam's fulfilling of the conditions of that covenant; but the making of them did not in the least degree depend on that ground. They had their whole origin, their sole foundation, in the infinite and absolute sovereignty of the grace of Jehovah. The whole mystery of Christ's undertaking and of His fulfilling all righteousness in the room of His elect is to be considered as the grand means, devised by an infinite wisdom, for bringing the promises to such an accomplishment as should redound in the highest degree possible to the glory of the divine perfections and to the honor of the holy law.

Of what unspeakably high importance the promissory part of the covenant is will appear if the following particulars are considered:

1. The covenant is in Scripture described to us as a cluster of free promises of grace and glory. To us it is, as it were, one continued promise, or constellation of promises, in which no mention is made of any proper condition. "This is the covenant . . . saith the Lord; I will put My laws into their mind, and write them in their hearts; and I will be to them a God, and they shall be to Me a people. And they shall not teach every man his neighbor, and every man his brother, saying 'Know the Lord';

The Promises of the Covenant of Grace

for all shall know Me, from the least to the greatest. For I will be merciful to their unrighteousness, and their sins and their iniquities will I remember no more" (Hebrews 8:10-12). In this draft there are no proper conditions, no terms exacted from impotent man. It is all promise from beginning to end. Faith and repentance are both comprehended in this heavenly deed and comprehended under the form of benefits vouchsafed, not of tasks imposed. These promises, with the conditions of them, having been proposed to Christ as the last Adam, and not only accepted but their conditions fulfilled by Him, they come consequently in the gospel to be granted to us, and to be by faith received in and with Him.

Thus the promises are, by way of eminence, the covenant; they are the covenant of Jehovah the Father by which He has bound Himself to perform His part as the Son has already fulfilled His. Not one duty is, in the whole dispensation of the covenant, required of us but what God promises to work in us both to will and to do, and at the same time so to accept from us as graciously to reward. In this sense the covenant of grace is not conditional; it consists of an assemblage of absolute promises, of promises that were rendered absolute in consequence of the conditions of them having been already fulfilled. At the same time, when it is viewed in its full extent and in respect to Christ, the promises are strictly conditional. Nevertheless, as even the last Adam's fulfillment of the conditions comes to us in an absolute promise (Genesis 3:15; Daniel 9:24), so all the conditional promises of the covenant are, with regard to us, reductively absolute, which in the event will prove equivalent to their being strictly so.

2. The covenant is, in sacred Scripture, denominated from this part of it. It is there called the covenants of promise (Ephesians 2:12); the covenants, because though in itself it is but one

covenant, yet from the time of its first publication in Paradise it was often renewed, and as often as it was renewed it was renewed in the form of a promise. Though the covenant of works had a promise of life, yet it is nowhere denominated a covenant of promise; on the contrary, that covenant or, which is the same, the law as a covenant of works is, in its nature, contradistinguished from the promise. "If the inheritance," says the Apostle Paul, "be of the law, it is no more of promise" (Galatians 3:18). The promise of life in that covenant was suspended on the condition of works to be performed by men themselves; whereas, in the covenant of grace, eternal life is, on the ground of the perfect righteousness of Jesus Christ, promised to believing sinners freely without respect to any performances of theirs as proper conditions of it.

3. The conditions of the covenant were accompanied by promises performed and to be performed to Christ Himself as second Adam. His fulfilling of those conditions issued from His reception of the furniture and assistance that the Father had promised to afford Him, and terminated in His enjoyment of the acceptance and reward that the Father had promised to confer on Him (Isaiah 50:4, 7, 9; 53:10-12; Philippians 2:9-11).

4. The Lord has sworn that He will perform the promises of that covenant. "I," said Jehovah the Father, "have made a covenant with My chosen One, I have sworn unto David My Servant" (Psalm 89:3). "So have I sworn that I would not be wroth with thee, nor rebuke thee" (Isaiah 54:9). An apostle informs us that God, willing more abundantly to show unto the heirs of promise the immutability of His counsel, confirmed it by an oath (Hebrews 6:17, 18). In human affairs, a conscientious person will not swear when promising anything except in a matter of great moment. Of what inconceivable importance, then, must

the promises of the everlasting covenant be that Jehovah Himself has confirmed by His oath!

5. The glory of Christ as last Adam depended, and still depends, on the promises of the covenant. These were His security for it; in the faith of which He lived, while on earth, even in circumstances of the deepest abasement. For the joy that was set before Him in the promises He endured the cross, despising the shame (Hebrews 12:2). He paid the inestimable price of the redemption of sinners while as yet multitudes of them were not born, and even while several of them were imbruing their hands in His blood; but He relied on the promises of the covenant. When He was about to enter into the swelling waves of dereliction and death, He pleaded them (John 17:5). It was in the faith of the accomplishment of the promises that He began, carried on, and in due time finished His performance of the conditions.

6. The holiness and happiness of the redeemed, both in time and eternity, depend on the promises of the covenant. It is the promise of eternal life, comprising all the particular promises to the elect, that keeps them while unconverted from dying in that state and dropping down to the chambers of eternal death. It is the promise that makes redeeming mercy overtake and embrace them when, as fast as they can, they are fleeing from it. What is it but the promises, applied by the Spirit of Christ, that preserves grace in their hearts like a spark of fire in the midst of the ocean; so that, instead of being extinguished in the water, it increases into a most vehement flame? And what is it but the same promise that makes affliction, and even death itself, wear a smiling aspect to them (2 Samuel 23:5; Hosea 13:14 compared with 1 Corinthians 15:54, 55)?

7. Last, the great ends of the covenant—namely the glory of God, the honor of Christ and, in subservience to these, the salvation of lost sinners of mankind—are all attained by the per-

forming of the promises of it. As all the rivers meet in the sea, so the glory of God, the honor of Christ, and the salvation of sinners that issue from the whole of the covenant, meet together in the accomplishment of the promises. The promises with the performance of them were the grand object that the high Parties contracting had in view when they entered into covenant. It was room for them that the Father sought by proposing the covenant to the Son; and it was that which the Son designed to purchase by fulfilling the conditions of it to the Father. The conditions of the covenant were fulfilled on earth in little more than thirty-three years; but the promises have continued to be performed on earth, now nearly six thousand years, and will continue to be accomplished in heaven through all eternity. The making and administration of the covenant, as well as the fulfilling of the conditions, are subservient to the accomplishment of the promises. No wonder then that the Apostle Peter calls the promises of that august covenant exceedingly great and precious (2 Peter 1:4).

SECTION 1. A View of the Promises in General

The promises of the covenant of grace are in general of two kinds. In their immediate application some of them respect as their object Christ Himself as the Head and Representative of the elect and others of them, the elect, as represented by Him. But such is the indissoluble connection between Christ and the elect that every promise performed by Him terminates in their good, and every promise performed by them terminates in His glory.

In the first place, the promises of the former class, namely those that were to be performed by Christ as Mediator, were made to Christ Himself. Some of the promises were to have their direct and immediate effect on Christ Himself, the Cove-

The Promises of the Covenant of Grace

nant-head of His people; such as the promises of furniture for His work, and of a mediatorial interest in God as His God and portion. Just as, in the covenant of works, there were promises that were to have had their immediate effect on Adam himself, and were to have had no more than a mediate and indirect reference to his descendants, who should have lived after the condition of that covenant had been fulfilled; namely the promises of the continuance of natural life in vigor and comfort, and of spiritual life in favor and fellowship with God during the course of His perfect obedience in His state of probation.

The promises that were to have their direct and immediate effect on Christ Himself as the second Adam were, in the making of the covenant, made to Him solely. As they were to be performed by Himself, considered as the Head and Representative of His spiritual seed, so they were made by Him in that public capacity. This appears especially from Psalm 89:3 where Jehovah calls Him His chosen One, the Head-elect, chosen to represent elect sinners, and David His servant to whom, in that public capacity, He cut or made the covenant. It is clear that all the promises of furniture for His work, and of a subsequent reward, were made to Him in view of His fulfilling the conditions of the covenant. And therefore, since it was in the character of last Adam, Head of the covenant and Representative of His elect seed, that He was to fulfill the conditions, it was to Him in the same character that those promises were made.

The promises of this class then were made to Christ in that capacity, and to Him solely. As it was the peculiar burden imposed on Him that He should perform the conditional part of the covenant, so that was the peculiar honor put upon Him in the promissory part. In the elect company, of whom He is the federal Head, He shines above the rest as the sun at noon-day does, above the twinkling stars. He has a name that is above every name; in all things He has the pre-eminence; and He is anointed with the oil of gladness above His fellows. He is the antitypical Joseph who, in fulfilling the conditions of the covenant, was separated from his brethren and who, as the first born among many brethren, had a double portion in the promised land conferred on him. He is the Benjamin, at God's table with his brethren, whose mess of promises in the covenant is five times as much as any of theirs.

Still, however, as the honor and welfare of the Head redound to the comfort of the members, their interest, with regard to union and communion, being a joint interest, so the riches and honor settled on Christ by promise are a source of grace and glory, an enriching, an ennobling, treasure to His mystical members. The ointment poured upon the head cannot fail to go down to the skirts of the garments. Hence it is that prayer for the accomplishment of promises made to the glorious Mediator is, without ceasing, sent up to Jehovah by the whole multitude of the saints on earth. "Prayer also shall be made for him continually" (Psalm 72:15). Till the end of the world, this prayer will never cease to be offered up by the followers of the Lamb: "Thy kingdom come" (Matthew 6:10). Prayer for the enlargement of His spiritual kingdom began with Adam's embracing of the first promise, continued during the whole period of the Old Testament dispensation, has been incessantly made in the New Testament church now for almost eighteen hundred years, and will not cease till He Himself comes in the clouds of heaven with power and great glory. Hence too are the thanksgivings and shouts of praise presented to Jehovah by the mystical members of Christ for the accomplishment of promises to Him as their Covenant-head. No sooner does it appear that any of them are performed to Him than it is a matter of unfeigned joy to the saints; and the more of it that appears, their joy is the

The Promises of the Covenant of Grace 155

greater. The church, accordingly, is represented as singing an anthem of praise upon the performing of the promise of gathering the nations to Him (Psalm 98; Isaiah 12), of the promise of His victory over Antichrist (Revelation 19:1-5), and of the promise of converting His ancient people (Revelation 19:6-9). And when at last all the promises made to Him shall be accomplished, it will be to the church universal matter of a triumphant, of an everlasting song of praise.

In the second place, the promises of the latter class, namely they that were to have their immediate effect on the elect, were made to Christ primarily and to them secondarily; first, to the Head and next to the members, in and through Him. Is justification promised? It is first to Him and then to them in Him. "By the knowledge of Him shall My righteous Servant justify many" (Isaiah 53:11). Is the Spirit of sanctification promised? It is first to Him and next to them in Him. "I will put My Spirit upon Him and He shall show judgment to the Gentiles" (Matthew 12:18). Is glorification, or the full enjoyment of God, promised? It is primarily to Him and secondarily to them in Him. "If children then heirs, heirs of God and joint heirs with Christ" (Romans 7:17).

1. The promises that have their direct and immediate effect on the elect were, in making the covenant, made to Christ the last Adam primarily and principally. Jehovah did, in the covenant from eternity, promise grace and glory, all things that pertain to life and godliness, to the elect of mankind; but the promises of all these were originally and chiefly made to Christ their Covenant-head. All the promises of grace and glory center in Him; and all the promises of God in Him are yea, and in Him Amen, unto the glory of God (2 Corinthians 1:20). In Him, they are all yea; infallibly sure, invariably the same; and in Him they are all Amen; irrevocably confirmed by His death in order

that, in their proper time and order, they may be effectually and completely performed to the glory of Jehovah as a God of grace. The consequence is that He has not only an interest in the promises, but the chief interest; and that the interest of believers in them depends on their union with Him.

That those promises were made primarily and chiefly to Him as the Head and Representative of His spiritual seed will be evident if we consider,

First that, as in the covenant of works, God promised life to the natural posterity of the first Adam on condition of his perfect obedience, so, in the covenant of grace, He promised life to the spiritual offspring of the last Adam upon condition of His unsinning obedience as their Representative. For, says the Apostle Paul, "as in Adam all die, even so in Christ shall all be made alive" (1 Corinthians 15:22). "By the righteousness of One the free gift came upon all men unto justification of life" (Romans 5:18). But the promise of life for the natural posterity of Adam was primarily made to Adam himself as their representative while as yet none of them was in existence; and they were to have it performed to them only in and through him to whom it was made. In like manner the promise of life for the spiritual offspring of Christ was primarily and chiefly made to Christ Himself before any of them existed, and to them only in and through Him. Accordingly it is declared in Titus 1:2 that the comprehensive promise of eternal life on which believers build all their hope was made before the world began. And to whom could it then have been made primarily and immediately but to Christ Himself, the Covenant-head of His people? Hence are these words of the eternal Father cited once and again above: "I have made a covenant with" or, as it is in the original, "to My chosen One" (Psalm 89:3). It is as if He had said, "I have made a covenant, binding Myself by solemn promise to My chosen One for certain benefits to His spiritual seed upon the conditions therein settled." Christ, therefore, was the primary receiver of all the promises of the eternal covenant.

Second, it will be further evident if we consider that Christ the last Adam is constituted the Heir of all things. His almighty Father has appointed Him heir of all things (Hebrews 1:2) according to this promise of the covenant. "I will make Him My first-born" (Psalm 89:27), as if He had said, "I will treat Him as the first-born of My family. I will appoint Him heir of all my possessions." Now if Christ as the first-born is, by the promise of the Father, appointed heir of all things He is consequently heir of the promises. Believers are called heirs of promise (Hebrews 6:17); but He is the chief, the primary heir, and they in and through Him are secondary heirs. Hence, in view of this great promise of the covenant, "I will be their God," He uttered that consoling declaration, "I ascend unto My Father and your Father, and to My God and your God" (John 20:17). For, as the Apostle Paul informs us, "if children then heirs, heirs of God and joint heirs with Christ" (Romans 8:17). The promises of all things then were made not immediately to them in their own persons, but immediately and primarily to Him. God appointed the first Adam heir and lord of all things here below so that he was, as it were, the heir of God Himself. But by violating the covenant of works he forfeited all; he lost all. The Lord, therefore, constituted a new heir of all things and, by a new covenant, invested Him with the whole inheritance. It descended to Him, indeed, with a burden; there was a great debt upon it; but by agreeing to fulfill the conditions of the contract He engaged to discharge the whole sum.

Third, it will appear still more clear if we consider that those promises comprise a special part of the reward secured by the covenant to the last Adam. We read that for the joy that was set before Him, He endured the cross, despising the shame (Hebrews 12:2). A special part of the joy set before Him was to consist in this: He shall see His seed. "He shall see of the travail of His soul" (Isaiah 53:10, 11). "At the name of Jesus every knee shall bow . . . every tongue shall confess that He is Lord, to the glory of God the Father" (Philippians 2:10, 11). Now, to whom could the reward designed for Christ the last Adam be chiefly promised with so much propriety as to Himself, who was to work the work? To Him that reward was of debt by virtue of the promises of it, which made it due to Him upon His fulfilling the conditions. Moreover, the benefits of the covenant that are conferred on the children of the second Adam are doubtless to be viewed as a reward of debt to Him as well as a reward of grace to them. And considering those benefits in the first of these views there is no more impropriety in making, for instance, the promise of a new heart, or of taking away the stony heart, to the last Adam than in a physician's making a promise, on certain terms, to a father to cure his diseased children; the children, surely, cannot regard such a promise as made to them otherwise than secondarily, or through their father.

Fourth, to conclude, the Apostle Paul expressly affirms that the promises of the covenant were made to Christ. In Galatians 3:16 he thus writes: "Now to Abraham and his seed were the promises made. He saith not, 'and to seeds,' as of many, but as of one, 'And to thy seed,' which is Christ." The promises here meant are those that are mentioned in the context, such as the promises of the blessing of the Spirit, and of the inheritance (vs. 14, 18), promises that are received through faith (verse 14). These, he informs us, were made to the seed of Abraham, that seed which is Christ. By Christ here is principally meant Christ personal, Christ the glorious Head of the body, that seed who (vs. 13) was made a curse for us and in whom (verse 14) the nations should be blessed. Christ mystical, the Church, cannot be that seed of Abraham who was made a curse for us, and who redeemed us from the curse of the law; nor that seed through whom the blessings should come on the Gentiles. The word "seed" in verse 16 has the same meaning that it has in verse 19, in which our apostle proposes and answers this question: "Wherefore then serveth the law?" It was added, says he, because of transgressions, till the seed should come to whom the promise was made. If by the seed here that was to come we understand Christ mystical, our apostle must be understood to say, "The law was added because of transgressions till Christ mystical, the Church, should come in the flesh," which is absurd. It is Christ personal, then, that here, and in the 16th verse, is meant by the seed to whom the promises were made. This is fully confirmed by the following passages that inform us that Jehovah's covenant of grace was made with Christ, and at the same time explain that covenant by promises of the eternal happiness of His seed: "I have made a covenant with My chosen One . . . Thy seed will I establish forever. My covenant shall stand fast with Him; His seed also will I make to endure forever. I will not lie unto David; His seed shall endure forever" (Psalm 89:3, 4, 28, 29, 35, 36).

The promises, then, that have their immediate effect on his spiritual seed, were made primarily to Christ Himself. And, indeed, nothing can be more natural or more reasonable than to make a promise to a father on behalf of his offspring.

2. The promises of the covenant that have their direct and immediate effect on the elect are made to themselves secondarily in and through Christ. While they are presented or directed in offer to sinners of mankind in common who hear the gospel, they are made to the elect of God in and under Christ, their Head of righteousness and life. This is evident from these,

among many other declarations of Scripture: "In hope of eternal life, which God that cannot lie promised before the world began" (Titus 1:2). "And this is the promise that He hath promised us, even eternal life" (1 John 2:25). In the making or establishing of the covenant, the promises were made to Him; in the application of it they are made to them in Him. As He the second Adam has a primary and fundamental interest in the promises for the elect, so they have a secondary and derived interest in them in and under Him.

There was from all eternity, according to the covenant, a legal union between Christ and His elect seed; in consequence of which their debt to the law and justice of God became His and the promises made to Him became theirs. On the one hand, the Lord laid on Him the iniquity of them all (Isaiah 53:6); on the other, grace was given them in Christ Jesus before the world began (2 Timothy 1:9); in time, a spiritual and vital union commences between Him and them, upon His taking possession of them by His Spirit, and His beginning to dwell in their heart by faith. Their legal union invested them with a right to the promises in Christ their Covenant-head; their spiritual union constitutes their title to them in their own persons as being actual members of His mystical body. In respect of the former, eternal life is said to have been given them in Christ Jesus before the world began (Titus 1:2; 2 Timothy 1:9); in regard to the latter, the promise is represented as given to them who believe (Galatians 3:22); believers are called the heirs of promise (Hebrews 6:17) and partakers of the promise in Christ by the gospel (Ephesians 3:6).

Thus it is manifest that those promises are made to the spiritual seed of the second Adam as well as to Himself; though primarily to Him as the federal Representative on whom the fulfilling of the conditions was imposed; and but secondarily to them as the party represented, who were to enjoy the benefits promised. Hence it plainly follows that they were strictly conditional to Christ, and that they are absolutely free to His people in the same manner as the promise of life in the covenant of works, which was properly conditional to Adam, would, in the event of his having performed the condition, be absolutely free to his posterity. Thus the infinite merit of Christ and the boundless grace of God meet together in that glorious covenant. An infinite satisfaction for sin is given to divine justice; and in the channel of it the super-abounding grace of God flows to sinners freely. The performing of the promises was purchased at the full value, while no part of the inestimable price was advanced by us. Accordingly, we obtain precious faith, with all other spiritual graces and benefits, through the righteousness of our God and Savior Jesus Christ (2 Peter 1:1) as the proper condition of them. And His divine power has given, has freely or of mere grace given unto us, all things that pertain unto life and godliness (2 Peter 1:3).

SECTION 2. A More Particular View of the Promises

Having taken a general view of the promises it will be proper now that I take a more particular survey of them, and first, of the promises peculiar to Christ Himself. These are many and various, but they may all be comprised in these three: the promise of assistance in His arduous work, of the acceptance of it, and of a glorious reward for it.

First, Christ the second Adam had, in making the covenant with Him, a promise given Him of assistance in His arduous work. "Mine arm," said the omnipotent Father, "shall strengthen Him" (Psalm 89:21). "Behold My Servant whom I uphold. I the Lord have called Thee in righteousness, and will hold Thine hand, and will keep Thee, and give Thee for a covenant of the people" (Isaiah 42:1, 6). The Father promised to Him not only that a holy human nature should be formed for Him, but that His human nature, in His state of humiliation, should, by the immeasurable fullness of the Holy Spirit, be furnished and strengthened for His service. In the faith of that promised assistance He went through even the most difficult parts of it. "I gave My back," said He, "to the smiters, and My cheeks to them that plucked off the hair; I hid not my face from shame and spitting. For the Lord God will help Me." And again: "Behold the Lord God will help Me; who is he that shall condemn Me" (Isaiah 50:6, 7, 9). Accordingly, when He was in His agony in the garden, there appeared an angel unto Him from heaven, strengthening Him (Luke 22:43).

Second, He had a promise likewise of the acceptance of His work as soon as it should be finished, of the full acceptance of it as a complete performance of the conditions of the covenant, entitling Him to the promised reward (Isaiah 42:21). Accordingly, in view of the sure performance of His work, the full acceptance of it was first, at His baptism, proclaimed by a voice from heaven, saying, "This is My beloved Son in whom I am well pleased" (Matthew 3:17), and was afterwards proclaimed at His transfiguration on the mount a little before His last sufferings (Matthew 17:5). This promise of the acceptance of His work comprises two promises—the promise of His resurrection from the dead and of His justification in the Spirit.

(1). It comprehends the promise of His resurrection from the dead: "Thou wilt not leave My soul in hell; neither wilt Thou suffer Thine holy One to see corruption" (Psalm 16:10). These words are, by the Apostle Peter, cited and expounded of God's raising up of Christ from the dead (Acts 2:27-32). It was settled in the covenant that as Christ the second Adam should die in order to satisfy divine justice, so God the Father should bring Him again from the dead in consideration, as well as in testimony, of that satisfaction whenever it should be made by His blood (Hebrews 13:20). God, then, by raising up the Lord Jesus from the dead, substantially or in effect declared His acceptance of the work performed by Him. That God who had laid Him up judicially in the prison of the grave brought Him out again; that He sent an angel to roll away the stone from the door of the tomb, and so dismissed Him legally, is a demonstrative evidence that the debt that He had covenanted to discharge was completely paid, and that His payment of it was accepted.

(2). It comprises also the promise of His justification in the Spirit. "He is near that justifieth me" (Psalm 50:8). The accomplishment of the promise implied in these words is declared by the Apostle Paul: "God," says he, "was manifest in the flesh, justified in the Spirit" (1 Timothy 3:16). Jesus the immaculate Lamb of God, having no sins of His own to be pardoned, needed no personal justification on His own account; but, seeing He was the Surety of elect sinners and had the iniquity of them all laid on Him, it was promised in the covenant that as soon as He finished the work that the Father gave Him to do He should have an official justification. Having cleared the debt that had been charged upon Him and that He had engaged to clear, He, according to the promise, received an ample discharge from it under the hand and seal of Jehovah the Father. Having, by His obedience and death, answered all the demands of the law and justice, He was publicly and judicially acquitted from all the charges that had been laid to Him and, as the righteous Head and Representative of His church, was accepted by God the Judge of all. By the concurrence of the power of the eternal Spirit, with His own power as the eternal Son, He was raised again for the justification of His person and cause, and at the same time for our justification from all the offences that had been imputed to Him and for which He, as our Surety, had been delivered up to death (Romans 4:25). This is the ground of the security of all who believe on Him, against the law's demand of infinite satisfaction for sin, and of perfect obedience as the condition of eternal life.

Last, He had the promise also of a glorious reward for His work. This was to be conferred on Him as a just recompense for His work when finished. There was joy set before Him in the promise for which He willingly endured the cross and despised the shame (Hebrews 12:2). His work was the greatest that ever was performed, and His reward the highest that ever was promised. That promise of a glorious reward that the eternal Father, in making the covenant, gave Him comprised:

1. The promise of a new and mediatorial interest in God as His God and Father. "He shall cry unto me, Thou art my Father, my God, and the rock of my salvation" (Psalm 89:26). Our Lord Jesus, as the second person in the glorious Godhead, was the eternal Son of the Father, His Son by eternal generation; so that He had Jehovah the first person for His Father by an eternal as well as by a necessary birthright. But, in addition to this, a new relation was constituted between God the Father and Him, considered as the Covenant-head of believers, founded on His fulfilling of the conditions of the covenant by which relation He became heir of God as His heritage (Psalm 16:6). Hence we read that believers, being heirs of God, are joint heirs with Christ (Romans 8:17). They are joint heirs with Christ, who is the primary heir; for by His surety-righteousness He purchased the fruition of God as a God and Father. I do not mean that He purchased it for Himself; the man Christ Jesus needed not to do that inasmuch as, by the personal union of the human with the Divine nature, He had already an infinitely perfect title to eternal life, or, which is the same, to the everlasting enjoyment of

God for Himself; but He purchased it for sinners of mankind who had lost all personal interest in God, and who could neither be happy without it, nor recover it otherwise than in His right.

2. It included the promise of a most glorious exaltation to the right hand of the Majesty on high. Jehovah the Father promised to Him that, as a reward of His humiliation and bond service, He would exalt Him to the unparalleled dignity of becoming His honorary Servant, the great Administrator of the covenant to His people. "Behold," said He, "My Servant shall deal prudently, He shall be exalted and extolled, and be very high" (Isaiah 52:13). And again, "I will . . . give Thee for a covenant of the people" (Isaiah 49:8). In fulfilling the conditions of the covenant, He made Himself of no reputation, took upon Him the form of a bond servant, and so humbled Himself as to become obedient unto death, even the death of the cross. Wherefore God, according to His promise, highly exalted Him and gave Him a name, as the high Administrator of the covenant, which is above every name; that at (or rather in) the name of Jesus, every knee should bow (Philippians 2:7–10). It was according to His promise to Him that the Father exalted Him in the human nature to supreme and universal dominion; that He set Him at His own right hand in the heavenly places, far above all principality and power and might and dominion, and every name that is named not only in this world, but also in that which is to come (Ephesians 2:20, 21).

3. It also comprehended the promise of His inheriting, as the primary heir, all things. This is the promise of His eternal Father: "I will make him my first born" (Psalm 89:27). This great promise Jehovah has accomplished for Him; for the Apostle Paul informs us that God has appointed Him heir of all things (Hebrews 1:2); and Christ Himself publicly acknowledged

that, according to that promise, He was put in possession of all. "All things," said He, "are delivered unto Me of My Father" (Matthew 11:27). And again, "The Father loveth the Son, and hath given all things into His hand" (John 3:35). Thus, as the performance of the Father's promise to Him, He has treasures sufficient to support the unparalleled dignity conferred on Him.

4. It comprised, likewise, the promise of a spiritual seed to Him, innumerable as the stars of heaven. "So," said Jehovah, "shall thy seed be" (Genesis 15:5), so many as the stars of the sky in multitude and as the sand which is by the seashore innumerable (Hebrews 11:12). And again, "He shall see his seed" (Isaiah 53:10), even the whole multitude of the children whom God gave to Him who were all to be born again to newness of life, in consequence of His enduring the pangs of death and so were to bear His image, as a son bears that of his father. He was like a corn of wheat to fall into the ground and die; but the promise on that condition secured to Him His bringing forth of much fruit (John 12:24).

5. Once more, it included the promise of complete victory and dominion in His glorified humanity over all His and His people's enemies. "I," said the Father, "will beat down his foes before his face, and plague them that hate him" (Psalm 89:23). In the quarrel of the intended heirs of promise, He was to encounter Satan, sin, and death; and no sooner did He begin the conflict with them than the wicked race of mankind too began to war against Him. But He had the promise of the loving Father that although He should be the first that would fall and die on the field of battle, yet His death should be the destruction of the dominion of Satan, of the strength of sin, and of the power of death, over them who believe; and that all who would presume to support that sinking interest should fall under him. Hence are these words of Jehovah the Father to Him, "Sit thou

at My right hand, until I make thine enemies thy footstool" (Psalm 110:1); and these words of the Apostle Paul concerning Him: "He must reign till He hath put all enemies under His feet" (1 Corinthians 15:25).

So much concerning these three great promises, the promises of Divine assistance, acceptance, and reward, that were to have their immediate effect on Christ Himself, the last Adam. In reference to them, it may further be in few words observed that the promise of furniture for, and assistance in His work having been performed to Christ antecedently to His performance of that work depended entirely, together with the eternal election of His spiritual seed, on the free and sovereign love of God the Father; whereas the promises of the acceptance and reward of His work, in His glorious exaltation, and in their eternal redemption, depend immediately on His fulfilling the broken law in their stead.

It will be proper, next, to take a more particular view of the promises that have their immediate effect, or their direct fulfillment, on the elect of God. These are indeed exceedingly numerous as well as great and precious; but yet they may all be comprehended in this one, *The Promise of Eternal Life*. For thus it is written, "In hope of eternal life which God that cannot lie, promised before the world began" (Titus 1:2); and "this is the promise that He hath promised us, even eternal life" (1 John 2:25). The great, the all-comprehensive promise in the everlasting covenant then to the spiritual seed of Christ is the promise of eternal life made from everlasting to Him as last Adam and to them in and under Him.

If we consider in one point of view eternal life as promised in the covenant, it may be viewed on the one hand as implying a death, or a being dead to the law as a covenant of works (Galatians 2:19), to sin in the love, power, and practice of it (Romans

6:2), and to the world as a portion for the soul or a supreme object of affection (Galatians 6:14); and on the other as an endless life of perfect holiness in conformity to the last Adam, and of perfect happiness in communion with Him; and that from a covenant-God as the glorious cause of it, on Him as the almighty Sustainer of it, with Him as the most intimate Friend, the most affectionate Father, in Him as the center and sum, and to Him as the chief, the ultimate end of it.

In another point of view, eternal life as promised in the covenant comprehends as the matter of it all the happiness of which a human soul is or ever will be capable, the everlasting duration of that happiness, and all the appointed means of it.

First, it comprises all true happiness, or all that real blessedness, of which the soul of man is or ever will be capable. The promise of life is a promise of true felicity, of real blessedness. It is of the same comprehension as this glorious promise of Jehovah: "I will be to them a God and they shall be to Me a people" (Hebrews 8:10). This promise, "I will be to them a God," is a promise of a saving interest in God the Father as their God and Father, and in all the perfections of His nature. It is a promise that His wisdom shall direct them, His power protect them, His justice acquit them, His holiness sanctify them, His mercy pity and relieve them, His goodness supply all their wants, and His truth perform all His promises to them; a promise that His infinity and all-sufficiency shall be the extent of their inheritance, His eternity the duration of their happiness, His unchangeableness their security for all the salvation of the covenant, and His providence theirs to make all things work together for good to them (Romans 8:28).

It is a promise too of a saving interest in God the Son as their almighty Savior, and in His righteousness and fullness. He who has the Son has life; such a one is an heir of the grace of life. Hereby it is promised that He will be life to the dead, light to the blind, liberty to the captives, clothing to the naked, food the hungry, drink to the thirsty, a Physician to the sick, and a treasure to the poor; that He will be a Prophet to the ignorant, a Priest to the guilty, a Redeemer to the enslaved, a Deliverer to the tempted, a Strength to the weak, an example to His followers, a Comforter to the disconsolate, a Rest to the weary, and a Father to the fatherless.

It is a promise likewise of a special interest in God the Holy Spirit and in all His saving graces and influences. It is a promise that He will be to them, and in them, the Spirit of regeneration, of sanctification, and of consolation; the Spirit of faith and repentance, of grace and supplication, of wisdom and revelation; the Spirit of life, of light, and of liberty; of power, of love, and of a sound mind; and the Spirit of adoption, of holiness, and of glory. While Jehovah, Father, Son and Holy Spirit is, according to this promise, the covenant-God of all who are interested in His covenant, they, according to the same promise, are His covenant-people. They are His chosen, His peculiar, His redeemed, His willing people; a people who resign themselves to Him, who are all righteous; in whose heart is His law, and whom He has formed for Himself that they may show forth His praise; a people who are so near to Him as to be in covenant with Him and who praise Him with their hearts, their lips, and their lives; a people in whom He delights, whom He comforts, and whom He will never cast off.

The promise, then, "I will be to them a God, and they shall be to Me a people," or, which upon the whole is the same, the promise of eternal life, is a promise of all true happiness. The word "life" is often used in the Scripture to express happiness. In the style of the covenant of works it is so employed: "The man which doth those things shall live [that is, shall be happy] by them" (Romans 10:5). It is so used likewise in the phraseology of the covenant of grace. The just by his faith shall live, or, shall be happy (Habakkuk 2:4). The damned in hell have an existence that will endure to all eternity; but in the language of inspiration they are said not to see life because their existence is not a happy but a miserable one. It is manifest from the sacred oracles that the death threatened in the covenant of works comprised all misery both in time and in eternity; consequently the life on the contrary promised in that covenant comprehended all happiness both in this and in the world to come. Seeing then that the life promised in the covenant of grace was designed to repair the loss that sinners had sustained by their breach of the covenant of works, it must in its comprehension be as extensive as the death to which thereby they became liable. God therefore, in promising eternal life to His elect in Christ, has promised them all true happiness.

In promising eternal life He has promised them the happiness of the whole man, soul and body. And therefore, from the doctrine of the covenant, our blessed Lord proved against the Sadducees the resurrection of the body (Matthew 22:31, 32). Though the soul is the principal part of the man, it is not, however, the only part therein provided for. In virtue of the covenant the body also is for the Lord, and the Lord for the body. As the body partook of the death threatened in the first covenant, so it does and will partake of the life promised in the second. Since, in fulfilling the conditions of this covenant, the incarnate Redeemer gave His life a ransom for the bodies of His people, the life that is laid out and secured in the promises of it must extend to them as well as to their souls.

Second, the promise of eternal life includes the everlasting continuance of that happiness. It is not only life that is promised to the spiritual seed of Christ, but life for evermore (Psalm

133:3); life which, from the first moment in which it is given, will never be lost throughout the revolving ages of eternity. Eternal life is not in Scripture restricted to the state of glory in the celestial mansions. The life that is imparted to a sinner in the first moment of his vital union with Christ is there said to be life eternal; it is the same eternal life that is promised in the covenant of grace, according to those consoling passages: "He that believeth on the Son hath everlasting life" (John 3:36). "Verily, verily, I say unto you, he that heareth My word and believeth on Him that sent Me hath everlasting life" (John 5:24). Accordingly, from this promise, "the just by his faith shall live" (Habakkuk 2:4), our apostle proves the perseverance of the saints (Hebrews 10:38), a clear evidence that their perseverance in grace during their state of imperfection, and that in the midst of innumerable snares and enemies in this evil world is a part of that life eternal promised in the covenant, as well as the happiness of the heavenly world.

Thus then the promise of eternal life in the covenant of grace is a promise of the life that now is, and of that which is to come (1 Timothy 4:8). It is a promise of the life that now is. The life of justification, sanctification, and consolation, which the saints in this world enjoy, is eternal life begun. Were we to estimate happiness by the frowns, or even by the smiles, of common providence, no man, while in this world, could be counted happy. But the Scriptures teach us to form our estimate of it in another way, namely by a saving interest in the Lord Jesus, the blessed Head of the covenant; and they declare those people to be happy whose God is the Lord, however great or however many the afflictions are that are between them and the grave (Hebrews 10:38); so that the eternal life promised in the covenant is happiness which is begun in this world; the welfare of both soul and body, happily begun and infallibly to be carried on and completed.

It is a promise too of the life that is to come, of the same eternal life perfected, with respect to soul and body, in the heavenly world. There the promise of eternal life is to receive its full accomplishment in that ineffable and endless blessedness that consists in the perfect vision and fruition of Jehovah and the Lamb for evermore.

Third, and last, it comprehends all the appointed means of that endless felicity. It is a promise of all the appointed means by which that happiness of soul and body is to be begun, advanced, and consummated; whether outward, or inward; whether Paul or Apollos, or Cephas, or the world, or life, or death, or things present, or things to come; all are by promise theirs who believe; for they are Christ's; and Christ is God's (1 Corinthians 3:22, 23). The same comprehensive promise that secures the inestimable benefit itself secures also all the appointed means by which the enjoyment of it is to be attained. All the benefits included in the promise of eternal life may be arranged in these two classes: the means and the end. This, however, is always to be so understood as that those that are the means of attaining one promised benefit are oftentimes the end of attaining another. As the whole of true religion or internal holiness in this world is a special part of that eternal life that is promised in the covenant, and is usually denominated grace, so all this together is, according to the covenant, made subservient to glory, though not in the same manner and degree. Some promised blessings are instrumental means merely of other blessings that follow; they are, in their nature and use, so framed as merely to serve the attaining of eternal glory in heaven. Of this kind, faith appears to be the chief; as it is essential to the nature of it, that one, arrived at the years of understanding, believe with application the record which God has given of His Son, and so receive of His fullness, grace for grace (John 1:16). Other blessings again are either previously requisite to, or certain approaches toward, eternal glory, and so are parts of the end; yet as it is in this world that they are conferred on believers, they are also means of attaining the perfection of eternal life in the world to come. To this class, sanctification and spiritual consolation belong.

Thus the promise of eternal life in the covenant of grace is a promise of all true happiness, and of all the divinely appointed means of attaining it.

That this all-comprehensive promise of eternal life to the spiritual seed of Christ may be the better understood, it will be proper, next, to consider it in reference to three distinct periods: first, before their vital union with Christ; second, between the first moment of their union with Him and their death; and last, from death throughout eternity. In the first of these periods, eternal life, according to the promise, is on its way toward them; but in their own persons they have neither title to it nor possession of it. In the third, they have a full possession of it as well as a complete title to it. Of the operation of the promise of it, in the first and last periods, we know but very little; and indeed, not much of it, even in the middle period. It is like a river issuing from a remote and hidden spring, and running far under ground; then rising above ground and running on till it loses itself in the extended ocean. The hidden spring whence the promise of eternal life to His elect issues is the sovereign, the free, the boundless grace of God, that grace that was given them in Christ Jesus before the world began (2 Timothy 1:9). It runs under ground, undiscoverable, even by the elect themselves, until the moment of their vital union with Christ by faith; then rising, it runs on, as it were, above ground in visible and salutary streams till death; and after death, it flows full and clear throughout eternity.

I shall now, as was proposed, consider the great promise of eternal life in reference to each of these its distinct periods.

SECTION 3. Of the Promise of Eternal Life to the Elect as Having Its Effect on Them BEFORE Their Vital Union with Christ

When we view the promise of eternal life as performed to the elect, or as having effect on them before their spiritual union with the last Adam, we discern two leading branches of it: a promise of their preservation during the continuance of their natural state and a promise of the Spirit of life to them.

First, the promise of eternal life in the covenant to the elect comprises a promise of their preservation in their natural state till the happy moment of their vital union with Jesus Christ by which they will be settled in a state of grace; or a promise of divine security from whatever might tend to obstruct their participating, in due time, of eternal life. This, then, is a promise that they shall be brought forth into natural life (Isaiah 53:10). While the curse of the broken law, as it were, thrusts them forth into being as children of fallen Adam, the promise of eternal life secretly draws them forth into existence in order that they may, in due time, participate in the salvation of the last Adam. It is likewise a promise that, though innumerable dangers incessantly surround them after they are brought into existence, yet their natural life shall be preserved until the appointed moment of their spiritual union with the Lord Jesus. "When I passed by thee," said Jehovah, "and saw thee polluted in thine own blood, I said unto thee, when thou wast in thy blood, 'Live';" or, as it is in several approved versions translated more agreeably to the sacred original, "I said to thee, 'Live in thy blood' " (Ezekiel

The Promises of the Covenant of Grace   175

16:6). In this illustrious and consoling passage is represented under the figure of an exposed infant the natural state, the miserable condition, in which Jehovah found Israel and in which He still finds His elect, of whom ancient Israel were typical. Here, and in the context, is intimated to us by the Holy Spirit a twofold passing by this miserable outcast, a passing by her at two distant times. The first was on the day in which she was born and exposed (verses 4, 5, 6); the second after she was grown up and become marriageable, at which time she was actually married (verses 7, 8). The former relates to the time of the elect's coming, in their natural state, into the world, that is, of their being born into it, and of their beginning to think and act in it as reasonable creatures; the latter, to the time prefixed in the purpose of Jehovah when, by means of the law in the hand of the Spirit, convincing them of sin and misery, their breasts, as it were, are fashioned, upon which ensues their spiritual marriage with the Lord Jesus. But how was the exposed infant in the meantime preserved so that she did not perish in such a forlorn condition? Why, though no arm of protection seemed to be stretched out, yet a word was spoken that completely secured the continuance of her life, even in a case which, according to course of nature, was deadly. At His first passing by her in the day she was born and cast out, Jehovah said to her, "Live in thy blood." It is as if He had said, "Though you are lying in the open field, in your blood, your navel not having been dressed, so that, according to the course of nature, your blood and spirits must quickly fail and this the day of your birth prove the day of your death, yet I say unto you, 'LIVE.' You shall not die in that condition, but on the contrary grow up in it, being preserved till the happy moment of your designed marriage."

Now, this promise of the preservation of the elect while in their natural state is a promise:

1. That their natural life shall be continued till they are made partakers of spiritual life in the last Adam, their covenant-head. Jehovah has said that they shall live in their blood, that they shall live, though in the blood of their natural state. And therefore, whatever dangers should encompass them, though a thousand should fall at their side and ten thousand at their right hand, it is impossible that so much as one of them should die before that time; for by the promise of the covenant an unseen guard is placed around them to protect them. It is in virtue of this defense that during all the time they are in their natural state—whether conceived in the womb or born into the world or in the midst of the dangers of infancy, childhood, youth, or whatever age they arrive at—they are therein preserved safe. It is this that, so long as they are unregenerate, so often makes them return in safety, even from the gates of death; when either by diseases or accidents their case is in their own eyes, and in the eyes of friends and physicians, altogether hopeless. Though the elect malefactor was, in his natural state, nailed to the cross, yet death could have no access to separate his soul from his body till after he was by faith united to Christ and made partaker of spiritual life in Him.

2. It is a promise that no gravestone, fixing them beyond recovery, under spiritual death, shall be laid on them. The sin against the Holy Ghost, that unpardonable sin, is, as it were a gravestone that, on whomsoever it is laid renders from that moment their case irrecoverable; so that henceforth it becomes utterly impossible for them ever to rise from the grave of spiritual death. He who shall blaspheme against the Holy Ghost never has forgiveness, but is in danger, or, is guilty of, eternal damnation (Mark 3:29). Though the elect, while in their natural state, being dead in sins as much as others are, may, through the strength of reigning and raging lusts, so putrefy in their graves as

The Promises of the Covenant of Grace 177

to become most abominable in the sight of God and saints, yet that promise of the covenant renders it impossible that this gravestone should ever be laid over them. An invincible guard is set around their souls as well as their bodies by which that is effectually prevented, as may be inferred from these words of Him who cannot lie, "Insomuch that (if it were possible) they shall deceive the very elect" (Matthew 24:24). Satan, so long as they continue his captives, may instigate them to go prodigious lengths in wickedness, as he did Manasseh and Saul of Tarsus; but, though he drove these and many others of them exceedingly far in sin, he could not urge them to go the length of that sin.

3. Once more, it is a promise that, to ensure more effectually their preservation while in their natural state, they shall not only be under the common care of providence, as mankind in general are, but shall be secretly under the special and gracious care of it, though still in themselves children of wrath even as others; it is a promise that, in order to their living while in their blood, they shall then, as well as afterwards, be the objects of special providence. It is a promise that, under the care of special providence, all that befalls them during their state of alienation from the life of God shall, by His infinite wisdom, love, and faithfulness, be so managed as either to prove the occasion or the means of forwarding their vital union with Christ. In a few words, it is a promise that all things in their lot shall be so conducted as either directly or indirectly to pave the way for their entering, at the moment prefixed in the covenant, on the begun possession of eternal life (Ezekiel 20:37; Hosea 2:14; Acts 9:1-18; Philemon 10-19).

This promise that Jehovah will preserve His elect so long as He permits them to remain under the guilt and dominion of sin, like the rest of the promises, is performed to them on the ground of the perfect righteousness of Christ the last Adam; so it is closely connected with and, as it were, grafted on the promise of assistance made in the covenant to Him; and especially on that of the preservation of His body from corruption in the grave by which divine support was ensured to Him during all the time that their iniquity and the wrath due for it were to press upon Him. And thus in the covenant the cases both of the Head and of the members were jointly provided for (Isaiah 7:14, 15; Psalm 16:10, 11).

Second, the promise of eternal life to the elect includes likewise a promise of the quickening Spirit, or Spirit of life, to be imparted to them at the precise moment prefixed for that purpose in the covenant with regard to each of them. That happy moment of time is what the Lord in Ezekiel 16:8 calls, "Thy time, and the time of love." In making the covenant Jehovah the Father made this promise to Christ and to the elect in Him: "I will pour My Spirit upon Thy seed" (Isaiah 44:8); and again, "I will put My Spirit within you" (Ezekiel 36:27). The elect of God were, like the rest of children of Adam, dead in their sins, and could not otherwise be made spiritually alive than by the Spirit of life communicated to them. This quickening Spirit, however, they could not have from a holy and righteous God but on condition that all the demands of law and justice were completely answered for them. In the covenant, therefore, Christ their glorious Representative undertook to fulfill all righteousness in their stead that thereby He might purchase for them the inhabitation and operation of the Holy Spirit, upon which was made the promise of the Spirit, the leading fruit of Christ's purchase, called therefore by way of eminence the promise of His Father (Luke 24:49). In token of this, the Spirit was most eminently poured out at the ascension of the Lord Jesus when He as our great High Priest carried the blood of His sacrifice into the most holy place not made with hands (Acts 2:2-18).

Now, concerning that promise of the Spirit of life, it will be proper to observe that it is a promise of spiritual life and a promise of faith.

It is a promise of spiritual life to the elect dead in their sins. No sooner does the promise of the Spirit begin to be performed to a soul morally dead, or dead in sins, than that soul is quickened and raised to spiritual life. This commencement of spiritual life in the soul is, at the same time, the beginning of life eternal. It is the lighting of the sacred lamp of spiritual life in the dead and benighted soul that can never be again extinguished, but continues thenceforth to burn with increasing luster forever and ever. That promise is thus expressed: "Thy dead men shall live" (Isaiah 26:19). And that it belongs to the promise of the quickening Spirit is evident from these reviving words: "I will put My Spirit in you, and ye shall live (Ezekiel 37:14).

The immediate effect of this promise is the quickening of the dead soul by the Spirit of Christ passively received. For the Apostle Paul says, "God, who is rich in mercy, for His great love wherewith He loved us, even when we were dead in sins, hath quickened us together with Christ" (Ephesians 2:4, 5). This quickening of the dead soul is what we mean by regeneration, or being born again. All who are born again are born of the Spirit (John 3:8), and so are born of God. They are "born not of blood, nor of the will of the flesh, nor of the will of man, but of God" (John 1:13). Sinners in their unregenerate state are lifeless and motionless. They are no more able to believe in Christ, to repent of sin, to perform one spiritually good work, than a dead body is to speak or walk. But when, in virtue of that promise, the Spirit of life in Christ Jesus enters at the time of love into a soul dead in sin, He so quickens it that it is no more spiritually dead, but alive to God, having those spiritual powers and principles again put into it that were lost by the breach of the first covenant.

It is a promise of faith, a promise that the spiritual seed of Christ shall believe in Him and so come to Him. "Thy people shall be wiling in the day of Thy power" (Psalm 110:3). "In His name shall the Gentiles trust" (Matthew 12:21). "A seed shall serve him . . . they shall come (Psalm 22:30, 31). Jehovah the Father has promised that, when His incarnate Son would make His soul an offering for sin, He should see His seed and that, seeing the travail of His soul, He should be satisfied (Isaiah 53:10, 11). Therefore, whoever they are that do not believe, all who were represented in the covenant shall assuredly be enabled to believe; for our blessed Lord Himself, upon the credit of that promise, declared that all whom the Father gave Him would come to Him (John 6:37). Now this also belongs to the promise of the Spirit who, therefore, is called the Spirit of faith (2 Corinthians 4:13), as being the great efficient cause of it (Zechariah 12:10).

The effect of this promise when performed is actual believing; not only, in adult persons, the principle and habit, but the act or begun exercise of faith. This is produced by the quickening Spirit in the soul, immediately out of the spiritual life given it, by the communication of Himself thereto. When, as the Spirit of faith, He enters the soul, He inlays it with the whole Word of God, the gospel as well as the law; and by His almighty power, deeply impressing the heart therewith, He transforms it into a conformity or suitableness to both. We accordingly read that the hour now is when the dead shall hear the voice of the Son of God (John 5:25); and that "as many as received Him, to them gave He power to become the sons of God . . . which were born . . . of God" (John 1:12, 13). As in receiving Christ passively the sinner, who was but a moment ago spiritually dead, is quickened; so, being quickened, He receives Christ actually. Christ the last Adam, by His quickening Spirit, comes into the dead soul; and so He is passively received, even as one who has power to raise the dead to life comes into a house where none is to be found but a dead man; none to open the door to him, none to desire him to come in or to welcome him. But Christ being so received as now to be within, the dead soul is quickened and by faith actually embraces Him in like manner, as the restorer of the dead man to life would immediately be embraced by him, and a thousand times be welcomed to his habitation. As the Lord God breathed into the first man the breath of life, so that he who was before but a lifeless piece of clay became a living soul, and showed that he had a soul or spirit put into his body by beginning to breathe through his nostrils, so the Lord Jesus, in the time of love, puts His Spirit into the soul dead in sins, which immediately shows itself to be alive by embracing and trusting in Him as offered in the gospel, and now beheld in His transcendent comeliness and suitableness. Thus the spiritual and vital union between Christ and the soul is completed. Christ first apprehends the soul, and by His Spirit unites Himself to it; then the soul, thus apprehended and quickened, apprehends and applies Him as offered in the gospel and by faith is united to Him.

Now the promise of the quickening Spirit, in both these branches of it, appears to be grafted on the promise made to Christ Himself of God's uniting the human to the divine nature in His adorable Person, and especially on that of His reuniting his soul to his body in his resurrection from the dead. It appears, I say, to be grafted on the promise made to Him of uniting the human to the divine nature in His glorious person; for the union of the persons of the elect to His person depends on the union of their nature to His nature as residing in His person. It seems especially to be grafted on the promise made to Christ of God's reuniting His soul to His body in His triumphant resurrection. It is so connected with this promise that the one cannot be separated from the other. The promise of His resurrection, like the oil upon Aaron's head, runs down to the skirts of His garments in the promise of quickening likewise the members of His body mystical. This is evident from these, among other passages of Scripture: "Thy dead men shall live, together with my dead body, shall they arise" (Isaiah 26:19). "But God . . . even when we were dead in sin, hath quickened us together with Christ, and hath raised us up together" (Ephesians 2:4, 5, 6). The Lord Jesus, in the everlasting covenant, became the Head of a dead body, of a body of elect sinners dead in sins in order that He might restore it to life; and being thereby legally united to that dead body, so that death might, at the appointed time, have access to extend itself from it to Him as the Head; He had a promise made to Him of a resurrection to life, both for Himself and His members. When the time appointed was come, death mustered all its forces and made a furious attack upon the Head of the body, the only part which remained alive. Having, with its sting, pierced Him to the heart on His cross, it brought Him likewise to the dust of death, and so it had them all, both Head and members, dead together. Thus the conditions of the covenant were fulfilled.

Now the promises in their turn fall next to be performed, particularly the promise that, after death had exhausted all its force on the Head, He should be raised again from the grave; and that, as death had extended itself from the members to the Head, so life should in its turn diffuse itself from the Head to the members so that they, together with His dead body, might arise. It was in virtue of this promise that the spirit or soul which animated Christ's body, and which He yielded upon on the accursed tree, returned again into His blessed body; upon which, on the morning of the third day, He came forth out of the grave; and it is in virtue of the same promise that the Spirit of life enters into the dead souls of elect sinners, upon which they also begin to live and to believe. The precise moment of the return of the Spirit, both into the Head and into each of the members, was prefixed in the covenant; so that, as it was not possible that the body of the Lord Jesus should be held in the grave after the morning of the third day, so neither is it possible that His elect can be held under the power of spiritual death, after the time prefixed for their passing, each from death to life. "After two days will he revive us, in the third day he will raise us up, and we shall live in his sight" (Hosea 6:2).

Thus the promise of eternal life to the elect operates in this dark period of their days, their natural state, which dark period terminates here. It now appears and, like a clear and salutary stream, runs henceforth above ground.

SECTION 4. Of the Promise of Eternal Life, as Performed to the Elect, From the First Moment of Their Vital Union with Christ Until Death

When the promise of eternal life, as performed to the elect from the commencement of their vital union with Christ until death, is considered, the following branches of it are the most remarkable: The promise of justification, the promise of a new and saving relation to God, of sanctification, of spiritual comfort, of perseverance in grace, and of temporal good things.

First, the promise of eternal life to the elect comprises that of the justification of life, a promise to be accomplished to each of them the moment he begins to be vitally united to Christ as

Jehovah his Righteousness. This great promise is recorded in these, as well as in many other passages of Scripture. "By the obedience of One shall many be made righteous" (Romans 5:19). "By the knowledge of Him shall My righteous Servant justify many" (Isaiah 53:11). "In the Lord shall all the seed of Israel be justified" (Isaiah 45:25). This promise of a free, full, irrevocable, and everlasting justification upon their union with the last Adam and the imputation of His surety-righteousness to them is the leading promise of this period. The immediate effect of its accomplishment is that the sinner, legally dead under the condemning sentence or curse of the broken covenant of works, becomes legally alive. This is the beginning of that life which is received from Christ by faith. There is a life that is received from Christ previous to the begun exercise of faith whereby one is enabled to believe that has been described above; and there is a life that is received from Him by faith according to these words of John: "that, believing, ye might have life through His name" (John 20:31). This last is by our blessed Lord Himself expressly called eternal life: "He that heareth My word and believeth on Him that sent Me hath everlasting life, and shall not come into condemnation, but is passed from death to life" (John 5:24).

The elect of God were, for their breach of the covenant of innocence as well as for their personal sins, laid under the curse and so were dead in law. And they could not be restored to life in the eye of the law but on condition of fulfilling the righteousness of the law, which they not being able to do for themselves, Christ the last Adam undertook in the covenant of grace to fulfill it for them, upon which was made the promise of their justification. This promise having its full effect upon their believing, the curse is removed and they are personally and actually justified. Thus restored to life in the eyes of the law, they are now legally alive. They live in law. This kind of life received by faith is, as was hinted above, everlasting; for according to the covenant that is the charter or instrument of justification, the curse can never any more return upon them so much as for a moment. For thus said Jehovah, "With everlasting kindness will I have mercy on thee; for as I have sworn that the waters of Noah should no more go over the earth, so have I sworn that I would not be wroth with thee, nor rebuke thee" (Isaiah 54:8, 9).

Of the promise of justification, there are these two branches: a promise of the pardon of sin and of acceptance as righteous.

First is a promise of the pardon of sin, or of deliverance from the guilt of eternal wrath. "I," said Jehovah, "will be merciful to their unrighteousness, and their sins and their iniquities will I remember no more" (Hebrews 8:12). The sins of the elect being in the everlasting covenant imputed to Christ, who, in legal estimation, becoming one with them undertook that their debt transferred to Him should be discharged by Himself, a promise was thereupon made of pardon to each of them. And as soon as by faith they became spiritually and mystically one with Him they, in consequence of that union, have communion with Him in His righteousness, upon which His infinite satisfaction for sin becomes theirs and so is imputed to them. It is on account of it only, and not of any doings or sufferings of their own, that the promise of pardon is, according that eternal contract, accomplished to them. Hence are these consoling words of our great apostle, "In whom we have redemption through His blood, the forgiveness of sins, according to the riches of His grace (Ephesians 1:7).

Now this is life to the sinner who was dead in law, a pardon put into the hand of the condemned criminal, disarming with respect to him the law of its curse and death of its sting, causing him to lift up his head off the block and to retire with acclamations of praise for the mercy of the King eternal, and for the merit of His Son; and it is eternal life, for all his sins, past, present, and future are freely, fully, and irrevocably pardoned as to the guilt of eternal wrath, or so far as they are transgressions of the law as a covenant of works (Psalm 103:3). In the act of justification, which is completed at once and not carried on gradually, like a work of time, his past and present sins are formally pardoned and in the same act a non-imputing of his future sins, as to the guilt of eternal wrath, is secured to him. Hence are these words of the Apostle Paul that he cited from the 32nd Psalm: "Blessed are they whose iniquities are forgiven, and whose sins are covered; blessed is the man to whom the Lord will not impute sin" (Romans 4:7, 8). And since the gifts and calling of God, are without repentance (Romans 11:29), He will never revoke His act of remission.

The other branch of the promise of justification is a promise of acceptance as righteous in the sight of God; it is a promise of a full and irrevocable acceptance of the persons of believers into a state both of favor with God, and of complete title to life eternal, begun here in grace and perfected hereafter in glory. Accordingly we read that "By the obedience of One shall many be made righteous" (Romans 5:19), that the Lord is well pleased for His righteousness' sake (Isaiah 42:21); that Christ is His beloved Son, in whom He is well pleased (Matthew 3:17); and that "He hath made us accepted in the beloved" (Ephesians 1:6). The righteous Lord, who loves righteousness and whose judgment is necessarily according to truth, cannot accept sinners as righteous without a righteousness so perfect as fully to answer all the demands of His holy law. They who are not perfectly righteous in law can never pass for righteous ones in His view, whose justice as well as omniscience is infinite. "In Thy sight," said the Psalmist, "shall no man living be justified" (Psalm 143:2); that is, as the Apostle Paul explains it, "be justified by the deeds of the law" (Romans 3:20). But Christ as last Adam having, in the covenant, engaged to fulfill all righteousness for His elect seed, who of themselves could fulfill none, a promise was thereupon made that God would account them righteous, and accept them as righteous in His sight, for His righteousness, which through faith becomes truly theirs, and that by a twofold right: First, by the right of a free gift received. Inasmuch as the righteousness of Jesus Christ is, in the gospel, offered as a free gift to sinners, this glorious gift is by faith actually received. Hence it is called the gift of righteousness (Romans 5:17), and the righteousness of God, revealed from faith to faith (Romans 1:17), in order that it may by faith be received. Second, it is theirs too by right of communion with Christ as their Surety and their Husband. When sinners are by faith united to Him, they have communion, or a joint interest with Him in His righteousness. "That I may be found in Him," said our apostle, "not having mine own righteousness, which is of the law, but that which is through the faith of Christ, the righteousness which is of God by faith" (Philippians 3:9). By the right then of a free gift received, and the right of communion with Christ as Jehovah their Righteousness, the holiness of His human nature, the obedience of His life, and the satisfaction given to justice by His death, being the constituent articles of that surety-righteousness, are imputed to believers or legally accounted theirs; and it is on account of these solely that they are by God accepted as righteous. Seeing "It is the righteousness of God, which is by faith of Jesus Christ, unto all, and upon all them that believe" (Romans 3:22), they are made the righteousness of God in Him (2 Corinthians 5:21).

Here likewise is life to the sinner dead in law, righteousness to justification of life (Romans 5:18), everlasting righteousness (Daniel 9:24), a garment that never waxes old, that is never rent, never tarnished, but from the moment it is put on continues throughout eternity in its original luster. That life, therefore, to which it entitles the believers, cannot but be everlasting. Grace cannot but reign through such a divine righteousness to eternal life for, being once put on, it is never again put off so much as for one moment during the ages either of time or of eternity.

Now the promise of justification in both these branches of it is connected with and grafted on the promise of complete justification made to Christ Himself. The conditions of the covenant having been fulfilled, the blessed Head was, according to the promise, justified, and the members are justified in and under Him. First, He received from the hand of justice a full discharge for the whole debt; and then, they pleading it by faith, each for himself, are in their own persons discharged (Isaiah 50:8; Romans 4:25).

The promise of eternal life to the elect comprises the promise of a new and saving relationship to God into which they, upon their being justified, are brought. Having, by the breach of the covenant of works, fallen under a spiritual and a legal death, they fell likewise under a relative death. That happy and honorable relationship that had originally subsisted between God and them was dissolved; and it could not be constituted again so long as they lay under the condemning sentence of the law. But upon Christ's undertaking in the covenant of grace to fulfill all righteousness, the price of the purchase of every saving benefit, this promise was made. No sooner, therefore, do they so come to Christ by faith as to be united to Him, and justified for His righteousness imputed to them, than God meets them in Him, the appointed place of meeting. There, with the entire safety of His honor, He takes them by the hand, admits them into special favor, and joins them again to Himself in a saving and honorable relationship. Thus they have a relative life, according to the-

The Promises of the Covenant of Grace

se words of the holy Psalmist: "In his favor is life" (Psalm 30:5). Now this life, as well as the former, is eternal inasmuch as the happy relation once begun is forever indissoluble. For as the undertaking of the second Adam was surer than that of the first, so the bond of the second covenant is, in the same proportion, more firm than the bond of the first.

Of this promise of a new and saving relation to God in Christ there are these three leading branches: the promise of reconciliation, the promise of adoption, and the promise that God will be their God.

First there is the promise of reconciliation between God and them, or of a new and saving relationship to Him as their reconciled and reconciling Friend. "I will make," said Jehovah, "a covenant of peace with them; it shall be an everlasting covenant with them" (Ezekiel 37:26). The elect of God were all in a state of enmity against Him; their carnal mind was not merely an enemy, but enmity itself against a holy God, enmity in the abstract (Romans 8:7). On their part, there was real enmity against God, and on His part legal enmity against them, such as a judge has against a condemned malefactor whom, notwithstanding, he may on other accounts tenderly love. But Christ the second Adam having in the covenant undertaken to make atonement for their sins by the sacrifice of Himself, the Father made thereupon a promise of peace and reconciliation with them. Hence we read that Christ made peace by the blood of His cross (Colossians 1:20), and that believers are reconciled to God by the death of His Son (Romans 5:20), inasmuch as by His death He purchased reconciliation for them, which was promised on that condition.

This precious promise is accomplished to every one who is justified. No sooner is the believing sinner pardoned and accepted as righteous than he is brought into a state of peace with

God, as the Apostle Paul says, "Being justified by faith, we have peace with God through our Lord Jesus Christ" (Romans 5:1). The Lord the righteous Judge lays down His legal enmity against him, never to be taken up again; and besides, He takes him into a bond of friendship so that he is not only at peace with God, but is "the friend of God." While God in Christ is the reconciled Friend of the believer, he is the friend of God. "Abraham believed God, and it was imputed unto him for righteousness; and he was called the friend of God" (James 2:23).

Now this promise is grafted on the promise of justification or acceptance, made to Christ Himself for His infinite atonement being accepted as well pleasing to God, and He being discharged from the infinite debt for which He became responsible, the reconciliation as well as the pardon. Of those who are by faith united to Him it is a native and necessary consequence. "God was in Christ, reconciling the world unto Himself, not imputing their trespasses unto them" (2 Corinthians 5:19); and again, "He hath made us accepted in the beloved" (Ephesians 1:6).

Another branch of that promise is the promise of adoption into the family of God, or of a new and saving relationship to Him as their Father. It shall be said unto them, "Ye are the sons of the living God" (Hosea 1:10). This is more than even the former. It is more to be the son than to be the friend of God. It was shown above how all the children of Adam were, by the covenant of works, constituted the hired servants of God; how, by the breach of that covenant, they reduced themselves to the low condition of bond servants under the curse of it, and how Christ consented to have that state of servitude transferred from His spiritual offspring to Himself. Now, on consideration of His taking on Him the form of a bond servant for them, the promise of adopting them into the family of God was made, for thus it is written, "God sent forth His Son, made of a woman, made under the law, to redeem that were under the law, that we might receive the adoption of sons" (Galatians 4:4, 5).

No sooner are they justified by faith and reconciled to God than this promise is accomplished to them inasmuch as then Christ's service is imputed to them and a way is at the same time opened through their reconciliation to God for their adoption into His family. "Being justified by faith, we have peace with God through our Lord Jesus Christ; by whom also we have access by faith into this grace wherein we stand" (Romans 5:1, 2). "As many as received Him, to them gave He power to become the sons of God" (John 1:12). Then it is that they are admitted as children into the family of the living God, that He becomes their Father in Christ and they, His sons and daughters, to abide in His house forever (John 8:35), and to have a covenant-right to all the privileges of that exalted relationship.

This promise is grafted on the promise made to Christ as last Adam of a new interest in God as His Father according to His own words to Mary Magdalene, "I ascend unto My Father and your Father" (John 20:7). For by the Spirit of adoption they who are justified and reconciled call God their Father in the right of Christ Jesus, their elder Brother, spiritual Husband, and Covenant-head.

The promise of God's being their God, or of a new and saving relationship to Him as their God, is the last and highest branch of it. "I," said the Lord, "will be to them a God" (Hebrews 8:10). "I will say to them which were not My people, 'Thou art My people'; and they shall say, 'Thou art my God' " (Hosea 2:23). This is more than justification, reconciliation, or even adoption. It is the highest degree of relationship to the infinitely glorious Jehovah, to which it is possible for a sinful creature to be exalted. The elect were by nature without God (Ephesians 2:12). But inasmuch as the eternal Son of God did, in the everlasting covenant, engage to give Himself a ransom for them, and so, in their nature, perfectly to fulfill the law by His holy incarnation, righteous life, and satisfactory death—a price of infinite value, infinitely more precious than all created objects whatever, whether pardons, or graces, or comforts, or heavenly mansions—there was, upon that high condition, a promise made of God's bestowing HIMSELF on them as the only equivalent reward of that service. By the second Adam the service was performed, and so the exceedingly great reward was purchased for them. Hence Jehovah said to Abraham, "I am . . . thy exceeding great reward" (Genesis 15:1).

Now, to believers being justified, reconciled, and adopted, this boundless inheritance falls as the accomplishment of that promise. Hence are these consoling words of our apostle: "If children, then heirs; heirs of God" (Romans 8:17); and if a son, then an heir of God through Christ (Galatians 4:7). Jehovah Himself, by becoming their God, becomes their inheritance. They have a covenant-right to Him, a saving interest in Him, and are possessed of Him as their own peculiar property; property, the amount of which the highest angels around the celestial throne will never be able fully to comprehend. Not only are all the works and creatures of God in the heavens and on the earth, in the seas and in all deep places theirs (1 Corinthians 3:22), but He Himself is theirs, which is infinitely more than they all—as the bridegroom himself is more than all his marriage-robes or large possessions. All His transcendently glorious attributes, as was observed above, are theirs; these are all on their side, all engaged to secure, to promote, to perfect their everlasting welfare. Whatever His infinite wisdom, His eternal power, His immaculate holiness, His inflexible justice, His immense goodness, His inviolable faithfulness, can do to render them happy shall most assuredly be done. He is theirs too, in all His endearing relations. He is not only their Friend and their Father, but their Lord and their God, to be confessed and served by them; their King, to bestow of His grace, to rule in their hearts, and to destroy their enemies; their Shepherd to keep them from want, to restore their souls, and to make them to lie down in green pastures; their Protector, to cover, to shield them from evil; their Husband, to dwell with them, to provide for them, to commend, to cherish them; and their Head, to communicate life to them and confer dignity on them. All the Persons of the glorious Godhead are theirs. The Father, with all His redeeming love, the Son, with all His boundless grace, and the Holy Spirit, with all His saving influence, belong to them. "Thy Maker is thine husband (the Lord of hosts is His name)" or, as it is in the sacred original, "Thy Makers are thy husbands; Jehovah of hosts is His name" (Isaiah 55:5).

This great and precious promise is grafted on the promise made to Christ Himself of a new and mediatorial interest in God as His God. Jehovah is by purchase the God of the blessed Mediator, and becomes the covenant-God of believers in and through Him: "I ascend," said He, "to My God and your God" (John 20:17). The last Adam, having fulfilled the conditions of the eternal covenant, falls heir to this great and goodly heritage; and they become heirs of it in Him. "If children, then heirs, heirs of God and joint heirs with Christ" (Romans 8:17).

In the third place, the promise of eternal life to the elect comprehends likewise a promise of the sanctification of their nature and life. "I," said Jehovah, "will take away the stony heart out of your flesh, and I will give you an heart of flesh; and cause you to walk in My statutes, and ye shall keep My judgments and do them" (Ezekiel 36:26, 27). By their breach of the covenant of innocence they lost the moral image of God. The faculties of their souls and the members of their bodies were thereby so corrupted that they could neither do, nor speak, nor so much as think anything that is spiritually good; and it was entirely beyond their power ever to make themselves again holy. It is to no purpose for them to try to mend or make their heart better; it is impossible to make it better for there is no degree of good remaining in it (Romans 7:18). It may be renewed or made anew, but cannot be improved or made better. The depraved heart must be taken away, and a new heart be given them (Ezekiel 36:26; Ephesians 4:22, 23, 24). The curse of the broken law lying upon them dissolved all saving relationship between God and their souls and so obstructed all saving communication with heaven; for it hindered, in point of justice, all sanctifying influences from heaven to them. The awful curse fixed an impassable gulf between God and them, so that sanctifying influences could not pass from Him to them, nor could their prayers pass from them to Him. It is because the curse cannot be removed from fallen angels and damned souls in hell that they are beyond all possibility of ever receiving sanctifying influences from above. In this deplorable condition all the seed of Adam should have forever continued if Christ Jesus had not, as the Representative of the elect, undertaken in the covenant of grace to remove that bar, to fill up that gulf, and by His own obedience and death to found a new and saving relationship between God and them. This He as last Adam engaged to do, upon which the Father by promise secured their sanctification. He promised that a seed should serve Christ (Psalm 22:30), and that His people should be wiling in the day of His power, in the beauties of holiness (Psalm 110:3).

This promise of sanctification is the principal promise of the covenant made to Christ for His elect seed. Among the other promises of that class, it shines as the moon among the twinkling stars. Sanctification is the chief subordinate end of the covenant, standing in it next to the glory of Jehovah, which is the chief ultimate of it. All the foregoing promises—the promise of preservation, of the quickening Spirit, of faith, of justification, and of a new and saving relation to God—tend thereto, and stand related to it as means to their end. They are all fulfilled to elect sinners on purpose to render them holy. And all the subsequent promises, even the promise of glorification itself, are but the promise of sanctification extended.

This is evident from the descriptions given us in holy writ of the promissory part of the covenant respecting the spiritual seed of Christ. "To remember," said Zacharias, "His holy covenant, the oath which He sware to our father Abraham, that He would grant unto us that we, being delivered out of the hands of our enemies, might serve Him without fear, in holiness and righteousness before Him all the days of our life" (Luke 1:72-75). Here we have the covenant or oath sworn to Abraham as a type of Christ in which His seed, their serving Jehovah in holiness and righteousness all the days of their life, is represented as the main object sworn by the Father to the second Adam, and their being delivered from their enemies as the means employed for that end. And by comparing the 10th with the 12th verse of the 8th chapter of the epistle to the Hebrews, it appears that God's writing of His law in their heart is set on the front as the first object in the divine intention, though the last in execution. This is evident likewise from the nature of the thing itself. For the great object that Satan aimed at in seducing our first parents to sin was the defacing of the image of God in them, so that the human race might no longer resemble God, but resemble himself; and the mystery of God for the recovery of lost sinners is then, and not till then, finished when holiness restored to them is brought to perfection.

From all this it is obvious that the sanctification of all who shall ever enter heaven is, in the covenant, secured on the firmest grounds, infinitely beyond the possibility of failure; that the unsanctified have no personal interest in the covenant, and that the less holy the believer is the less is the promise of eternal life in the covenant fulfilled to him. The sanctification of sinners is the great design of that holy covenant. It is that which the Father, Son, and Holy Spirit, next to the glory of redeeming grace, had principally in their view; and the promise of it is, in respect of sinners, the chief, the capital branch of the promise of eternal life to them.

Now at the time appointed in the counsel of peace for every elect sinner, this promise is graciously fulfilled to him. Being justified and received into a new and saving relation to God in Christ as his Friend, Father, and God, he is sanctified. The gulf, with respect to him, being filled up, every legal bar being removed and his saving relationship to the High and Holy One being established, the communication between God and him is opened, and sanctifying influences flow freely, for the sanctification of his spirit, soul, and body.

This sanctification is by some called the second regeneration, according to the following passages compared together: "Christ also loved the church, and gave Himself for it, that He might sanctify and cleanse it with the washing of water" (Ephesians 5:25, 26). "According to His mercy He saved us by the washing of regeneration, and renewing of the Holy Ghost" (Titus 3:5). "If any man be in Christ, he is a new creature" (2 Corinthians 5:17). As in regeneration, when taken strictly for the quickening of the soul dead in sin, and by some, called the first regeneration, new vital powers are infused; so in regeneration, when taken largely for the forming of the new creature in all its distinct members and called the second regeneration, new qualities or habits of grace are formed and strengthened. This second regeneration is the same as the renewing of the Holy Ghost, that second renewing mentioned in our shorter Catechism, under the heading of sanctification. In our sanctification we are there said to be renewed in the whole man, after the image of God.

Of what has now been discoursed this is the sum: the sinner being united to Christ by faith, in consequence of the Spirit of life from Christ communicated to him, and being thereupon justified and related to God as his Friend, Father and God, a predominant measure of every spiritual grace, from the immeasurable fullness of grace in Christ the Head, is derived to him, being now a member of His mystical body, and that, by the same Holy Spirit that dwells in the Head and in the members, by this the man becomes not only a living, but a new creature. Old things are passed away, and all things in him, are become new. He is renewed in the whole man after the image of God, and so is sanctified wholly in spirit, soul, and body. For the immediate effect of that communication of grace from the fullness of Christ is the sealing of the person with the image of Christ the incarnate Son (Romans 8:29). As the wax receives character for character in the seal applied to it, so does he receive grace for grace in Jesus Christ. The restored image of God is expressed on him immediately from Christ the last Adam, who is the image of the invisible God, just as Eve, by her being created after the image of Adam, was made in the image of God. Hence Jehovah said respecting the man, "I will make him an help meet for him" (Genesis 2:18); the Hebrew word means "as before him," that is, in his own likeness, as if he had sat for his picture. Compare with this what our apostle says in 1 Corinthians 11:7, 8: "He (that is, the man) is the image and glory of God; but the woman is the glory of the man. For the man is not of the woman; but the woman, of the man." And likewise in 2 Corinthians

8:23: "Our brethren . . . are the messengers of the churches, and the glory of Christ." Thus the sinner's being united to Christ the last Adam issues as really in his becoming one spirit, or in his being of the same holy and spiritual nature with Him, as Eve's being formed out of the first Adam issued in her becoming one flesh with him, or "bone of his bones, and flesh of his flesh" (Genesis 2:23). When the Apostle Paul, in allusion to this, was speaking of the spiritual union between Christ and the believers at Ephesus, he said to them, "We are members of His body, of His flesh, and of His bones" (Ephesians 5:30).

And indeed, from the account given us of it in the holy Scriptures, we see that the sanctification of a sinner has a special relationship to Christ the last Adam, and to His Spirit. It has, at the same time, an immediate dependence on the sinner's relative state in the favor of God, and so is no less a mystery than his justification. It is only from the oracles of God that we learn the mystery of the sanctification of a sinner. There we are informed that this great and gracious work is, by the Holy Spirit, wrought on the souls of men in and after believing. "In whom also, after that ye believed (or when ye believed), ye were sealed with that Holy Spirit of promise" (Ephesians 1:13). Faith is the appointed instrument of sanctification. We are sanctified by faith in the holy Lord Jesus (Acts 26:18). By faith it is that of his fullness we receive, even grace for grace (John 1:16). And the grace that is received by faith is at the same time communicated by the Spirit of Christ, who thereby renews us after His image, and so glorifies Him by imparting to us grace from His fullness (John 16:14); so that, "beholding as in a glass the glory of the Lord Jesus, we are changed into the same image, from glory to glory, even as by the Spirit of the Lord" (2 Corinthians 3:18).

It likewise depends on our union with Christ, for it is, by the Spirit, produced on the souls of men only in a state of union with Him. They who are sanctified are sanctified in Christ Jesus (1 Corinthians 1:2). They are created in Christ Jesus unto good works (Ephesians 2:10). The Lord Jesus is such a stock as changes the graft into its own nature. "Therefore, if any man be in Christ, he is a new creature" (1 Corinthians 5:17). It depends too on our justification and reconciliation with God. The blood of Christ with which, according to the Scriptures (1 Peter 1:2; 1 John 1:7; Revelation 1:5), we are sanctified, is effective of our sanctification inasmuch as it is the meritorious cause of it; and so the sanctifying virtue of that infinitely precious blood arises from its atoning virtue. It sanctifies us because it justifies and reconciles us to God. "How much more," says our apostle, "shall the blood of Christ, who through the eternal Spirit offered Himself without spot to God, purge your conscience from dead works to serve the living God?" (Hebrews 9:14). And again, "The very God of peace sanctify you wholly" (1 Thessalonians 5:23). It also depends on our adoption inasmuch as it is, upon our being adopted into the family of God, that we receive the Spirit of His Son, conforming us to His image, as our elder brother. "For whom He did foreknow, He also did predestinate, to be conformed to the image of His Son, that He might be the first-born among many brethren" (Romans 8:29). And, "because ye are sons, God hath sent forth the Spirit of His Son into your hearts, crying, 'Abba, Father' " (Galatians 4:6). In few words, it presupposes God's having become our God. "I sware unto thee, and entered into a covenant with thee, saith the Lord God, and thou becamest mine. Then washed I thee with water; yea, I thoroughly washed away thy blood from thee, and I anointed thee with oil" (Ezekiel 16:8, 9).

But although in the work of sanctification there is communicated, out of the overflowing fullness of grace in Jesus Christ, a predominant measure of every grace, yet not a full measure of any grace. Hence it is that although we are thereby renewed in the whole man, yet we are still at the same time unrenewed in the whole man in respect of two general and opposite parts that, for that reason, are called the renewed and the unrenewed part. For by that communication of grace, for grace in the man Christ, we are indeed renewed in every particular part; yet the measure of none of the spiritual graces being full in any soul while in this world, we are not renewed completely in any part; but on the contrary have remainders of corruption still dwelling in every part. They dwell in all the faculties of the soul, and in all the members of the body as the organs of the soul. Thus the two contrary principles of grace and corruption are in them who are sanctified, being together in such a manner that in every particular part where the one is the other is by it, just as in the twilight, darkness and light are together in every part of the visible heavens. What believers have while in this world of that gracious work on them, they have but in part. It is not perfect (1 Corinthians 13:9, 10). Though the new man is put on, the old man is still to be put off (Ephesians 4:22, 24). There is flesh as well as sprit in the holiest of the saints (Galatians 5:17) who, therefore, look forth but as the morning (Song of Songs 6:10); or, as the original word more properly signifies, as the dawn or daybreak. Still, however, as the dawn differs from the thick darkness, they differ from unsanctified persons in whom there is no dawn, but gross darkness (Isaiah 8:20; Romans 7:14-24).

Notwithstanding, as it is a predominant measure of every grace that is communicated, this work of sanctification issues in dying to sin and in living to righteousness.

It issues in dying to sin, or in mortifying the body of sin. A mortification thereby seizes, and never stops in its progress till it spreads through the whole body of sin. By means of that communication of sanctifying grace from Christ the Head, though it is far from being full, the old man or corruption of nature receives a mortal wound. The vital and reigning power of the whole body of sin is destroyed; inasmuch as a reigning principle of grace is, in opposition to it, set up and thereby strengthened in the soul. Hence Paul says to the believers in Rome, "Sin shall not have dominion over you; for ye are not under the law but under grace" (Romans 6:14). Not only is the pollution of sin, by the application of the blood of Christ in the hand of the Spirit, purged off but, by the restored image of the Son of God, so far as it goes, a man becomes personally upright and holy (Titus 3:5 compared with Colossians 3:10). And thus he is, in respect of his unrenewed part, put into a state of death; for our apostle, in writing to the saints at Colossae, says, "Ye are dead" (Colossians 3:3); and in writing to those in Rome he says, "Reckon ye also yourselves to be dead indeed unto sin" (Romans 6:11). This state of death is similar to that which a crucified man is in who, having been nailed to the cross, cannot come down, but must continue on it till he expires. "Knowing this," says our apostle, "that our old man is crucified with Him, that the body of sin might be destroyed" (Romans 6:6).

It issues likewise in the believer's living to righteousness. By means of the same communication of sanctifying grace from Christ his federal Head, a man is endued with such habits of grace as are the immediate principles of holy actions. The holy law is written in his heart. His heart is circumcised to love the Lord his God with all his heart and with all his soul. And thus, in respect of his renewed part, he is vivified; he is put into a state of life unto righteousness, being dead indeed unto sin, but alive unto God though Jesus Christ our Lord (Romans 6:11). The Apostle Paul says of himself, "I am crucified with Christ; nevertheless I live; yet not I, but Christ liveth in me" (Galatians 2:20). This state of spiritual life is that newness of life mentioned by our apostle, to which the elect sinner is not only quickened but made to rise and come forth out of the grave of sin. You are risen with Him through the faith of the operation of God (Colossians 2:12). That like as Christ was raised up from the dead by the glory of the Father, even so we also should walk in newness of life (Romans 6:4). And, as it is a spiritual and new life, so it is an eternal life; for the grace communicated from Christ to the believer, for that purpose, shall be in him a well of water springing up into everlasting life (John 4:14).

Here let it be carefully attended to that this death to sin and life to righteousness proceed from communion with Christ the last Adam in His death and resurrection. His death and resurrection possess a virtue to render the members of His mystical body conformable to Him in them. These have a virtue to effect or produce in them a dying to sin, as Christ died for sin, and a rising from the grave of sin to a new manner of life to be continued during their stay in this world, and perfected in the world to come, as He rose from the grave to a new manner of life which was continued till His ascension to heaven. To this purpose are these words of the Apostle Paul: "That I may know Him, and the power of His resurrection, and the fellowship of His sufferings, being made conformable unto His death" (Philippians 3:10). "Therefore, we are buried with Him by baptism unto death; that like of the Father, even so we also should walk in newness of life. For if we have been planted together in the likeness of His death, we shall be also in the likeness of His resurrection" (Romans 6:4, 5). Seeing that, in the sin and death of the first Adam, there is such a malignant efficacy as renders his natural posterity conformable to Him therein, to their depravity and defilement; why should it be thought incredible that there should be such a benign virtue in the death and resurrection of the last Adam as should render His spiritual offspring conformable to Him in both to their sanctification? The death and resurrection of Christ, having this transforming virtue, because He died and rose again as a public person, and in consequence of His divine nature merited this conformation of His mystical members to His image" (Romans 6:4-12; Ephesians 2:5, 6); and both begin to have this effect on these as soon as they begin, by the Holy Spirit, to be applied to them.

The case of the justification and sanctification of a sinner is much like that of releasing a man who has been imprisoned for debt. When the surety's payment of the debt is by the judge judicially applied to the prisoner and sustained as a legal discharge of his debt, in the very first moment of that application the prisoner becomes legally free; he is now no longer a prisoner in point of right, though he still continues in prison till one sent by the judge applies it to him actually by opening the prison doors and setting him at liberty. In like manner, the death of Christ and His resurrection considered as the evidence of His having thereby fully satisfied divine justice, being judicially applied by God the righteous Judge to a sinner the moment he begins to believe; they have an immediate effect on him, bringing him into a relative state of happiness in justification, and to a new relation to the Lord as his Friend, Father, and God, so that he is thereby, in point of right, freed from the dominion and defilement of sin as well as he is in point of fact delivered from the guilt of it. By that application he becomes dead to sin and alive to righteousness legally, or in law. For, says our apostle, "in that He (that is, Christ) died, He died unto sin once; but in that He liveth, He liveth unto God. Likewise reckon ye also yourselves to be dead indeed unto sin, but alive unto God, through Jesus Christ our Lord" (1 Corinthians 15:56). The curse that, as a legal obstacle to sanctifying grace to him, out of the fullness of Christ his federal Head, conformable to Christ in both. Thus they have a mediate effect on him, constituting him in sanctification, really and personally holy. Hence are these consoling declarations of our apostle: "Buried with Him in baptism, wherein also you are risen with Him" (Colossians 2:12). "For by one Spirit we are all baptized into one body" (1 Corinthians 12:13). "The law of the Spirit of life in Christ Jesus hath made me free from the law of sin and death" (Romans 8:2).

Under the law there was a twofold sprinkling of the blood of the sacrifices, called the blood of the covenant. First, it was sprinkled on the altar to make atonement to Jehovah for the people; and next it was sprinkled on the people themselves, for their purification (Exodus 24:6, 8). The purifying virtue of it proceeded from its atoning virtue. Accordingly, a twofold application, or sprinkling of the blood of Christ, was thereby typified; one, for our justification and reconciliation with God, which is mentioned in Hebrews 12:22, 24. "But ye are come . . . to the blood of sprinkling, that speaketh better things than that of Abel, "namely in that it speaks for pardon, whereas that of Abel spoke for vengeance; and another for our sanctification, which is mentioned in 1 Peter 1:2 and called "sanctification of the Spirit unto obedience, and sprinkling of the blood of Jesus Christ." Now it is this sanctification that has a special relationship to Christ and to His blood and Spirit, that is to be regarded as the only true sanctification of a sinner.

Though the branches of the great promise of sanctification are manifold, spreading as wide as the all-extensive precepts of the holy law, yet the principal branches of it are these two: the promise of repentance unto life and the promise of actual grace for all holy obedience.

One principal branch of the promise of sanctification is the promise of repentance unto life; not of that legal repentance that goes before saving faith, and is common both to believers

The Promises of the Covenant of Grace

and unbelievers, but of that evangelical repentance, the seeds of which are, in our larger Catechism, said to be put into the heart in sanctification; which therefore, in the order of nature, follows saving faith and justification. "Then shall ye remember your own evil ways, and your doings that were not good, and shall loathe yourselves in your own sight, for your iniquities, and for your abominations" (Ezekiel 36:31). "All the ends of the world shall remember, and turn unto the Lord" (Psalm 22:27). "They shall look upon him whom they have pierced, and they shall mourn for him" (Zechariah 12:10).

The spiritual seed of Christ were, in consequence of their breach of the covenant of works, children of wrath even as others. The first Adam left them as so many lost sheep straying on the mountains of vanity, and ready to become the prey of that roaring lion that goes about seeking whom he may devour. All they like sheep have gone astray; they have turned every one to his own way (Isaiah 53:6). All of them had lost the way, and none of them could find it again. They had departed from the Lord, and they neither would, nor could, return to Him. They had turned to Him the back and not the face, and had become so obstinate, so inflexible, that they could not turn about to Him, nor do their duty to Him. They had lost their eyes and could not discern the way to return. To do good they had no knowledge (Jeremiah 4:22). They had lost, if I may so say, the power of their limbs; and although they had known the way they could no more return, than the Ethiopian could change his sin or the leopard his spots (Jeremiah 13:23); and withal they had lost heart to return. Having made themselves the enemies of God, and God their enemy, so that His face was set against them, they could not endure to approach Him. Consequently, though they had been able, they never would have returned; but each of them would have said, "There is no hope. No, for I have loved strangers, and after them will I go" (Jeremiah 2:25). Therefore, had not the all-compassionate Mediator interposed, they would have continued perpetually to wander. Had not the Lord Jesus taken up the desperate case, there would never have been a returning sinner of Adam's rebellious race; there would never have been a true penitent, a heart kindly softened in godly sorrow for sin, turning to God with irreconcilable hatred of all sin as sin, among the fallen race of Adam more than among the fallen angels. But, upon condition of the second Adam's walking with God, that whole way of unsinning obedience to the law as a covenant from which they had gone aside, and of His bearing their iniquities, a promise was made of granting them repentance unto life, or of gathering together in one the children of God that were scattered abroad (John 11:52). Accordingly, upon His ascension into heaven, it was found that God in performance of that promise had to the Gentiles granted repentance unto life (Acts 11:18).

Now when a man is justified by faith and personally related to God in Christ as his Friend, Father, and God, he, according to that promise, is sanctified and so brought to the exercise of evangelical repentance. Having come to Christ by faith, he comes back to God by Him in repentance (Hebrews 7:25). Hence in the Scripture it is called repentance toward God, and is the great end to which faith toward our Lord Jesus Christ is the means (Acts 20:21). Then, and never till then, it is that the heart is set on, in the exercise of that true, that evangelical repentance, which is acceptable to God through Jesus Christ. "I," said Jehovah, "will establish My covenant with thee . . . that thou mayest remember, and be confounded, and never open thy mouth any more because of thy shame, when I am pacified toward thee for all that thou hast done" (Ezekiel 16:62, 63). And again, "Then will I sprinkle clean water upon you, and ye shall be clean... I will take away the stony heart out of your flesh, and I will give you an heart of flesh... And ye shall be My people, and I will be your God... Then shall ye remember your own evil ways, and your doings that were not good, and shall loathe yourselves in your own sight" (Ezekiel 36:25, 26, 28, 31). For then it is that the infinite loveliness and love of God to the soul, which before lay concealed, shine forth more or less brightly and, being discerned by the eye of faith, warm the heart with love to God in return. "We love Him," said an apostle, "because He first loved us" (1 John 4:19).

This marvelous love shed abroad, and warm on the heart, melts it down into the exercise of true repentance as it did in that instance of the woman who, being forgiven much, loved much, and showed her love by washing her Savior's feet with her tears, and wiping them with the hairs of her head (Luke 7:38, 47). The hard heart is then laid, as it were, on the soft bed of the free grace and redeeming love of God in Christ; and the word of the law, inlaid with that of the gospel, falls upon it, saying, "Break, for the Lord is merciful. Rent your heart... and turn unto the Lord your God; for He is gracious and merciful, slow to anger, and of great kindness" (Joel 2:13). This, like a hammer, breaks the rock in pieces. The man, as was shown above, being renewed in the whole man, and brought into a state of death to sin and of life to righteousness, his new nature reveals itself in an ingenuous and entire turning from all sin to the Lord his God. By faith, he turns to God in Christ as his portion wherein he chooses to rest; by repentance, he turns to Him as his Lord or Master whom he resolves to serve. He turns not from one sin to another (Hosea 7:16), but from all sin to God. He turns from all sin, not merely in life and behavior, but in heart and affection. He returns, with self-loathing and blushing and tears, to his place and duty in the family of his reconciled

Father. His heart is filled not only with shame and sorrow for his having offended such a gracious and merciful God by his sin, but with universal and irreconcilable hatred of sin. He hates it not only as a hurtful thing that would destroy him, but as a filthy, loathsome thing that defiles him. He loathes it as the abominable thing that God hates, as the very opposite of the spotless holiness of Jehovah expressed in His law, and as the only deformity of the immortal soul. He also loathes himself for it, condemns himself, smites on his thigh as if he would break the limbs by which he walked on in it, and smites on his breast as if he would bruise the heart out of which it proceeds (Jeremiah 31:18, 19; Luke 15:21 and 18:13). In a few words, he returns to the love of God, and to his duty to Him; and that with full purpose of and endeavor after new obedience; with a heart inclined to keep the statutes of the Lord always, even to the end; and filled with carefulness in the practice of good works, with vehement desire after them, and with zeal for the acceptable performance of them (2 Corinthians 7:11).

The other principal branch of the promise of sanctification is the promise of actual grace, or of seasonable supplies of grace for all holy obedience. "I," said Jehovah, "will strengthen them in the Lord, and they shall walk up and down in His name" (Zechariah 10:12). "I will cause you to walk in My statutes, and ye shall keep My judgments and do them" (Ezekiel 36:27). God had planted the first Adam, a noble vine, wholly a right seed. He had made him, as it were, a green tree full of sap for producing fruits of righteousness. But by violating the covenant of life he and all his posterity in him withered and died under the curse; so that no fruits of holiness could be any more expected from them. But the last Adam, having engaged His heart to satisfy divine justice by enduring the awful curse, a promise of raising them up again to walk in newness of life was thereupon made; and it is performed partly in the habitual sanctification of believers, or their being renewed in the whole man immediately upon their vital union with Christ. For, though sanctification does, in order of nature, follow justification, and a saving relationship to God as a Friend, Father, and God, yet, in the order of time, it is as early as these are. At the same instant in which a sinner is justified, he begins to be sanctified. But even though believers are habitually sanctified, or have the habits of grace by the Holy Spirit infused into them, still they are not able merely upon that stock, or in the strength of those habits that they have already received, to produce any fruits of true holiness. They cannot otherwise be active in new or spiritual obedience than by receiving for that purpose new and continued supplies of actual grace. Of themselves, as our blessed Lord teaches, they, even they, renewed as they are, can do nothing (John 15:4, 5). And the Apostle Paul, though holy in a very eminent degree, yet makes, in his own name and in that of all other saints, this humble acknowledgment: "Not that we are sufficient of ourselves to think anything as of ourselves, but our sufficiency is of God" (2 Corinthians 3:5); for, as he says in another epistle, "it is God which worketh in us both to will and to do" (Philippians 3:13). This is not more wonderful in the economy of grace than it is in that of nature; that good seed, though sown in the most fruitful soil, yet cannot spring up or produce fruit without fructifying influences from the heavens; or that though we have a natural power of motion, yet we cannot actually move so much as a finger without a common providential influence from God, in (or by) whom we live and move, as well as have our being (Acts 17:28). Accordingly the promise, as was said, is a promise not only of habitual, but of actual sanctification; a promise of actual grace and strength for acts of holy obedience; and when it is fulfilled to a believer, he is enabled to perform obedience acceptably in every act of dying to sin and of living to righteousness.

Such a sufficient allowance of grace is thus made and secured in the covenant for believers as renders it possible for them, even in this world, acceptably to perform obedience to the moral law as the law of Christ, and that in all the parts of it; so that no corruption in their heart is so strong but they may get it acceptably mortified; no duty is so difficult but they may get it acceptably performed; and no affliction of body, or even of soul, is so heavy but they may get it acceptably endured. If it had not been so, the Lord Jesus would not have made their doing whatsoever He commands the distinguishing character of His friends (John 15:14). The Apostle Paul indeed denies that we are sufficient of ourselves; but at the same time he affirms that our sufficiency is of God (2 Corinthians 3:5). This the Lord Himself taught him in his own case: "My grace is sufficient for thee; for My strength is made perfect in weakness" (2 Corinthians 12:9). And truly if it were not so the yoke of Christ could not be easy nor His burden light (Matthew 11:30); but should be, like the yoke and burden of the law as a covenant, grievous to be borne. But His commandments are not grievous (1 John 5:3). Epaphras was not mistaken when he supposed and even prayed that the believers at Colossae might stand complete in all the will of God (Colossians 4:12). Nor was it a proud or empty boast that the Apostle Paul made when he said, "I can do all things through Christ which strengtheneth me" (Philippians 4:13).

What has now been advanced is nowise inconsistent with the doctrine of the imperfection of the saint's obedience in this world; which, as it is fully evident from the holy Scriptures, has also an additional testimony to its truth in the experience of all to whom it is given spiritually to discern the holiness of Jehovah, the spirituality of His law, and the depravity of their own

The Promises of the Covenant of Grace

heart. But I believe that this doctrine, as several other doctrines of Scripture are, is, through the cunning artifices of Satan, a stumbling block to many because they do not advert to the sufficient allowance of grace made in the promises of the covenant; and that by this means many sinners are snared, and the hands of many saints weakened in the practice of holiness.

To break that snare, and to set the matter in a clear point of view, the following things are carefully to be distinguished:

We must distinguish between performing obedience perfectly and performing it acceptably. No man is able in this world to perform obedience perfectly (Philippians 3:12); but every true Christian is enabled to perform it acceptably. "He that feareth Him, and worketh righteousness, is accepted with Him" (Acts 10:35). In confounding these a snare is laid. The sinner who is hardened through the deceitfulness of sin says, "There is none who performs obedience perfectly; and I am sure I do many things, though not all things that are commanded." Now that the real Christian does not perform obedience perfectly is indeed true; but that he does not perform it acceptably, as is the case of the secure and crafty sinner whose obedience is not universal, and therefore not sincere, is altogether false. They who are masters of families know well how to make this distinction in their domestic affairs. If a servant reveals a real and habitual willingness to obey the commands of his master, he will accept his work, though it is not done in every point as he would have it to be. In like manner, if there is first a willing mind, discovered by sincere endeavors to please the Lord, it is, for the sake of Christ, accepted according to what that man has (2 Corinthians 8:12). But if a servant will entirely neglect to put his hand to a piece of work which he is commanded to do, because he cannot in every respect so do it as his master would have it done, this is justly counted a contempt of his master's authority. And what other account can sinners suppose will be made in heaven of their conduct in instances of unquestionable duty that they entirely neglect, and of known sin in which they freely indulge themselves?

We must also distinguish between yielding obedience in all the parts of it and in all the degrees of those parts. The latter, indeed, no man is in this world able to do (Ecclesiastes 7:20); the former, every true Christian may do, yea, and as far as those parts are known to him actually does (James 3:2). By confounding these a snare is laid for the unwary. "The very best of men," says the crafty sinner, "do, in many things, come short of the obedience required of them, and so indeed do I." Now, that the saints come short of the highest degrees of every part of obedience required of them is indeed true; but that they come short of any of the parts themselves, so far as these are known to them, which is the case of the artful sinner, seeking a pretext here for his sin, is false. In this, the least of the saints distinguish themselves from the most splendid of hypocrites, as David showed himself to be of another spirit than Saul by fulfilling all the will of God in the several parts of it, which Saul did not do (Acts 13:22). It is here as it is in the case of a family consisting of pliable children and of stubborn servants: the master of the family prescribes different pieces of work to be done by them all. His adult children, who have attained perfect skill in their employment, do them all exactly to his mind; and thus the saints in heaven obey. His younger children, who are but learning to work, do, from regard to their father's command, put their hand indeed to every one of them, but they can do none of them exactly right; and thus it is with the saints on earth. His refractory servants put their hand to some, but quite neglect others of them; and this is the way of the wicked and slothful servant who seeks shelter here for his indolence and partiality in obedience.

Once more, we ought carefully to distinguish between ability in ourselves for performing acceptably all the parts of obedience and strength for that purpose in Christ to be derived by faith. Neither sinners nor saints have the one (Romans 5:6; 2 Corinthians 3:5), but all true believers have the other. They have all their strength in Christ Jesus their Covenant-head; for, says our apostle, "Ye are complete in Him, which is the head of all principality and power" (Colossians 2:10). And again, "I can do all things through Christ which strengtheneth me" (Philippians 4:13). This ability for performing acceptably every part of duty is offered to all who hear the gospel; so that whosoever will may warrantably take and use it (Matthew 11:28, 29). When a considerate master orders his servant to go and do a particular piece of work, it will not excuse the servant's neglect of it that he had not instruments wherewith to do it; for he will reckon that his ordering of him to do the work implied that he allowed him the instruments without which it could not be done, and that he ought to have asked them from him. Here also lies a destructive snare to many. We of ourselves, say they, can do nothing; and so the slothful sinner hides his hand in his bosom and attempts to do nothing, but having laid his head on his downy pillow sleeps to death on the bed of carnal ease and security. Oh, that men would but open their eyes and see how destructive this piece of deceit is! No man will be able hereby to excuse his not performing holy obedience, and that in all its parts.

On the contrary, this conduct of his will subject him to a twofold guilt—one, of neglecting that which he was commanded to do, and another, of despising the grace offered to him to enable him to perform it acceptably. And so he shall be justly condemned, not because he could not, but because he would not accept grace to enable him to obey.

In the covenant of works only perfect obedience could be accepted; and suitable provision of strength for such obedience was made in it to our first parents. God made man upright, able perfectly to obey the law. Accordingly, the holy law justly requires perfection of obedience still upon the ground of that provision that was originally made for the same, though it is now lost, seeing it was lost by man's own fault. But in the covenant of grace, which is adapted to our fallen condition, sincere obedience, performed by one already justified, may, notwithstanding the imperfections that attend it, be graciously accepted. Accordingly, provision is therein made of such a sufficiency of grace that every part of duty required of believers may thereby, even in this world, be done—though not indeed as it should be done, yet so as it may be accepted; accepted, I say, not indeed for its own sake, nor yet for the sake of the worker, but only for the sake of Christ Jesus. In His name it is required to be done; and it is presented as a spiritual sacrifice, acceptable to God by Him (1 Peter 2:5). Still, however, that sufficiency of grace for acceptable obedience is not lodged in believers themselves, but in the last Adam their federal Head, in whom they have it, as the branches have a sufficiency of vital juice in the vine for causing them to yield fruit in their season. "Surely, shall one say, In the Lord have I righteousness and strength" (Isaiah 14:24). "Thou, therefore, my son, be strong in the grace that is in Christ Jesus" (2 Timothy 2:1). They derive and receive it into their heart by the confidence of faith, embracing the promise. "Blessed is the man that trusteth in the Lord, and whose hope the Lord is; for he shall be as a tree planted by the waters" (Jeremiah 17:7, 8). "The Lord is my strength and my shield; my heart trusted in Him, and I am helped" (Psalm 28:7). Indeed, every command of the Lord Jesus, in His administration of this covenant, supposes an allowance of grace sufficient for enabling believers to yield obedience to it in an acceptable manner. A declaration and grant of grace, accordingly, stand on the front of the Ten Commandments. "I am the Lord thy God . . . Thou shalt have no other gods before Me" (Exodus 20:2, 3). If the law, without the gospel, came to us, we might indeed have some excuse to offer for not doing what we are commanded to do; yet not so powerful, but that it would be easily overthrown, as in the case of the heathens (Romans 2:12). But since, along with the law requiring obedience, the gospel also comes to us, showing us how we may be enabled acceptably to obey the law, and containing a free offer to us of ability on Christ Jesus for that purpose, we are inexcusable if we do not obey. The plea of the wicked and slothful servant is rejected; and he is justly condemned, not merely for omitting to obey, but for refusing to accept the strength that is graciously offered him to enable him to obey.

Seeing then that God has not given to His professing people the command of sanctification to be obeyed, without the promise of sanctification to be believed; that He has not said, "Wash ye, make you clean," without saying at the same time, "I will sprinkle clean water upon you, and ye shall be clean" (Ezekiel 36:25), no man has ground to imagine that he so much as attempts to comply with the true design of the command of sanctification if he does not first believe and embrace the promise of it. He who tries, with the niter and soap of his own faithless endeavors, to wash himself clean mistakes the true intent of the command of sanctification as it stands in sacred Scripture; and that, as much as the command of a considerate master would be mistaken by his imprudent servant who, should, without taking spade or any other instrument proper to dig with, try to dig in it with his fingers.

Let us then cordially and constantly believe with application the great promise of sanctification exhibited to us in the gospel that we may be able and willing to yield acceptable obedience to the commandments of the law; for where there is no expectation of grace to enable us to perform acceptably our duty, there can be no suitable endeavors to perform it. If the heart is without hope of sufficient supplies of strength for that purpose, the hands will hang down, the knees will become feeble; and the consequence inevitably must be either a ceasing from the duty altogether or else such a very faint performance of it as will be unacceptable to God. On the contrary, the lively faith of that promise will, in the hand of the Holy Spirit, remove the pretenses of sloth, will quicken to all holy obedience, and will derive strength for every good work. "Having therefore these promises, dearly beloved, let us cleanse ourselves from all filthiness of the flesh and spirit, perfecting holiness in the fear of God" (2 Corinthians 7:1).

I have only further to observe, concerning the promise of sanctification, that it is closely connected with or grafted on the great promise made to Christ of His being Himself to be filled in the human nature with an immeasurable fullness of the Holy Spirit and of His resurrection from the dead. It is grafted, I say, on the promise made to Him of an immeasurable fullness of the Holy Spirit. It was, in the covenant, promised to Him that the Spirit of Jehovah should rest upon Him, etc. (Isaiah 11:2, 3). For it pleased the Father that in Him, as the Covenant-head of His redeemed, should all fullness dwell (Colossians 1:19). It is by grace received out of His fullness that believers are, according to the promise, so sanctified as to be conformed to His moral image, and so to bear the image of the heavenly. It is also grafted on the promise made to Him of a glorious resurrection from the grave. The conditions of life in the covenant having been fulfilled by Him, He as the glorious Head of the body was according to that promise brought again from the dead and lives unto God, death having no more dominion over Him. And it is in virtue hereof that His mystical members also are brought again to repentance from dead works and to newness of life. Hence they are said to be begotten again to a lively hope by the resurrection of Jesus Christ from the dead (1 Peter 1:3) inasmuch as they are risen with Him (Colossians 3:1) to walk in newness of life (Romans 6:4, 5) according to this promise: "Thy dead men shall live, together with my dead body shall they arise . . . and the earth shall cast out the dead" (Isaiah 26:19); first, the blessed Head Jesus Christ, the first-born from the dead, and, next, the members of His mystical body after Him in their order. In the third day, He will raise us up, and we shall live in His sight (Hosea 6:2). So much for the promise of sanctification.

I proceed now to observe that the promise of eternal life to the elect comprehends the promise of spiritual comfort to them while they continue to pass through this valley of tears.

By spiritual comfort is meant that spiritual and supernatural consolation, that invigorating, enlivening, enlarging or cheering of the heart of an exercised Christian by the Spirit of Christ, that disposes him to joy in God through our Lord Jesus Christ, and with holy courage to press toward more resemblance to Christ, and more communion with Him. It does not consist in rapture or ecstasy, but in that refreshing and consoling delight of soul that, under the influences of the Holy Spirit, arises from the consideration of what God in Christ is to him who believes, of what He has done for him, and of what He hath promised still to do in him and to him (2 Corinthians 1:4, 5). The promise hereof is accordingly a leading branch of the promise of eternal life. It is therefore called everlasting consolation (2 Thessalonians 2:16). To live comfortably is indeed to live. Reprobate souls in hell do exist, and shall continue through all eternity to exist; but they are never said in Scripture to live because they are far from existing comfortably. Spiritual consolation, then, is spiritual life in enjoyment. Everlasting consolation, so far as attained in this world, is the begun and progressive enjoyment of justification, of a new and saving relationship to God in Christ as one's Friend, Father, and God, and of sanctification (Romans 5:1, 2, 11). It is one of the constituent parts of the fruit of the Spirit in every sanctified soul. The fruit of the Spirit, says the Apostle Paul, is love, joy, peace, etc. (Galatians 5:22). While the Lord Jesus is, according to the covenant, the great dispenser of comfort to him who trusts in Him, and is therefore called the Consolation of Israel, the Holy Spirit, as residing in the believer, is the immediate Author of it, and is for that reason called the Comforter (John 14:16, 26). By His effectual application of the Word, of the righteousness, and of the fullness of Christ to the soul of the believer, He fills him with the joy of faith, with joy and peace in believing, and even with joy unspeakable and full of glory.

The elect of God, by their breach of covenant in the first Adam, as well as by their other innumerable transgressions, forfeited all their comfort and were justly condemned to everlasting sorrow as a part of the punishment due for their disobedience.

The Lord the righteous Judge was to have rendered to them, in common with other sinners, indignation and wrath, tribulation and anguish (Romans 2:8, 9). He was to have given them, while they continued in this world, trouble and anguish, a trembling heart, and failing of eyes, and sorrow of mind; and then to have cast them into outer darkness; where, through all eternity, there would be weeping and gnashing of teeth (Matthew 8:12). But on the ground of Christ the second Adam's having undertaken to bear their griefs and carry their sorrows, a promise of everlasting consolation was made for them; and as soon as by faith they are united to Him it begins to be made good to them. Jehovah the God of all comfort has left on record these, among His other promise to them: "The Lord shall comfort Zion; He will comfort all her waste places" (Isaiah 51:3). "I, even I, am He that comforteth you" (Isaiah 51:12). "I will lead him also, and will restore comforts unto him, and to his mourners" (Isaiah 57:18). "As one whom his mother comforteth, so will I comfort you; and ye shall be comforted in Jerusalem" (Isaiah 66:13). "I will turn their mourning into joy, and will comfort them, and make them rejoice from their sorrow" (Jeremiah 31:13). "I will bring her into the wilderness, and speak comfortably unto her" (Hosea 2:14).

This consolation the believer receives by the exercise of faith, feasting on Christ in the promise. The God of hope fills Him with all joy and peace in believing (Romans 15:13). When he is enabled to trust in the Lord Jesus for all his salvation, and especially for all necessary comfort, and to say, "The Lord my God will enlighten my darkness" (Psalm 18:28); "Thou wilt comfort me on every side" (Psalm 71:21); it will be unto him according to his faith. It comforts his heart to be enabled to trust that Christ, according to the promises, saves and will save him; and besides, the renewed exercise of confidence in Him for all necessary comfort in the performance of duty is the appointed means of deriving fresh supplies of it from His fullness into the soul (Psalm 28:7). The way to grow in spiritual consolation is by the exercise of direct, unsuspecting confidence in Christ, the glorious dispenser of it, to take it fresh out of the fountain. If the believer were more willing than he is to take in this manner spiritual comfort; he should have more of it and be more established in it. If he were more exercised than he is in forsaking the love and the practice of every sin he should soon attain more communion with the Holy Spirit in His consoling influences. Any sin persisted in for a season, though it should not be a known sin, will be as a worm at the root of spiritual comfort.

That comfort of joy in the Holy Ghost that is genuine is distinguished from the counterfeit joy of hypocrites by its enlivening (Nehemiah 8:10), enlarging (Psalm 119:32), humbling (Job 42:5, 6), and sanctifying influence on the heart (2 Corinthians 3:18). The joy of hypocrites, on the other hand, has effects entirely the reverse of these. It lulls the soul asleep in carnal security and inspires it with courage to continue in the love and practice of some secret iniquity. Whereas true comfort fills the heart with courage in its opposition to all sin, and with fervent zeal for the glory of God, the honor of Christ, the diffusion of gospel-knowledge, and the practice of universal holiness.

Now, the promise of spiritual comfort to the elect of God seems to be grafted on the promise of Christ the last Adam's being made full of joy with the countenance of His eternal Father. "Thou shalt make me full of joy with thy countenance" (Acts 2:28). In fulfilling that promise to Him, God the Father, His covenant-God, anointed Him with the oil of gladness above His fellows (Psalm 45:7). And with regard to believers, we read (Matthew 25:21) that, when according to the promise of eternal life they are exalted to the perfection of spiritual joy in the mansions of glory, they enter into the joy of their Lord; so that the promise of everlasting consolation is accomplished to them by admitting them to a perfect and everlasting participation of His joy as their covenant-head.

The promise of eternal life to the elect comprehends also the promise of perseverance in grace, a privilege to be conferred on all the spiritual seed of Christ; so that being once brought, in their justification, saving relationship to God, sanctification, and spiritual comfort, into a state of grace, they shall never be left to fall away from it, either totally or finally. That great promise, Jehovah thus expresses: "I will make an everlasting covenant with them, that I will not turn away from the to do them good; but I will put My fear in their hearts that they shall not depart from Me" (Jeremiah 32:40). Here, they are on both sides secured against falling away. Jehovah promises on the one hand that He will not turn away from them to do them good and, on the other, that He will put His fear so in their hearts that they shall not depart from Him. Thus He engages for them as well as for Himself. Glorious engagement! Encouraging promise! A promise infinitely more precious than all the treasures of this world. That the inestimable benefit here promised is comprised in the promise of eternal life is evident from an apostle's quoting from Habakkuk 3:4 a promise of that life, to prove that justified persons are not of them who draw back unto perdition. "Now the just by faith, shall live" (Hebrews 10:38). So great are the advantages that Satan has against the saints, and so manifold are the snares that are laid for them in this present evil world; so corrupt, so inconstant, so deceitful are the hearts of the holiest of them while here below, and so very tender is the bud of grace that is implanted in them, that if their perseverance, instead of having been secured by promise in the covenant, had been made a proper condition of the covenant, and so been left to the determination of their own will, they would no more have been able to preserve the habit of grace alive in their heart than to keep a spark of fire alive in the midst of a mighty ocean. In that case they might all have drawn back to perdition; and the second Adam, notwithstanding His having fulfilled all righteousness to merit for them eternal life, might have to all eternity remained a Prophet without disciples, a King without subjects, a Brother without brethren, and a Head without members. But the honor of the great Redeemer and the redemption of His elect seed were objects too important to be exposed to such uncertainty. That perseverance in a state of innocence in which the first Adam failed, and which was made a condition of the covenant of grace, the second Adam as the Representative of His people, undertook to finish; upon which was made the promise that they should persevere in a state of holiness to the end. Accordingly, by His having persevered to the end in a course of perfect obedience to the law as their Surety, He merited for them this inestimable blessing. The perseverance of the second Adam, therefore, in His obedience to the law as a covenant, is the legal ground on which, in virtue of the faithfulness of Jehovah, pledged in the promise the perseverance in grace of the saints, is infallibly secured to them.

This great promise begins to be performed to them as soon as they are united to Jesus Christ; and it continues to be performed till their death, when their souls, made perfect in holiness, are received up into glory; yea, properly speaking, death is not the last, but as it were the middle term of their perseverance; for after death the promise of it continues to be performed far more gloriously than even before. Upon their union with the second Adam, and communion with Him in that righteousness in which He persevered till it was finished, they are confirmed in their justification in their saving relationship to God, in their sanctification, and in their spiritual consolation, so that they cannot fall away; just as the natural posterity of the first Adam would, upon his having persevered in fulfilling the condition of the first covenant till it had been completely fulfilled, have been confirmed in holiness and happiness. As then the natural seed of the first Adam, in the case now reposed, would have been infallibly confirmed in a state of holiness, as the reward of his continued obedience; so the spiritual seed of the last Adam are so confirmed as to persevere in grace, and that as the reward of his continued and finished obedience.

Now of the praise of the saint's perseverance in grace, there are two leading branches.

The first branch is a promise that continued influences of grace shall be afforded to each of them. "I the Lord do keep it, I will water it every moment" (Isaiah 27:3). Their stock of inherent grace would soon fail if they were left to live upon it without fresh supplies continually coming in to them from the fullness of Christ (John 15:5, 6; Luke 22:32). Adam in his innocent state had a far larger stock of inherent grace than any of the saints in this world has and yet he lost it all. But the grace of Christ in His spiritual seed cannot be lost because, according to the promise, continued influences of it are secured for them and conferred on them. Preserving influences of grace are hereby secured for them and continue to be imparted to them by which the grace formerly given them is kept from languishing so as to die out of their heart. While they are sanctified by God the Father, they are preserved in Jesus Christ (Jude 1) and are kept by the power of God through faith, unto salvation (1 Peter 1:5). Strengthening influences also continue to be communicated to them by which the grace preserved is strengthened, and so increased as gradually to rise superior to corruption from within and to temptation from without. "They shall revive as the corn, and grow as the vine" (Hosea 14:7). Exciting influences likewise continue to be conferred on them by which the grace preserved and strengthened is, in every time of need, stirred up to exercise, or when they are performing duty put in motion toward its infinitely glorious Object (Ezekiel 36:27; John 16:13, 14). Thus their faith is never suffered totally to fail, but is preserved, strengthened, and excited to exercise, and all the other graces of the Spirit with it and by means of it. All this is effected by new and continued supplies of grace communicated to them by the Spirit from Christ their Head of in fluencies, from whom all the body, by joints and bands, having nourishment ministered and knit together increases with the increase of God (Colossians 2:19).

The other leading branch of the promise of their perseverance is a promise of the continued pardon of the sins that they daily commit, by which emergent grounds of the Lord's pleading a controversy with them are from time to time so done away that a total rupture is prevented. "I," said Jehovah, "will be merciful to their unrighteousness" (Hebrews 8:12). "I will pardon all their iniquities" (Jeremiah 33:8). Though justified persons have no need of any new formal act of pardon with regard to their state, but only of a manifestation or intimation of their former pardon to their conscience (since the pardon given them in their justification is perfect and irrevocable (John 13:10), though by their later sins they often lose sight of it), yet with respect to their daily behavior they have continual need of one formal act of pardon after another because they are daily, alas, incurring new guilt. He that is washed, said our Savior, needs not save to wash his feet, but is clean every whit (John 13:10). For though the sins of them who are justified in the sight of God cannot expose them any more to the guilt of eternal wrath, nevertheless they do bring them under the guilt of fatherly displeasure, or of that anger of God as their covenant-God and Father whom they provoke by sinning against Him (Psalm 89:30-32; Isaiah 57:17, 18). They therefore need daily thus to pray: "Our Father which art in heaven . . . forgive us our debts" (Matthew 6:9, 12), give us renewed intimations of our deliverance in justification, from the guilt of eternal wrath, and grant us also deliverance from the guilt of fatherly anger which by our iniquities we daily incur.

This continued pardon of the sins of their daily conduct is graciously conferred on them upon the renewed actings of their faith in Jesus Christ, and of their repentance toward God; yet not for their faith or repentance, but for the sake of Christ, as Jehovah their Righteousness, in like manner as their first pardon was given them (1 John 1:7). Applying, by the renewed exercise of faith, the blood of the Lamb of God anew to the heart, they are thereby constrained to the renewed exercise of true repentance. With grief, shame, and self-abhorrence, as well as with hatred of all their sins, they sincerely turn from them to God as their God in Christ. Looking anew by faith upon Him whom they have pierced, they, renewing their repentance, mourn for Him and so receive this forgiveness. For though the exercise of true repentance does not, in the order of nature, go before, but follows after the pardon of sin in justification, yet not only does faith, but repentance too, go before the renewed forgivenesses conferred on them who are already justified. Accordingly, in a passage above cited, the Apostle John says, "If we walk in the light as He is in the light . . . the blood of Jesus Christ His Son cleanseth us from all sin. If we confess our sins, He is faithful and just to forgive us our sins, and to cleanse us from all unrighteousness" (1 John 1:7, 9). The children of God are therefore enjoined to pray thus: "Our Father which art in heaven; . . . forgive us our sins; for we also forgive every one that is indebted to us" (Luke 11:2, 4); or, "Forgive us our debts, as we forgive our debtors" (Matthew 6:12), to intimate to them that they must first forgive others their trespasses if they would justly expect that God as their heavenly Father would thus forgive their own.

But it is far otherwise, with regard to the pardon that is in justification. That pardon is not the consequence but, on the contrary, the source of their forgiveness of others (Matthew 18:32, 33). Their cordial and acceptable forgiveness of others flows from true Christian love to them; and this again issues from pure love to God in Christ, which is kindled in their heart by His pardoning mercy to them, apprehended by faith (Luke 7:47; Ephesians 4:32). The reason of the difference between this pardon in justification and those renewed forgivenesses that follow, in the relation of each to true repentance, is this: unjustified persons are under the guilt of vindictive wrath, which seeks not their amendment but their destruction. Until that, therefore, is removed in justification, there can be no true amendment, no evangelical, no acceptable repentance in the heart or life of a sinner; for these, being in fact a restoration of him to eternal life, are inconsistent with his being at the same time legally doomed to everlasting destruction or eternal death. On the contrary, they who are already justified are only under the guilt of fatherly displeasure, which seeks not the destruction but the amendment of the guilty. It is therefore not taken away till after they renew the exercise of repentance, or turn in an acceptable manner from their iniquity to God; and this is the very amendment that their heavenly Father seeks by showing His displeasure against them for their sin, as is manifest in the case of David, Hezekiah, Jonah, Peter, and others of the saints.

Thus, then, are the saints made to persevere in grace. The promise of continued influences secures the preservation and the renewed exercise of their grace, especially of their faith and repentance; and the promise of continued forgiveness of sin to them, believing and repenting, secures a removal of the guilt of fatherly anger. The Spirit of Christ always dwells in them and so continues to be an inviolable bond of their spiritual union with Him; and thus residing in them, He restores, He raises them up when they fall, and so stirs up the sacred fire of grace in their heart that, for a time, lay hiden under the ashes of remaining corruption. Then they renew the exercise of their faith; they again believe with application the promise of the forgiveness of all their sins, as to the guilt of eternal wrath; and this melts down their heart into tears of evangelical repentance. They also believe the promise of the continued pardon as to the guilt of fatherly displeasure, of the sins that are the grounds of the Lord's present controversy with them; and thereby, from time to time, they receive this continued pardon. Thus are they kept, by the power and grace of a promising God, through faith unto salvation (1 Peter 1:5).

This perseverance of the saints depends not upon their own free-will, but upon the immutability of the decree of election flowing from the free and unchangeable love of God the Father; upon the efficacy of the merit and intercession of Jesus Christ; the abiding of the Spirit, and of the seed of God within them; and the nature of the covenant of grace (*Westminster Confession of Faith*: Chapter 16, Section 2).

The promise of the perseverance of the saints in grace seems to be grafted on that of Christ's perseverance in fulfilling all righteousness as their Surety. Jehovah the Father promised to Him that He would so uphold Him, and that His arm should so strengthen Him, that He should at no time fail or be discouraged (Isaiah 42:1, 4). This promise, being made to Him as the federal Head and Representative of His spiritual offspring, ensures the preservation, support, and safe conduct not only of the Head, but also of the members, and that in all their respective temptations, conflicts, and perils until they are forever set beyond the reach of danger. It appears to be grafted also on the Father's promise to Him of the perpetual security of His heavenly life. As the Covenant-head of His mystical body, He asked life of His eternal Father, and He gave it Him, even length of days forever and ever (Psalm 21:4). Hence He said to His disciples, and under them to all who should believe in Him, "Because I live, ye shall live also" (John 14:19). To the same purpose our apostle said to the believers at Colossae, "Your life is hid with Christ in God. When Christ who is our life shall appear, then shall ye also appear with Him in glory" (Colossians 3:3, 4).

In the sixth and last place, the promise of eternal life to the elect, when viewed as in this period, comprises a promise of temporal good things to be conferred on them in such measure as God shall see most proper for their good, in subservience to His own glory. This promise stands connected in the covenant with the promises of spiritual blessings. "I will also save you," said Jehovah, "from all your uncleannesses; and I will call for the corn, and will increase it, and lay no famine upon you" (Ezekiel 36:29). "I will even betroth thee unto Me in faithfulness; and thou shalt know the Lord . . . I will hear the heavens; and they shall hear the earth; and the earth shall hear the corn, and the wine, and the oil; and they shall hear Jezreel" (Hosea 2:20, 21, 22). This, though far indeed from being the main thing contained in the promissory part of the covenant, is yet such an addition thereto as the condition of the children of God while in this world renders necessary (Matthew 6:32, 33).

By the covenant of works into which God had entered with man, He made ample provision for his temporal as well as for his spiritual and eternal welfare. He invested him with a covenant-right to the creatures in the air, the earth, and the sea, and with dominion over them, granting him full authority soberly to use them, and equitably to dispose of them for his own benefit in subservience to the divine glory. That dominion over the creatures was to be possessed in subordination to Him as the sovereign Lord of all, and according to the tenor of that covenant was to be firm and irrevocable so long as he should continue in his obedience, but was to be forfeited the moment he should break the covenant (Genesis 1:28; 2:17). But man being

The Promises of the Covenant of Grace

in that honor did not continue. He violated the covenant, and so fell from his right of dominion over the creatures. He transgressed, and by transgression he forfeited his covenant-right to life itself, and to all the supports and comforts of it. In this condition, with respect to these things, are all the descendants of Adam while in their natural state Whatever portion of the necessities or comforts of life they possess, they have no covenant-right to it. All the right that they have is merely a providential, a precarious right, such as a condemned criminal has to bread and water so long as his prince pleases to have his execution delayed. This is a most uncertain, a most uncomfortable tenure. Still, however, it is so far available that they are not, strictly speaking, to be considered as violent possessors of temporal good things; they have the same right to them that they have to their forfeited life while, by the disposal of divine providence, it is permitted to remain in their possession. The very worst of men, therefore, may warrantably eat and drink and partake of the other necessaries of life; whatever Satan, in the hour of temptation, may suggest to the contrary, yea, it is their duty to do it; and they disobey the sixth commandment of the moral law, which is, "Thou shalt not kill," if they do it not.

But Christ the second Adam having engaged, in the room of His spiritual seed, fully to endure the curse, and perfectly to obey the precept of the law, a promise upon that ground was made of restoring to them their forfeited life, with all the means and comforts of it, and especially a promise of all the good things necessary for the support and convenience of their temporal life till at death they should be conveyed home to their Father's house. This promise begins to be performed to them as soon as they begin to be vitally united to the last Adam. Then, their federal relationship to the first Adam is legally dissolved. The forfeiture is taken off and a new covenant-right to the creatures is conferred on them. Hence our apostle said to the saints at Corinth, "All things are yours . . . all are yours; and ye are Christ's; and Christ is God's" (1 Corinthians 3:22, 23). This covenant-right to the creatures continues as long as they continue to have need of them; and whether it is a small portion or a great of these good things that the all-wise Administrator of the covenant bestows on them, they from that moment hold it by a new and a sure tenure; it is theirs, secured by the charter of a covenant, ordered in all things and sure.

This promise then of temporal good things is a promise that believers shall possess them, as far as their need of them shall require (Philippians 4:19); of which need not they themselves, but their infinitely wise and gracious Father is the proper Judge (Matthew 6:32). Accordingly, there are two leading branches of the promise, namely a promise of protection from all the evil things, and a promise of provision of all the good things of this life.

The first branch of it is a promise of protection from all the evil things of this life. "There shall no evil befall thee . . . for He shall give His angels charge over thee, to keep thee in all thy ways" (Psalm 91:10, 11). "The Lord shall preserve thy going out and thy coming in, from this time forth and even for evermore" (Psalm 121:8). "The same Lord that is a sun to cherish will be a shield to protect them" (Psalm 84:11). "He will be unto them a wall of fire round about, to cherish them and to keep off and frighten away their enemies" (Zechariah 2:5).

The covenant affords a broad covert for the protection of believers. "He shall cover thee with his feathers, and under His wings shalt thou trust" (Psalm 91:4). The covert of the covenant is spread out over their bodies to preserve the health and vigor of them as long as these are requisite for the purposes of the divine glory and of their own good. "Fear the Lord and depart

The Promises of the Covenant of Grace 231

from evil. It shall be health to thy navel, and marrow to thy bones" (Proverbs 3:7, 8). "My sayings . . . are life unto those that find them, and health to all their flesh" (Proverbs 4:20, 22). This covert is stretched out over their life as long as the Lord has any employment for them in this world, to preserve it safe until their work is done. In sickness they are tenderly cared for; and at the fittest time their diseases are removed and they are raised up (Psalm 41:3; 103:3, 5; Job 5:18, 19). They are preserved safe in the midst of snares, and delivered from enemies who seek their life (Psalm 41:2). Yea, even when death the last enemy rides in triumph, having by sword or pestilence or otherwise made havoc on every side of them, they are found safe under the shelter of the covenant (Psalm 91:5-7). This covert is stretched out over their reputation among men. "Thou shalt be hid from the scourge of the tongue" (Job 5:21). Either the virulent tongues of malignant persons will not reach them, or they will not be able to make the filth of reproach stick to them, or if they will be permitted to make it stick for a time, the covert of the covenant will wipe it all off at length so that their righteousness shall be brought forth as the light, and their judgment as the noon-day (Psalm 37:6). It is also stretched out over their habitations. "Neither shall any plague come nigh thy dwelling" (Psalm 91:10). It surrounds their substance too, making a hedge about all that they have on every side (Job 1:10). Yea, and there is a lap of it to spread over their widows and children when they themselves are gone. "Leave thy fatherless children, I will preserve them alive and let thy widows trust in Me" (Jeremiah 49:11).

The last branch of it is a promise of provision, or of a supply of all the good things necessary for the life that now is; and of these, an issuing forth from redeeming mercy through the channel of the everlasting covenant. "They that seek the Lord shall not want of any good thing" (Psalm 34:10). Having this promise, the saints, whatever the straits be into which they are at any time brought, may confidently trust in their covenant-God for a suitable supply of the good things of this life. Food for their bodies is hereby secured to them; and when this is by faith perceived, it cannot fail, however small as to quantity, or mean as to quality, their provision is, to give it the sweetest relish. They may not indeed be feasted, but they shall be fed. "Verily thou shalt be fed" (Psalm 37:3). "They shall be fed to the full; they shall be satisfied" (Joel 2:26); and even days of amine will not hinder this their satisfaction. In the days of famine they shall be satisfied (Psalm 37:19). His bread shall be given him; his waters shall be sure (Isaiah 33:16). It is not here said how much or how little of each will be afforded but, as it is in the original, his bread shall be given him; that precise quantity and quality of bread which infinite wisdom and love see fittest for him, will be afforded him. His water, that water which in the making of the covenant was, by unbounded wisdom and liberality, set apart for him shall be sure. That portion, be it ever so great or ever so small, of the good things of this life that his gracious Father, according to the promise, affords him, is at the time not only good but best for him. Nothing of the kind could, at that time, be so conducive to his real welfare. As sleep also is requisite to refresh their bodies, it is secured for them by promise. "Thou shalt lie down, and thy sleep shall be sweet" (Proverbs 3:24). "He giveth his beloved sleep" (Psalm 127:2). They need clothing, and it likewise is promised. "If God so clothe the grass of the field, which today is, and tomorrow is cast into the oven; shall he not much more clothe you, O ye of little faith?" (Matthew 6:30) Having by covenant made to them a new grant of life which is more than meat, and of a body which is more than raiment (Matthew 6:25) He will not deny them the less, especially since

The Promises of the Covenant of Grace

these are necessary for the support of the greater. Hence our first parents, after the fall, having accepted the promise of life, had, with that new grant of it, food and clothing bestowed on them (Genesis 3:15, 18, 21). In few words, a blessing on the works of their hands and success in their lawful callings are by promise secured to them (Isaiah 65:21-23). Not only will their covenant-God give them that which is good, but He will withhold no good thing from them (Psalm 84:11).

Now, this promise seems to be grafted on the promise made to Christ Himself of preservation during His state of humiliation (Isaiah 49:8), and likewise on that of His inheriting all things. He is His Father's first-born (Psalm 89:21) for He has appointed Him heir of all things (Hebrews 1:2) and has appointed them who are united to Him to be joint heirs with Him, and so to inherit also all things (Revelation 21:7). That estate and honor which the first Adam, by his violation of the covenant of works, had forfeited for himself and his family were, in the covenant of grace, made over by promise to Christ the second Adam, for Himself and His spiritual seed upon condition of His surety-righteousness. Accordingly, no sooner was that consummate righteousness fulfilled than the whole ancient estate of the family, together with all the honors belonging to it, was recovered. The original dominion over the creatures was restored in the person of the second Adam; and all His spiritual offspring participate of it in Him. This the Holy Spirit teaches in the 8th Psalm: "What is man that Thou art mindful of him? And the Son of man, that Thou visitest him? For Thou hast made him a little lower than the angels, and hast crowned him with glory and honor. Thou madest him to have dominion over the works of Thy hands; Thou hast put all things under his feet; all sheep and oxen, yea, and the beasts of the field; the fowl of the air, and the fish of the sea, and whatsoever passeth through the paths of the seas."

Here we imagine the sacred writer to be setting forth the pre-eminence of man in general above the rest of the creation, or the honorable state of the first Adam, and all mankind in him, at his creation; but in Hebrews 2:6-8 we are informed that the supremacy conferred on the second Adam over all the creatures in heaven and earth, to the participation of which He admits His mystical members is the subject there treated of. Accordingly, when Abraham had the promise that he should be heir of the world, we are informed that he had it through the righteousness of faith (Romans 4:13). But Abraham was a type of Messiah, and at the same time the father of all them that believe, who are all blessed with him (Romans 4:11). This promise, therefore, was primarily to Christ through the righteousness fulfilled by Him, and secondarily to believers through the same righteousness applied by faith. As in virtue of the promise that He should be heir of all things, made to Him as the last Adam, He had a covenant-right to all things in heaven and earth; so in virtue of the promise that they should be joint heirs with Him, believers have a covenant-right with Him to all temporal good things.

SECTION 5. Of the Promise of Eternal Life as Performed to the Elect from DEATH Throughout ETERNITY.

Of the promise of eternal life to the elect, as accomplished to them from the moment of their death through all eternity, there are three principal branches: first, the promise of a blessed death; next, of an honorable judgment at the last day; and, last, of everlasting blessedness in the heavenly world.

The first principal branch of it is the promise of a blessed, a happy death, to the dying believer. This comprises:

1. A promise of disarming death of its sting. It comprehends a promise of disarming death to the dying saint so that it shall be utterly unable to give him a hostile or a destructive stroke. "O death, I will be thy plagues" (Hosea 13:14). This consoling promise He performs to the believer by disarming to him death of its sting. When sin, by the first Adam, entered into the world, death quickly followed. Sin armed death with an empoisoning sting by which it could kill at once both the soul and the body of the sinner. The righteous law, with its dreadful curse, fixed that sting in the hand of death having first so sharpened it that it could not fail of doing execution. But Christ the second Adam, having undertaken to endure, in the room of His people the curse of the law, and so to die for them, a promise of disarming death to them was thereupon made; for since the condescending Surety endured the pains of death armed with its sting it behooved the principal to be set free from the obligation of suffering the same in their own persons. Thus the covenant secures believers from receiving the smallest hurt by the stroke of death. Death strikes them indeed, but it can give them no stroke except one that is friendly and beneficial to them. It does strike, but it cannot sting them. Some have observed that when the bee strikes its sting into a dead body it still retains it; but when it thrusts it into a living body it often leaves and loses it. So death, thrusting its sting into Christ's body, in which there was no spiritual death, left and lost it there with respect to his mystical members.

2. It includes a promise that death thus deprived of its sting shall be sanctified and sweetened to the dying believer. Death to believers is removed from the curse of the covenant of works to the promise of the covenant of grace; and as its place is changed so is its nature. So much is its nature altered by being matter of promise to the saints that it is become quite a new and another

thing to them. It is so sanctified to them as to be a mean of introducing them into the perfection of holiness and happiness; so changed as to be of excellent use to them, affording them a free and a quick passage to everlasting rest in the full enjoyment of Jehovah, Father, Son, and Holy Spirit. As death entered into the world by sin, so sin goes out from the world of the elect by death. Sin entered into them at the union of their souls with their bodies; and it will be finally cast out of them at the dissolution of that union. Hence death is, in Scripture, represented as gain to the saints and as such is found in the inventory of their treasure. "All things," said our apostle, "are yours, whether . . . life, or death, or things present, or things to come; all are yours" (1 Corinthians 3:21, 22). Hence also are these words of the same holy apostle: "I am in a strait between two, having a desire to depart, and to be with Christ, which is far better" (Philippians 1:23). And again, "For we know that if our earthly house of this tabernacle were dissolved, we have a building of God, an house not made with hands, eternal in the heavens" (2 Corinthians 5:1). The covenant of grace did not make death, but found it in the world as the just punishment of breaking the covenant of life; and from being an old enemy as it was, the second Adam did, according to that covenant, convert it into a new servant to Himself and His people. It accordingly serves the unspeakably important purpose of introducing them into their heavenly Father's house. And indeed, it is nowise unsuitable, either to their present state or to their future prospects, to leave this evil world by dying; and so to leave it not because they are legally summoned, but because they are graciously invited; not because they must, but because they desire to depart and to be with Christ.

3. It comprehends a promise that death to the believer shall in the resurrection be finally destroyed: "O death," said Jehovah,

"I will be thy plagues; O grave, I will be thy destruction" (Hosea 13:14). When death had by sin entered into the world, then followed the grave as death's attendant to keep fast his prisoners for him till the judgment of the great day. This office the grave performs for death in the case of all who die under the guilt and dominion of sin. But Christ the second Adam, in the covenant of grace, undertook to go down instead of His people, as death's prisoner, into the grave, and there to lie till all their debt to divine justice should be completely discharged; upon which a promise was made of a glorious resurrection to them, by which they should at the last day be fully and forever set beyond the reach of death. Then shall be brought to pass the saying that is written, "Death is swallowed up in victory." And then will all the redeemed, with inconceivable triumph, sing, "O death, where is thy sting? O grave, where is thy victory" (1 Corinthians 15:54, 55)? Thus the covenant ensures the fashioning anew of their dissolved bodies, the returning of their departed spirits into them, and their coming forth from their graves incorruptible, glorious, spiritual and immortal (1 Corinthians 15:42-44). In the faith of this, the dying believer may, with holy composure and comfort, consider the grave as a place of retreat or a bed of repose, out of which he shall after a while come forth with ineffable transports of joy.

Now this promise to the saints of a blessed death, or of death disarmed of its sting of death sanctified, and of death finally destroyed, appears to be grafted, first, on the promise of safety in and of victory over death, made to Christ Himself. "He," said Jehovah the Father, "will swallow up death in victory; and the Lord God will wipe away tears from off all faces" (Isaiah 25:8). Christ the second Adam encountered death armed with its sting in order to disarm it to His spiritual seed. He received into His own soul and body the empoisoning sting of it that they might, according to the covenant, be secured from it. The promise, therefore, of victory over death, made to Him, ensures the disarming of it to them. And as the promise renders them safe and, in their encounter with that last enemy, secures to them the victory, so the lively faith of that promise is a means of delivering them, in the prospect of it, from slavish and disquieting fear.

Second, it seems to be grafted likewise on the promise of a triumphant resurrection made to Christ Himself. "Thy dead men shall live, together with My dead body shall they arise" (Isaiah 26:19). The promise of a resurrection being made to Him as a public person, it must have effect also on His mystical members who were represented by Him. Hence the Psalmist said of himself, "My flesh shall rest in hope," that is, shall rest in the grave in hope of a glorious resurrection because Jesus that holy One was not to see corruption (Psalm 16:9, 10 with Acts 13:35); thereby comforting himself in the assured prospect that the resurrection of Messiah his covenant-head would secure his happy resurrection as a member of His mystical body. Such an indissoluble connection, indeed, is there according to the covenant between the resurrection of the Head and that of the members after it, and in virtue of it that if the dead do not rise, then Christ is not raised (1 Corinthians 15:16).

The second principal branch of the promise of eternal life to the elect, as accomplished to them from death throughout eternity, is a promise of an honorable judgment to be passed upon them at the great day. "He shall call to the heavens from above, and to the earth, that He may judge His people. Gather My saints together unto Me, those that have made a covenant with Me by sacrifice" (Psalm 50:4, 5). No sooner shall they be raised up in glory from their graves than by the ministry of angels they are gathered together from among the wicked into one glorious assembly. While the wicked shall be left on the earth, they, on the contrary, shall be caught up together in the clouds to meet the Lord in the air. Ascending in one august company to meet their Lord, to welcome Him to His throne of judgment, and to wait on Him as His illustrious attendants, they shall be placed in a situation the most honorable. The glorious Judge, seated on His imperial throne, white as the snow and fiery as the flame, will, as a token of His affection for them, as a mark of honor conferred on them, and as a pledge of the glory to which He is about to exalt them, set them on His right hand.

Then they shall be openly acknowledged by Him as their sovereign Lord (Matthew 10:32). He will acknowledge them to be His own. He will confess the relationship in which He and they stand to each other. "They shall be Mine," acknowledged to be Mine, saith the Lord of hosts, "in that day when I make up My jewels" (Malachi 3:17). He will then, in the most public manner, own them as the blessed of His Father, for whom the kingdom was prepared. He now acknowledges all that are His secretly by regarding them as His, by His Spirit's testimony of their sonship, by the seal of His image impressed on them, and before His Father in whose presence He appears, interceding for them as His own (John 17:9, 10). But He will then acknowledge them openly in their own hearing and in the hearing of assembled worlds, so that devils and wicked men shall see clearly that they are the men whom the King delights to honor. He will confess them before His Father and the holy angels, saying in effect to His eternal Father, "Behold I, and the children which Thou hast given Me" (Hebrews 2:13).

They shall then also be openly acquitted by Him as their righteous Judge. By this cheering sentence passed on them, "Come ye blessed of My Father, inherit the kingdom prepared for you from the foundation of the world" (Matthew 25:34), they shall not only be acquitted from all the false aspersions that are now cast upon them in this world (1 Corinthians 4:5), and have all their sins declaratorily pardoned (Acts 3:19), but shall be adjudged to life eternal. Their acquittal from every charge of guilt and from every effect of iniquity will at that day be pronounced in the most public and solemn manner. That their comfort and honor may be the more abundant, and the shame and confusion of the wicked (Isaiah 66:5) the more overwhelming, the saints shall be acquitted, not in secret as formerly, but from the imperial throne, in the presence of Jehovah, of angels, and of men. The white stone and the new name will, in the most public and honorable manner, be given them; and so the mouths of all who accused them shall be finally stopped.

They, being themselves openly acquitted, shall be honored to be assessors with Christ in judging wicked men and angels. "Do ye not know," says an apostle, "that the saints shall judge the world? . . . Know ye not that we shall judge angels?" (1 Corinthians 6:2, 3) This high office, being a part of the exalted honor of the glorious Head of the body redounding to all the members, they shall be honored to judge the world by way of fellowship with Him, and of approbation of the righteous sentence that He will then pronounce against them. They will all consequently, with one accord, say "Amen" to the tremendous doom of the wicked, the righteous parent to that of the wicked child, and the godly husband to that of the ungodly spouse (Revelation 3:21 and 19:3).

This promise of an honorable judgment to the saints appears to be closely connected with that of Christ's being, in the human nature, the prime minister of heaven, and of His having supreme dominion over all the creatures in heaven, earth, and hell (1 Thessalonians 4:6, 17; Colossians 3:4).

The third and last principal branch of the promise of eternal life to the elect as accomplished to them, from death throughout eternity, is the promise of eternal happiness in heaven, to commence in the soul at death and to be completed in both soul and body at the last day. "Many of them that sleep in the dust of the earth shall awake, some to everlasting life" (Daniel 12:2). Eternal life in the mansions of glory, to be conferred after death on every one of the spiritual offspring of Christ, was revealed more sparingly under the Old Testament than it is under the New (2 Timothy 1:10); yet even then it was revealed so clearly that all the godly Patriarchs lived and died in the faith of it (Hebrews 11:13, 14). Believers before Abraham saw it in the promise of the seed of the woman who was to bruise the head of the serpent; and after Abraham they saw it likewise in the promise of Canaan. But now, by the gospel, this life and immortality are set in a much clearer point of view. By the breach of the covenant of works eternal life in heaven was forfeited; the celestial paradise was lost to the first Adam, and to all his posterity in him, in token of which he was expelled from the earthy paradise. But the second Adam having, in the covenant of grace, undertaken to redeem the forfeited inheritance, a new promise of it was made in behalf of His spiritual seed; and though they are not immediately put in possession of it, yet in the first moment of their vital union with Christ an irreversible title thereto is conferred on them; and when they do attain the possession it is not bestowed on them all at once, but in different degrees and at two different periods, according to these two leading branches of the promise of it: a promise of conveying their souls into heaven at death and a promise of translating them there, soul and body, at the last day.

The first leading branch of it is a promise of conveying their souls, separate from their bodies, into heaven, there perfectly to see and enjoy their covenant God. This promise is accomplished to them immediately after their death. It was expressly declared and applied by our almighty Redeemer to the penitent malefactor on the cross. "Verily, I say unto thee, Today shalt thou be with Me in paradise" (Luke 23:43). It was in the faith of it that the everlasting covenant was, to David, even in the near prospect of death, all his salvation and all his desire (2 Samuel 23:5); and that the holy Apostle Paul, knowing that he was to be with Christ upon his departure hence, had a desire to depart that he might be with Him (Philippians 1:23). In consequence, indeed, of violating the covenant of works, the spiritual seed of Christ, as well as the rest of mankind, fell under the curse of it; and that awful sentence would have operated in cutting them asunder as covenant-breakers but, having been executed fully on Christ, their condescending Surety, so as to part asunder His holy soul and body, it can no more have any such effect on them. Therefore, though others die in virtue of the curse, separating their souls from their bodies, consigning the one to the prison of hell and the other to that of the grave till the Day of Judgment, yet they do not so die. Redeemed as they are from the curse of the law, they shall never see death under such a form (John 8:51); but they die in conformity to Christ, their covenant-Head who died, and who is the first-born from the dead (Colossians 1:18), as well as the first-fruits of them that slept, whom every man in his own order is to follow (1 Corinthians 15:20, 23). In consequence of their fellowship with Christ in His death, the union between their souls and mortal bodies is dissolved and their souls are dismissed into glory, there to dwell until their bodies lying in the grave shall, in virtue of their communion with Him in His resurrection, put on the bright robes of incorruption, immortality, and glory.

The Promises of the Covenant of Grace 243

The next and last leading branch of the promise of eternal life in heaven is a promise of translating the saints there, soul and body, to be ever with the Lord. This great, this transporting promise is to be accomplished to them at the last day. "Many of them that sleep in the dust of the earth shall awake, some to everlasting life . . . And they that be wise shall shine as the brightness of the firmament; and they that turn many to righteousness (or rather, they who pronounce many righteous. The verb is in the form hiphil, and in that form it signifies to justify, to pronounce or declare righteous), as the stars forever and ever" (Daniel 12:2, 3). And, said our great Redeemer, "The hour is coming in which all that are in the graves shall hear His voice, and shall come forth; they that have done good unto the resurrection of life" (John 5:28, 29; Matthew 25:46). Having come forth to the resurrection of life they shall shine, not only as the stars forever and ever, but as the sun in the kingdom of their Father (Matthew 13:43). They shall then, in their whole man, begin fully to enjoy Jehovah, their covenant God; by attaining such a perfect knowledge of Him as will have no other limits set to it than what arise from the limited capacity of the creature (1 Corinthians 13:12). They shall know Him perfectly by sight, which will satisfy the understanding, and by experience, which will satisfy the will and the affections. They shall thenceforth, with the eyes of their body, have a blissful sight of that transcendently glorious body which, with its soul, is united to the divine nature in the person of the eternal Son (Job 19:27), and with the eyes of their understanding a beatific vision of the infinitely glorious Jehovah, three in one, and one in three (Matthew 5:8; 1 John 3:2). As the accomplishment of the promise to them, they shall be blessed with the most clear, the most complete, the most intuitive, knowledge of God and divine things of which creatures can be capable. Here they have only a sight, as it were, of His back parts; but then they shall see His face (Revelation 22:4), and shall incessantly and eternally feed the eyes of their souls upon Him (Psalm 17:15). They shall be admitted to look into His heart and there to have a perfectly clear, distinct, and assimilating view of that redeeming, that astonishing love, that He had for them from eternity, and will have to them forever (Jeremiah 31:3). Moreover, they shall then know God as their chief good, by experience, which will completely satisfy their will and their affections. Their understandings will rest in the contemplation of eternal truth, their wills in the fruition of infinite good. The Lamb, who is in the midst of the throne, shall feed them, and shall lead them unto living fountains of waters (Revelation 7:17). They shall participate in the fullest measure of the overflowing goodness of God, not so much in the streams as in the fountain; and they shall have, in their inmost souls, the liveliest sensation of that goodness. The immeasurable fullness of God, who is their infinitely rich inheritance, their exceeding great reward, will ever stand open to them; and the consequences of the free communication and full participation of it will be perfect likeness to God, and the most unspeakable joy. "I shall be satisfied," said the psalmist, "when I awake with Thy likeness" (Psalm 17:15). And an apostle said, "We shall be like Him; for we shall see Him as He is" (1 John 3:2). "In Thy presence is fullness of joy, at Thy right hand there are pleasures for evermore" (Psalm 16:11).

Eternity is the knot, as it were, that binds the bundle of life together. The undoubted certainty, therefore, that the saints in heaven will have that their enjoyment of God in Christ, and their likeness to Him, shall continue throughout eternity, will be accompanied with the most ineffable and transporting joy (Revelation 7:17).

Thus the saints will, in the upper sanctuary, enjoy in perfection the whole of that eternal life that God, who cannot lie, promised before the world began. A conditional promise of it was, in the covenant of works, given to man; but by his failing to fulfill the condition that inestimable benefit was forfeited; and so the gates of heaven were shut against Adam and all his natural posterity. But the blessed second Adam, having engaged to fulfill the conditions of the covenant of grace that were stated from the high demands that the broken covenant of works made on His spiritual seed, a new and absolute promise of it was made in their favor. To His fulfillment of those conditions, the accomplishment of this great promise is entirely owing. No righteousness but His could ever have sufficed to reduce the forfeiture and to purchase a new right; and His does it so effectually as fully to ensure the putting of all His elect seed in actual and complete possession of life eternal. They, therefore, who receive abundance of grace, and of the gift of righteousness, shall reign in life by one, Jesus Christ (Romans 5:17).

This is that promise of the eternal covenant that is the consummation of all the other promises of it, and is therefore the last of all in fulfilling. The saints under the Old Testament died in the faith of it; and it is not yet performed to them; nay, even the saints under the New Testament died, and still die, in the belief of it, not having it performed to them until at the last day it is accomplished to the whole elect together. It still remains to be an object of faith to the church triumphant, whose flesh must rest in hope till that day, as well as to the church militant. In order to confirm, however, the faith of the church universal in the accomplishment of it, as soon as all the elect seed should be gathered in some memorable pledges of it were given, such as the translating of Enoch, soul and body, into heaven in the age of the Patriarchs, of Elijah in the time of the law, and of the last Adam Himself in the time of the gospel.

Now the former branch of this transcendently glorious promise to the elect is grafted on the promise of the Father's acceptance of Christ Himself, when He should finish the work that He gave Him to do in confidence of that promised acceptance. Christ, when He was dying, commended His spirit or soul into the hands of His Father (Luke 23:46) and informed the penitent malefactor that he was to be with Him in paradise on that very day, though it was then near the close of it (Luke 23:43). It is remarkable that the words in which He commended His soul to His Father were those of David: "Into Thy hand I commit My Spirit" (Psalm 31:5), thereby intimating that the Father's reception of the souls of believers at their death depends on His reception of his soul. When the Father received His soul He, according to the covenant, received it as a public soul, representing the souls of all the seed. Hence the psalmist, when speaking of Messiah says, "Thou wilt not leave my soul in hell" (Psalm 16:10 compared with Acts 2:31). In the promise, then, of the Father's acceptance of Christ's soul when He should make it an offering for sin, was comprised a promise of His reception of the souls of all who were represented by Him.

The latter part of the promise appears to be grafted on the promise of Christ's high exaltation to the right hand of the Father, by which was ensured to Him His triumphant ascension in soul and body, and entrance into His glory. Ought not Christ, said our great Redeemer Himself, to have suffered these things, and to enter into His glory (Luke 24:26)? His suffering was requisite in respect of the conditions of the covenant that He engaged to fulfill to His Father; and His entering into His glory was necessary, in regard of the promise of it that the Father engaged to perform to Him. Now Christ the last Adam, ascended

The Promises of the Covenant of Grace 247

and entered into glory as a public person, as a forerunner entering for us (Hebrews 6:20). The promise, therefore, in virtue of which He ascended and entered into His glory, comprehends at the same time a promise of the ascension and entrance into glory of all His spiritual seed who are, therefore, said to sit together in heavenly places in Him (Ephesians 2:6). Then, and not till then, will the promise be fully accomplished to Him, when all the members of His mystical body shall be there personally, together with their Head; when, completely delivered from death, they shall there sit and reign together with Him in life eternal.

So much for the promise of eternal life, as performed from death throughout eternity.

From what has been discoursed in this chapter, the reader may see that sanctification is inseparable from justification. They are both promised in the covenant. They are both parts of that eternal life that the Father promised to the Son as last Adam on behalf of His spiritual seed upon condition of His fulfilling in their stead all the righteousness of the law. That consummate righteousness, He as their Surety fulfilled for them. Nothing now remains, therefore, but that the promise in all its branches be performed to them. The performance of the promise of justification, then, must be accompanied by the performance of that of sanctification. One may as soon pretend to separate weight from stone or heat from the fire as to separate sanctification from justification. There is, therefore, no foundation for this cavil that justification on the ground of righteousness imputed sets a man free from his obligation to duty.

Here I cannot deny myself the pleasure of extracting the following passage from Mr. Ralph Erskine's excellent sermon on "Christ the People's Covenant":

> If there be any person here that never found this doctrine of grace to have any other tendency than to lead him to licentiousness, I will pledge my life, he is not a believer, but a person ignorant of the mystery of the gospel. But what say you, believer? Cannot your experience bear witness to God and His gracious covenant that however vile and unholy you find yourself to be, yet, when the new covenant-cord of free grace is wrapped about your heart, does it draw you to the love of sin or to the love of holiness? The more lively faith you have, of Christ's being your treasure, your righteousness, your covenant, your all for debt and duty both, do you not find holiness the more lovely to you, and His love constraining you the more to delight in His service? Let the Word of God, and the experience of the saints in agreeableness thereto, decide matters of this sort.

Again, were the promises of the covenant of grace made to Christ upon condition of His fulfilling all righteousness as the Surety of His people? And was He, being a Divine person, incapable of failing, in what He engaged to fulfill? It follows that there was no proper penalty in that covenant. A penalty is not an essential part of a proper covenant. It is but accidental only arising not from the nature of a covenant itself, but from the nature of the parties covenanting who, being fallible, may be in danger of failing either in the condition or in the promise; in which case a penalty is usually annexed to secure on the one hand the performance of the condition, and on the other that of the promise. Since, therefore, the party contracting on the side of man in that divine covenant on whom it lay to fulfill the conditions was infallible, as was the party contracting on the side of heaven on whom it depended to perform the promise, there was no place for a penalty, strictly so called, as there was none for any in the covenant of works but upon the one side. It is true, indeed, the persons contracted for are fallible; but then

The Promises of the Covenant of Grace

the fulfilling of the conditions properly so called did not lie on them, but on the second Adam who, having taken these entirely on Himself, fulfilled them, and that completely. No sooner are elect sinners, by the Spirit of faith, vitally united to Him than the promise of the eternal covenant, notwithstanding all their innumerable failures, stands sure to them and must continue so to stand because the conditions of the covenant are already fulfilled by Him, their glorious Surety, and are judicially sustained as fulfilled for them. And though, as long as they remain in this world, they are fallible with regard to their actions, yet, from the moment of their spiritual union with Christ, they are infallible with respect to their state; they can no more fall from their state of grace than the spirits of just men made perfect can from their state of glory. In their case, then, there is no place for condemnation to eternal wrath (Romans 8:1), the only penalty by which they could lose their title to the promise of the covenant. They indeed deserve condemnation, and, for their sins, they are often liable to God's fatherly anger and fatherly chastisement; but, inasmuch as by these there is no interruption of their right to the promise, and as they are not vindictive but medicinal, they cannot be counted a proper penalty of the covenant of grace. They belong only to the promise and to the administration of it (Psalm 89:30-34; Hebrews 12:5-7). Where the condition of a contract is perfectly fulfilled and legally sustained in favor of the party who is to receive the benefit promised, it is manifest there can be no more place for a proper penalty on that side; and so it is in the case of believers here.

From what has been advanced above it may also be inferred that all the benefits of the covenant of grace are the sure mercies of David (Romans 8:1). All of them are mercies, free, unmixed mercies. All of them to you, reader, if you indeed believe, are gifts of free grace, gifts without respect to any worthiness in you;

for the covenant, from the first to the last, is to you a covenant of infinitely free and glorious grace (Ephesians 2:7, 8). The receiving of you into glory, after all your works are performed, is as much of grace as was the quickening of you when, being dead in sin, you could do no good work. Your faith and your works, your grace and your glory, your temporal and your eternal benefits, are all equally of free grace. They are all secured to you by the promise of that covenant that was made before the world began, and are all given to you on the ground of a righteousness that you had no hand in fulfilling. All of them are the mercies of David; of Messiah, the Son, and the antitype of David. The holiness of His nature, the righteousness of His life, and the satisfaction for sin, given by His death, are the only channel in which the grace of the covenant, bringing with it all those mercies, flows. Upon these alone, and upon nothing in you, whether before or after conversion, is the promise of them founded. Your believing through grace, while others remain still in unbelief; your seeing God in the light of glory, while multitudes are cast into outer darkness; the bread that you eat and the water that you drink in this world, together with the hidden manna of which you will eat, and the living fountains of water of which you will drink in the world to come—all are equally the purchase of your dear Redeemer's blood.

Finally, they are all sure mercies. Those of them that believers already posses, they could not fail of possessing; and those of them that they have not yet received are as sure to them as if they had it already in hand (2 Samuel 23:5). Common mercies are tottering, uncertain comforts; but covenant-mercies are sure. The former may flow in abundance for a while, and yet at length be completely dried up; but the spring of the latter, when once it is opened, still continue without interruption forever to flow. The promise of eternal mercy is sure, infinitely sure, to all the seed and cannot fail of being accomplished to them; it is sure, from the immutable truth of Jehovah as well as from His infinite justice in respect of the second Adam. "If his children," said Jehovah, "forsake My law . . . then will I visit their transgression with the rod, and their iniquity with stripes. Nevertheless, my loving kindness (or mercy) will I not utterly take from him" (Psalm 89:30-33). One would have thought that this promise should have been thus expressed: "My mercy will I not utterly take from them. But all the mercies respecting them, having been primarily promised to Him, it behooved them to be taken from him, before they could, from them."

To conclude: Were all the promises of the covenant made to Christ? And are they all in Him, Yea and Amen? Then it follows that they, in and with Him, are freely offered to sinners of mankind in common who hear the gospel. Reader, Christ and all the precious promises in Him are by Jehovah graciously offered, and in the offer are directed to you for your acceptance (Acts 2:39; Hebrews 4:1). The authentic offer brings them all within your reach, and affords you a divine, an authoritative warrant, to come as a sinner and to accept Him, and them in Him. Come, then; come as you are; come without delay; come without looking into your heart or into your life for any good thing to recommend you; and, upon the warrant of the free, full, and particular offer so embrace the promises in Christ as cordially to trust in Him for the performance of them to your soul. Do not come on the ground of any good disposition wrought in you, or of any good work done by you, for these afford you no right. But come as a sinner upon the warrant of the unlimited grant and call of the gospel, and trust in the Lord Jesus for all the grace of the promise.

After you have begun, continue to trust in Him. The believer's turning away his eye from Christ and the covenant is the cause why he begins to sink under his pressure. His departing from Christ his living Redeemer by an evil heart of unbelief issues for ordinary in his being torn asunder with a thousand anxieties. O beware of disbelieving the promise, of distrusting the grace of a promising God, lest He measures to you according to your opinion of Him. Since the spotless righteousness of Jesus Christ is likewise offered to you, and since the offer affords you an immediate warrant to receive it, oh, rely on it for a right to the blessings promised. Trust with assured confidence that the promises will be fulfilled to you on the ground of that righteousness only that is yours in offer, and not on the ground of any works that you yourself have done. Do not even rely on your acts of faith for a title to the grace of the promise, but wholly on the righteousness revealed from faith to faith. So shall you be an heir of promise, and shall reign in life eternal by one, Jesus Christ.

5

The Administration of the Covenant of Grace

By the administration of that august covenant is meant the entire management of it. It comprises the exhibition or offer of the covenant, together with all that is necessary to be done in order to make those sinners of mankind, who were represented by Christ, partakers of the purchased and promised benefits of it. Seeing this glorious covenant is that on which the salvation of sinners depends, and according to which all the dispensations of Jehovah toward them, for carrying on and completing that gracious design, are regulated; and seeing it was withal a compact entered into between the Father and the Son before the world began, and so is in itself, the deepest secret (Psalm 25:14); it is requisite that there be an administration of it by which it may be rendered effectual, for all the gracious purposes for which it was made.

That the reader may have a proper and distinct view of this, it will be requisite that we consider the glorious Party on whom the administration of the covenant was devolved, the object of that administration, the ends, and the form and order of it.

SECTION 1. The Party to Whom the Administration of the Covenant of Grace Was Committed

First, I am to consider the glorious Party on whom the administration of the covenant was devolved. The nature and high importance of this administration are such that none except one of the high contracting Parties in the covenant was fit to be entrusted with it. The administration of the covenant, therefore, was devolved on no mere man or angel, but on Christ the last Adam; and He has it as one of His high prerogatives made over to Him in the covenant itself. It was herein made over to Him by promise, particularly by the promise of a glorious exaltation, to be the honorary Servant of the Father or Prime Minister of Heaven. Accordingly we read that the last Adam was made a quickening Spirit (1 Corinthians 15:45), and that He was to be given for a covenant of the people, or rather, as in the original, a covenant of people (Isaiah 49:8). He was divinely constituted the Covenant-head of vital influences to His spiritual seed. The living Father gave to Him as last Adam to have life in Himself; so that He quickens whom He will and gives eternal life to as many as were given Him. He gave, and still gives, Him for a covenant of people. Thus giving, according to the usual phraseology of sacred Scripture, implies a divine settlement or constitution. Thus in Isaiah 49:16 Jehovah said, "I will also give thee for a light to the Gentiles, that thou mayest be My salvation to the end of the earth"; that is, "I will set or constitute thee for a light;" even as He set (Hebrew "gave") the sun and moon in the firmament of the heaven to give light upon the earth (Genesis 1:17). To give Christ, then, for a covenant of people is to constitute or appoint Him the covenant whereby people, any people, whether Jews or Gentiles, may become the covenant-people of God, and as such receive all the blessings of the covenant. Thus the Lord Jesus as last Adam is the great and gracious ordinance of Jehovah for the redemption of sinners of mankind to Him, and for putting them in possession of all the blessings of His covenant; in like manner as the sun is the ordinance of God for light to this world, to whose light all the inhabitants of it have a right of access, though still it gives no light to the blind, nor to them who, because they hate the light, choose to dwell in darkness. This unparalleled honor was secured to Him by the promise of the covenant in consideration of His fulfilling the infinitely arduous conditions of it.

That Christ the last Adam was, by the authority of Jehovah the Father, constituted a covenant of the people implies, as was just now hinted, first, that He was thereby constituted the Administrator of the covenant of grace. As He had the charge of purchasing all the benefits promised therein so, according to the eternal purpose of Jehovah, He had the honor of distributing and bestowing them. None of the blessings of the covenant are to be received but from His hand. He obtained them from the Father, and sinners must receive them from Him. That this is included in the phrase is evident from these words in Isaiah 49:8, 9 (compared with chapter 42:6,7), which immediately follow and express the end of that divine constitution: "To establish the earth, to cause to inherit the desolate heritages; that thou mayest say to the prisoners, 'Go forth'; to them that are in darkness, 'show yourselves.' " Second, it implies that the whole of the covenant is in Him. He therefore who has Christ has the covenant, the whole of the covenant; and he who does not have Christ has neither part nor lot in it. A distributor of one's goods must have them in his own custody; he must have power of them, as Joseph who, that he might distribute corn to the people, had all the corn in Egypt at his command. The Lord Jesus is such an Administrator of the covenant as has in Himself and at His entire disposal the whole of the covenant. This, as well as the former, appears to be included in that unusual expression occurring only in the two passages compared above; and that it is so is confirmed by these words which in one of the places immediately follow: "to establish the earth."

A covenant is an establishing, a confirming object. When the covenant of works was broken, the foundations of the earth were, as it were, loosened or disjointed so that it could no longer stand firm till Christ was given or set for a covenant to establish it again. It is, in virtue of His having the whole of the covenant in Himself, that He bears up the pillars thereof. And no sooner will His administration of the covenant on the earth be at an end than the earth shall cease to be established by Him, and so shall be dissolved by fire.

Thus it is manifest that the administration of the covenant of grace was devolved on Christ the last Adam inasmuch as He was made a quickening Spirit and was given for a covenant of the people, which implies that He was divinely constituted the Administrator of the covenant, and that the whole of the covenant is in Him.

QUESTION. But for what purposes was the administration of the covenant committed to Him?

ANSWER 1. That thereby a brighter display of the glory of God in the salvation of His elect might be afforded. It was devolved on Him for the honor of the High and Holy One in order that He might have no immediate dealing with creatures who had been sinners against Him even after their sanctification should become perfect, but that His infinite holiness, justice, love, and mercy toward them might forever shine forth through His only begotten Son in their nature as the Mediator between Him and them. It was in the face of Jesus Christ, the glorious Administrator of the covenant, that the infinite glory of Jehovah, the God of the covenant, was to shine forth (2 Corinthians

The Administration of the Covenant of Grace

4:6; Hebrews 1:3). Accordingly in Him, the glory of His immaculate holiness, of His tremendous justice, of His matchless love, of His boundless grace, and of His infinite mercy shines, and will forever shine with the most resplendent, the most astonishing luster. "God was in Christ reconciling the world unto Himself" (2 Corinthians 5:19). From a throne of grace, established upon the firm foundation of justice fully satisfied by Him, and of judgment fully executed on Him, the infinite Jehovah, in the most glorious manner, confers pardon and peace, grace and glory; confers them freely, without any merit in the receivers, and yet, not without a sufficient compensation to His injured honor.

ANSWER 2. Again, He was entrusted with it as a reward of His finished work. His eternal Father committed it to Him in order that the innumerable multitude of the redeemed and all the concerns of their salvation might forever depend on Him. When Joseph was a bondservant, he behaved himself with all prudence, meekness, patience, and faithfulness in that low condition which was afterwards, by divine providence, richly rewarded with honor in his being advanced to be the prime minister of Egypt, having the administration of the whole kingdom entrusted to him (Psalm 105:17-22). In this he was an eminent type of Christ. The Lord Jesus willingly submitted Himself to the very lowest depth of meanness and disgrace. He took upon Himself the form of a bondservant, and in that form so humbled Himself as to become obedient unto death, even the death of the cross; and that in order to fulfill the conditions of the covenant for the glory of His Father and the redemption of His people. Therefore He was, in the human nature, exalted to the highest possible honor. He was exalted to be the Prime Minister of heaven, to have the whole administration of the covenant entrusted to Him that under His eternal Father He might be the Head over all things to the church. Hereby a name was given

Him that is above every name, whether of men or of angels. Principalities and powers are made subject to Him; and all things are put under His feet (Philippians 2:7-9; Ephesians 1:20-23). It is in reference to this that He is often, in Scripture, called the Father's Servant, namely His honorary Servant, and that His honor in that character is often promised to be made very great (Isaiah 49:6; 3:13-15; Zechariah 6:12, 13).

And seeing the everlasting covenant will continue to be the rule of God's dispensation toward His redeemed through eternity, Christ the last Adam is to enjoy the unparalleled dignity of having the administration of that august covenant ledged in His incarnate person forevermore. For unto the Son He said, "Thy throne, O God, is for ever and ever" (Hebrews 1:8). And again, "He shall reign over the house of Jacob forever, and of His kingdom there shall be no end" (Luke 1:33). The time comes, indeed, in which He will deliver up the kingdom to God, even the Father; in which He will deliver up or present to Him the whole church and every member of it, brought by His administration of the covenant to the perfection of life eternal. "Then cometh the end" (1 Corinthians 15:24), namely the end of the world, but not the end of His administration; for in His being constituted Administrator of the covenant "there was given Him dominion, and glory, and a kingdom . . . His dominion is an everlasting dominion, which shall not pass away as the world shall, and His kingdom that which shall not be destroyed" (Daniel 7:14). Scarcely could He be said to give eternal life to as many as were given Him by the Father if He only conferred on them the first-fruits of that life and not the full harvest. When the redeemed shall reign forever and ever, surely the Redeemer shall not cease to reign. The Lord Jesus will, indeed, deliver up the kingdom to God the Father; but, as the Father did not cease to reign when all power in heaven and on earth was given to the

Son as Mediator, so neither will the Son cease to reign when He shall have delivered up the kingdom to the Father; as the reign of the Father is not then to begin, so the reign of the Son is not then to terminate.

We are informed that when all things shall be subdued to Him, then shall the Son also Himself be subject to Him that put all things under Him, that God may be all in all (1 Corinthians 15:28). By this it is not meant that Christ's power over all flesh ends, nor that His subjection to the Father begins with the general resurrection; but that after the resurrection, when He will give an account of all that He has done for the redemption of His people, that subjection to the Father as His honorary Servant, or as Administrator of the eternal covenant, shall be more clearly manifested to the whole intelligent creation.

ANSWER 3. Last, it was devolved on Him in order to suit the condition of His people and to secure and sweeten their eternal redemption. The whole of their fellowship with God, whether in time or in eternity, is through Him who is and will continue to be their Brother as well as their Lord (John 10:7, 9 and 14:6; Ephesians 2:18 and 3:12; Hebrews 10:19-22; 1 Peter 2:5). In the person of Christ, the glorious Administrator of the covenant, returning sinners have to do with a God, the splendor of whose infinite majesty which the guilty are not able to behold, is veiled with the robe of a spotless humanity. An alluring sweetness appears in the countenance of Immanuel, that benign Administrator. While He is full of grace and truth (John 1:14), He is at the same time fairer than the children of men (Psalm 45:2). In Him they may see the redemption of their soul, so precious, so dear to the God who made them that He Himself would put on their nature in order to establish by His own blood an everlasting covenant of peace between Jehovah and them. He is a real man, of the same family of Adam with themselves, to whom, therefore, they may freely and confidently approach, joining themselves to Him as the Head, and to God in Him as the God of the covenant. And He is at the same time the true God, infinitely able and willing, notwithstanding their utter unworthiness, to make the covenant effectual for their eternal salvation.

SECTION 2. The Object of the Administration of the Covenant

In the second place, I am to consider, as was proposed, the object of Christ's administration of the eternal covenant. As it is a covenant of infinite, of overflowing grace, it is in some things administered to sinners of mankind indefinitely, without the consideration of them either as elect or as reprobate. The elect only were the party represented by the second Adam; and to them only is the administration of the covenant effectual for salvation. But it is sinners of mankind indefinitely that are the object of the administration, the party to whom Christ is empowered by commission from the Father externally to administer the covenant. He is divinely authorized to administer it to any sinners of the race of Adam without exception, to receive them into the bond of it, and to bestow on them the benefits of it. Accordingly, He administers it to sinners indefinitely in the unlimited offers of the gospel, which is good tidings of great joy to all people (Luke 2:10); and in which, all without exception, are declared welcome to receive Himself, and all the blessings of the covenant in Him. The election of particular persons is a secret not to be discovered in the administration of the covenant, according to the settled order of it, till after the sinner has taken hold of the covenant, and so come personally into the bond of it. The extent, therefore, of that administration to sinners indefinitely is not founded on election, but on the intrinsic sufficiency of the obedience and death of the Divine Redeemer for the salvation even of all men; on His relation of a Kinsman-redeemer to sinners of mankind as such; and on all men's having in them the moral characters of those for whom He obeyed and suffered. Neither is it regulated by election, but by the fullness of power in heaven and on earth given to the last Adam, as a reward of His having become obedient, even to the death of the cross.

1. The extent of Christ's administration of the covenant to sinners indefinitely is founded on the intrinsic sufficiency of His obedience and death for the salvation even of all the human race (Romans 1:17; Luke 14:22, 23; Mark 16:15). The consummate righteousness of our divine Surety comprises the very utmost of what law and justice could require in order to repair the breach of the covenant of works and to merit justification and salvation for sinners of mankind. Though the Lord Jesus came into this world to redeem only a part of mankind, yet He did not, as their Surety, come to fulfill only a part of the law or to endure only a part of the punishment due for their iniquity. Nothing less could have sufficed for the redemption of any one of them than a fulfilling of the whole precept and a bearing of the whole penalty of the violated law; nor could anything more, in the nature of the case, have been required for the redemption of all the sinners who are under that broken covenant. And while none are justified simply as the elect of God, but as sinners of mankind, betaking themselves by faith to that consummate, that infinitely meritorious righteousness, all these are equally as well as fully warranted wherever the gospel is published so to betake themselves to it. The intrinsic value and sufficiency, then, of the surety-righteousness of Jesus Christ is a ground of sufficient validity for the most free, full, and extensive offers of salvation to sinners of mankind.

2. The extent thereof is also founded on His standing in the relationship of a Kinsman-redeemer to sinners of mankind as such, and that both in His person and in His offices. In the glorious constitution of His person as Immanuel, God-man, our Lord Jesus stands in the general and equal relationship of a Kinsman-redeemer to sinners of mankind as such. This relationship does not arise from any act of Christ's intention respecting them, but from the constitution of His person, He being God-man, a Redeemer in human nature. From the act of His Father's will in giving them to Him, as well as from the act of His own in covenanting to redeem them, Christ indeed stands in the special relationship of a Redeemer to the elect of God, which peculiar relationship is entirely abstracted from the offer made of Him in the gospel to them in common with others. But as He is God manifest in the flesh, sustaining the public character of a Redeemer, made in man's nature under the law, His person stands thereby in the endearing relationship of Kinsman-redeemer to sinners of mankind in common, and that without any distinction between elect sinners and others; for the elect are no otherwise men, and no otherwise sinners, than the rest of mankind are. In His mediatorial offices likewise Christ stands in the relationship of a Kinsman-redeemer to mankind in general. His offices do, in the glorious nature of them, stand in an equal relation or suitableness to the need of perishing sinners of the human race as such. The relation and suitableness that result from the nature of those offices must belong to sinners in common, without any distinction between the elect and the non-elect, because the cases and wants of the elect are of the very same nature as those of the rest of mankind.

From the common relationship of a Kinsman-redeemer, then, in which Christ stands to mankind in general, He, in His person and offices, is fully qualified for being received and rest-

The Administration of the Covenant of Grace 263

ed on for salvation by any, or even by all of them, which is a ground of sufficient validity for extending the fullest and freest offers of righteousness and salvation in the gospel to all of them without distinction.

3. Last, the extent of that administration to sinners of mankind indefinitely appears in a considerable degree to be founded on all men's having the moral characters of those for whom the great Redeemer died. All the children of fallen Adam, while in their natural state, are said in Scripture to be, without exception, unjust, ungodly, sinners, enemies, persons without strength, and even dead in trespasses and sins. They are all represented not only as men and sons of man, but as simple ones who love simplicity, scorners who delight in scorning, fools who hate knowledge, and rebels who are stout-hearted and far from righteousness. They are all declared to be a corrupt, a wicked, a backsliding, a disobedient, and a gainsaying people; to be laboring and heavy laden with a burden of guilt and of insensibility as well as of trouble; to be thirsting for happiness in vanity, or in anything else where it is not to be found, spending their money for that which is not bread and their labor for that which satisfieth not; and to be prisoners in darkness, lost, and self-destroyed. Since these, then, according to the Spirit of inspiration, are the moral characters not only of the elect in their natural state for whom Christ died, but of all the rest of mankind He administers the covenant in the offers and calls of the gospel to sinners of mankind indefinitely.

In order to elucidate and confirm this consoling truth, that Christ as last Adam is authorized thus to administer the covenant to sinners of the family of Adam in common, without the consideration of them either as elect or non-elect, let the following particulars be considered.

PARTICULAR 1. The gift or grant that the Father made of Christ crucified as His gracious ordinance for salvation to sinners of mankind is general and unlimited. When the Israelites in the wilderness had on a certain occasion rebelled, many of them were bitten by fiery serpents. In that case the Lord instituted an ordinance for their cure, namely a serpent of brass, lifted up upon a pole, and He made a grant of it to the whole congregation, promising that whosoever would, by looking upon it, use it for the purpose of being healed should live. The grant was expressed in the most ample terms. "It shall come to pass that every one that is bitten, when he looketh upon it, shall live" (Numbers 21:8). No person in the camp who needed a cure was excepted. In like manner, all mankind being stung by that old serpent the devil, and sin as his deadly poison being left in them, God appointed Christ to be His great ordinance for their cure, and made a grant of Him as such to the lost race of Adam, promising that whosoever of them will, by believing in Him, make use of Him for that purpose shall be saved. In that divine grant, none of the world of mankind is excepted. This is clear from these words of our blessed Lord Himself: "As Moses lifted up the serpent in the wilderness, even so must the Son of man be lifted up; that whosoever believeth in Him should not perish, but have eternal life. For God so loved the world that He gave His only begotten Son, that whosoever believeth in Him should not perish, but have everlasting life" (John 3:14-16). Now the administration of the covenant as a reward of Christ's obedience unto death, being settled in pursuance of this grant therein made, the object of the former must be as extensive as that of the latter.

PARTICULAR 2. Christ's commission from the Father to administer the covenant is expressed in the most ample terms; and He is invested for that purpose with the most extensive

The Administration of the Covenant of Grace

powers. His commission is expressed in terms the most ample. "The Spirit of the Lord God," said He, "is upon Me, because the Lord hath anointed Me to preach good tidings unto the meek. He hath sent Me to bind the broken-hearted, to proclaim liberty to the captives, and the opening of the prison to them that are bound" (Isaiah 61:1-3 with Luke 4:18, 19). Here, His commission is to administer the covenant not only to the meek, the poor, the bruised, and broken-hearted who might be supposed to have some good qualities to recommend them, but to the captives, the blind, the prisoners, and the bond men who had sold their inheritance, and even themselves, for a thing of naught. No sort of sinners can well be imagined that does not fall under one or another of these denominations. The terms are too general to admit any exception. He is given for a covenant of people, not of this or that class of people, but of people indefinitely; so that none on earth are excepted from His administering the covenant to them. Inasmuch as He is the ordinance of God for taking away the sin of the world, He is empowered to administer it to a guilty, lost world (John 1:29; Mark 16:15, 16). Accordingly, from His fullness of power He issues out the unlimited offer and call of the gospel by which all without exception who hear the gospel are warranted, and in which all are declared welcome to come to Him for the grace of the covenant. "All things," said He, "are delivered unto Me of My Father. Come unto Me, all ye that labor and are heavy laden, and I will give you rest" (Matthew 11:27, 28). And again, "All power is given unto Me in heaven and in earth. Go ye, therefore, and teach all nations, baptizing them in the name of the Father, and of the Son, and of the Holy Ghost" (Matthew 28:18, 19).

PARTICULAR 3. Christ executes His commission in an unrestrained, unlimited manner. He administers the covenant to any sinners of the human race; not to this or that class of them, under this or that appellation; but to men and the sons of man to any men or to men indefinitely. "Unto you, O men, I call; and my voice is to the sons of man" (Proverbs 8:4). The gospel in which He administers the covenant is good tidings to all people (Luke 2:10); and the gospel-feast is a feast made to all people (Isaiah 25:6), though many, not relishing the tidings, never taste of the feast. Accordingly, He commissioned His apostles for that purpose in terms than which none can be imagined more unlimited. "Go ye into all the world, and preach the gospel to *every creature*" (Mark 16:15). The Jews were accustomed to call man the creature, as being by way of eminence the creature of God. By "every creature," then, is meant every man and every woman, without exception. The gospel, therefore, in and by which Christ executes His high commission, is to be preached, and the covenant is thereby to be exhibited or offered to every human creature.

PARTICULAR 4. Though the Lord Jesus saves none eventually but the elect of God, yet He is by office the Savior of the world, equally fit for every sinner of mankind in the world, to whom they are all warranted by God to come for salvation. We know, said the Samaritans, that this is indeed the Christ, the Savior of the world (John 4:42). His salvation is a common salvation (Jude 3), and His gospel, which is an exhibition of His eternal covenant, is grace that brings salvation in offer to all men who hear it (Titus 2:11). Considered, indeed, as an actual and eventual Savior, He is the Savior only of the body (Ephesians 5:23); but considered as an official Savior, or a Savior by office, He is the Savior of the world. To explain my meaning, suppose, for instance, that one has received a commission to be the physician of a society; he is, in virtue of that commission, the physician by office of the whole society; and so he stands related to every member of it as his or her physician. At the same time he is not actually or eventually a healer to any of them but those who employ him. Though many of that society should not employ him at all, but on every occasion call another physician, yet he is still their physician by office. Though not choosing to call him they should even die of their diseases, yet still it is true that he was their physician; they might have employed him and have had the benefit of his medicines. It was entirely their own fault, therefore, that they were not cured by him. In like manner, Christ the second Adam has a patent from the Sovereign of heaven constituting Him the Savior of the world; by the sovereign authority of Jehovah the Father He is invested with that high office. "We have seen, and do testify," says an apostle, "that the Father sent the Son to be the Savior of the world" (1 John 4:14). No sinner, therefore, to whom the gospel has come shall perish for want of a Savior. Christ Jesus, O sinner, is the Savior of the world. He is by office your Savior and my Savior, be our case ever so deplorable. Let no man say, "Alas! I have nothing to do with Jesus, nor He with me; for I am a sinner, a great sinner, a lost sinner, the chief of sinners." Be it known to you that your being a sinner of mankind is a proof, not indeed that He is your Savior in possession, but that He is your Savior in offer, your Savior by office. If therefore you resolve to employ another Savior in preference to Him, or to pine away in your disease rather than commit yourself to Him as the physician of souls, you do it upon your peril (Mark 16:16).

He is constituted the great Burden-bearer, whose office it is to give rest to them who labor and are heavy laden (Psalm 55:22; Matthew 11:28). Sinners of mankind in common are they, properly speaking, who labor and are heavy laden. They spend their labor for that which does not satisfy; they are laden with iniquity, yea, heavy laden; and not the less, but the more so, that they are not duly sensible of it. The Lord Jesus, then, stands in the relationship of a Savior by office to the world of mankind, or to sinners of mankind indefinitely, who therefore are the object of His administration of the covenant.

PARTICULAR 5. Finally, if Christ's administration of the covenant were not thus general, some sinners of mankind could have no more warrant to trust in Him for their salvation than fallen angels have; contrary to the uniform tenor of the gospel (John 3:16; Mark 16:15; Revelation 22:17). They, doubtless, have no warrant to take hold of the covenant or trust in Jesus for salvation to whom He is not authorized externally to administer the covenant. But who of mankind-sinners can those excepted persons be? Not heathens or infidels, who do not hear and do not know the gospel; for though in the unfathomable depth of sovereign wisdom that warrant to believe is not intimated to them, yet it really extends to them as persons included in that universal term "whosoever" (John 3:16; Revelation 22:18). And, indeed, if it did not extend to them and to all of them, ministers of the gospel could not lawfully preach or offer the covenant to them, any more than a courier could lawfully proclaim and offer his prince's indemnity to criminals who have no concern in it, but are excepted out of it. The ministerial gospel-offer is undoubtedly null as far as it exceeds the limits of the object of Christ's administration of the covenant; for so far, it would exceed the limits of the Father's original and authentic gospel-offer (John 6:32), and so would cease to afford a divine warrant to sinners to believe in Jesus. Neither are any sinners who hear the gospel excepted; for their not taking hold of the covenant by believing in Christ is the greatest sin, and the greatest as well as surest cause of the condemnation of all who, hearing the gospel, do not believe in Him (Proverbs 8:36; John 3:19, 36; Mark 16:16). But were any of them excepted, it could not be

The Administration of the Covenant of Grace

the sin of such not to believe or trust in Him; for it can never be a man's sin not to do a thing that he has no warrant from God to do. If every hearer of the gospel had not a revealed warrant to take hold of the covenant by believing in Jesus, no hearer of it could justly be condemned for refusing to believe in Him. Much less are the non-elect excepted; for if they were, not only should their unbelief cease to be their sin, but the elect themselves could never warrantably begin to believe till after their election were revealed to them, which would be quite contrary to the settled order of grace in the covenant. For none can, according to the covenant, truly believe or trust in Jesus for all their salvation till once they begin to see their warrant inasmuch as that warrant is the stated ground of faith; but a man's guarantee in the Lord Jesus of his election is not to be attained till after he has begun to believe.

It is plain, therefore, that sinners of mankind indefinitely are the object of Christ's external administration of the covenant; that He is authorized so to administer it to you who read this and to every sinner of the family of Adam, however numerous or aggravated his sins may have been; and that every man must either take hold of Jehovah's covenant by accepting Christ as His righteousness and strength offered to him in the gospel or perish externally as a proud despiser of Christ and of the eternal covenant administered by Him.

SECTION 3. The Ends of the Administration of the Covenant

The ends for which Christ the last Adam administers the covenant of grace are the bringing of sinners personally into the bond of it, the managing of them who are already instated therein, according to it while they remain in this world, and the completion of their happiness according to it in the world to come.

1. The first end is the bringing of sinners personally into the bond of the covenant: "And now, saith the Lord that formed me from the womb to be His Servant, to bring Jacob again to Him, Though Israel be not gathered, yet shall I be glorious in the eyes of the Lord, and my God shall be my strength" (Isaiah 49:5). Though the covenant was settled from eternity, long before we could either consent or dissent, yet by the constitution thereof it is provided that even to the end of time any sinner's receiving of that covenant by faith shall be as valid to enter him into it as if he had subscribed it personally at the making of it (John 3:36). In the offers of the gospel, it is left open to sinners of mankind in order that any of them entering into it may occupy his place in it under Christ the Head, and so become personally confederate with Jehovah, as well as interested in life eternal. There is room enough in the covenant, under the infinitely great name of the last Adam, for every sinner of mankind to subscribe his little name. Though, therefore, since the time that Eve, by believing the promise, first set down her name, whereby she then became to be the mother of all living (Genesis 3:20), many have subscribed under that glorious name, each of them saying, "I am the Lord's" (Isaiah 44:5); yet the voice of the gospel still is, and to the end of time will be, and yet there is room (Luke 14:22). Now the blessed Mediator was authorized to treat with sinners, those rebels against heaven and subjects of Satan's kingdom, in order to bring them over to God again, and for that purpose to administer the covenant to them by proposing it to them and gathering them into the bond of it. Hence, having gone forth upon that embassy, He testifies His earnestness in the work. "O Jerusalem, Jerusalem . . . how often would I have gathered thy children" (Matthew 23:37).

2. The second end is the management of them who are already instated in the covenant, according to it while they con-

tinue in this world; when sinners are, by Christ's administration, brought into the bond of the covenant they are not henceforth entrusted with the management of themselves and of their stock but their whole stock is lodged with Him as the sovereign and solemn Manager of it; and they themselves are committed to His oversight as the great Shepherd and Bishop of souls (1 Peter 2:25). Whatever they need they must receive it from His hand; whatever blessings they hope to enjoy He is to dispense them to them. Are they to be justified? He is to pronounce the sentence, "Thy sins be forgiven thee" (Matthew 9:2, 6). Are they to be adopted? He it is who gives them power to become the sons and daughters of God (John 1:12). Are they to be washed and sanctified? He is commissioned to sanctify and cleanse them (Ephesians 5:26), to give repentance to them as well as forgiveness of sins (Acts 5:31). Are they to be comforted on every side? As the consolation of Israel, He it is who said to them, "I, even I, am He that comforteth you" (Isaiah 51:12). Are they to be made to persevere in grace? Those whom the Father gave Him, He is to keep so that none of them can be lost (John 17:12). Are they to be tenderly cared for, with regard to their temporal concerns? The care of all these is devolved on Him. He is the antitypical Joseph, who has all the stores of the covenant in His hand; and respecting Him the Father said to them, as Pharaoh did to his famishing subjects when they cried to him for bread, "Go unto Joseph" (Genesis 41:55). In a word, are they to receive commands or directions concerning their duty? It is from Him that they must receive all their orders respecting duty in every particular. They must receive the law at His mouth since, according to the covenant, it is by Him that Jehovah speaks to them. God the Father, therefore, has given a solemn charge to all the people of the covenant, saying, "This is My beloved Son, in whom I am well pleased; hear ye Him" (Matthew

17:5). "Beware of him, and obey his voice, provoke him not . . . for My name is in him" (Exodus 23:21).

3. Finally, the third end is the completion of their felicity, according to the covenant, in the heavenly world. One blessed end of His administration of the covenant is that He may present His elect seed to Himself a glorious Church, not having spot or wrinkle, or any such thing (Ephesians 5:27). It is, indeed, a ground of unspeakable consolation to the saints that the blessed Mediator administers the covenant in this world so that, however remote the place is to which they may be driven, they can never be driven to any corner to which His administration does not reach. The most comfortable part, however, of His administration is performed in the heavenly world; for it is there that the promises of the eternal covenant are fully accomplished. It is this that makes heaven so desirable to the saints. The passage from the one world to the other is indeed a dangerous and a gloomy one. Who can, without terror and trembling, think of the cold and deep waters of the Jordan of death, and of the gloomy mansions of the grave! But at the same time, the people of Christ should consider that He has business in that passage as well as on each side of it. The line of the covenant is extended straight through it, forming a path by which the ransomed of the Lord safely pass through; so that there also is the scene of the last Adam's administration of the covenant. He has the keys of hell and of death (Revelation 1:18). It reveals great weakness to think that a merciful and faithful Redeemer only stands, as it were, on the other side of the river, pointing to the departing believer how to direct his course, and ready to receive him as soon as he reaches the shore. Nay, verily, it is incumbent upon Him, as Administration of the covenant, even to go into the water with the passenger, to take him by the arm and, going between him and the stream, to break the force of it

The Administration of the Covenant of Grace

to him, and so to bring him safely to shore. "Though I walk," says David, "through the valley of the shadow of death, I will fear no evil; for Thou art with me" (Psalm 23:4). He did not say, "Light is with me, or light is afforded me in the dark valley to dispel the gloom," but, "Thou art with me; Thou Thyself, the fountain of light." Oh, how effectual must this be, when firmly believed, to render that gloomy passage lightsome and even desirable! When the Israelites were passing over to Canaan, the ark of the covenant went *first* into Jordan, and was *last* in coming out, staying there till after all the people had safely passed over (Joshua 3:4-17). The ark being a type of Messiah, as Canaan was of heaven and Jordan of death, this instructs us that our faithful Redeemer will have business in the passage between this and the heavenly world so long as there is one of His redeemed to pass that way; or until the last soul within the bond of the covenant has landed safely on the other side.

When this is done, He will administer the covenant to them there also, completing their blessedness by a perfect accomplishment of all the promises of it to them. Jesus, said an apostle, is the Author and Finisher of our faith (Hebrews 12:2). In these words he alluded to the races, famous among the ancient Greeks, in which there was one who opened the race, ran it, and went on the head of all the rest of the runners, and another who was set on a throne at the end of the course and awarded the prize to him who won it. In the Christian race, the Lord Jesus performs both these parts. As performer of the conditions of the covenant in the course of His obedience, in which He endured the cross, despising the shame, He is the Author, the chief Leader of our faith; and in bringing many sons unto glory He, as the Captain or chief Leader, goes on ahead of them (Hebrews 2:10) and is therefore called the Forerunner (Hebrews 6:20). Then, as Administration of the covenant, He is the Finisher of our faith, the perfecter of that which concerns us who, being set down at the right hand of the throne of God, bestows the crown on them who so run as to obtain. Thus it is His office to set the crown of glory that does not fade away on the heads of those who, by His grace, He has made more than conquerors. From His hand the holy Apostle Paul, expected it. Henceforth, said he, there is laid up for me a crown of righteousness, which the Lord, the righteous Judge, the Lord Jesus to whom all judgment is committed, shall give me at that day (2 Timothy 4:8). To Him as Administrator of the covenant, it also belongs to grant to them who overcome to sit with Him on His throne (Revelation 3:21). I therefore humbly apprehend that the passage in Matthew 20:23 may safely be read without the supplement: "To sit on My right hand and on My left is not Mine to give, but for whom it is prepared of My Father" (The conjunction rendered "but" in the passage here cited is likewise used in an exceptive sense in 2 Corinthians 2:5 and in Mark 9:8).

The fullness of power given to the second Adam comprehends all power in heaven as well as on earth (Matthew 28:18). Hence He prepares in His Father's house a place for each of His saints, having it as Administrator of the covenant wholly at His disposal. And He is to administer the covenant to them not only at their entrance into the mansions of bliss, but during all the revolutions of eternity, seeing He is to remain the bond of union and the medium of communication between God and them for evermore (Revelation 7:17; Hebrews 7:25).

Seeing then that these are the ends of the Administration devolved on the last Adam, it is manifest that the elect only are the object of the more special, internal, and efficacious administration of that eternal covenant; and that it is externally administered to others in order to subserve the salvation of the elect and the glory of Jehovah, Father, Son, and Holy Spirit, in that great salvation (1 Corinthians 3:21, 22; Ephesians 4:1113; 2 Corinthians 4:15).

SECTION 4. The Nature and Form of Christ's Administration of the Covenant

Of the nature and form of the administration of the covenant we may have a distinct view by considering the relationships in which Christ the last Adam stands to the covenant as Administrator of it. We have already seen that He became the Mediator of the covenant, both substantial and official, and that His official mediation runs through the whole of that divine contract; and we have also taken notice of a fourfold relationship of His to it, namely of His being the Servant of the Father, according to it; the Kinsman-redeemer of His elect in it; the Surety and the sacrificing Priest of it. These parts of His mediation relate to the conditions of the covenant, and so belong to the making of it. It will be proper now to consider His other relationships to it, namely those parts of His mediation that, as they respect the promises of the covenant, belong to the administration of it, and they are these five: He is the Trustee, the Testator, the interceding Priest, the Prophet, and the King of the covenant. Each of these is a letter of that name which is above every name given to Him by the Father as a reward of His obedience unto death. As the Trustee of the covenant He received from the Father, for the benefit of His people, all the purchased and promised benefits of it. Having these all in His hands, He as the Testator thereof bequeaths them as His legacies to sinners of mankind. As the Executor of His own testament, He, in the characters of their interceding Priest, instructing Prophet, and almighty King, confers His inestimable legacies upon His elect seed. In considering these in their order, the nature and form of His administration of the covenant will plainly appear.

1. Christ the Trustee of the Covenant of Grace

The last Adam as Administrator is, in the first place, the Trustee of the covenant, having the covenant itself and all the blessings of it committed to His trust. "For it pleased the Father that in Him should all fullness dwell" (Colossians 1:19). For this, the greatest of all trusts, infinitely too great for any mere man or angel, our divine Redeemer was perfectly well qualified; and so He was set over the house of God, having all the precious things of it committed to His care. That which is sealed up from the highest angels of light He has full access to. To Him it is entrusted to loose the seals, for He is worthy (Revelation 5:2-5). A holy and a jealous God put no such trust in His servants, and His angels He charged with folly (Job 4:18); for, as they were naturally fallible, it was possible for them to betray their trust. But it pleased Him from everlasting to entrust the blessed Mediator, as an infallible Administrator, with all the fullness of the covenant.

This high trust was indispensably requisite to the exercise of His administration. And therefore upon His engagement to fulfill the conditions of the covenant (accounted in heaven as sure, as if they had already been actually fulfilled), all the blessings of it were not only transferred to Him in point of right, but were delivered to Him in actual possession so that, according to the method therein settled, He might freely dispense them to sinners. "The Father loveth the Son, and hath given all things into His hand" (John 3:35). "All things are delivered unto Me of My Father . . . Come unto Me, all ye that labor and are heavy laden, and I will give you rest" (Matthew 11:27, 28). Hence He was ready to begin, and He actually entered upon His administration of the covenant on that very day in which the first Adam fell; though the solemnity of His investiture or taking possession was delayed till His ascension to heaven when, in human na-

The Administration of the Covenant of Grace

ture, He was set down at the right hand of the throne of God (Genesis 3:8, 15 compared with Psalm 68:18 and with Ephesians 1:20-22).

Thus the infinite and overflowing fullness of the covenant is in Him; and therefore that fullness is in Scripture called "the unsearchable riches of Christ." Seeing that these riches are unsearchable, and are therefore incapable of being so explored by any created understanding as to be, either in their value or variety, fully calculated, I shall, agreeably to what has been observed in a foregoing chapter, attempt merely to unlock them by explaining the following particulars:

PARTICULAR 1. The invisible guard of the covenant is entirely at His disposal. All power over natural and over spiritual things is given to Him that He may manage the whole, for the preservation and the restraint of them who are afterwards to be brought into the bond of the covenant while as yet they are strangers to it and neither perceive the invincible guard that surrounds them nor the glorious Commander of it. "The Father . . . hath committed all judgment unto the Son" (John 5:22). "Thus saith the Lord, As the new wine is found in the cluster, and one saith, Destroy it not; for a blessing is in it; so will I do for my servants' sake, that I may not destroy them all" (Isaiah 65:8). "I taught Ephraim also to go, taking them by their arms; but they knew not that I healed them" (Hosea 11:3). During their state of spiritual blindness they are sometimes in the most imminent danger of losing their lives, and at other times narrowly escape a torrent of strong temptations, threatening to sweep them away; and yet the force of these is, by some means or other, broken, and they are brought back from the very brink of eternal destruction. At the same time, they themselves never truly know whose debtors they are for those deliverances, nor do they discern the merciful design of redeeming love in them until converting grace has reached their hearts; and then they hear the Captain of that guard saying to each of them, as He did to Cyrus, "I girded thee, though thou hast not known me" (Isaiah 45:5). "The mountain was full of horses and chariots of fire, round about Elisha and his servant; while yet the servant saw none of them, but only saw those that came against them, till the Lord opened his eyes" (2 Kings 6:17).

PARTICULAR 2. The quickening Spirit of the covenant is in Him, whereby He causes sinners dead in sins to live a spiritual life. The quickening influences of the Spirit, having been purchased by the meritorious life and satisfactory death of the second Adam, all the fullness of them was, according to the covenant, lodged in Him. Hence He proposed Himself to the angel of the inanimate church in Sardis as One who had the seven Spirits of God (Revelation 3:1). And He said to the Jews, "The dead shall hear the voice of the Son of God, and they that hear shall live" (John 5:25); that is, dead souls shall so hear His voice as to be quickened by it and, being quickened to spiritual life, shall believe in Him. The first Adam, having been made a living soul, was capable to transmit natural life; but since he was not made a quickening Spirit he was not able to restore life after it was once lost; but on the contrary, the last Adam was made a quickening Spirit that He might restore spiritual life to sinners who were spiritually dead. He is, therefore, according to the covenant, a living and a life-giving Head, a Head of spiritual and eternal life to all His mystical members. With Him, as the Trustee of the covenant, is the fountain of life; in His light, souls when they are quickened see light (Psalm 36:9). The sin of the first Adam put out the lights of the whole world; his natural descendants were all left by him as so many extinguished candles. But the last Adam is constituted and set up a flaming lamp to light them again; and as many of them as it touches immediately

The Administration of the Covenant of Grace 279

begin to flame; and could they all but touch it (and none of them is forbidden) they should all be lighted again, and shine as lights in the world with the light of spiritual life.

PARTICULAR 3. The justifying righteousness of the covenant is also in Him. "This, therefore, is His name whereby He shall be called, JEHOVAH our RIGHTEOUSNESS" (Jeremiah 23:6). The beautiful garment of original righteousness was, as it were, worn to pieces on the back of the first Adam, so that there was nothing of that kind left for any of his natural offspring, as it is written, "There is none righteous, no not one" (Romans 3:10). But Christ the second Adam, having by His holy nature, righteous life, and satisfactory death wrought out all the righteousness that the law in its covenant-form required, brought it in and presented it to His eternal Father (Daniel 9:24 compared with Leviticus 16:15). The Father, having accepted it as the righteousness of His eternal covenant for justifying all who believe, entrusted the glorious Worker thereof with it and lodged it in His hands as the Administrator of that covenant. Hence He is said to be made unto us righteousness (1 Corinthians 1:30), namely by a divine constitution, just as He was made a covenant of the people. A declaration of this is in the gospel made to sinners for a ground of faith. "Surely shall one say, 'In the Lord have I righteousness' (Hebrew: "Only in Jehovah (of me he hath said) are righteousnesses," or, "is all righteousness" (Isaiah 45:24). These are the words of Messiah, in which He gives an account of the divine constitution respecting Himself (verse 23 with Romans 14:10, 11). The gospel of Christ, therefore, is called the ministration of righteousness (2 Corinthians 3:9). Thus He is entrusted with His own consummate righteousness that He may, according to the covenant, administer it to guilty sinners for their justification (Romans 5:18).

PARTICULAR 4. The new covenant-right and relation to God as a Friend, Father, and God are in Him as the exalted Mediator. As Trustee of the covenant He was entrusted with and possessed of all the fullness of God that, as the Administrator, He might communicate it to all who should believe in Him. "In Him," said the Apostle Paul, "dwelleth all the fullness of the Godhead bodily. And ye are complete in Him who is the Head" (Colossians 2:9, 10). As the only begotten of the Father, our Lord Jesus had a natural, a necessary, an indefeasible right to all the fullness of the Godhead inasmuch as the divine nature, with all the perfections of the glorious Godhead in their utmost fullness, resided and do reside substantially in His incarnate person. But besides that He as the second Adam purchased by His obedience unto death a new right to all that fullness; and the same was consequently entrusted to Him in order that it might be imparted by Him to all the members of His mystical body. Thus the peace of the covenant, that peace of God that surpasses all understanding, is in Him (Ephesians 2:14; Philippians 4:7). The sonship of the covenant, the adoption of children, is in Him as the first-born among many brethren (John 1:12; Romans 8:29). The covenant interest in God as one's own God is likewise in Him (John 20:17). As these inestimable privileges are all under His hand as the Trustee, and all in Him as the Storehouse of the covenant; the only way to attain the possession of them is by faith to receive, and to be united to Him.

PARTICULAR 5. The sanctifying grace of the covenant by which believing sinners are rendered holy is in Him. "It pleased the Father that in Him should all fullness dwell" (Colossians 1:19). "And of His fullness," says the evangelist John, "have all we received, even grace for grace" (John 1:16). All fullness of sanctifying influence, having been purchased by Him as the Surety, was lodged with Him as the Trustee of the covenant.

The Administration of the Covenant of Grace 281

Hence He is said to be made unto us sanctification (1 Corinthians 1:30). Accordingly, out of His pierced side came there forth blood and water—blood to remove the guilt and water to wash away the pollution of sin. It was prophesied concerning Him that He should be a fountain opened for sin and for uncleanness; not a vessel of that water of purification which, however full it might be, would lack as much as it should communicate, but a fountain, an inexhaustible spring, to supply the necessities of the unclean without the least diminution of its contents. "For God giveth not the Spirit by measure unto Him" (John 3:34). There is therefore in Him, our Covenant-head, such an overflowing fullness of the Spirit of holiness as is, by the infinite efficacy of it, sufficient to sanctify the whole race of Adam. There is grace enough in Him to mollify and melt down the hardest hearts to evangelical repentance (Acts 5:31); to subdue and mortify the strongest corruptions (Galatians 5:34); and to quicken and strengthen believers for all spiritual obedience (2 Timothy 2:1).

PARTICULAR 6. The comforting grace of the covenant is in Him. All comforting influences of grace are, according to the covenant, treasured up in Him. He is, by the Father, the God of all comfort, entrusted with all those spiritual influences that serve to invigorate, enliven, enlarge, or solace the hearts of His redeemed. Hence He is in Scripture called "the Consolation of Israel" (Luke 2:25). It is by Him that the consolation of the saints abounds (2 Corinthians 1:5). He it is who, as Administrator of the covenant, sends forth from the Father the Comforter to abide with them forever (John 14:16). Accordingly, He said to all who believe in Him, "I, even I, am He that comforteth you" (Isaiah 51:12). The Apostle Paul thus prays for the Thessalonians: "Now our Lord Jesus Christ Himself, and God even our Father, which . . . hath given us everlasting consolation, and good hope through grace, comfort your hearts" (2 Thessalonians 2:16, 17). This is one of the cheering promises that, in Jesus Christ as Trustee of the covenant, are all yea and Amen. "As one whom his mother comforteth, so will I comfort you; and ye shall be comforted in Jerusalem" (Isaiah 66:13).

PARTICULAR 7. The establishing grace of the covenant that causes all who are within the bond of it, however inconstant they are in themselves to persevere steadfastly to the end, is in Him. Hence we are informed that they who are sanctified by God the Father are preserved in Jesus Christ (Jude verse 1). In the covenant, He is constituted the Head of influences to all His mystical members; and therefore they are all to have nourishment ministered by Him (Colossians 2:19). The dispensing of continued pardon, so necessary for them in this their state of imperfection, is also committed to Him as Trustee of the covenant. "Him hath God exalted with His right hand, to be a Prince and a Savior, for to give repentance to Israel, and forgiveness of sins" (Acts 5:31). Thus having all fullness of grace in Himself to communicate to them, suited to all their exigencies, whether in respect of the guilt or of the power of remaining sin, He is completely furnished for preserving and establishing them in their state and exercise of grace to the end.

PARTICULAR 8. The temporal good things of the covenant are all in His hand; so that it belongs to Him to afford His people sufficient provision and protection while they remain in this world. A promise was in the covenant made to Him that He should, as the first-born of the family of heaven, inherit all things; and therefore, as was observed above, in His person as the last Adam, the ancient and forfeited dominion over the creatures was restored. As the high Trustee of the covenant, the inheritance of the world and of all things that are in it, was by the Father delivered into His hands so that He as Mediator is not only in right, but in fact, Lord of the world, having supreme dominion over all the creatures and all the comforts in it, from the least of them to the greatest. This He Himself declares: "All things are delivered unto Me of My Father" (Matthew 11:27). "All power is given unto Me in heaven and in earth" (Matthew 28:18). To encourage His ancient people, when oppressed by poverty, to persist, notwithstanding in building the second temple He said to them, "The silver is mine, and the gold is mine" (Haggai 2:8). That these are the words of Messiah is evident from verse 6 compared with Hebrews 11:26. Accordingly, from these words of the Psalmist, "The earth is the Lord's, and the fullness thereof" (Psalm 24:1), the Apostle Paul evidences the right of true believers to the creatures (1 Corinthians 10:25, 26). The sun, moon, and stars, the earth, sea, and air, with all that in them is, are deposited in the hands of Christ as the Trustee of the covenant; so that He is empowered to dispose of them all according to the covenant for the glory of God and welfare of the saints.

PARTICULAR 9. All fullness of power over death and the grave is committed to Him, by which He can completely disarm and destroy death, and so bring to pass a glorious resurrection of His mystical members. "I," says the glorious Trustee of the covenant, "have the keys of hell, and of death" (Revelation 1:18). Death and the grave are, indeed, mighty conquerors, and none of the guilty sons of Adam is able to resist them; yet, mighty as they are, they are far from being absolute potentates; there is One above them to whose orders they must strictly adhere. Death may, indeed, enter within the boundaries of the covenant, and carry off the children of the second Adam as well as others; but at the border it must drop its sting and enter without it. The whole power of death is now in the hands of the almighty Redeemer; and He will not suffer it to enter there, armed with its sting. And the time comes in which He will say to the grave, "Give up"; and then its bars will burst in sunder, its gates fly open, and it will yield up to Him its numerous inhabitants; for, as Administrator of the covenant, He is entrusted with infinite power over death and the grave.

PARTICULAR 10. Finally, the complete and everlasting happiness of the covenant is in His hand, by which He renders the souls of His redeemed perfectly blessed, immediately after death, and their souls and bodies reunited, perfectly blessed, at the last day. All power in heaven is given to Him. His eternal Father has constituted Him the glorious repository of life eternal; the inexhaustible fountain, whence it will forever stream forth to all the heirs of promise. The dispensing of it to the redeemed throughout an endless eternity is entrusted to Him. Hence are these consoling declarations: "God hath given to us eternal life; and this life is in His Son" (1 John 5:11). "Thou hast given Him power over all flesh, that He should give eternal life to as many as Thou hast given Him" (John 17:2). His Father, in making the covenant with Him, entrusted Him with eternal life; and His people, in taking hold of the covenant, trust in Him for the same. In the immediate prospect of dying, they commit their souls to this faithful Trustee, as Stephen did, each of them saying, "Lord Jesus, receive my spirit" (Acts 7:59). Keeping that which each of them commits to Him against the great day, He will then solemnly receive them, soul and body, into His heavenly kingdom and glory.

Thus, Christ the last Adam is the glorious Trustee to whose trust the infinite fullness of the covenant is committed for the benefit of His chosen seed.

2. *Christ the Testator of the Covenant*

Our Lord Jesus as last Adam is constituted the Testator as well as the Trustee of the covenant of grace (Hebrews 9:16, 17).

The Administration of the Covenant of Grace 285

By the conditions of the covenant God had a sufficient recompense made to Him for the wrong done by sinners to His manifested glory; and by the promises Christ had unsearchable riches to communicate to them by which they might be rendered unspeakably happy; and being, according to the covenant, to die, He early made His testament as a deed or conveyance of those to each of them. In so doing He turned the promissory part of the covenant respecting them into a testament in their favor. "This cup," says He to all who believe in Him, "is the new testament in My blood which is shed for you" (Luke 22:20).

A testament among men is the declaration of a man's latter will concerning the disposal of his property after his decease. By the testament of Christ, therefore, we are to understand the declaration of His will respecting the disposal or conveyance of the inestimable blessings that He purchased by His obedience and death. Although that divine contract, so often mentioned above, was strictly federal, as established between the Father and the Son, yet it is also strictly testamentary as it is confirmed by the death of Christ and exhibited to sinners of mankind. All the essentials of a testament are to be found in it such as a Testator who by His death confirmed it, a seed to be constituted heirs, an inheritance to be conveyed, and a deed or conveyance legally drawn and duly ratified so as to be pleadable in behalf of the legatees. The benefits of the covenant, considered as offered and promised by Christ, are so many legacies in respect of the freeness with which they are bestowed on the children of the covenant. The spiritual seed of Christ are, properly speaking, the legatees. They do not rely on their own, but on His righteousness; they do not plead their faith nor their works, but His testament, as the ground of their claim of right. And, as in testaments among men, he who accepts any one of the articles thereby obliges himself to accept and adhere to the whole; so he who accepts any one promise of the new covenant or testament must accept and cleave to all the promises; and when once accepted the promises and privileges of it must be used for the acceptable performance of all the duties consequent upon a saving interest in them.

Hence it is manifest that Christ's making of His testament belongs to the administration of the covenant committed to Him for the glorious purpose of rendering sinners of mankind partakers of the inestimable blessings of it, yea, and that it is the first and fundamental act of that administration, laid as a foundation of all the other acts of it, which are only so many means employed in executing the testament. Upon His undertaking to fulfill the conditions of the covenant, the Father disposed of the blessings contained in the promise of it to Him; and the blessings thus disposed of were, as was already observed, actually delivered into His hand as the appointed Trustee of the covenant. Now having them all thus in His hand, He made a disposition of them to needy sinners by way of testament. "I appoint unto you," said He, "a kingdom, as My Father hath appointed unto Me," or, "I dispose of a kingdom to you, as My Father hath disposed of it to Me." The verb in the original signifies to dispose or dispose of; and it conveys the notion both of a federal and of a testamentary disposition. Of the former kind was the disposition made by the Father to Christ as last Adam, namely a federal or covenant-disposition as being made to Him on a most onerous cause, a condition properly so called, viz. the making of His soul an offering for sin (Isaiah 53:10). This could not be a testamentary disposition because where a testament is there must also of necessity be the death of the testator (Hebrews 9:16), which, it is manifest, could have no place in the case of the Father. Of the latter sort is the disposition made by Christ to sinners of mankind, namely a testamentary disposition that must,

The Administration of the Covenant of Grace 287

in its very nature, be a deed or conveyance of grace and bounty without conditions properly so-called. Sinners were utterly unable to fulfill such conditions; and therefore it was indispensably requisite that it should be a testament, or testamentary disposition.

In order to elucidate the nature of this testament that it is of infinite importance for sinners to know, it will be proper to consider the making of it, the legatees, the legacies, and the Executor.

First, as to the making of Christ's testament, let it be carefully attended to that, though the covenant was made from eternity, the testament was not made till after the beginning of time. Christ made His testament only in the character of Administrator of the covenant; but He did not enter upon His administration of the covenant till after time began. He was indeed from all eternity the Trustee of the covenant, which high trust was previously necessary to His administration; yet inasmuch as His commencing as Testator of the covenant was an act of His administration of it, there could be no place for that until He had an opportunity to administer the covenant—and that He could not have till after the covenant of works was broken. This will appear evident if the reader adverts to the nature of a testament among men, which is not only a will, but a will declared, testified, and signified by word or writ or some other external sign pleadable by the legatees in order to their obtaining of the legacies therein bequeathed to them.

The testament of our Lord Jesus is, with respect to substance, but one. The Testator is one, and the inheritance one, and so is the testament in which that inheritance is bequeathed. With regard to the legacies disposed of, the testament is only one; but with respect to the circumstances of it, and the means by which the legatees are put in possession of the legacies, it is twofold, and is denominated the first or old, and the second or new testament (2 Corinthians 3:14; Hebrews 9:15). Hence are these words of an apostle, cited from Jeremiah 31:31: "Behold, the days come, saith the Lord, when I will make a new covenant with the house of Israel, and with the house of Judah; not according to the covenant that I made with their fathers in the day when I took them by the hand to lead them out of the land of Egypt. In that He saith, 'A new covenant,' He hath made the first old" (Hebrews 8:8, 9, 13). The apostle's meaning in these verses would be more obvious were they rendered, as some have rendered them, "Behold, the days come, saith the Lord, when I will make [Gr. consummate, perfect] a new testament to the house of Israel, and to the house of Judah; not according to the testament that I made to their fathers, etc. In that He saith, 'A new testament,' He hath made the first old." Compare herewith Hebrews 9:18. (See William Bell's *Sermons on Various Subjects*, p. 177, published in 1817).

The Old Testament, published before His incarnation, is the declaration of the last will of our dying Savior in which He freely bequeaths His unsearchable riches to sinners of mankind, confirmed by His typical death in innumerable sacrifices of divine institution, sealed with the seals of circumcision and the Passover, and continued in the church till the fullness of time when He Himself was to be manifested in the flesh (Hebrews 9:20; Romans 4:11; 1 Corinthians 5:7; Luke 16:16). His testament in this form was originally expressed by word of mouth, which kind of testament is called a nuncupative testament, or a testament verbally pronounced; but afterwards it was committed to writing so that there were not only words of the testament to be heard, but books of the testament to be read, by the legatees. In that part of sacred writ called the Old Testament we have this

The Administration of the Covenant of Grace 289

testament written out in proper form (Hebrews 9:19, 20; 2 Peter 1:21; Romans 15:4).

The New Testament, published after His incarnation, is the declaration of the same last will of our dying Redeemer in which He freely bequeaths His unsearchable riches of grace and glory to poor sinners, confirmed by His own death on the cross, sealed with the seals of baptism and the Lord's supper, and to be continued in the church till the end of time (2 Corinthians 3:6; Hebrews 9:16; 1 Corinthians 11:23-26). This also was originally delivered by word of mouth during the time of His public ministry, in the course of which He declared His will concerning the blessings to be enjoyed by all who should believe on Him. The Apostle Paul informs us that the great salvation offered in the gospel, at the first, began to be spoken by the Lord (Hebrews 2:3). It also was afterwards committed to writing; and now we have it likewise a written testament in that part of Scripture that is called the New Testament (John 20:31).

As to the original date of the first or old testament of Christ, we find that it was of a date as early as the nature and circumstances of it could admit. It was made in paradise on the very day in which the first Adam fell, and made in the cool or wind of the day (Genesis 3:8), that is, in the cool or the windy part of the evening, called in Exodus 23:6 the time between the two evenings, or between three and six of the clock in the evening. That was the time in which the second Adam did, in the promise that He the Seed of the woman should bruise the serpent's head, while it should bruise His heel (Genesis 3:15), foreshow His death and declare His will that the benefits to be purchased thereby should be conferred on the elect seed. As there could be no need of any of His legacies before Adam fell, Christ did not till then begin to be a Testator; but on the very day, and perhaps in the very hour, in which the former began to be poor, the latter began to form and publish His testament. Some, unwilling to think of their death, delay the making of their testaments until they be stretched on a deathbed; but so willing was Christ the second Adam to die for sinners that He set His house in order and so prepared for death on the very day that the first Adam deserved to die. The business of the offended Majesty of heaven and of the fallen world of mankind required haste. The whole fabric of this world was, by the sin of the first Adam, so unhinged as to be hastening to dissolution, and mankind about to perish in the ruins, until the last Adam went under and so bore up the pillars thereof as to establish the earth again (Isaiah 49:8). In paradise, therefore, in the cool of the day He made His testament in few words, bequeathing the benefits of the covenant of grace to needy sinners (Genesis 3:15), and typically went in under that infinite weight of divine wrath that was pressing down the whole world. This testament was afterwards renewed to Abraham, to whom the promises were made (Galatians 3:16), which are comprehended in this phrase, "the covenants (or testaments) of promise" (Ephesians 2:12). It was also renewed to Israel in the wilderness when Moses sprinkled them with blood, saying, "This is the blood of the testament, which God hath enjoined unto you" (Hebrews 9:19, 20). This then was the old or first testament of Christ, upon which all who believed during four thousand years built their faith and hope of attaining the legacies therein bequeathed.

The Apostle Paul says that a testament is of no strength at all while the testator lives (Hebrews 9:17). Was the testament of Christ, then, of no force during the space of four thousand years? Yes, it was of force; for it was preconfirmed, or confirmed before, of God in Christ (Galatians 3:17). The confirmation of a testament is declared in Scripture to be by the death of the Testator. Now there was a two-fold death of Christ as Testator, one

The Administration of the Covenant of Grace 291

typical and another real. In respect of His typical death He was the Lamb slain from the foundation of the world (Revelation 13:8), having died typically in the sacrifices that continued to be offered under the patriarchal and Jewish dispensation. It was by that typical death of the glorious Testator that His testament was preconfirmed (death simply was all that was required to confirm a testament, but since covenants anciently were initiated and ratified by a sacrifice, or at best cut in two, a bloody death was deemed requisite to confirm a covenant). Since then the blood of Christ is, especially in Matthew 26:28, called the blood of the *diatheke*, which signifies a covenant as well as a testament, His bloody death ought to be considered not only as that of the Testator, but also as that of the Priest of the covenant; for so far as it was bloody and availed as a propitiatory sacrifice, it ratified the covenant of grace and reconciliation; but so far as it was death simply, it ratified the absolute promise of that same covenant, as turned into a testament. This double relation of the death of our Lord Jesus proves that when we meet with *diatheke* in the writings of the New Testament, we ought not to stop in the precise signification of a testament only, but ought also to join the signification of a covenant; in order that the efficacy, and especially the satisfactory virtue, of His death may the more fully appear; so that, from the day in which it was first made, it was of force for the legatees' obtaining of the legacies therein bequeathed.

In the second place, I now proceed to consider the legatees, or persons to whom the legacies were left.

In order to know distinctly who the legatees are, it will be requisite again to advert to the meaning of a testament among men. The testament of a dying man is his last will, declared and attested, in which he disposes of his property, or appoints to whom it shall be given after his death. In his testament he transfers or bequeaths his possessions to those whom he ordains to possess them after he ceases himself to possess them any longer; or in other words, his testament is his last will, directing the disposal of his possessions after his decease. In like manner, the testament of our Lord Jesus is His will, declaring how He would have His unsearchable riches disposed of, or to whom He bequeaths them. Now by consulting His testament we find that He therein disposes of them in a twofold way: first, in the way of giving them in offer, or of offering them to all sinners of mankind who hear the gospel; and next, in the way of giving them in possession to some of those sinners. While He bequeaths or disposes of them in possession to some, He disposes of them in offer to all to whom the testament is intimated, or the gospel preached.

1. Christ in His testament disposes of His legacies in the way of granting them in offer to all sinners of mankind who hear the gospel. He so disposes of them as to offer them to sinners in common. He ordains that they should be offered to all to whom the gospel is preached, and that all should be invited, and even commanded, so to believe on Him as to receive them (Isaiah 55:1-3; Revelation 22:17). As He so disposes of them as to offer them to hearers of the gospel in common, it is observable that they to whom they are offered are in His testament described not by their personal names, nor are they denominated from their places of abode or callings in life, but from their natural state and disposition, or from their moral character. As was hinted above they are denominated men, sons of man, the people, enemies, sinners, self destroyers, prisoners, persons who thirst for happiness, and yet spend their money for that which is not bread, and their labor for that which does not satisfy. Hence all of these descriptions to whom the testament is read or preached have a full warrant to claim and take into possession

by faith all the legacies that are therein offered. The authentic offer to all in common affords to all a divine, an equal warrant to take possession. In this sense the testament may be, and is by many, called a deed of gift or grant (it has been so called by several of our own divines, and is frequently so by Lutheran-divines in Germany and other places abroad). That is a testamentary deed in which the unsearchable riches of Christ are so disposed of as to be granted in offer to sinners of mankind indefinitely. Hence it is that the legacies of Christ's testament, even with respect to unbelievers, are in Scripture called their own, that is to say, their own in offer. "They that observe lying vanities forsake their own mercy" (Jonah 2:8). To the elder brother in the parable the father said, "Son . . . all that I have is thine" (Luke 15:31). "Who shall give you that which is your own" (Luke 16:12)? The promises of Christ in His testament are directed in offer to sinners of mankind, as the promise of Canaan was to the Israelites in Egypt, indefinitely. "Say unto the children of Israel, I am the Lord . . . I will bring you in unto the land, concerning which I did swear to give it, to Abraham, to Isaac, and to Jacob; and I will give it you for an heritage" (Exodus 6:6, 8). This promise of entering into the typical rest of Canaan was left them; it was directed or offered to them in common. Those of them who cordially believed it with application to themselves, and trusted in Jehovah for the performance of it, entered in according to their faith; those who believed it not perished in the wilderness; and they came short of it not because it was not left them, but because, though it was left or offered to them as well as to those who entered, yet they believed it not. So we see, says an apostle, that they could not enter in because of unbelief (Hebrews 3:19). This could be no ground of imputation on the faithfulness of Jehovah for, in promises as well as in covenants properly so called, it is requisite that there be a mutual consent to the thing promised. The party to whom a promise is directed, his acceptance of it is necessary to complete the obligation of the promise to fulfill his promise to him; for when one man makes a promise of a benefit to another he cannot reasonably be supposed either to bind himself thereby to obtrude that benefit on the other against his will, or yet to give it up as a thing that he intends to abandon at any rate. Accordingly the apostle, when admonishing the Hebrew Christians to guard against unbelief, proposes to them the case of the ancient Israelites having a promise of Canaan left them, and yet coming short of it through unbelief. "Let us therefore fear," says he, "lest a promise being left us of entering into his rest, any of you should seem to come short of it" (Hebrews 4:1). Thus the legacies in the testament of our dying Redeemer are so disposed of as to be granted in offer to sinners of mankind indefinitely.

2. Christ in His testament disposes of His riches of grace and glory to some sinners of mankind in possession. He ordains them to be possessed by some, and at the same time appoints how they are to be enjoyed by them and how long. When He said to His disciples, "I appoint unto you a kingdom, as My Father hath appointed unto Me," the original verb employed by the sacred historian signifies to ordain or appoint as well as to dispose of. In His testament then, Christ the last Adam, ordains His unsearchable riches to be enjoyed by persons under certain general descriptions, expressive of their natural condition and character. He so bequeaths or disposes of them as to secure the possession or fruition of them. He ordains and leaves them to be possessed and, at the same time, declares who shall inherit them. Hence He said to His disconsolate disciples, "Peace I leave with you, My peace I give unto you" (John 14:27). This is the main object intended by Christ's testamentary disposition; for it is His will, declaring how He will have His unsearchable

riches disposed of as to the enjoyment of them after His death, whether typical or real; or His will declaring who shall be His heirs, or who shall inherit in and after Him. Taking the testament of Christ then in the strict and proper sense of the term, according to the nature of testaments among men, the elect, or they who will eventually believe on Him, are the legatees to whom His legacies were ordained. They only, for whom He died, and for whom He intercedes, are in this view to be considered as the objects of His testamentary disposition and of the legacies bequeathed. He could not appoint His legacies but to those for whom He purchased them. The legatees then to whom Christ has left His inestimable legacies are His elect seed, the children whom God has given Him. The legacies of His testament are left to the children of the covenant, of whom He as last Adam is the everlasting Father as well as the federal Representative. For these, He designed them; for these, He purchased them. The kingdom that, in His testament, He appoints to them is a kingdom prepared for them, a kingdom that, as the appointed heirs of it, they are to inherit in and through Him. Were His testamentary disposition, in this strict sense, supposed to be more extensive we must suppose it to be so far, vain, and unworthy of Him. But to suppose this would be to ascribe an intention to Him that He knew would, and which He resolved should, be frustrated. Moreover, if all the hearers of the gospel were in this sense the legatees, they should all be put in possession of the legacies bequeathed; but this is far from being the case. While the legacies are, in the testament, bequeathed to the elect under descriptions of character that are common to them with the rest of mankind, such as, sinners, enemies, unjust, ungodly, stout-hearted, far from righteousness, rebellious, lost, self-destroyed, etc., they being, by the Spirit convincing them of sin and misery, made to know that these characters belong to them, come and by faith take into possession the legacies left to them. In few words, as the promissory part of the covenant respecting the elect was, by the dying Savior turned into a testament, it necessarily follows that the legatees can be none other than those to whom the promises were originally made by the Father; the promissory part of the covenant regulating the testamentary (Matthew 20:23; John 6:37 and 17:2). To whomsoever the promises were made in Christ to them, and to them only, are the promises made by Him; otherwise His promises would be more extensive with respect to their objects than his Father's were; that is to say, He would promise eternal life to persons to whom His Father never did. But this would not be compatible either with His delegated power, or with His faithfulness in promising. His elect seed then are, strictly speaking, His legatees; the elect are the secret, and true believers are the open legatees of His testament.

Third, it will be proper now to take a view of the legacies that, in the testament of our dying Redeemer, are bequeathed to the legatees. Such is their number that it cannot be told; and such is the value of each that it cannot by a finite understanding be estimated. Every benefit of God's covenant is a legacy in Christ's testament. Whatever, according to that eternal covenant, is laid up in Christ and laid out in the promise is a legacy bequeathed in His testamentary deed. They are all constituent parts of the inheritance of the saints, of that inestimable portion to the eternal enjoyment of which they were chosen in Christ Jesus. They are infinitely sufficient to render them unspeakably rich and honorable and happy in time and throughout eternity. They are all to be received by faith. The general clause of the testament is, "According to your faith, be in unto you" (Matthew 9:29). Unable fully to reckon up the particulars, let it suffice briefly to mention a few of the most comprehensive of them.

PARTICULAR 1. A personal and saving interest in the blessed Testator Himself is one. In His testament He makes over to all the elect seed <u>Himself</u> as their Covenant-head, their Redeemer, their ALL IN ALL (Romans 8:32). While He offers to all who hear the gospel a personal interest in Himself, He leaves it as an inestimable legacy to them who believe in Him. No creature in heaven or upon earth can calculate the value of this legacy. The Lord Jesus Himself is the uncreated, the overflowing fountain of all that can render one rich or great or noble or happy. He therefore who has the Son has life, eternal life.

PARTICULAR 2. The quickening Spirit is another of those inestimable legacies. By the Spirit the sinner is quickened or made spiritually alive, and so is enabled to believe in the blessed Testator, and cordially to acquiesce in His testamentary will. Hear the words of the testament: "A new Spirit will I put within you . . . I will put My Spirit within you and cause you to walk in My statutes" (Ezekiel 36:26, 27). "Turn you at My reproof; behold, I will pour out My Spirit unto you" (Proverbs 1:23). The Lord Jesus has the seven Spirits of God, an immeasurable fullness of the Spirit to communicate; and in His testament He has left the same to sinners of Adam's posterity. Oh, how suitable a legacy is this to sinners dead in sins! Here is quickening influence. Here is spiritual life for our dead souls. The Spirit of Christ Jesus is the Spirit of life, making us free from the law of sin and death (Romans 8:2). He calls Himself the living bread that gives life unto the world. The Spirit of life is in that bread, and it is by eating of it that our souls live (John 6:33, 57, 63), that they walk with God in newness of life and serve Him in newness of spirit. Where then should we go for life but to Jesus the last Adam, who is the Executer of His own testament? We have derived death from the first Adam, and we cannot live again but by deriving life from the second (John 6:53, 68).

PARTICULAR 3. A complete and everlasting righteousness for the justification of our persons is another of His legacies. He makes in His testament an offer or grant of it to be received by faith. Hence we read of the gift of righteousness (Romans 5:17) and of the righteousness of God as revealed from faith to faith (Romans 1:17). No sooner do we begin with the heart to believe than the consummate righteousness of the blessed Testator is imputed to us (Isaiah 54:17); and the happy consequence is a plenary remission of sin and an indefeasible title to life. He bequeaths to us not only a saving interest in Himself, but in His service and suffering. Many when about to die used to leave suits of mourning to their poor friends. But our dying Redeemer left to His legatees beautiful garments (Isaiah 52:1), garments of salvation, a robe of righteousness (Isaiah 61:10), and white raiment (Revelation 3:18) as suits of rejoicing; for though He was dead yet He is now alive and lives for evermore. The first Adam left us naked to our shame, yet we need not suffer the shame of our nakedness to appear; for in the testament of the second Adam sufficient clothing is left to us, clothing of wrought gold, raiment of needlework (Psalm 14:13, 14), and change of raiment (Zechariah 3:4). O the transcendent luster, the surpassing splendor, the immense value, of that immaculate, that consummate RIGHTEOUSNESS that our condescending Testator has bequeathed to us! Nothing now remains but that we receive it as His legacy and with adoring gratitude put it on. A holy God cannot admit us into His presence in our spiritual nakedness. The holy law required us to appear before Him in unspotted holiness of nature and unsinning righteousness of life, with full satisfaction to His justice for the sins that we have committed against Him. But how can we afford to make such an appearance? All our righteousness is as filthy rags. Our case, however, is not hopeless. Christ the heir of all things has by His testament left to us the holiness of His human nature, the righteousness of His humbled life, and the infinite satisfaction made by His suffering of death. He has made these one undivided gift of righteousness that in His testament He bequeaths to us. How then shall we escape if, refusing to accept this inestimable legacy, we continue to trample on the wondrous loving kindness of our divine Testator?

PARTICULAR 4. A covenant-interest in Jehovah as a Friend, a Father, and a God is also one of them. He bequeaths to all His people a covenant-interest in God as a Friend. He leaves to them peace and reconciliation with God. "Peace I leave with you, My peace I give unto you" (John 14:27). He likewise, by His testament, leaves to them the exalted honors of adoption, or of a new covenant-interest in God as a Father. "I ascend," says He, "to My Father and your Father" (John 20:17). Nor is that all: He leaves as a legacy to them a new covenant-interest with Himself, in God as an all-sufficient God. "I ascend . . . to My God and your God." What a boundless, what a glorious legacy is this! Who can fully estimate what is comprehended in this infinitely great promise, "I will be to them a God" (Hebrews 8:10)? Surely all blessedness for time and for eternity is wrapped up in it. "Happy is that people whose God is the Lord" (Psalm 144:15). The first Adam left his whole family without God in the world (Ephesians 2:12). This was an unspeakable loss to them and, for any thing that their own righteousness or strength could do to retrieve it, a loss, absolutely irrecoverable. But the last Adam, having recovered for His spiritual children the forfeited interest in God, bequeaths it in His testament to them. If children, then heirs; heirs of God and joint heirs with Christ To His covenant-seed He leaves for a legacy all the adorable Persons of the Godhead to be theirs, and all the glorious perfections of the Godhead to be employed for their welfare; all the purposes, all the promises, all the providences, of Jehovah, to ensure their temporal and their eternal blessedness. Nothing, reader, can make you come short of this infinitely rich legacy, but unbelief. Come then, O come without delay to the gracious Executor and, upon the warrant of the unlimited offer contained in the testament, accept as a free gift your immense legacy.

PARTICULAR 5. The Spirit of grace, to make them resemble their gracious God and Father, is another inestimable legacy. In that divine testament sanctifying grace is left and offered to us in order that our nature may be thereby renewed (Ezekiel 36:25-27), that the image of God may, by grace received answering to grace in the man Christ Jesus (John 1:16), be stamped on our soul, and that we may be enabled in the faith of redeeming mercy to grow in the habit and exercise of evangelical repentance (Zechariah 12:10; Ezekiel 36:31), to mortify the deeds of the body (Romans 8:13), and to walk worthy of the Lord to all pleasing. Enlightening grace also is therein bequeathed by which we may spiritually discern the good and the duty of the covenant (John 16:13); exciting race to stir up the graces of the Spirit to lively exercise; strengthening grace to enable us successfully to maintain the struggle against corruptions within and temptations from without (Ephesians 3:16); comforting race in all our difficulties, trials, and tribulations (Psalm 94:19; John 16:7, 14); and establishing grace by which, being once in Christ, we are forever kept from falling away, either totally or finally (1 John 2:17; 1 Thessalonians 3:13). In few words, Christ, having by His testament made over to us the Spirit of grace in all His rich variety of gracious influences, all grace suited to our necessities lies open to us. None, therefore, who read or hear the gospel continue destitute of grace but because they will not come to Christ for the grace offered in His testament (John 5:40).

PARTICULAR 6. A suitable portion of the good things of this life, such as infinite wisdom sees to be necessary, is one of those legacies. The Lord Jesus having, by testamentary disposition, appointed to believing sinners a kingdom, superadded to it all these things (Matthew 6:33). He added them as appendages, or as things given over and above. His testamentary promise to every believer is, "His bread shall be given him, his waters shall be sure" (Isaiah 33:16). "Verily thou shalt be fed" (Psalm 37:3). These promises, primarily made in the covenant to Himself, He in His testament left, and as it were endorsed to us, to be fulfilled to all who by faith will embrace the testament and claim them upon it. Believers, therefore, should trust in Christ for their temporal comforts as well as for their spiritual supplies; they should, in the exercise of faith, plead the testament for the former as well as for the latter. Those temporal good things, however scanty in measure, that the saints in the exercise of faith receive out of the hand of the Lord Jesus, and in virtue of His testament, are far more sweet and satisfying to them than all the treasures of the world can be to a worldling. "A little that a righteous man hath in that way, is better than the riches of many wicked" (Psalm 37:16); for he has it as a part of the purchase of his Testator's blood, and with the enriching blessing of his heavenly Father.

PARTICULAR 7. A blessed death, or death deprived of its sting, is also one of them. Death, says our apostle, is yours (1 Corinthians 3:22). To the saints death is gain; for being hereby absent from the body they are present with the Lord (2 Corinthians 5:9). Men in their testaments make provision for the life of their legatees to render that comfortable, but they can leave them nothing to make their death comfortable; whereas in the testament of Christ special provision is made for His legatees in death as well as in life, in the faith of which the saints have welcomed that grim, that ghastly messenger (Hebrews 11:13). Our great Redeemer, being about to encounter death, armed with its sting, and that in all the strength imparted to it by the broken law, was perfectly sure of gaining the victory. In that prospect, making His testament, He appointed it as an article therein that His legatees should, by means of faith in Him, be set free from the sting of death. A precious legacy this was, which He could well afford to leave to them because He purchased it by His own death; and which He can and will confer on them seeing, as the Executor of His own testament, all fullness of power over death and the grave is in His hand. How lamentable the reflection that sinners, knowing they must die, continue, notwithstanding, to slight the testament and the kindness of their best friend, who has made ample provision against a case in which none else can afford the smallest help!

PARTICULAR 8. A glorious resurrection at the last day is likewise one of them. The words, the reviving words, of the almighty Testator, are express: "I will ransom them from the power of the grave; I will redeem them from death; O death, I will be thy plagues; O grave, I will be thy destruction; repentance shall be hid from mine eyes" (Hosea 13:14). "Thy dead men shall live, together with my dead body shall they arise" (Isaiah 26:19). As sure as He rose, they also shall rise; and shall have their bodies fashioned like unto His glorious body, according to the working whereby He is able even to subdue all things unto Himself (Philippians 3:21; 1 Corinthians 15:48, 49). Not so much as one of them will be lost or left in the gloomy grave.

PARTICULAR 9. Finally, the completion of eternal life, beyond death and the grave, is also one of those legacies. "He that eateth of this bread," saith the great Testator, "shall live forever"

(John 6:58); and again, "I give unto My sheep eternal life" (John 10:28). In His testament He made provision not only for the life that now is, but for that which is to come. He bequeathed in it a kingdom, a celestial, an everlasting kingdom. Into that everlasting kingdom an entrance shall, according to it, be administered to the legatees abundantly (2 Peter 1:11). This was to be the issue and end of the other legacies already mentioned. In this they will all infallibly terminate. As certainly as the divine Testator purchased and bequeathed this unbounded, this transcendently glorious inheritance, the legatees shall enjoy it, and that through all eternity; for it comprehends not only the perfect happiness of the soul in its separate state, but the complete blessedness of the soul and body reunited forevermore. It is indeed a goodly heritage, an inheritance incorruptible and undefiled, and unfading (1 Peter 1:4). It is called the inheritance of the saints in light (Colossians 1:12), an inheritance that is all light, glory, and joy and which cannot be enjoyed even by saints themselves otherwise than in that glorious light of perfect knowledge, holiness, and happiness in which Jehovah and the Lamb forever dwell. What a legacy is this for you, O believers! Who can conceive? Who can calculate? Who can express the amount of it? Oh, the immense value! Oh, the riches of the glory of that inheritance that is bequeathed to the saints! How boundless are the treasures of the Lord Jesus, the Heir of all things, that infinitely gracious Testator!

These are the chief, the comprehensive legacies of Christ's testament. Of entering more particularly into a detail of them there would be no end. Readers, you have the book of the testament, both old and new, in your hands. Read it diligently; read it frequently, as the testament of the dying Savior, signed, sealed, and ratified; and in every page, you will discover more or less of His infinite treasure. At the same time, remember that it nearly concerns you, and each of you. By preaching the word of the testament, as well as by putting a copy of it in to your hands, it is lawfully intimated to you: the inestimable legacies bequeathed in it are freely, fully, and particularly offered to you; and you are called, as men and the sons of men, as sinners and the chief of sinners, to come to Christ as the gracious Executor, and by faith to take possession of them. Happy, unspeakably happy shall you be, if you cordially comply with the gracious invitation. But if you refuse, it shall be more tolerable for Sodom and Gomorrah, for Tyre and Sidon, in the day of judgment than for you (Matthew 11:22).

In the fourth and last place, it will be proper, as was proposed, to take a view of the great and glorious Executor of that testament. In testaments among men, the testator and the executor are always different persons because the testator dying cannot live again to execute his will. One or more, therefore, of them who survive him must be nominated for that purpose. But of that there is no necessity here. Christ the second Adam could well afford to be the Executor of His own testament and did not need to appoint another to discharge that office. He was the Lord of death as well as the Prince of life; and it was not possible that He should be holden of death (Acts 2:24). Though He was indeed to die to ratify the testament, yet He was quickly to rise again from the dead to execute the same. "I am He," said the incarnate Redeemer, "that liveth, and was dead; and, behold, I am alive for evermore, Amen, and have the keys of hell and of death" (Revelation 1:18). Even while He was in the grave He was capable of executing His testament, for He was God as well as man. He had a divine life that could not even for a moment be lost. And His executing of it then, when His human nature was under the power of death, was nearly the same as His

The Administration of the Covenant of Grace 305

executing of it before He had actually assumed the human nature at all.

That the Lord Jesus is indeed the Executor of His own testament is evident from His being, by His eternal Father, constituted the Administrator of the covenant, to dispense the blessings of it as high Steward of the house of Heaven; and also, from the acts of His administration both in this world and that which is to come; for it is He who has delegated authority to bestow grace, both real and relative, on sinners, and to confer glory on saints; which are the executing of his testament as well as the administering of the covenant; for, though the Holy Spirit applies the legacies of it, and the ministers of the gospel are instruments of that application, yet the Spirit in that capacity is His Spirit, and the ministers His ministers. Whosoever, then, would have any spiritual benefit from the testament of Jesus Christ, or would participate in the inestimable legacies therein bequeathed, must have recourse to Him for them. Hence the call of the gospel to needy sinners constantly is to come to Christ by faith that they may have life; and the complaint against those who refuse to comply with the gracious invitation, and so forsake their own mercy, is that they will not come to Him for life (John 5:10). The whole life of believers must be a life of faith in Him (Galatians 2:20), of coming to Him (1 Peter 2:4), so that, according to their daily necessities, they may daily receive of those legacies from His hand as the great Executer of the testament.

Christ the second Adam, having as Testator bequeathed and offered His unsearchable riches to sinners of mankind, executes His testament by conferring on His elect seed the inestimable legacies therein disposed of, answerably to their need, and that, in the threefold character of an interceding Priest, of a Prophet, and of a King.

3. Christ the Interceding Priest of the Covenant

First, He executes His testament, or effectually confers on the elect the legacies of His testament in the character of an Advocate or interceding Priest.

As in order to fulfill the conditions of the covenant, Christ the second Adam became the sacrificing Priest of it; so in order to administer the blessings of the covenant, He became the interceding Priest of it. His exercise of the priestly office lies, according to the covenant, as the foundation of His exercise of the other two offices. Though His first dealing with sinners is as a Prophet, yet their first dealing with Him is as a Priest. The intercession of Christ did not, indeed, take its place in the making of the covenant; the sovereign grace of God made the motion for a covenant of grace freely. The breach between a holy God and sinful man was of another nature than to be made up merely by intercession. Mere intercession might have moved mercy, but could not have satisfied justice which, demanding a sacrifice for sin, could not be satisfied with pleading, but with paying a ransom. Without shedding of blood is no remission (Hebrews 9:22). Neither does Christ's offering of sacrifice take its place in the administration of the covenant. There is no need of any new sacrifice there; "for by one offering, He hath perfected forever them that are sanctified" (Hebrews 10:14); but His offering of sacrifice took its place properly in the making of the covenant, and in the fulfillment of the conditions of it, and His intercession in the administration of the covenant, and in the performance of the promises of it. Accordingly, for the administration of the covenant in general, and for the execution of His testament in particular, He was constituted the Advocate or Intercessor of the covenant (Psalm 110:4; Isaiah 53:12; Romans 8:34).

When God had, in the space of six days, finished His work of creating this world, He, on the seventh day, rested from all

The Administration of the Covenant of Grace

His work that He had made; He ceased from creating any new kinds of being. But He has ever since been most particularly employed about the world that He had made. It has never for a moment been out of His sight, nor out of His hand He is perpetually preserving and governing all His creatures and all their actions. In like manner, Christ the last Adam has ceased from His work of performing the conditionary part of the covenant. He has entered into His rest (Hebrews 4:10). He has nothing more of that kind to do. His work of obedience and suffering could not admit either of alteration or addition. But, as the interceding Priest of the covenant, He is continually employed about that finished work. He has it constantly in His view and on His heart. Without ever forgetting or neglecting it, He is every moment most intent upon having the whole design of it accomplished in due time (Hebrews 7:25).

And, indeed, there was great need of His being an Intercessor for that purpose. An infinitely holy God and sinful creatures could neither come together into a state of reconciliation, nor consistently with the honor of His perfections continue in it for a moment without an interceding Priest. Christ, therefore, having in the covenant been appointed to sustain that high character, is entered into heaven itself, now to appear in the presence of God for us (Hebrews 9:24), to present the blood and to manage the business of the covenant for our salvation. On account of their ignorance, guilt, and unworthiness, His legatees cannot prosecute their own claim before God the Judge of all. Christ, therefore, as the Advocate or Intercessor of the covenant, wills and pleads on the ground of His perfect righteousness, fulfilled in their stead, that the legacies bequeathed may, at the prefixed moment of grace, be conferred on each of them. None of the promises of the covenant are, in His intercession, ever forgotten or overlooked by Him. The Father could abate nothing to Him in the conditionary part of the covenant; and He will abate nothing in the promissory part. His intercession is always effectual: the Father hears Him always (John 11:42). He gives Him His heart's desire and does not withhold the request of His lips (Psalm 21:2). Hence it is clear that the object of His intercession is not so extensive as the object of His external administration of the covenant; but that it is restricted to them whom He as last Adam represented in that eternal transaction. This is very agreeable to the nature of the divine contrivance for the redemption of sinners; and is, as it were, one clause in the constitution of the administration, peculiarly in favor of the objects of electing love. This the glorious Intercessor Himself teaches us: "I pray not," says He, "for the world, but for them which Thou hast given Me; for them which shall believe on Me, through their word. Father, I will that they also whom Thou hast given Me be with Me where I am" (John 17:9, 20, 24).

Now the acts of Christ's administration of the covenant as the interceding Priest of it are especially the following:

(1) He, by His interest in the court of heaven, effectually secures the bringing of His elect at the time appointed into their covenant-state of union and communion with Himself, and of peace and favor with God. "Neither pray I for these alone, but for them also which shall believe on Me through their word, that they all may be one, as Thou Father art in Me and I in thee; that they also may be one in us" (John 17:20, 21). The elect are all by nature even as others are in a state of enmity and rebellion against the Lord; but by means of the intercession of Christ peace is made and maintained between heaven and them. He, by the blood of His sacrifice, purchased it for them. His intercession at the right hand of the throne of God is the spring that puts all the wheels in motion, that are set at going in the time of love, for bringing the sinner out of a state of nature into a state

of grace. Providence paves the way for the conversion of the man; the Word affects him with irresistible efficacy while on others it falls like rain on a flinty rock, going off as fast as it comes on; the business of his salvation is deeply laid to heart by him; the law does its office upon him, and so does the gospel; and these continue to cooperate till he is brought into a new state and has become a new creature. Whence did all this proceed? Why, the man had, at the court of heaven, an unknown Friend who spoke for him to the King.

(2) He appears for them, and in their name takes possession of heaven, and of all the other blessings of the covenant to which, in consequence of union with Him and communion with Him in His righteousness they are entitled. "God hath raised us up together," says our apostle, "and made us sit together in heavenly places in Christ Jesus" (Ephesians 2:6); and again, "Whither the forerunner is for us entered, even Jesus, made an High Priest forever" (Hebrews 6:20). The moment that a man by believing takes hold of the covenant he begins to have a covenant-right to all; "for if children, then heirs; heirs of God, and joint heirs with Christ" (Romans 8:17). Still, however, in the case of most of the children of God, the possession seems to be delayed till long after that moment. But it ought to be considered that possession may be taken by a man not only in his own person, but in the person of another. One may by his attorney take possession of an estate that he never saw; and a minor may by his representative be put in possession of that which he is not yet qualified to have in his own hand. In like manner, though a believer's possession of all in his own person is indeed delayed yet, in this respect, it is not put off one moment after his beginning to believe; for his exalted Intercessor acts for him in the whole affair. Nothing can occur to hinder this mode of possession for so much as one moment after union with Christ

by faith; for the covenant of promise is a sure charter and conveys an undoubted right. The believing sinner, though on earth, by faith pleads it before God the Judge of all in heaven; and Christ, as His Representative and Intercessor, is there to take possession in his name. Every believer, therefore, may justly reckon that though he has nothing, he yet possesses all things (2 Corinthians 6:10) and is complete in Him (Colossians 2:10).

(3) He maintains the peace and friendship that subsist between God and them while they are in this ensnaring world. Having by the sacrifice of Himself purchased peace with God for them, and having by His intercession brought them into a state of peace, He does not leave it to them to maintain the same. If He did, it would soon be at an end. There are so many failures on their part while they have sin dwelling in them that their own consciences have, every hour, matter of accusation against them. The devil too is an incessant accuser of the brethren. But the Lord Jesus appears continually before the throne, and so intercedes for them that however much they may, for their sins, fall under God's fatherly anger, yet a total breach of peace between Him and them is always prevented (Luke 22:32). Upon the ground of His infinite satisfaction for them, He answers all accusations against them and makes up all emergent differences between them and their covenant-God. Hence one apostle says, "If any man sin, we have an Advocate with the Father, Jesus Christ the righteous; and He is the propitiation for our sins" (1 John 2:1, 2); and another, upon this ground, triumphs over all their accusers, saying, "Who shall lay any thing to the charge of God's elect? It is God that justifieth; who is he that condemneth? It is Christ that died, yea rather, that is risen again . . . who also maketh intercession for us" (Romans 8:33, 34). All grounds of controversy between them and God are thereby removed; their state of peace with God is inviolably maintained

though, for their correction, they may for a season lose the comfort of it. Having once, in Christ His beloved Son, become their Friend, He may indeed for their iniquities, severely chastise them; but He never, even in a way of legal enmity, far less in a way of real enmity, becomes their enemy again (Isaiah 54:9, 10; Romans 8:1).

(4) He procures for them, notwithstanding their remaining ignorance, imperfection, and unworthiness, access to God and acceptance with Him. The saints on earth always have business in the court of heaven; yet being sinful they in themselves are altogether unworthy, as well as unfit, to come into the presence of the King eternal. But the great Intercessor of the covenant introduces them, procuring them access by His interest in the court. For through Him, says an apostle, we have access by one Spirit unto the Father (Ephesians 2:18); and we have boldness and access with confidence by the faith of Him (Ephesians 3:12). He, notwithstanding the sinfulness that cleaves to them, makes their persons accepted. They are made accepted in the Beloved (Ephesians 1:6). In Him also they have an altar that sanctifies their gifts (Hebrews 13:10). Their spiritual sacrifices, therefore, though they are not without blemishes, are still acceptable to God by Jesus Christ (1 Peter 2:5). Their prayers offered up in faith, though smelling strong of the remains of corruption, yet, being by the great Intercessor perfumed with the incense of His infinite merit, are accepted in heaven and have gracious answers returned to them (Revelation 8:3). Their best services that, however costly, cannot be accepted for their own worth because imperfect are, through His intercession, accepted as sincere, being washed and made white in the blood of the Lamb (Revelation 7:14).

(5) Finally, He procures for them an entrance into heaven in due time, and an everlasting continuance of their state of

perfect blessedness there (John 17:4). Christ the second Adam was, by His eternal Father, constituted a Priest forever (Psalm 110:4); and yet, after His having once offered up Himself a sacrifice for the sins of His people, He offered no more sacrifice. He must therefore be not a sacrificing but an interceding Priest forever; as our apostle explains it, "He ever liveth to make intercession for them" (Hebrews 7:25). Seeing the spirits of just men are made perfect, there is, after death, no more any moral imperfection cleaving to their souls (Hebrews 12:23); and there will be, after the resurrection, no more any imperfection about their bodies (1 Corinthians 15:53, 54). The subject as well as the effect then of Christ's intercession forever must be the everlasting continuance of their perfect happiness. The ground on which He eternally wills the continuation of their happy state in heaven is that eternal redemption was obtained for them by the sacrifice of Himself on earth (Hebrews 9:12). The infinite merit of His obedience and sacrifice will be eternally presented before Jehovah in the holy place where, in their nature, He is continually to appear in the presence of God for them (Hebrews 9:24); and this will be their everlasting security for the continuance of their perfect blessedness. This consummate felicity, issuing from the merit of His sacrifice as their Priest, will be eternally communicated to them by Him as their Prophet and their King; for these mediatorial offices will never be set aside; the execution of them will never be at an end. As He is to be a Priest forever, so shall He be the light of the heavenly city (Revelation 21:23); and of His kingdom there shall be no end (Luke 1:33). The communion of the redeemed with God in heaven will, in a manner suited to their state of perfection, be still in and through the glorious Mediator (Revelation 7:17).

4. Christ the Prophet of the Covenant

As Christ in His Priestly office bore the burden of performing the conditions of the covenant, so in His Prophetical office He has the honor of publishing the promises of it. The covenant being an eternal contract that no creature had access to witness, the existence of it was an absolute secret to the whole creation. And seeing that it was a mystery of the manifold wisdom of God (Ephesians 3:10), no creature, whether human or angelic, was qualified to unfold the nature of it. On these accounts a sacred writer calls it the wisdom of God in a mystery, even the hidden wisdom that God ordained before the world" (1 Corinthians 2:7). Hence it is evident that it was necessary to constitute a prophet of such a covenant, and that none but a divine person was qualified to be the original prophet of it, especially when it is considered that by reason of the spiritual blindness of the persons to whom it was to be revealed a mere objective revelation of it could not be sufficient for them (1 Corinthians 2:14). Christ the last Adam, therefore, as Administrator of the covenant and Executor of His testament, was constituted the Prophet of it, He being the same of whom, according to the testimony of an apostle, Moses truly said unto the fathers, "a Prophet shall the Lord your God raise up unto you, of your brethren, like unto me" (Acts 3:2). Whoever else were at any time prophets thereof, He only was the primary Prophet of it. "No man hath seen God at any time; the only begotten Son, which is in the bosom of the Father, He hath declared Him" (John 1:18).

In this illustrious character the Lord Jesus was constituted the Messenger, the Interpreter, and the Witness of the covenant. Since by reason of their blindness and weakness His legatees cannot of themselves discern the glorious mysteries of His covenant and testament, He, in this threefold capacity, reveals these to them.

(1) In the character of a Prophet, He was constituted the Messenger of the covenant (Malachi 3:1). The declarations respecting the covenant are good news from a far country; and He it is who, as the Messenger of the covenant, brings us these glad tidings. He brings the good news of that divine treaty of peace into the world, and by the authority of heaven proclaims the treaty to sinners, offers them the benefit of it, and deals with them to accept the same. He is the Messenger, then, or Angel of the covenant, that transcendently illustrious One whom the Father sent to negotiate a peace and to settle a correspondence between heaven and earth. He is the uncreated Angel who received a commission from Jehovah the Father to bring, by a covenant of grace, sinners back to Him who had revolted from Him by violating the covenant of works. Accordingly, the doctrine of that eternal covenant that is all our salvation began to be spoken by the Lord (Hebrews 2:3). Doubtless this must have been a covenant of unparalleled importance that required such a Messenger.

(2) In that illustrious character He was also constituted the Interpreter of the covenant to show it to sinful men (Job 33:23). Since we are unable of ourselves spiritually to know them, He, being constituted an Interpreter, one among a thousand, explains to us the terms of His covenant and the articles of His testament. We are not only ignorant of the eternal covenant, but it is very difficult for us to understand it. It is therefore necessary that it be revealed *in* us as well as *to* us (Galatians 1:16). It lies so far beyond the reach of our natural understanding that we cannot in a spiritual manner discern it, unless the Son of God give us an understanding, a supernatural, a spiritual understanding, that we may know Him who is true (1 John 5:20). They who will so understand it must be all taught of God (John 6:45, 46), that is, of God manifested in the flesh. Christ

the last Adam then is, by the Father, constituted the great Interpreter, Expounder, or Teacher of the mystery of the covenant; and all the children of God must be His disciples and learn of Him.

(3) Last, in the capacity of a Prophet He was also appointed the Witness of the covenant. "Behold, saith Jehovah, I have given him for a witness to the people" (Isaiah 55:4). God knew the world to be a guilty world whose consciences witnessed that they deserved to die, and that, therefore, they would be very slow of heart to believe the good tidings from heaven concerning the covenant of peace, especially those that are contrary to the dictates of a defiled conscience and of a depraved self-love. He, therefore, would give them a Witness who was competent to attest the truth of these and He pitched on His own Son Jesus Christ for that purpose. Christ was a Son of Adam, and therefore was the more qualified to attest it to men. He was the eternal Son of God and so was not liable to any mistake in His testimony. He was an eyewitness to the eternal contract and therefore in giving testimony concerning it He could speak that which He had seen with His Father (John 8:38). He came down from heaven where the covenant was made to earth in favor of which it was made. He therefore could witness on earth that which He had seen about it in heaven. "He that cometh from heaven is above all; and what he hath seen and heard, that he testifieth" (John 3:31, 32). In Him we have a twofold witness, which is full evidence in law. He is the Amen, the faithful and true Witness (Revelation 3:14). We have in Him the witness of man, in respect of which He is the faithful Witness, and the witness of God, in respect whereof He is the true Witness, the truth itself; and in relation to both these, He is the Amen whose testimony confirms and determines in law the truth of the matter in question. Hence He said to the Pharisees, "I am one that

bear witness of Myself" (John 8:18). Christ as a divine Witness in respect of His Godhead is here said to bear witness of Himself as Mediator and man, appearing in the world and revealing the doctrines of the covenant. Those doctrines He solemnly attests to us; He declares them in His Word (John 20:31); He confirms them by solemn asseverations and oaths (John 3:3, 5; Hebrews 6:17, 18); He exemplifies them in His Person and work (John 1:14 and 14:6); He ratifies them by His sufferings and death (Hebrews 9:16; John 18:37); and He seals them by the sacraments that He instituted.

Now Christ's administration of the covenant as the Prophet thereof in the three characters above mentioned, includes the following particulars:

PARTICULAR 1. His revealing and offering of the covenant in His Word to sinners in order to bring them personally into the bond of it. This He did from the day on which Adam fell, is now doing, and will continue to do till the end of time. He began the Old Testament dispensation of the covenant in person. Appearing in human form, He in paradise gave with His own mouth the first intimation and made the first offer of the covenant that ever was made in the world (Genesis 3:8, 15). He carried it on by prophets and ordinary ministers whom He commissioned and furnished with gifts for the purpose. The former of these He employed to write, as well as to speak of it, in His name; and by both He spoke to sinners of mankind, revealing and exhibiting the covenant to them. Thus He conducted that glorious work to the salvation of them who believed in the Patriarchal ages before and after the flood and during all the time from Moses until the end of the Old Testament dispensation. Then He also began in His own person the New Testament dispensation. Having become incarnate, He applied Himself with unparalleled ardor to this work. He came a Light

The Administration of the Covenant of Grace 317

into the world. Though He was born King of the Jews, and though many of them would have had Him to ascend their throne, yet He chose rather to appear in the character of a Prophet and preach the gospel that He might thereby declare and offer the covenant to lost sinners. Hence He is called a Minister of the circumcision for the truth of God (Romans 15:8). Of Him, in this character particularly, Solomon that royal preacher was a type (Ecclesiastes 1:1). This also, especially after His ascension, He did, and still does carry on, partly by His apostles and other extraordinary ministers whom He commissioned to write as well as to speak in His name, and partly by ordinary ministers of the gospel, to be continued in the church for that purpose till the end of the world (Ephesians 4:11-13). Thus He is, at this day administering the covenant to sinners by affording them His written Word and by sending forth ministers in His name to preach the gospel to them. By these means He speaks from heaven (Hebrews 12:25) to sinners, revealing and offering the covenant to them; and so He carries on the work to the salvation of all who believe (2 Corinthians 5:20 and 2:15, 16). Therefore the offer of the covenant made to us in the gospel is *His* offer; and though the Word is ministered to us by men of like passions as ourselves, they are the voice only of Him. He is the Speaker.

PARTICULAR 2. It includes His making, by His Holy Spirit, that revelation and offer of the covenant effectual for the illumination and conversion of His elect seed. "By them," says an apostle, "that have preached the gospel unto you with the Holy Ghost sent down from heaven" (1 Peter 1:12). That great Prophet of the covenant can teach effectually the most indocile of the children of Adam. He causes light to shine forth not only in a dark world by His Word, but in dark understandings by His Spirit; for the fullness of the Spirit of light is in Him; and He has eye-salve for them who are spiritually blind (Revelation 3:18). "He knoweth them that are His" (2 Timothy 2:19), for whom He covenanted with the Father, and received from Him the promise of the Spirit; and at the time appointed He so enlightens their mind as to deliver them from the power of intellectual darkness and to bring them into His marvelous light. This He does by bringing His Word home with power to their heart through the almighty operation of His Spirit, opening the eyes of their understanding.

He first, by His Holy Spirit as a Spirit of conviction and fear, brings home to their conscience the holy law in the commands and curses of it as of divine authority, and as binding on them in particular. The consequence is that they are convinced of their sin and misery. They now begin to see that of all evils sin is the greatest, and that of all sinners they are the chief. They now discern that their sin, with regard to the Object of it, is an infinite evil, and that they deserve for it the infinite wrath of Jehovah. Hence they begin to be filled with remorse, anxiety, and terror. They pant for deliverance, feel their absolute, their extreme need of Jesus, with His righteousness and strength, and despair of salvation by any other (Acts 2:37; 16:30). And next, by the same Spirit communicated from Himself and acting within them as the Spirit of life, He powerfully brings home to their heart and conscience the free offer and promise of eternal life in Himself to sinners of mankind as recorded in the gospel; clearing and demonstrating the same to them to be the sure, the infallible word of Jehovah, and His word of grace to them in particular. "Ye received it not," says the Apostle Paul, "as the word of men, but (as it is in truth) the word of God" (1 Thessalonians 2:13). "For our gospel came not unto you in word only, but also in power, and in the Holy Ghost, and in much assurance" (1 Thessalonians 1:5). It is this demonstration of the Spirit that clearly evidences to them the grounds on which they are to believe the record with application to themselves, "as," says the same apostle, "my preaching was . . . in demonstration of the Spirit, and of power; that your faith should not stand in the wisdom of men, but in the power of God" (1 Corinthians 2:4, 5). It is an internal attestation of the truth of the gospel to them, altogether different from the clearest external evidence of it; according to these consoling words of our great Redeemer Himself, "Even the Spirit of truth, which proceedeth from the Father, He shall testify of Me. And ye also shall bear witness" (John 15:26, 27). Hereby, attaining a spiritual knowledge of the Savior in His transcendent amiableness, suitableness, and sufficiency, exhibited to them in the gospel, they are enabled with the heart to believe in Him. While the Spirit thus applies the word of the gospel to them, He enables them so to accept and embrace that faithful word as to apply it and the grace offered in it to themselves, as those converts did of whom we read in Acts 2:38, 39, 41.

PARTICULAR 3. It comprehends His instructing and directing believers by His Word and Spirit during their continuance on earth. The whole scheme of redemption, even that mystery of the manifold wisdom of God, is delineated in the covenant. There is, then, still more and more of it to be learned by the children of the covenant; and Christ is the great Prophet to teach them the knowledge of it. "The secret of the Lord," says the psalmist, "is with them that fear Him; and He will show them His covenant" (Psalm 25:14). Believers, by reason of darkness remaining in their mind while in this world, are apt to lose sight of the high contracting parties of the covenant; but the divine Prophet thereof shows them the Father, and by the Spirit of wisdom and revelation in the knowledge of Him manifests Himself to them, not as He does to the world. The arduous conditions of the covenant, the obedience and death of the blessed Surety that are the sole foundation of their title to life eternal, cannot be kept suitably in view but by means of spiritual light from Him. It is only in His light that they can at any time have a believing and solacing view of the precious promises or inestimable blessings of the covenant. By reason of the ignorance of the gospel-offer that still remains in them, they are often in their exercise ready to lose sight of it as their warrant to trust in Him at all times for their whole salvation; but He shines upon that offer, letting them, from time to time, see it in the light of His Word and Spirit, and making them so to know the gift of God (John 4:10) as to perceive with certainty that they are thereby warranted to come daily as sinners and take hold of the covenant afresh. The duties of the covenant, of which the moral law (which is exceeding broad) is the rule, are manifold; and though they are clear in themselves, yet they are sometimes so dark and intricate to us that we cannot clearly distinguish between sin and duty. But the children of the covenant have an infallible, a condescending Teacher whom they may on every occasion consult, and of whom they may in every point learn how to direct their course. "The meek will He guide in judgment; and the meek will He teach his way" (Psalm 25:9). Apply then, O believer, this precious promise, "I will guide thee continually"; and, in the exercise of humble confidence placed in Him who is given for a Leader to the people (Isaiah 55:4), say, "Thou wilt guide me with Thy counsel" (Psalm 73:24 and 48:14), "This God will be My guide even unto death."

The darkness that is introduced into the mind by sin is such that nothing but the illuminating grace of the new covenant can effectually remove it. Spiritual light, therefore, is a benefit of the covenant, purchased by the blood of Jesus Christ, and is entrusted to Him that He may, as the great Prophet of the covenant, dispense it to benighted souls. Whether the reader is under the midnight-darkness of a state of nature, or under the twilight-darkness of their imperfection of a state of grace, let him then, in all cases, come to the Lord Jesus, who is given for a Light to the Gentiles and, trusting in Him, say, "When I sit in darkness the Lord will be a light to me; He will bring me forth to the light, and I shall behold His righteousness" (Micah 7:8, 9).

PARTICULAR 4. Finally, it includes His communicating to them in their heavenly state the light of perfect knowledge. In the noonday of glory the Lamb is the light of the heavenly city (Revelation 21:23). As He will continue through all eternity to be invested with His prophetic office, so the perpetuity of the light of perfect knowledge in the redeemed will depend on His continued influence in the execution of that office. Hence, continuing to enjoy the blissful vision of Him and of the glory of Jehovah shining forth in Him, they will be filled, as far as their expanded capacities will admit, with the perfect knowledge of His will in all wisdom and spiritual understanding. As the Sun of Righteousness, He will through endless ages shine forth among them in all His resplendent luster, and will irradiate their minds with the refulgent beams of His uncreated glory. The continuance of that light of perfect knowledge in them, probably with increasing brightness throughout eternity, will doubtless depend upon their being filled with incessant emanations of light from Him; and indeed a failing of these even for a moment would leave them in utter darkness. But there shall be no night there; for the glory of God will lighten it, and the Lamb will be the light, the everlasting light thereof (Revelation 22:5 and 21:23). From the perpetual execution of His prophetic office in the church above, each of the redeemed will, through all eternity, have to say in a far loftier strain than he could ever say it in time, "The Lord is my light and my salvation" (Psalm 27:1). Then, believer, your knowledge of God will be so perfect as to have no limit set to it but what will arise from your finite capacity. You shall know Him by sight, which will satisfy your understanding, and by experience that will satisfy your will. You shall be forever contemplating the adorable Jehovah, Father, Son, and Holy Spirit, together with His infinite love, His unchangeable truths, and His wonderful works, and that with the most cordial complacence and the most adoring wonder (Psalm 16:11). To what astonishing degrees of knowledge will He who is the fountain of uncreated light, the brightness of the Father's glory, exalt His redeemed in the heavenly sanctuary! No more seeing as through a glass darkly, but beholding with open face the glory of the Lord they will be perfectly satisfied and sanctified at once. What heart of man can conceive, what tongue or pen of angels can describe, what they will see when they shall behold His face in righteousness and see Him as He is, when the Lord shall be their everlasting light and their God their glory!

5. Christ the King of the Covenant

Seeing the legatees of Christ are by nature rebellious, enslaved, and miserable, He as the King of the covenant powerfully imparts to them the legacies bequeathed by Him. In a manner suited to His princely state, He bestows on them an abundance of grace with the gift of righteousness, and so exalts them to reign with Him in life eternal.

The covenant of grace is an object of such unspeakable importance to the glory of God and the good of souls, and at the same time of such general concern to the human race that the administration of it requires one to be invested with kingly authority for the due accomplishment of it. The natural disposition of the objects of that administration, together with the nature of the thing itself, which chiefly relates to the inner man and the disposal of the greatest of divine favors, at once sets aside the greatest of men and the highest of angels as being no more able to discharge that office than to create a world. The Father's choice, therefore, freely fell upon His only begotten Son the last Adam; and He appointed Him as King of the covenant.

Jehovah considered as Creator and Preserver is King of the world by an original and underived, a necessary right; and He can no more divest Himself of His supreme dominion over it than of His being. This is that essential kingdom that belongs equally, as well as necessarily, to the three Persons in the ever-blessed Godhead.

But the kingdom of which I here treat is a delegated and derived one that the exalted Mediator holds of His Father by the tenure of the covenant in order that He may be fully qualified to administer that covenant, and so to execute His testament. This is declared in Psalm 2:6: "Yet have I set my King upon my holy hill of Zion." Now the great design of that administration is to gather sinners of mankind together into one mystical body within the bond of the covenant, and to exalt them to the progressive enjoyment of the blessings of it in grace and to the perfect fruition of them in glory. That mystical body is the kingdom of the covenant, a spiritual kingdom that was to subdue, and be raised out of the rebellious world of mankind, and of which Christ the last Adam was, by the Father, appointed the sole King and Head.

In subservience to this spiritual kingdom, the kingdom of providence throughout the world was also given in trust to Him. Being constituted the Head of the body the church, He was made the Head over all things to the church (Ephesians 1:22, 23). He was appointed to rule not only in and over His willing subjects, but in the midst of His enemies (Psalm 110:2). The entire management of the wheels of providence throughout the world was devolved upon the righteous King of Zion in order that His dispensations of providence might subserve His dispensation of grace. To the same hand to which the Father committed the spiritual government of the church, He also committed the providential government of the world for the good of the church. "All power," said the Lord Jesus, "is given unto Me in heaven and on earth" (Matthew 28:18). "The Father hath committed all judgment unto the Son" (John 5:22) so that the Lamb is Lord of lords and King of kings (Revelation 17:14); and by Him kings reign and princes decree justice; by Him princes rule and nobles, even all the judges of the earth (Proverbs 8:15, 16). This headship or supremacy over the world was indispensably requisite to His administration of the covenant as Head of the church. The great ends of His administration of it could not otherwise be attained. Being accordingly invested with that universal dominion, He puts down and sets up in the kingdoms of men as He sees meet for subserving the great designs of the covenant. Of what importance this is, in His administration of it, we may learn from His own words: "For your sake," that is, for the sake of the Israelitish church, "I have sent to Babylon, and have brought down all their nobles and the Chaldeans whose cry is in the ships. I am . . . the Creator of Israel, your King" (Isaiah 43:14, 15). Thus the King of Zion, by His providence, manages all things in the world as well as in the church. He is, therefore, the Governor among the nations as well as the Ruler in Jacob to the ends of the earth (Psalm 22:28; 59:13). His ruling without as well as within the church was typified by that of David who, for the benefit of his own kingdom, the kingdom of Israel, was by Jehovah made the head of the heathen (Psalm 18:43). For David smote the Philistines, and subdued them; and the Moabites, and the Syrians, and all they of Edom, became David's servants (2 Samuel 8:1, 2, 6. 14). As the Lord Jesus has a right to set up His kingdom of grace in every part of the world; so wherever He knows that any of His elect are to reside, though it should be in the remotest corner, and at the distance of many generations after this, there He is, in the mean time, mysteriously directing events toward that gracious object.

His mediatorial kingdom cannot supersede or supply the place of His essential kingdom as God over all; it cannot suspend, even for a moment, the natural and necessary influence of His Godhead. He has a distinct, though at the same time a conjoined, administration of both these kingdoms. The difference between His divine government and His mediatorial one does not lie in the objects of the one and of the other; for the objects of both are materially the same; but it lies in the manner of the administration. By His divine government He orders all persons and things in their natural course toward their natural ends; but by His mediatorial government He orders the same persons and things, so far as He is graciously pleased, in a supernatural course toward supernatural ends. He makes all natural objects, even the worst, subserve the best interests of the church, and of every true believer.

Having premised these things in general, it will be proper now particularly to show how Christ administers the covenant, considered as the King of Zion. In this capacity, he administers it:

(1) By appointing ordinances and officers for bringing sinners personally into the bond of it, and for establishing them therein. He appoints officers of His spiritual kingdom to dispense the ordinances of it in His name and by His authority. The ordinances that were dispensed under the Old Testament, as the reader will see in the next chapter, are different from

those under the New. This has produced different forms of the external administration of the covenant, the old form that is done away, and the new, that will continue till the consummation of all things. Both were from the same high authority and for attaining the same great designs of the covenant, agreeably to the different periods for which they were appointed; and they are to be found in the sacred Volume, the book of the manner of the kingdom. It was the same Lord Jesus, the Angel of the covenant, who spoke to Moses on Mount Sinai (Acts 7:38), who instituted the ordinances of the New Testament church, and who gave some apostles, and some prophets, and some evangelists, and some pastors and teachers for the perfecting of the saints, for the work of the ministry, for the edifying of the body of Christ (Ephesians 4:11, 12). As King of Zion, He established in His church not only a system of ordinances, of doctrine, worship, government, and discipline, but likewise a succession of ordinary office-bearers, besides some at first who were extraordinary, to dispense those ordinances. By these means He still gathers multitudes of mankind into a visible church state and maintains them in that state.

(2) In the same character He administers it by issuing forth His royal proclamation, calling and affording a warrant to sinners to come by faith to Him, and so to receive a full and perpetual interest in all the benefits bequeathed by Him. In virtue of His regal authority, He by His messengers openly declares it in the gospel to be His sovereign pleasure that whosoever will come to Him, and by faith be untied to Him as the Head of the covenant, shall without delay be received into the bond thereof, and under Him have a sure title to all the blessings of it. The commission that He gave to His apostles was this: "Go ye unto all the world, and preach the gospel to every creature. He that believeth and is baptized shall be saved" (Mark 16:15, 16). In

The Administration of the Covenant of Grace 327

the gospel the covenant is published and offered in His name to every sinner of mankind to whose ears the sound of it reaches; and sinners in common are, by the high authority of this heavenly King, called and commanded to touch His royal scepter and accept His offered grace. His offer and call afford them a warrant to accept it, and His command that they believe in Him imposes a firm obligation upon them so that they cannot refuse without downright disobedience to His royal authority. The promises are set before them in the unlimited offer of His gospel to the end that whosoever will may by faith apply and plead them. The proclamation of the gracious King of Zion is not a publication of the secrets of election; but, seeing that the promises of the covenant, that are to be infallibly accomplished to some, are in His testament directed to sinners indefinitely, in order that they may be fulfilled to every one who will by faith embrace them, it is to be regarded as a public and lawful intimation of His testament. This intimation is the appointed means of producing and increasing faith, and of bringing sinners thereby into the bond of the covenant; for "faith cometh by hearing" (Romans 10:17).

Hence it comes to pass that while the promises are thus administered to all without exception, use is made of conditional phrases in the administration of them; though in the covenant as such there are, strictly speaking, no conditions but what were fulfilled by our condescending Surety in His own person. The word of the covenant, affording an equal warrant for believing to the elect and to the non-elect, to them who certainly will believe and to them who will continue in unbelief, the administering of it equally to both must inevitably be by exhibiting the promises to them in common; which renders it necessary that they for the most part be at length resolved into conditional expressions. Thus Jehovah, in the promises, said to all the hearers of the gospel, "Ye shall be My people, and I will be your God. I will betroth thee unto Me forever." Some believe and apply the same, and are thereupon personally interested in the covenant; others, who have as good a revealed warrant to believe with application as the former have, yet do not believe and so come short of the promise. Now to address alike the words or promises of the covenant to those in common who will treat them so differently, it necessarily follows that they be resolved into such expressions as these: "Believe on the Lord Jesus Christ and thou shalt be saved. He that believeth on the Son hath everlasting life; and he that believeth not the Son shall not see life. He that believeth and is baptized shall be saved." At the same time, let it be remembered that the covenant itself is an object quite different from the form of its external administration.

(3) In the same character He administers the covenant by effectually subduing the elect to Himself so as to give them a full title to the benefits of it, as well as a begun possession of them. By the power of His Spirit, He so applies His Word as to make it operate on them like a sword piercing their souls, conquering their natural aversion, and making them willing to submit to Him and embrace the covenant. We read that out of His mouth went a sharp two-edged sword (Revelation 1:16). What that sword is, and how strong the arm is by which it is wielded, may be learned from its being by the Apostle Paul called the sword of the Spirit (Ephesians 6:17); and what the effect of it is, when managed by that arm of the Lord revealed, is declared by the prophet Isaiah, "I will pour my Spirit upon thy seed . . . and they shall spring up . . . one shall say I am the Lord's," etc. (Isaiah 44:3-5); and by the psalmist, "Thy people shall be willing in the day of Thy power" (Psalm 110:3). The Lord Jesus imparts to each of them at the time appointed in His eternal counsel the Spirit of the covenant, secured for them by

The Administration of the Covenant of Grace

promise. And thereby they are quickened, inclined, and enabled with the heart to believe in Him. And seeing He finds them prisoners, He opens the prison doors and, by His almighty Spirit applying to them His satisfaction for sin, He breaks the yoke of sin, Satan, and death from off their neck. His satisfaction thus applied has that powerful effect, inasmuch as then the law in reference to them has complete satisfaction. For the law being satisfied, the strength of sin is broken; and the strength of sin being broken the sting of death is removed; and the sting of death being removed, Satan loses his power over them; and the power of Satan over them being lost the present evil world that is his kingdom can no longer retain them. Thus are they delivered from the power of darkness and translated into the kingdom of God's dear Son (Colossians 1:13). From that time forth, although they are in the world, yet they are no more of the world, but are strangers and pilgrims in it and are living members of the invisible kingdom of Christ, a society to whom the world is an irreconcilable enemy (John 15:19). Herein the Lord Jesus does, in a peculiar manner, show Himself a King mighty in battle in that, by the power of His grace, He subdues the most rebellious and stubborn to the most cordial, the most unreserved, obedience to Himself. By implanting faith and all other spiritual graces in their heart, He begins the good work of grace in them. And though this good work of grace is the same in all of them as to the matter of it, there is however a difference as to the manner. There is always a conviction of sin and misery by the law; but the degrees of impression which that makes are very different. In some, it is only a breaking of their legal and their carnal rest; in others, it is a filling of them with the terrors of the Almighty so that each of them has reason to say, "The sorrows of death compassed me, and the pains of hell gat hold upon me; I found trouble and sorrow" (Psalm 116:3). Some are long exercised in this way; others are conducted speedily to a happy issue; while others again are sweetly led to the Savior at once under a joint discovery of sin and salvation.

(4) In the character of a King He administers it by gathering His converted elect along with others into a visible church-state in which, by regulations suited to their various circumstances, He governs them to His own honor and to their spiritual advantage. "Unto him shall the gathering of the people be" (Genesis 49:10). Thus is erected the visible church or visible kingdom of Christ in the world, a society separated from the visible kingdom of Satan, professing faith in Jesus, and obedience to Him, and externally bearing His badge with the signs of His covenant. Among them is the ordinary seat of His administration of the covenant, the ordinary means and offers of salvation. They have the Scriptures and the Sabbaths, the preaching of the gospel and the sacraments. In their land, the voice of the turtle and the singing of birds are heard while in the rest of the world a perpetual winter reigns. Among them are found the communion of saints and a church-government, divinely instituted for checking disorder, suppressing iniquity, and encouraging righteousness. Christ is the only King and Head of this church. It is His free, spiritual and independent kingdom, in its nature entirely different from the kingdoms of this world, and in nothing subordinate to them. He has established in it a system or ordinances and a succession of ordinary office-bearers for administering those ordinances. By these means He still gathers believing sinners, along with others of mankind, into a visible church and maintains them in that state.

(5) Last, in the same capacity He administers the covenant by so governing His true and voluntary subjects, according to it, as to preserve and manifest His royal prerogatives and to secure their privileges. "The government shall be upon His

shoulder" (Isaiah 9:6). "The Lord is our King; He will save us" (Isaiah 33:22). Of His government of them there are various acts, the chief of which are the following:

First, He gives them in their justification a legal and full title to all the inestimable treasures of the covenant; and in their adoption, a filial and honorary title to them (Titus 3:7; Jeremiah 3:19; Romans 8:17).

Second, He gives them the laws of the covenant. He not only intimates these to them externally by His Word, but reveals them to them internally by His Spirit. By His Holy Spirit He so writes them on the fleshly tables of their hearts as to leave a legible and an indelible copy of them there. "I will put my laws," He said, "into their mind, and write them in their hearts" (Hebrews 8:10). These laws of the covenant are the Ten Commandments, which were originally given to Adam in his creation, and were afterwards at his settlement in paradise vested with the form of the covenant of works. They are now standing without that form in the covenant of grace, given to believers in Christ as the instrument of His government of them, and as the rule of their duty to Him, to which, by the grace of the covenant, they are to be always conformed. The effecting of that was by the Father entrusted to Christ Himself as Administrator of the covenant. Accordingly He by His Word and Spirit effects it in a manner suited to their nature and state as rational creatures, making these laws in their spirituality and extent known to them as a rule of life; to the obedience of which they stand immutably bound by the supreme authority and stupendous love of their creating and redeeming God; and at the same time, inclining and enabling them to perform sincere obedience to them. Thus, as the King of saints, He gives them the same moral law as a rule of life to be obeyed for Him that He Himself as their Surety obeyed as a covenant of works for them; the same law that He perfectly obeyed for life to them to be sincerely, and in due time perfectly, obeyed from life, for Him and God in Him (1 Corinthians 9:21).

Third, He graciously bestows on them in the course of their obedience the rewards of the covenant. These He confers on them not indeed for their worth, or for the sake of their good works, but as a reward originally due to Himself as their Surety, and due to them merely as united to and accepted in Him. In (though not for) the keeping of them there is great reward (Psalm 19:11). He indeed obliges His true subjects to labor, but not to labor in the fire or for vanity, as the servants of sin do; they are to work like the ox treading out the corn, which was not to be muzzled, but was to have access at once to work and to eat. The work, now done acceptably to the King of Zion, has a reward of grace in this world as well as in that which is to come. In the order of the covenant that our heavenly King observes in His administration, privilege follows duty as the gracious reward of it. He, accordingly, proposes the privilege of spiritual comfort to encourage to the duty of mourning for sin. "Blessed are they that mourn; for they shall be comforted" (Matthew 5:4). He also proposes the special manifestations of His love to His people in order to excite them to universal holiness: "He that hath my commandments and keepeth them . . . shall be loved of My Father, and I will love him and will manifest Myself to him" (John 14:21).

To excite likewise to the same holiness of heart and life, He proposes a full reward in the world to come. "So run that ye may obtain" (1 Corinthians 9:24). "To him that overcometh will I grant to sit with Me in My throne" (Revelation 3:21). In dispensing to His saints privilege on the back of duty performed He observes, as was already hinted, the settled order of the covenant. Not that the order of the covenant is in every particular

The Administration of the Covenant of Grace 333

first duty and then privilege; nay, it is first privilege, next duty, then privilege again; and so on until privilege and duty come both to perfection in heaven, and are so interwoven as never to be distinguished from each other anymore (1 John 3:2). Dreadful would the case of the elect be if it were otherwise! Verily, if it were, they could neither be brought into the covenant nor kept within it for a moment. For how can dead sinners begin to believe before they are privileged with the quickening spirit? And how can fallen saints renew their faith and repentance before they are privileged with new supplies of grace? "Without Me," said the Redeemer, "you can do nothing" (John 15:5).

Thus then the matter stands: The leading privilege brings duty after it; then follow, according to the order of the covenant, further privileges on the back of duty. Now these further privileges are the rewards of which I speak. In Scripture they are called rewards, even with regard to the saints themselves, because they are dispensed to working saints after they do their work. Still, however, they are as far from being rewards properly so called, which on account of a man's work are of debt to him, as the first or leading privilege is, which produces the working. According to the proper notion of reward, both the former and the latter are equally the reward of Christ's finished work.

Fourth, He ministers to them, in case of disobedience, the discipline of the covenant. Although He is as fully reconciled now as He will ever afterwards be to their persons, yet He is nowise reconciled to their sins. Nay, these, from their peculiar aggravations, are more provoking to Him than ever the sins of others. They have therefore to endure chastening; "for whom the Lord loveth He chasteneth, and scourgeth every son whom He receiveth" (Hebrews 12:6, 7). The discipline that He administers to them is fatherly chastisement. This, their state of imperfection, while in this world, is rendered necessary to their spiritual welfare; and therefore in the covenant it is ensured for them (Psalm 89:30, 32, 33, 34). It belongs to the promises of the covenant, and especially to the promise of sanctification because it is at no time vindictive, but always salutary, being an appointed means of promoting holiness in them (Hebrews 12:10). Thus it serves to purge iniquity and take away sin (Isaiah 27:9) in that, as a fire melting down in their view the varnish of the defiling objects of the world around them, and as a looking-glass, showing them their own moral pollution, it excites them by faith to wash in the laver of redeeming blood.

As to the nature of that discipline ministered by the King of Zion, it comprehends all manner of strokes on the outward and inward man. First, I will speak of the outward man. Not to speak of the contempt and reproach of the poverty and misery to which the believer is liable for his transgression; his iniquity exposes him to all those plagues, maladies, and torments, that are incidental to sinful flesh; and these may be inflicted upon him not only by the hand of Christ Himself, but sometimes, as in the case of Job, by the hand of Satan. Yea, and Christ may pursue His controversy with an offending believer even to death itself, so that his natural life may go in the cause of his disobedience (1 Corinthians 11:30). To this may be added the marks of the divine indignation against his sin set, as in the case of David's family, upon some or all of his relations.

Next, I will speak of the inward man. The believer is, for his transgression, liable to be deprived of the sense and comfort of the exercise, and even of some degree of his spiritual graces; of the comfortable sense of the Savior's love to him, and of actual communion with God in his performance of duties. He is liable to fall under desertion, or a withdrawing of the light of God's gracious countenance; to be left to walk in darkness, and to go mourning without the sun; to be thrown into horrors and ago-

The Administration of the Covenant of Grace 335

nies of conscience, pierced in his spirit with the arrows of the Almighty, compassed about and distracted with the terrors of the Lord, and to be seized with dreadful apprehensions of his revenging wrath against him so as to be brought to the brink of absolute despair. Although the casting of the believer in to hell is not within the compass of the discipline of the covenant, yet the casting of a kind of hell into the believer, making him to roar by reason of the disquietness of his heart (Psalm 38:8), is within the compass of it. And what is more dreadful still, it comprehends his being harassed with horrible temptation, and his being suffered to fall into one sin, and that perhaps a gross sin, for the punishment of another, as were David and Peter.

All these in themselves, and in their natural influence, are the deserved fruits of his sin, and so are included in testamentary threats against it. He is, in case of disobedience, particularly and directly threatened with them, in order to move him the more diligently to guard against sin. They are inflicted by the righteous King of Zion upon His beloved subjects, not for the satisfaction of divine justice but for the important purposes of making sin bitter to them, of correcting them, and of stirring them up to the frequent exercise of faith and repentance. By the sovereign grace of the covenant, thus opening their heart in renewed penitence, the tears of godly sorrow for sin issue forth the more forcibly, as waters do that have long been dammed up. These bitter streams, by thus running in the channel of the covenant, become healing waters. Those sharp swords are, by the grace of the covenant, beaten into plowshares and those piercing spears into pruning hooks. Although then they are comprised in testamentary threats against their sin; yet, as managed by infinite wisdom, love, and power, for promoting their holiness and happiness, they are mercies purchased by Christ, and are contained in promises to their persons as objects of redeeming love. His displeasure and controversy with them, manifested thereby, do, strictly speaking, aim at their sins (Psalm 89:32, 33) and not at their persons, however much they sometimes dread the contrary. Their persons are never for a moment the real objects of divine displeasure, even under their severest chastisements. All these are still from love, unchangeable love, to their persons (Zephaniah 3:17).

Fifth, He dispenses to them the forgivenesses promised in the covenant. The pardoning of crimes against the law of Jehovah is one of the royal prerogatives of the King of Zion. "Him hath God exalted with His right hand to be a Prince . . . to give repentance to Israel, and forgiveness of sins" (Acts 5:31). Hence He, according to the covenant, gives them the first pardon, removing, in their justification, the guilt of revenging wrath; and He likewise dispenses to them the subsequent forgivenesses, removing, upon their renewed acts of faith and repentance, the guilt of paternal displeasure. The Father having committed all judgment unto the Son, divine favors are, according to the tenor of the covenant, conferred on the saints, not only for His sake, but by His hand (Isaiah 43:25).

Sixth, He also affords them the protection of the covenant while they are in this world among their enemies. "The Lord," said believers in old time, "is our defense; and the holy One of Israel is our King" (Psalm 89:18). Satan, the prince of this world, is their enemy; and he is a subtle, powerful, and malicious enemy. But Christ the King of Zion is their friend (Song of Songs 5:16), and He takes them under His protection. He is infinitely wise, and can take the wise in His own craftiness; infinitely strong, and can bind the strong man armed. The world joins Satan in opposing them, but shall not, either by force or by fraud, prevail to destroy them; for infinitely greater is He than the prince and power of the world (1 John 4:4). Their worst enemies, the remains of corruption, are never absent from them, are always near them, always within them. In the depth of unsearchable wisdom, these are not expelled during the present life, but are left in them for their trial and exercise, and especially for the discovery of the infinite power and grace of their almighty King. By preserving alive in them the feeble spark of holy fire in the midst of an ocean of corruption, and causing it even to increase and make headway against the same till it dries it all up in the soul, He manifests the exceeding greatness of His power (Romans 7:24, 25). Thus their perseverance in the state, in the habit, and in the exercise of grace is infallibly secured. They cannot but be safely and finally protected for they are perpetually in Christ's hand, and in His Father's hand, hands out of which none is able to pluck them (John 10:28, 29). Besides, as King of Zion, He restrains and conquers all their enemies (1 Corinthians 15:25). He has them all in chains so that they can act no further against His true subjects than He sees proper to permit; and at His pleasure He restrains them, bounding them, as to the kind, degree, and continuance of all their enterprises and attacks upon His people (Job 1:12; 2:6). He also overrules and disappoints their wicked designs. He sets limits to their fury, and brings out of it a revenue of glory to Himself (Psalm 76:10). Having already conquered them in His own person as the Head of the body mystical (Colossians 2:15), He goes forth conquering, and to conquer them daily, in His members.

Seventh, finally, He confers on them, in an authoritative manner, the complete happiness promised in the covenant. He will thus bestow it on them at the last day. Then shall the King say unto them on His right hand, "Come, ye blessed of My Father, inherit the kingdom, prepared for you from the foundation of the world" (Matthew 25:34). And He will forever secure them in the possession of it by His eternal glorification and government of them in the heavenly Zion (Revelation 7:17; 3:21; Isaiah 9:7). Having as a Priest purchased for them a crown of life, a kingdom that cannot be moved, and having as Prophet revealed it to them, He as a King will in a way of sovereign authority put them in full and everlasting possession of it; and so He will forever complete the peace and felicity of His covenant-people.

Thus I have treated Christ's administration of the covenant as King of Zion.

6

The Dispensations of the Covenant of Grace

By a dispensation of this covenant is meant a distributing or dealing out of the benefits of it to sinners of mankind; or, which is nearly the same, a particular mode of administering it to sinners and saints. Christ the last Adam is the great Dispenser or Distributor of the grace of the covenant. And in His dispensing of it the following objects concur:

First, the word of the covenant by which He declares His thoughts and offers His benefits to sinners, and which may be distinguished into the law and the gospel.

Second, the ordinances of the covenant, in which He deals with sinners and they with Him for the effectual application of His Word, and of the benefits therein presented to them.

Third, the spirit of the covenant, by whose influences the Word and the ordinances are made effectual for bringing them into the bond of the covenant, for making them actual partakers of the benefits of it, and capable of employing them for His glory and the glory of God in Him.

Fourth, faith, by which they, being quickened and actuated, receive the Word, the ordinances, and the Spirit of the covenant.

There are two dispensations of the covenant of grace, or two modes in which the grace of it is externally administered. The one is called the Old Testament-dispensation; the other, the New Testament-dispensation. The former is, by the Apostle Paul, called the first and the old testament; the latter is by him called the second and the new testament (Hebrews 8:7, 13). By the old testament, or as it is sometimes termed the old covenant, we are not to understand the covenant of works, but that dispensation of the covenant of grace that was before the coming of Messiah in the flesh. By the new testament or new covenant is meant that dispensation of the same covenant of grace that began soon after Christ's coming in the flesh, and is to continue till His second coming. The former commenced in the beginning of time, almost as soon as man fell (Genesis 3:15), and continued till the fullness of time (Hebrews 9:15); the latter began in the fullness of time, and is to continue till the end of time (Galatians 4:4; Luke 22:29).

The covenant of grace was, before the incarnation of Christ, dispensed by promises (Romans 15:8), by prophecies (Acts 3:20, 24), by sacrifices (Hebrews 10:1), by circumcision (Romans 4:11), by the Passover (1 Corinthians 5:7), and by other types and ordinances that all foreshadowed Christ to come (Hebrews 8:9; 10 throughout), and were for that time sufficient, by the operation of the Holy Spirit, to build up the elect in their faith in the promised Messiah (1 Corinthians 10:1-4), by whom they had full remission of sins and everlasting salvation (Galatians 3:7-9, 14). The dispensation, under which these were introduced and continued, was the Old Testament.

Since the incarnation and death of Christ, who is the substance of all those shadows, the covenant of grace is dispensed by "the preaching of the Word, and the administration of the sacraments of baptism and the Lord's Supper, in which grace

The Dispensations of the Covenant of Grace

and salvation are held forth in more fullness, evidence, and efficacy to all nations" (Larger Catechism, Question 35). The dispensation under which these ordinances were introduced and are still continued, is the New Testament (Matthew 28:19, 20; 1 Corinthians 1:23-25; Luke 22:20).

Various distinct periods of the Old Testament-dispensation are observable (Hebrews 1:1). The first period extended from Adam to Noah, in which the covenant of grace was embraced by faith and sealed by sacrifices offered up in faith. The death of Messiah, the just One, was prefigured by that of Abel, who was slain by his brother; and His ascension into heaven was foreshown by the translation of Enoch there.

The second was from Noah to Abraham. Noah was a preacher of righteousness. By him Christ preached to those spirits that are now in prison (2 Peter 2:5; 1 Peter 3:19). He was also an heir of the righteousness that is by faith (Hebrews 11:7). He was, as it were, the head of a new world, and so was an illustrious type of Him who as last Adam is the head of the church. A sacrifice of a sweet savor to Jehovah, typical of the sacrifice of Christ, was offered by him. Upon his offering of that sacrifice, a gracious covenant was divinely established with him and his sons and was sealed with the rainbow.

The third period extended from Abraham to Moses. The covenant of grace was solemnly renewed with Abraham, and was sealed with the new sacrament of circumcision. He was thereby constituted the father of all who believe, whether they be Jews or Gentiles (Romans 4:12); and so was made an illustrious type of Messiah, the everlasting Father of all true believers. The special favor of Jehovah to him was continued to Isaac his son, and to Jacob his grandson. To them he condescended often to reveal himself and to renew and confirm the promises made to that illustrious patriarch. And so the promises of the covenant, which had been formerly made to the church, now that they were renewed and amplified, became more full, clear, and particular.

The fourth and last period reached from Moses to Christ, or to John the forerunner of Christ. "The law was given by Moses, but grace and truth came by Jesus Christ" (John 1:17). "The law and the Prophets were until John; since that time, the kingdom of God is preached" (Luke 16:16). Under this period, the Son of God, from Mount Sinai, in the midst of thunders and lightening, and of a thick cloud, did, with terrible majesty, proclaim Himself the King and Lawgiver of Israel. The tabernacle and the Ark of the Covenant with the mercy seat, typical of His great atonement, were with exquisite skill framed. A multitude of typical ceremonies was added to the ancient simplicity of divine worship. The Israelites, in the wilderness of Arabia, were, during forty years, fed with manna from heaven and water from the rock; and afterwards they were introduced into the Promised Land, a type of the heavenly inheritance promised to the true Israel of God.

Seeing all the institutions of the former periods were, under the ministry of Moses, renewed and, by many additional ordinances, increased as well as formed into a system or scheme or worship; and seeing the covenant was then solemnly renewed with Israel at mount Sinai, and afterwards in the land of Moab—the form of the Old Testament-dispensation is, in Scripture, sometimes attributed to the ministry of Moses (Jeremiah 31:32). Circumcision in particular, though it was in the church long before his time, is, for the same reasons, represented as given by Moses. "Moses therefore gave you circumcision (not because it is of Moses, but of the fathers) and ye on the Sabbath-day, circumcise a man" (John 7:22).

The Dispensations of the Covenant of Grace 343

The ordinances of the Old Testament, being comparatively dark, carnal, and confined, and being appointed to represent Messiah as then to come, continued as to their obligation, living and vigorous, until His incarnation; languid and dying during the time of His humiliation, and especially of His public ministry; dead, after His death, and especially after His resurrection; and deadly or destructive after His full publication of the gospel and the destruction of the Jewish temple (Hebrews 7, 8, 9, 10 throughout).

It is evident that those ordinances were long since abolished. This is clear, first, from many predictions in Scripture (Jeremiah 3:16; 31:31, 32; Daniel 9:27; Malachi 1:11); second, from express declarations in Scripture (Acts 15:10, 28; Galatians 4:10, 11; 5:3, 4, 13; Colossians 2:14, 17; Hebrews 8:12, 18); third, from the nature of those ceremonies themselves. We are informed that, considered in themselves, they were not good; they pointed out Messiah not as come, but only as to come, and excluded the Gentiles from the church (Hebrews 10:1; Colossians 2:17; Galatians 3:24; Ephesians 2:14, 15); fourth, from the state of the Jewish nation which, for more than seventeen hundred years last past, has been such as to render the observance of those ceremonies in Jerusalem, or even in any part of Canaan, impossible (Luke 19:43, 44; 21: 20, 24; Romans 11:7-15, 20).

When it was in ancient prophecy foretold that priests, sacrifices, and a temple were to be in the New Testament church, those typical terms must be understood in a spiritual sense, agreeably to the nature of the New Testament economy (1 Peter 2:5; Hebrews 13:15; Romans 12:1). When we read that some of those ordinances were appointed to continue forever (Genesis 17:13; Exodus 12:24), we are to remember that the terms everlasting and forever sometimes signify no more, in the language of the Old Testament, than an indefinite time, or a long time, or the whole time of a particular state of things; and withal, that those typical ordinances do, in their antitypes, continue forever, in the fullest sense of the words.

The Old and New Testament-dispensations agree, and in a high degree resemble each other, first, in their Author, God in Christ (Hebrews 1:1); second, in the matter of them, the law and the gospel being the substance of both (Psalm 147:19; Galatians 3:8; Titus 2:11 and 3:8).

Third, they agree in this, that benefits of the same kind are offered and bestowed under both. Does the New Testament, for instance, contain a promise of the Spirit of life? So likewise did the Old (Proverbs 1:23). Does that contain a grant of union and communion with the blessed Redeemer? So did this (Job 19:25). Were the apostles of Christ under the New Testament authorized to proclaim pardon and acceptance through His meritorious righteousness? So also were His prophets under the Old (Job 33:24; Isaiah 1:18; Hosea 14:4). Does the Son of God under the New Testament offer to sinners the inestimable privilege of sonship? He likewise, under the Old Testament, received believing sinners into the family of God (Isaiah 63:16). Does Christ, the Head of influences to His church, offer, under the second Testament, regeneration and sanctification to sinners who hear the gospel? So did He under the first (Isaiah 55:1; Ezekiel 36:26, 27). Does He afford to His saints, under the new dispensation, persevering grace? He likewise under the old kept them as in a fortified city (Psalm 31:21). He preserved their souls (Psalm 121:7, 8). In few words, does He under the new economy bring life and immortality to light by the gospel, assuring His spiritual seed of the eternal inheritance? He also persuaded the saints, under the old, that He had prepared for them a city, "a city which hath foundations, whose builder and maker is God" (Hebrews 11:10). In the faith of this, one Old Testament saint said,

The Dispensations of the Covenant of Grace 345

"I shall dwell in the house of the Lord forever" (Psalm 23:6); and another, "Thou wilt afterwards receive me to glory" (Psalm 63:24).

Fourth, those dispensations agree in requiring the same chief end of duty (Psalm 91:7, 8), the same exercise of faith and repentance, and the same evangelical obedience in attending their respective ordinances (Isaiah 55:1-7; Matthew 11:28, 29; Revelation 22:17).

Fifth, they also agree in this respect, that the ordinances of both have of themselves no spiritual efficacy to convince and convert sinners, and hence are often least effectual when best dispensed, as by Moses, Isaiah, Christ Himself, etc. (Deuteronomy 29:4; Isaiah 6:9, 10; 49:4, 5; 53:1).

Sixth, they resemble each other in their being made effectual for salvation by the same means, namely (1.) by the blessing of Christ, which implies His sovereign appointment of them to be blessings to His people, and His rendering of them such by His all-powerful influence accompanying them (Exodus 20:24). (2.) By the working of His Spirit in preparing men for those ordinances in assisting them in their attendance on God in them, and in inclining and enabling them rightly to observe them (1 Corinthians 3:6, 7; 12:13). (3.) By the exercise of saving faith, corresponding to the influence of Christ and the working of His Spirit in discerning that which God discovers, in believing that which He declares, in receiving that which He offers, and in employing His manifestations, declarations, and offers to promote that holiness in all manner of conversation that He requires (Hebrews 4:2; 11:6).

The Old and the New Testament dispensations, at the same time, differ from each other, and that in various respects. An apostle informs us that if the first covenant had been faultless, then should no place have been sought for the second for finding fault with them. He said, "Behold, the days come, saith the Lord, when I will make a new covenant with the house of Israel, and with the house of Judah; not according to the covenant that I made with their fathers, in the day when I took them by the hand to lead them out of the land of Egypt" (Hebrews 8:7-9). Here he teaches us that the second covenant or second dispensation is not according that first covenant that Jehovah again and again renewed, and that He made with the Israelites at Sinai soon after He had led them out of the land of Egypt. While he tells us that the first covenant was comparatively faulty, he calls the second a better covenant, and says that it was established upon better promises (Hebrews 8:6); that is, it was formed into an authoritative establishment upon more spiritual, more heavenly, more absolute, and more extensive promises than those that were contained in the first; upon promises absolutely better than the temporal promises of the land of Canaan, and comparatively better than the spiritual promises of the first dispensation because in them the grace of Christ is held forth in more fullness, evidence, and efficacy to all nations than in those of the first.

Now the difference between these two covenants or testaments does not consist in the inheritance promised in each, as if Canaan only were the inheritance promised in the Old, and heaven the inheritance promised only in the New Testament. The inheritance of heaven was as really promised in the former as it is in the latter. In the Old Testament it was set forth under a variety of shadows and, during a certain period of that economy, under the type of the land of Canaan; in the New Testament it is exhibited clearly without the veil of typical ordinances or mystical representations. The one testament, then, differs from the other merely in this respect, that the one is a different mode of dispensing the same inheritance. Whatever in the dis-

The Dispensations of the Covenant of Grace

pensation of the inheritance was typical, and served to show that it was not yet purchased by the blood of the Testator, belonged to the Old Testament; whatever, on the contrary, in the dispensation of the same inheritance represents it as already purchased belongs to the New Testament.

But more particularly, these two testaments differ from each other, and the New is better than the Old:

1. In respect that under the New, Christ is exhibited as already incarnate, and as having already brought in an everlasting righteousness for the justification of them who believe. The faith of saints under the first testament centered on Messiah as yet to come, the faith of saints under the second centers on Him as already come. The saints under the old dispensation were called to believe that Messiah would die for the expiation of the guilt, and would bring in an everlasting righteousness for their complete justification; the saints under the new are bound to believe that He has already made reconciliation for their iniquity, and fulfilled all righteousness for their justification. The Old Testament church was required to believe that all the prophecies respecting the death, resurrection, and ascension of Messiah would be accomplished in due time; the New Testament church is required to believe that they are in Christ Jesus accomplished already (1 Peter 1:10-12). The church under the first testament was called to believe that Jehovah would fulfill both the conditions and the promises of the covenant in his time; the church under the second is bound to believe that God the Son, in human nature, has already fulfilled the conditions, that God the Father has already performed such of the promises as respected Christ personal, and that He will in due time perform such of them as respect Christ mystical.

2. The New Testament is better than the Old in respect of light. Under the old dispensation Moses, as the Apostle Paul

informs us, put a veil over his face so that the children of Israel could not steadfastly look to the end of that which is abolished, which veil is done away in Christ (2 Corinthians 3:13, 14); and in the last verse of the same chapter he says, "We all, with open face, beholding as in a glass the glory of the Lord, are changed into the same image, from glory to glory, even as by the Spirit of the Lord." When speaking of New Testament times, Jehovah promised that His people would teach no more every man his neighbor, and every man his brother, saying, "Know the Lord"; for that they should all know Him, from the least of them to the greatest of them (Jeremiah 31:34). The gospel under the new dispensation is preached clearly and in a new form, revealing and offering to sinners an incarnate Redeemer, and eternal redemption already obtained by Him. An internal and subjective light in the understanding, corresponding to those superior degrees of external revelation, in the Scriptures of the New Testament, is also by the Spirit conferred on believers. The Old Testament, on the other hand, was comparatively obscure. And indeed, what could reasonably have been expected, so long as the Sun of righteousness had not risen, but darkness, or at least obscure light? The Apostle Peter compares the word of prophecy under the Old Testament to a light shining in a dark place (2 Peter 1:19). By comparing it to a light or lamp he intimates that the Sun was not then risen. Our blessed Lord Himself, in the days of His humiliation accommodating His doctrine to that darker dispensation, scarcely ever spoke of any of the mysteries of His kingdom to the multitudes that heard Him but in parables (Matthew 13:34, 35).

3. The New Testament differs from, and is better than the Old, in respect of life. Christ is come that His people might have life, and that they might have it more abundantly (John 10:10). The Spirit of life was given them in greater measure after

Jesus ascended on high than ever He had been before (Ephesians 4:8, 11, 12). "The law was given by Moses, but grace and truth came by Jesus Christ" (John 1:17). The Lord Jesus having, according to the promise, put His laws into their mind and written them in their heart (Hebrews 8:10), His people now serve in newness of Spirit, and not in the oldness of the letter (Romans 7:6). Saints under the New Testament, then, are endued with superior degrees of spiritual life and vigor. The Old Testament, in comparison of the New, is called the ministration of death; and the New Testament, in comparison of the Old, is called the ministration of the Spirit who gives life. We are not however to imagine that the old economy was denominated the ministration of death, as if all who died under it were destined to eternal death; it was, on the contrary, the means of bringing many of them to the full enjoyment of eternal life. Nor was it so called, as if it announced nothing but death; for it set before them who were under it, life as well as death, the blessing as well as the curse. But a display of the covenant of works being, for gospel purposes, greatly prevalent in that economy, it is called the ministration of death because death was threatened in that part of it that exhibited the dreadful penalty of the covenant of works. It bore that name too because under it the communications of the Spirit as a Spirit of life were comparatively sparing. Whereas, since the last Adam rose from the dead to a new kind of life in his human nature, the power of His resurrection is, by the members of His mystical body, felt in a much greater degree than it was before.

4. The new dispensation excels the old in regard to evangelical liberty. The ordinances of the Old Testament were so very numerous and burdensome, and were enjoined under such severe threats as subjected the saints of those times to a comparative bondage. The Apostle Paul calls them a yoke of bondage

(Galatians 5:1) and the elements of the world under which the saints were in bondage (Galatians 4:3). Bondage and fear, therefore, prevailed under the old dispensation; whereas liberty and confidence in drawing near to God are predominant under the new. Though the saints under the first Testament had a promise that their debt of punishment should, by their blessed Surety, be completely paid, yet, seeing it was not then actually paid, there was a standing intimation of their debt-bond in the violated law that could not fail to strike them with terror. But now that the debt is actually discharged by the death of the condescending Surety, that bond is cancelled with His blood so that, instead of thunders and lightnings from Sinai, saints have invitations from Zion to draw near with a true heart in full assurance of faith (Hebrews 10:22). There is now in believers an internal liberty of spirit corresponding to their external liberty from the yoke of the ceremonial law. That internal liberty consists of more enlarged and distinct views of the justifying and sanctifying grace revealed in the promises of the new covenant, and of freedom from the dominion of the broken covenant of works as well as from that of sin, Satan, and the world (Romans 6:14; 8:1; Colossians 1:13, 14). We find, indeed, under the former economy many illustrious instances of access to God on special occasions; but for the most part the saints then were under what might be called bondage in comparison of the glorious liberty of the children of God under the latter.

5. The new economy differs from and excels the old in respect that saints under the new are favored with a higher and a more comfortable enjoyment of the Holy Spirit in His presence and influence than saints under the old. They are blessed with more exalted degrees of holiness. As they have more spiritual light put into their mind, so they have more of the love of God shed abroad in their heart and, consequently, more of that

The Dispensations of the Covenant of Grace 351

evangelical holiness that flows from it as the principle thereof (Isaiah 35 throughout; 62:12; 64:11, 12; Zechariah 12:8 and 14:20, 21). They have likewise higher degrees of spiritual comfort. The Holy Spirit, accommodating His influences to the nature of the new dispensation, fills them with more joy and peace in believing than were usually afforded under the old (Isaiah 40:1, 2; 55:12; 66:12-13; John 14:16; 2 Thessalonians 2:16), and favors them with greater filial boldness and intimacy with God (Hebrews 10:19). Their filial boldness, or confidence in God as their Father, is greater than that of Old Testament saints inasmuch as their adoption and the blessed effects of it are more clearly manifested to them. The Apostle Paul says to the believers in Rome, "Ye have not received the spirit of bondage again to fear; but ye have received the Spirit of adoption, whereby we cry, Abba, Father" (Romans 8:15).

6. The new dispensation is better than the old in regard to extent. The old was restricted to one nation; the new is extended to all nations (Romans 16:26). The ordinances of the Old Testament were as a middle wall of partition between Jews and Gentiles; but Christ Jesus, by His death, has broken down that wall (Ephesians 2:14) "Go ye, therefore," said He to His disciples, "and teach all nations, baptizing them in the name of the Father, and of the Son, and of the Holy Ghost" (Matthew 28:19); and again, "Go ye into all the world, and preach the gospel to every creature" (Mark 16:15). Every distinction of nation, of rank, of sex, and of place is now at an end (Isaiah 54:1-3; Galatians 3:28; Colossians 3:11).

7. Last, the New Testament dispensation is better than the Old in respect of duration. The Old decayed and vanished away; the New shall continue to the end of time. That yielded to a better dispensation even on earth; this shall give place only to the glory that is to be revealed and enjoyed in heaven. The present

dispensation of the covenant shall never give way to another in this world. Like the covenant of the day and of the night it shall not cease, but shall be continued as long as the sun. The blood of bulls and of goats was the blood of that testament that waxed old and vanished away; but the blood of Christ Jesus is the blood of the everlasting testament, a testament that cannot be made void, that cannot, until the consummation of all things, admit of a change (Matthew 28:20).

Should the reader now be disposed to ask why the old dispensation of the covenant was inferior to the new, it would be enough only to reply that the will of God determined it so to be. But besides, it might be observed that both in providence and in grace it is God's usual manner not to bring great objects to perfection all at once, but rather by degrees, and one of them after another, in order that His wisdom and power may shine forth the more conspicuously. In the creation of this world, for instance, He formed matter out of nothing first into a rude mass; next, by degrees, He out of that mass formed all the different orders of sublunary creatures, whether animate or inanimate, and imparted to them that variety, symmetry, and beauty in which He rested satisfied. In like manner, in the dispensation of His covenant and the formation of His church, He carries on His work from small beginnings till in process of time He brings it to such perfection as will reflect the highest honor upon His wisdom and His other perfections. If it was not unworthy of the only wise God to have produced something that is imperfect in the kingdom of grace, but which is afterwards to be made perfect in the kingdom of glory, neither was it unworthy of Him to have afforded fewer privileges and lower degrees of enjoyment to His saints under the Old Testament than to those under the New. Indeed, it would not be suitable to the wisdom and the grace of God that such marvelous light as shines in and by the gospel should break forth upon mankind all at once, but on the contrary that it should be poured forth by degrees, like that of the sun which does not in a moment, but by degrees, ascend to his meridian height and splendor. This an apostle intimates when he says, "God, who at sundry times, and in divers manners, spake in time past unto the fathers by the prophets, hath in these last days spoken unto us by His Son" (Hebrews 1:1, 2).

Since it pleased God that the mission of Christ should be delayed till the fullness of time, it is remarkable that the whole of the previous revelation of the covenant, being comparatively obscure, came under the idea of promise. The subsequent revelation of it again comes under the notion of testimony, or report of good tidings, and is usually called the gospel. These terms thus distinguished, however, refer to the dispensation rather than to the matter of the covenant, which was gospel in every age (Hebrews 4:2). The promise, as descriptive of the ancient revelation of the covenant, does not signify the promissory part of the covenant as distinguished from the conditional, but the manner of revelation. It was all exhibited in the form of promise respecting Messiah, His coming, His work, and the glory that was to follow. In the very first promise there was a revelation of the whole of the covenant, of the conditions promised, and even administration of it; for the bruising of the serpent's head by Messiah, the Seed of the woman, comprises not merely His triumphs on the cross, but all His victories in His dispensation of grace and providence till His enemies be made His footstool. Of this promise, the ceremonies and sacrifices under the law were intended to form an instructive explanation shadowing forth the good things to come. On this promise, all the successive revelations and prophecies were designed to be a commentary. While the church was under the promise, it behooved the administration of the covenant to correspond to the state in which it then was; and indeed the manner of instruction was most wisely adapted to that state. It was communicated by degrees to the saints according to their capacity of receiving it.

With respect to the matter of the covenant, there were three remarkable periods of revelation, bearing on the several parts of it, and calculated in a special manner to exhibit them to the faith of the church. These are commonly called the Abrahamic, the Sinaitic, and the Davidic covenants; for the term covenant is often in Scripture expressive of some special revelation of it; as it is by a revelation of it that it comes to be established, either with families, or with individuals. While the whole matter of the covenant, as intimated in the first discovery of it, was kept in view in each of those periods, the first had principally a reference to the promises, the second to the conditions, and the third to the administration of it.

1st, the covenant with Abraham chiefly related to the promises, or promised blessings of that eternal covenant. "In thee and in thy seed," said Jehovah to him, "shall all the families of the earth be blessed." Spiritual blessedness is evidently meant, or that eternal life of which believers as the seed of Abraham have become heirs. And their being heirs of this according to the promise is the same as their inheriting it, according to the covenant of grace in that period revealed to Abraham; for the promise of which we read in Galatians 3:29 does not signify the ancient dispensation, in which sense it could not be opposed to the law, but the promissory part of the covenant of grace. Even the assigning of Canaan to the natural seed of Abraham was designed to elucidate and confirm the promise of the eternal inheritance.

2nd, the covenant at Sinai principally referred to the conditions of the covenant of grace. It was not intended, as the carnal Jews imagined, to annul the promise, but to show what was necessary to be done in order to procure a title to the blessings promised, and to point out to the faith of the saints what would be done for that purpose by the adorable Surety. It demonstrated to all concerned that Jehovah was on no account to overlook the claims of law and justice in bestowing those blessings. That cursed is everyone who does not perform perfect obedience was His awful denunciation, and that full satisfaction for sin must be made was the voice of every sacrifice. The law in all its extent and spirituality was published at Sinai to show the people what it required, and to set forth those conditions that the Surety had covenanted to perform; that, despairing of life on the ground of their own performances, they might be driven to Messiah, and might rely on the conditions of the covenant of grace to be fulfilled by Him. Accordingly, the sacrifices then instituted, while they proclaimed that satisfaction for sin was necessary, were also types of the great atonement that was to be made.

3rd, the covenant of royalty made with David chiefly related to the administration of the covenant of grace. It was a typical disclosure of the covenant made with Messiah, in that part of it which respects his government, both special, as administered in His church, and general, as extended to the world for the good of His church. Nor was it merely a figurative revelation of the dominion that was to be exercised by Him in His exalted state, as predicted in the 18th and 89th Psalms, in which David is exhibited as typical of Him; it was also the method in which He exercised His administration in the ancient Church, and over the surrounding nations for her sake. His manner of exercising it was adapted to that period. Hence the royal throne, the temporal dominion, and the warlike achievements, all of which were to cease upon his appearing in our nature. But the government exercised was the same in kind as that which He now exercises in His administration of the covenant in His exalted state.

These successive revelations of the covenant were all introductory to its being established with Christ in our nature. Although it was made with Him from eternity in His divine person, yet it was necessary to its execution that it should likewise in all its parts be established with Him in His human nature as the Seed of Abraham and the Seed of David. By the revelation of the promises to Abraham, they terminated in Christ as the seed of Abraham. To Abraham and his seed were the promises made. The promises were the object of His faith as man, not indeed for himself, but for the children whom God had given Him. In virtue of the revelation of the conditions at Sinai, they terminated in Him as man inasmuch as he, being made of a woman, was made under the law. Being in our nature, under the precept, and by imputation of sin under the penalty of the law, it took hold of Him and said to Him what it had hitherto been saying to the Jewish church, "Perfect obedience and full satisfaction must be given." In virtue of the covenant of royalty, the administration, hitherto exercised by Him solely in His divine nature, also terminated in Him in His human nature, as the Seed of David. The Lord God was to give unto Him the throne of His father David (Luke 1:32). It was in His human nature as King of Zion that He was to inherit that administration that belonged to the throne of David.

Thus it appears that the New Testament dispensation is better than the Old in regard to light, life, liberty, comfort, extent, and duration.

Now from this view of the subject it may justly be inferred that unbelief and contempt of Christ are greater sins now than they were even under the old dispensation. Though they were the greatest of sins committed then, they are still greater transgressions now than they were then seeing they receive high aggravations from the superior light, life, liberty, comfort, and extent of the present dispensation. "He that despised Moses' law, died without mercy . . . Of how much sorer punishment, suppose ye," says an apostle, "shall he be thought worthy who hath trodden under foot the Son of God, and hath counted the blood of the covenant, wherewith he was sanctified, an unholy thing, and hath done despite unto the Spirit of grace?" (Hebrews 10:28, 29). "Consider, thou who believest not, that by thy unbelief thou not only makest the God of truth a liar (1 John 5:10), but treadest under foot the Son of God." God the Father, in His gracious offer of His Son to you, lays Him down, as it were, in the way between you and the place of torment; and by your unbelief and contempt of Him you are rushing over Him to eternal destruction. You trample on His Person and authority, on His oracles and ordinances; and instead of trusting for justification and salvation to that precious blood by which the covenant of grace was fulfilled and ratified, you, by your unbelief, profanely slight it and treat it as if it were not so holy as the blood of bulls and goats; or as if it were of no more value than the blood of a common man, or even of a malefactor, as the Jews, when they crucified Christ, accounted Him to be. Nay, if you have been convinced of the truth and grace of the gospel, you, by your obstinate unbelief, spitefully oppose and contemptuously vilify the Person, operation, and grace of the Holy Spirit. This, if not the unpardonable sin itself, is the very next step to it.

Now if one who presumptuously violated even the law of Moses was without mercy to be punished with death, how inconceivably more dreadful must that punishment be that you deserve for such contempt and rejection of the glorious grace of Christ! How, ah, how is it possible that you can escape the infinite vengeance of Jehovah through endless ages who continues to neglect such a great salvation as is offered to you in the glorious gospel! Be assured, it is infinitely dangerous to persist in sinning against the superior light and grace of the gospel. Oh, then, presume no longer to despise, to distrust Him who has already come in the name of the Lord to save, and who is infinitely able and willing to save to the uttermost all who come to him. "Believe on the Lord Jesus Christ, and thou shalt be saved" (Acts 16:31); come to Him for all His salvation, and He will in no wise cast you out (John 6:37).

Does the new dispensation of the covenant excel the old in respect that under the new Christ is exhibited as already incarnate, and as having already brought in everlasting righteousness for the justification and salvation of all who believe? It follows that it is comparatively easier to trust in Him for salvation now under the new than it was under the old. You therefore, believer, ought, in all your approaches to your reconciled Father, to draw near to Him not only in assurance, but in full assurance of faith, and to give all diligence to the full assurance of hope. Hold fast the beginning of your confidence in your faithful Redeemer, steadfast to the end, and pursue eagerly after an unshaken confidence in Him.

Is the present dispensation better than the former with regard to light? Then, beholding with open face as in a glass the glory of the Lord Jesus, be then, you who believe, changed into His image by advancing from glory to glory; from one degree of grace, which is the beginning of glory, to another (2 Corinthians 3:18). Trust that the Holy Spirit will, and pray that He may, take of the things, the glorious things of Christ, and show them to you. Walk in the light, as Christ is in the light, and you shall have increasing fellowship with Him (1 John 1:7).

Does the New Testament economy surpass the Old in respect of life? Is it the ministration of the Spirit who gives life?

See then what encouragement you have to trust in the Lord Jesus for daily communications of the Spirit of life from His fullness. Trusting that He gives, and will continue to give you, renewed supplies of the Spirit of life, walk in newness of life and serve in newness of spirit. Be always lively and active, diligent and fervent, in every good word and work.

Is it better than the former in regard to evangelical liberty? Stand fast then, believer, in the liberty wherewith Christ has made you free. Jesus the second Adam has made you free from the broken covenant of works. Resist with holy abhorrence the first motions of a legal spirit in your heart. You are brought into the glorious liberty of the children of God. Oh, receive by faith more and more of the spirit of adoption, whereby you may come boldly to the throne of grace, and as Jesus Himself did, cry, "Abba, Father." It is your bound duty to pursue after more holy reverence, more humble confidence, and more filial boldness in all your approaches to your covenant God and Father.

But further, is the present dispensation better than the former in respect that believers now have a more enlarged and comfortable enjoyment of the Holy Spirit than they had then? Learn hence, O Christian, that it is very unbecoming in you to indulge distrustful, despondent, and melancholy thoughts. Jesus is granted to you for your consolation. His Spirit is given to you for your Comforter. You ought then so to believe as to be filled with all joy and peace in believing, so to trust for your own salvation as to rejoice in Christ Jesus. If it was the duty of saints under the Old Testament to serve Jehovah with gladness (Psalm 100:2), it is still more your duty. "Oh, rejoice in the Lord always; and again I say, rejoice" (Philippians 4:4). Trust and pray for more spiritual comfort that you may be cheerful in all your obedience.

Finally, does the new economy surpass the old in regard to extent? You then who are believers and partakers of the inestimable blessings of the gospel should be zealous in promoting missions to infidel and heathen nations. By your prayers, your counsel, and your substance, you ought to exert yourself for the diffusion of evangelical knowledge among benighted nations in order that the spiritual kingdom of Christ may be universally extended.

7

The Way of a Sinner's Entering Into the Covenant so as to Become Personally Interested in It

Having in discoursing of the parties, the making, the conditions, the promises, the administration, and the dispensations of the covenant of grace, explained in some degree the nature of that divine contract, it will be necessary that I now proceed to answer a question of infinite importance to every son and daughter of Adam: How does a sinner pass from the covenant of works into the covenant of grace? Or how does a sinner so enter into the covenant of grace as to become personally and actually interested in that eternal covenant? The reader has already seen that a covenant was from all eternity entered into between Jehovah the Father and Christ the second Adam, a covenant of infinitely free grace made in favor of sinners of Adam's family who had destroyed themselves by violating the covenant of works. In that covenant, ample provision is made for their eternal salvation. The conditions of it, settled by the immutable justice and law of Jehovah, are indeed very high. There can be nothing, however, on that part to discourage them from essaying to enter into the covenant; for their inability having been from eternity foreseen, the performance of the arduous conditions was laid upon One who is mighty; and now these are completely performed by the second Adam, that mighty One. It is the promises only that remain to be fulfilled. Sinners of mankind are therefore invited to partake of the benefit of those promises; and that they may have ready access thereto the administration of the covenant is devolved upon the same almighty Redeemer. And He is entrusted with all the promises in order that He may fulfill them to believing sinners. He has already begun to fulfill them to all who have taken hold of the covenant; and He is ready to accomplish them to everyone who shall yet take hold of it.

Indeed the whole of the covenant is in Him. In Him is God the Contractor on the part of heaven (2 Corinthians 5:19). He Himself is the Contractor on the part of man. In Him are all the elect legally, and all true believers really. In Him also are the conditions of the covenant, and these as already performed. He is Jehovah our Righteousness (Jeremiah 23:6). In Him likewise all the promise of God are yea and Amen (2 Corinthians 1:20). They all meet in Him as the lines of a circle do in their center; and all are sure, nowise liable to fail or misgive, as the promise of the covenant of works did in the first Adam. He accordingly as King of Zion issues out His royal proclamations, bearing that whosoever will come to Him, and by faith unite with Him as Head of the covenant, shall be received into it and have in Him a right to all the blessings of it.

Thus the covenant is in the gospel brought near, so near as to be within the reach of every sinner who hears the gospel; so that everyone must either be a receiver or a rejecter of it. To reject it is inconceivably dangerous. Take hold of that covenant, sinners, for it is your life. You are under the broken covenant of works, where there is no life, no salvation for you. But the door of the covenant of grace is opened for you. Come, then, and enter into it without delay. Make your escape speedily from the dominion of the covenant of works under which you were born, and under which you have, till this moment, continued; which you cannot do otherwise than by embracing, and so entering into the bond of the covenant of grace offered to you in the gospel.

That you may, under the illuminating influences of the Holy Spirit, the more clearly discern your way into the covenant, it will be necessary to point out to you by what means a sinner enters into and is instated in it to everlasting salvation. This in general is by faith in Jesus Christ, by which one is spiritually united to Him as the Head of the covenant. But more particularly,

In the first place, sinners are personally and actually instated in the eternal covenant by their being spiritually united to Christ, the Head and Representative of His people in it (Isaiah 54:5, 9, 10; Ezekiel 16:8; Hosea 2:18-20). By that spiritual marriage-union Christ Himself, in His person, offices, and relations becomes theirs (Song of Songs 2:16; Philippians 3:8, 9). His performance of the conditions of the covenant becomes also theirs in law-reckoning (Isaiah 45:24, 25; Jeremiah 23:6; 2 Corinthians 5:21), and all the promised blessings of it become theirs in law-right (1 Corinthians 3:21-23).

The Lord Jesus, their Kinsman-redeemer, then brings sinners into the bond of the covenant by uniting them to Himself as their Husband, as their Head of righteousness and life, of justification and sanctification (Isaiah 54:5, 17; 61:10; Ephesians 2:10). They enter into it by uniting with Him the public Representative, with whom, as Contractor on the part of man, it was made. "I am," says He, "the door; by Me, if any man enter in, he shall be saved" (John 10:9). By this means the unity of the covenant and the representation in it are preserved entire. If men were to enter into the covenant by some other way, as for instance, by their accepting of terms (properly so called) proposed to them, and promising for themselves that they should fulfill the same; in that case, the representation in the covenant would be marred; and there would in effect be as many covenants of grace as the persons were who at different times entered into it; at least Christ's covenant would be one, and theirs would be another evidently distinct from it; the contrary of which was above evinced from the Oracles of truth. But the covenant of grace being made with Christ as last Adam, in the name of all who should be His, it evidently follows that the only way by which sinners can enter personally into the bond of it must be by becoming His, or by becoming related to Him the Head of the covenant as their Head. In what manner did we all enter personally into the covenant of works so as to participate in the awful curse of it? Was it not through our becoming, by ordinary generation, branches of the first administration, the root and representative of his posterity, in that covenant? Hereby every one of us was personally entered into and instated in it; and that before he was capable either of consenting to it or of dissenting from it. In like manner we enter personally into the covenant of grace so as to partake of the blessings of it by our becoming branches of the second Adam, the Root and Representative of His people therein. It is by our being engrafted into Christ that we are made partakers of the covenant and benefits of it. Hence it is that infants, though not capable of exercising faith, nor of knowing what the covenant is, yet having the Spirit of faith are personally entered into it and instated in it, inasmuch as by the Spirit of faith they are effectually united to Jesus Christ. As God the Father in making the covenant took Christ for all, for the conditions and for the parties that were to receive the promises, He being the second Adam; so sinners, in accepting the covenant, take Him

The Way of a Sinner's Entering Into the Covenant

for the whole of the covenant; the parts and the parties of it, being in Him as last Adam, God as well as man in one person. Accordingly, Jehovah the Father is said to give Christ the Son for a covenant of the people because in Him people may have the covenant and all the inestimable benefits of it. Spiritual union with Him is the foundation of all the communion that the saints have with Him as their Covenant-head, and with God in Him as their covenant-God.

In the last place, sinners are personally and actually instated in the covenant by faith, which is the instrument of that spiritual union with Christ. As the Lord Jesus, in a way of grace, brings elect sinners into the covenant by uniting Himself to them, so they, in a way of duty, enter into the bond of it by faith, uniting themselves to Him. The covenant of grace is in the gospel set forth to sinners. Jehovah in His offer of it says to them, "I will make an everlasting covenant with you, even the sure mercies of David." And to close it with them, or instate them personally in it, to all the purposes of salvation, all that is required of them is to hear, that is, to believe. "Hear, and your soul shall live" (Isaiah 55:3). He who believes is personally and actually within the covenant of grace; he who believes not is still under the covenant of works, where the first Adam left him. Faith is the mouth by which sinners expressly consent to the covenant, or consent that God in Christ should be their God and they His people. It is the hand with which they take hold of the covenant, each for himself, and close the bargain for their own salvation. Though while persons continue without the covenant, perfect obedience, on pain of the curse, is required of them, and more than that, suffering also, until divine justice is fully satisfied in virtue of the broken covenant of works; and though, after they are brought into the covenant, obedience to all the commands of the law, as a rule of duty, and submission to all the discipline of the covenant, are, in virtue of the covenant of grace into which they have entered, required of them, yet merely to enter them into the covenant and instate them in it to salvation, nothing is required of them but that they cordially believe in the Lord Jesus. "Believe on the Lord Jesus Christ, and thou shalt be saved" (Acts 16:31). "Only believe" (Mark 5:36). Do what they will, if they believe not, they remain in a state of condemnation; if they cordially believe, they thereby enter upon a state of justification and salvation. If they should say a thousand times with their lips only that they take hold of the covenant; if they should come under the most solemn engagements to be the Lord's, taking the same upon themselves in prayer or otherwise, and that in the most explicit terms; if they should even write their covenant, subscribe it, and then take the holy sacrament upon it to ratify all—yet if they do not with the heart believe on Jesus, they enter not into the covenant; they miss the hold of it, and remain still without the bond of it. Whereas if they should at this moment with the heart believe in Jesus, having no opportunity either to speak, pray, write, or receive the sacrament, yet the instant they so believe they begin to be personally and actually instated in the covenant, never to fall out of it, either in time or in eternity. God in Christ is their God. All the righteousness, all the promises, of the covenant are theirs. Although they had missed the grasp of the covenant hitherto a thousand times, yet now they have it sure and firm. These are the words of Him who cannot lie: "Verily, verily, I say unto you, He that believeth on Me *hath* everlasting life" (John 6:47).

That believing in Jesus Christ should be the appointed means of entering sinners into the covenant, and of instating them in it, is perfectly suitable to the nature and design of that august contract. While faith unites the sinner to Christ, the

The Way of a Sinner's Entering Into the Covenant

federal Representative of His people; and so preserves the unity of the covenant entire, it receives all the benefits of it as free gifts and so preserves the grace of it entire. By that means also the promise is made sure to all the seed (Romans 4:16). Faith is, in that great transaction, distinguished from works, as grace is from debt (Romans 4:4, 5). If any work of ours were that upon which we were personally interested in the covenant, and invested with a right to the promise, in that case the blessings of the covenant would be of debt to us, contrary to the declared intention of that glorious device of salvation, which is to exalt the sovereign grace of God and to take away all ground of boasting from the creature (Ephesians 2:8, 9). But as for faith, the nature of its efficacy in the affair is entirely adapted to that design of the covenant; inasmuch as it is a grace that gives nothing, but on the contrary receives everything; which takes all from Christ freely, without money and without price; relying for acceptance with God, solely on what He has done and suffered, and disclaiming entirely, in that point, all confidence in any doings or sufferings of our own. Thus the promise becomes sure to us for, whereas a plea founded upon any work of ours must be a very uncertain one, the plea of faith is ever sure and available, as being founded solely upon the finished work of Christ, that sure ground of title to life eternal.

It appears then that entering personally and formally into the covenant of grace is by uniting with Christ the Head of it, which uniting with Him, being by faith, it is manifest that it is by believing Him that sinners enter into that eternal covenant so as to be instated in it and saved according to it. They then who believe are thereby interested and instated in the covenant; they who believe not have no part in it. They remain still under the dreadful curse of the covenant of works.

QUESTION. Hence arises a very momentous question that it will be necessary to answer in order to direct sinners in their way into the covenant for salvation, namely, What is that faith or believing by which a person unties with Christ, and so enters into the covenant of grace?

ANSWER. To this I reply, faith or believing, according to the use of the term in Scripture, is TRUSTING. It is the trusting of a word spoken, of a person speaking, and of a thing spoken of, or exhibited to view. These Scripture-phrases, believing to and believing in convey the same meaning as trusting to and trusting in. The former phrases, however unusual with us in conversation, are yet very common in the original languages of the Scriptures.

1. A true faith, wrought in the heart of an elect sinner by the Holy Spirit, is a trusting to a word spoken, or a report. "Who," said the prophet Isaiah, "hath believed (Hebrew, believed to, or trusted to) our report" (Isaiah 53:1). "Our report," that is, our hearing, or words heard, namely the words of Messiah by His prophets and apostles. It is also a believing in or trusting in a word spoken. "Then believed they his words" (Psalm 106:12), Hebrew, "then believed they, or trusted they, in his words." Saving faith then is a trusting to and trusting in the word of Christ; that is, it is a believing or trusting that His Word contained in the Scriptures is divinely true. A counterfeit faith is little more than a suspicion or fear that the record of God concerning His Son may be true. A true faith, on the contrary, is a trusting that it is true, which includes not only a belief of it, but an approbation and a desire that it may be true to me. To trust to or in the word of Christ includes especially a cordial belief or persuasion that it is true. "By this faith, a Christian believes to be true whatsoever is revealed in the Word, for the authority of God Himself speaking therein"

The Way of a Sinner's Entering Into the Covenant

(Westminster Confession, chapter xiv, art. 2); or he believes that the record or testimony concerning the Lord Jesus and the covenant of grace is most true, and that, upon the authority of God who cannot lie, whose testimony it is. The Holy Spirit, in working divine faith, demonstrates to the mind the truth of the divine testimony so plainly as to produce a forcible persuasion of that truth, or a firm assent to the testimony as true. The consequence is that a man is as firmly persuaded that the doctrines and promises of the gospel are just what God has said they are as if he saw them with his eyes.

2. Faith is also a trusting to or in a person speaking to us. We read that the ancient Israelites believed (Hebrew, in) the Lord, and in His servant Moses (Exodus 14:31). We read too that He (God) did not believe in His servants; that is, as it is rendered in our translation, "He put no trust in His servants" (Job 4:18). Saving faith then is not only a believing or trusting in the word of Christ, but in Christ Himself as speaking to us and as offered to us in His Word. It is a believing in Him, or, which is the same, a trusting or putting trust in Him.

3. Last, faith is likewise a trusting to or in a thing spoken of or presented to view. In the style of the Holy Spirit, the phrase "Thou shalt not believe in thy life," signifies, as it is read in our translation, "Thou shalt have none assurance of thy life" (Deuteronomy 28:66); that is, no trust or assured confidence in it because no exemption from doubt with regard to the safety of it. Faith, accordingly, is a man's believing in or trusting in a thing spoken of or, in other words, his having assurance, or his being sure of it. Again, "Wilt thou (Hebrew) believe in him (the unicorn) that he will bring home thy seed, and gather it into thy barn?" (Job 39:12). That is, "Wilt thou trust in him that he will do it?" Hence it appears that genuine faith in the righteousness and fullness of Jesus Christ is a trusting in them, a trusting that

His righteousness will entitle me to eternal life and that His fullness will supply my various wants. The phraseology on this subject is the same in the New Testament as having been introduced into it from the Old. Learning then the meaning of the Holy Ghost in this matter from the words which He Himself teaches, I conclude that faith, so expressed by Him, is in general a trusting; that saving faith in particular is a trusting in the word spoken by Christ, in Christ Himself speaking, and in His righteousness and fullness spoken of in His Word.

Now there is a twofold word to be believed or trusted in by all who would enter personally into the covenant of grace, namely the word of the law and the word of the gospel. The believing of the former is the faith of the law; the believing of the latter is the faith of the gospel.

SECTION 1. The Faith of the Law as Preparatory to a Sinner's Entering Personally Into the Covenant

Both the law and the gospel occupy their respective stations in the administration of the covenant of grace; and therefore both must be believed, and that with application to ourselves. By believing the declarations of the law we, upon the authority of Jehovah impressed on our conscience, become deeply persuaded of our sin, our misery, and our utter inability to do anything for our own salvation. The faith of the law, according to the settled order of the administration of the covenant, is, in order of nature, necessarily antecedent to the faith of the gospel. It is like the hearing of the strong wind, the feeling of the earthquake, and the seeing of the fire in which, though the Lord was not, yet they served to prepare the prophet of old to hear the still small voice in which He was (1 Kings 19:11, 12). The faith of the law, therefore, as well as that of the gospel, is the work of the Spirit of Christ, though wrought by Him in a different manner. The former He works as a Spirit of bondage, convincing by the law of sin and misery (Romans 8:15; John 16:8); the latter He works as a Spirit of liberty, of wisdom and revelation, enlightening by the gospel the mind with the saving knowledge of Christ (1 Corinthians 3:17; Ephesians 1:17, 18); and both He works as a Spirit of regeneration.

If any man, then, would enter into the covenant of grace he must, first of all, have the faith of the law as a covenant of works; for which reason it is requisite that the law as well as the gospel be preached to sinners. Now the faith of the law consists in a firm belief of the following things:

1. It is a man's firm persuasion that he is a sinner, a transgressor of the commandments of the law, and therefore that he is exposed to the vengeance of the righteous Jehovah (Romans 3:20). The holy law pronounces him guilty; and he believes the report of the law with application to himself. His dejected and sorrowful heart does, by this faith, echo to the voice of the law, "guilty, guilty" (Romans 3:19). This faith rests not on the testimony of man, whether spoken or written, but it is a divine, a supernatural belief, founded on the testimony of God in His holy law; which is demonstrated by the spirit of bondage and the spirit of burning to be the voice of the eternal Jehovah, and His voice to him a sinner in particular. Believing the precepts of the righteous law in its covenant-form, requiring him to yield perfect obedience on pain of the tremendous curse, and that with application to himself, he is convinced of his sin upon the testimony of God who cannot lie.

Thus he believes, first, that he came into the world under the guilt of Adam's first sin imputed to him. He believes and is constrained to acknowledge that, having been represented by Adam in the covenant of works, he sinned in him, and so fell with him in his first transgression. He is persuaded that by the offense of one judgment came upon all men to condemnation; and that by the disobedience of one man many were made sinners, and he in particular (Romans 5:18, 19).

Second, he believes that he came into the world under the want of original righteousness; under the loss of the moral image of God, consisting of knowledge, righteousness, and true holiness, which image he had, by sinning in the first Adam, forfeited (Romans 3:10-12; Genesis 2:17); and he is, in proportion to the strength of that belief, convinced that any want of conformity in his nature to the holy law of God, is criminal, as well as any positive act of disobedience to it in his life. He begins to see, and with shame to confess, that his want of holiness in the faculties of his soul and members of his body renders his very nature, no less than his life, sinful, impure, and loathsome in the sight of an infinitely holy God.

Third, he also believes that he came into the world with a nature wholly corrupted; that, born in iniquity and conceived in sin (Psalm 51:5), his nature is entirely distorted, and even opposite to the holy nature and will of God, having in it the seeds of all actual transgressions. The holy law shining into the heart discovers various lusts there that the man never observed in it before; and at the same time, pressing hard upon the unholy heart, irritates them and so occasions their becoming tumultuous, and therefore more discernible. Thus a mystery of iniquity within his breast opens to his view that he never could before believe to have been there. "I was alive," said Paul, "without the law once; but when the commandment came, sin revived and I died" (Romans 7:9). He is now convinced that his heart is deceitful above all things and desperately wicked (Jeremiah 17:9); that the depravity of it is hereditary, natural, and inveterate, and that, unless it is wholly renewed, he cannot do so much as one good work.

Fourth, he likewise believes that his thoughts, his words, and his deeds are sinful, and therefore infinitely hateful in the sight of God, according to this testimony of the Holy Spirit: "They are all gone out of the way, they are together become unprofitable; there is none that doeth good, no not one" (Romans 3:12-16). In the exercise of that faith, he is deeply convinced that he in particular is gone out of the way of the holy commandment, and is walking in the way of sin, which is the way to endless destruction; that he lives in error (2 Peter 2:18); that the number of his errors, both of omission and of commission, none can understand; and that all his righteousness as well as unrighteousness are, in the sight of Jehovah, as filthy rags (Isaiah 64:6). In all these respects he firmly believes himself to be, in the sight of the High and Holy One, a most sinful and loathsome creature.

2. The faith of the law is a man's firm belief that by nature he is in a state of actual and absolute subjection to the covenant of works. He thereby believes that he is under an authoritative demand of perfect obedience for eternal life, to the law as a covenant, in every point, though he cannot yield the least real obedience to it in any point. Believing the commands of the law under that form with application to himself, he is deeply sensible that he in particular in a debtor to do the whole law (Galatians 5:3), by performing perfect obedience to all its righteous precepts as the condition of life; and that his having already violated the covenant of works does not in the least dissolve the obligation that lies upon him to continue in all things written in the book of the law to do them. Believing at the same time the curse of the law with application to himself, he is sure so long as he continues in his natural state that for every act of disobedience he is under a sentence of condemnation to death in all its dreadful extent and duration.

He is persuaded that every sin that he ever committed was committed against a God of infinite majesty and purity; that therefore it is an infinite evil, and as such deserves an infinite punishment; and that, seeing the law says, "Cursed is every one that continueth not in all things which are written in the law to do them" (Galatians 3:10), he in particular is under the curse by which he is doomed to suffer all that punishment. He can no longer regard the curse as a strange thing, belonging only to some who are monsters of wickedness and not to him; for the Spirit of the Lord applies it closely to him, so closely as if he had said, "You are the man." The consequence is that, like a man under a sentence of death pronounced upon him, he, under the pressure of it, utters with sighs his belief of it and says, "I am undone, I perish" (Luke 15:17).

3. Last, that faith is a man's firm persuasion that he is absolutely unable to deliver himself from sin and from the curse of the law. In the exercise of it he believes that in that point he is without strength (Romans 5:6), and therefore that he cannot, by any doings or sufferings of his own, either free himself from the curse of the law or so change his nature and life as to render them in the least degree acceptable to God. He believes with application to himself these humbling declarations of the Spirit of truth: "Who can bring a clean thing out of an unclean? Not one" (Job 14:4). "Can the Ethiopian change his skin, or the leopard his spots? Then may ye also do good that are accustomed to do evil" (Jeremiah 13:23). He is now, in his own view, not only a great sinner, but a sinner legally and morally dead (Romans 7:9; Ephesians 2:1); a sinner as incapable to help himself as a dead body is to rise and walk. In few words, he is convinced that for anything his own righteousness or strength can do for him his case is absolutely desperate, and that he has nothing to look for, according to the covenant of works under

The Way of a Sinner's Entering Into the Covenant

which divine justice finds him, but to be punished with everlasting destruction (2 Thessalonians 1:9). Thus the Holy Spirit, as a Spirit of burning (Isaiah 4:4) as well as a Spirit of bondage, consumes the self-confidence of the sinner. He burns up all his legal righteousness, root and branch, so as to leave no root under him, nor branch upon him.

This is the faith of the law; and the consequence of it is that the heart of the awakened sinner is broken with fearful apprehensions of the deserved wrath of almighty God. He sorrows for sin as the most destructive of all evils, and ardently desires to be delivered from it. He despairs of salvation from himself, and anxiously looks out for it another way (Acts 2:37; 16:30). That faith of the law paves the way for the faith of the gospel by which a sinner is united to Christ. In the hand of the Holy Spirit, it excites the sinner to flee for refuge to Christ, the hope set before him; or rather to flee from all refuges of lies. Not that it, or any of the consequences of it, is the condition of a sinner's welcome to Christ and the covenant of grace. His access to Christ and the covenant is declared free, without any conditions or qualifications required in him to afford him a sinner of mankind a warrant to come to Christ for righteousness and salvation. But though a sinner without the faith of the law will be welcome to Christ, yet Christ will not without it be welcome to him. Without it a sinner may come to the Lord Jesus; but if he does not have it, he will not come to Him.

By this faith it is that he is persuaded of his absolute and extreme need of Jesus and His grace, and of his having in himself those sinful and infamous characters under which men are in the gospel invited to come to Him for salvation (1 Timothy 1:13, 15; Romans 7:9-13; Matthew 11:28). It and the immediate consequences of it, then, are necessary, not to give sinners a right of access to Christ but, in the hand of the Spirit, to excite them to make immediate use of their privilege of free access to Him and the covenant of grace; inasmuch as none will, without them in a greater or less degree, be disposed to embrace Him and the covenant.

To explain my meaning, suppose a physician were to announce that he would administer medicines freely to all the sick of such a town or district who would apply to him. In such a case it is evident that none in that place will apply to him but they who are sensible of some distemper that cleaves to them; and yet that sense of their distemper is not the condition on which their welcome to that physician is suspended; nor is it necessary for his curing of them, but necessary merely for their employing him to cure them.

In calling sinners of mankind, then, to embrace Christ and the covenant of grace, they are called indirectly, and by consequence to exercise this faith of the law; they are called to believe that they are sinners in Adam, sinners by nature, and sinners by practice; that they are sinners lost under the curse of the law, and absolutely unable to save themselves. Yet it is not, strictly speaking, a saving faith, because it is not the instrument of instating them in the covenant. This is peculiar to the faith of the gospel, of which I now proceed briefly to discourse.

SECTION 2. The Faith of the Gospel by Which a Sinner Enters Personally into the Covenant.

That faith which is the instrument of uniting sinners to Jesus Christ is the faith of the gospel; for the gospel only is the ministration of righteousness (2 Corinthians 3:9). It is in the gospel only that the righteousness of God by faith is revealed to faith in order to be received by faith (Romans 1:17). The gospel only is that which, in the hand of the Spirit, conveys to lost sinners information of an almighty Savior, or His infinitely precious blood, and of the new covenant in His blood, and therefore is the only word by which saving faith is produced in the heart of a sinner (Galatians 3:2). It is the word of the gospel that the Lord Jesus, with His righteousness and salvation, according to the covenant, is to be embraced and believed on (Romans 10:6-9); so that the word of the gospel being received by believing, sinners who cordially believe have Christ and His covenant, with all the inestimable blessings of it. Saving faith is the echo of the quickened soul to the word of grace that brings salvation. It is a trusting or believing of the word of the gospel, of the person, that only Savior of lost sinners and of the thing therein set forth to sinners, namely His righteousness and fullness, to be believed on for salvation. This then is the faith of the gospel that the Apostle Paul for that reason calls the hearing of faith (Galatians 3:2). This is that believing by which, as a means or instrument, sinners are vitally united to the Savior, entered into the covenant, and instated therein to salvation.

Now, should the reader who is convinced of sin and solicitous for salvation ask what that faith of the gospel is by which a lost sinner under the curse of the law may untie with Christ, enter into the covenant of grace, and be so interested therein as to attain eternal life? I would answer, it is the faith of Christ's ability to save, the faith of the gospel-offer, the faith of our right thereby to trust in Him, and the faith of particular trust or confidence in Him for salvation to ourselves.

In the first place, it is the faith of the gospel is the belief of Christ's ability to save sinners of mankind.

It is a cordial belief or persuasion both of His natural and of His moral ability. It is a belief of His natural ability to save. When a man believes the gospel he believes that in Christ is all fullness of salvation for lost sinners. This is the constant report of the gospel concerning Him. The Apostle Paul says, "It pleased the Father that in Him should all fullness dwell" (Colossians 1:19). The same apostle also informs us that he preached among the Gentiles the unsearchable riches of Christ (Ephesians 3:8); and that Christ is able to save them to the uttermost who come unto God by Him (Hebrews 7:25). In the gospel, Jesus Christ is set forth as a Savior who is mighty, yea, almighty to save, infinitely able to save sinners from the sins of their heart and of their life, from the curse of the law and from the wrath of God (Isaiah 63:1). His righteousness is so perfect, so invaluable in itself, and in the estimation of His Father, as to be abundantly sufficient to purchase justification, sanctification, and the consummation of eternal life, even for sinners who in themselves deserve eternal death. His merit is sufficient to shelter from all that tempest of divine wrath that is ready, every moment, to fly forth against transgressors. "A man," says Isaiah, "shall be as an hiding place from the wind, and a covert from the tempest" (Isaiah 32:2). His Spirit is sufficient to regenerate the most depraved, to sanctify the most unholy (1 Corinthians 6:11). The faith of the gospel then is a firm belief of Christ's natural ability to save. It is a persuasion also of His moral ability or willingness to save even the chief of sinners. He complains that sinners will not come to Him that they may have life (John 5:40); which clearly implies that He Himself is willing to give life to all who come to Him. Saving faith then is a cordial belief on the ground of the divine testimony that the all-compassionate Jesus is willing, infinitely willing, to save sinners of mankind; that He is willing to be employed or trusted in by any of the family of Adam; that He is willing to execute His mediatorial offices in the complete salvation of the greatest of sinners; that He is willing to array in the robe of His righteousness, to cleanse in the fountain of His blood, to beautify with the comeliness of

The Way of a Sinner's Entering Into the Covenant

His grace, and to receive into the mansions of His glory every sinner who cordially confides in Him for all his salvation. In the great and precious promises of His testamentary covenant He says, "I will"; and those promises, in and with Himself, are offered or directed in offer to sinners indefinitely.

Now this faith of the natural and moral ability of Jesus to save is the general faith of the gospel, and is requisite to the exercise of the faith of particular application; for a man must first assent to the truth of a report, or believe a report to be true in itself, before he can trust that it is true to him; he must first believe an object to be good in itself before he can trust that it is good for him. The belief of the truth is necessary in order to the exercise of particular trust.

Where the faith of the gospel is so brought forward as to unite the sinner to Christ, the immediate effects of that general faith are no less important than necessary. These are, a high esteem of Christ and His holy covenant, an ardent desire of union and communion with Him, and of righteousness and salvation from Him. The man who thus believes is not indeed sensible that he has a special interest in Jesus and the covenant, but he is very desirous of having it. Without it, all other objects are insipid, yea, are nothing to him. His heart within him cries, "None but Christ; give me Christ, else I die." He is content to part with all for Christ, and to take Him instead of all. This is evident from the parables of the treasure hid in the field and of the pearl of great price, the finding of which excites one to sell all that he has and to buy them (Matthew 13:44-46).

This estimation and this desire of Christ, however, are somewhat different from those that follow upon the union and communion of the soul with Him after faith has taken possession of Him and of His inestimable benefits, and has attained a suitable and a realizing view of His transcendent amiableness and value (Psalm 73:25, 26; 1 Peter 2:7). The true source of all the former esteem and desire is the principle of self-preservation, accompanied with a discovery of Christ as suitable to the exigencies of the soul. The merchant man is seeking goodly pearls to enrich himself; and seeing that the one pearl will sufficiently answer that purpose he cannot rest until he possess it. The awakened sinner is hotly pursued by the curse of the law that is still thundering damnation in his ears. In the meantime he gains a distant view of the city of refuge; and therefore he advances toward it with all speed. But what is it that makes him run? It is a concern for life, precious life; a desire that he may not perish, but have eternal life. He cannot, surely, *before* the union with Christ be expected to act upon a more generous principle. For, says the Redeemer Himself, "Without Me," or, severed from Me, "ye can do nothing" (John 15:5). But let him not fear; he is welcome to the Savior, even though he comes to Him from no higher motive. The truth is, the Lord Jesus, by His Holy Spirit, stirs up the principle of self-preservation, being a principle in itself good, and employs it as a means of hastening the sinner forward to Himself. This is evident from His complaint cited above: "Ye will not come to Me that ye may have life" (John 5:40). Can it ever be imagined that the infinitely compassionate Savior will reject a miserable sinner coming to Him for life when yet He complains that sinners will not come to Him for that very purpose?

Second, the faith of the gospel is a cordial belief of the gospel-offer. In believing the gospel, the sinner believes that Christ with His righteousness and salvation is, by His eternal Father and Himself, offered to sinners who hear the gospel, and to him in particular. Jesus Christ says to all to whom the gospel comes, "My Father giveth you the true bread from heaven" (John 6:32). "Ho, every one that thirsteth, come ye to the waters,

The Way of a Sinner's Entering Into the Covenant

and he that hath no money; come ye, buy and eat," etc. (Isaiah 55:1). "Whosoever will, let him take the water of life freely" (Revelation 22:17). "Unto you, O men, I call; and my voice is to the sons of man" (Proverbs 8:4). "And saith the eternal Father, I will also give thee for a light to the Gentiles, that thou mayest be My salvation unto the end of the earth. I will preserve thee, and give thee for a covenant of the people" (Isaiah 49:6, 8). "Unto us," said the ancient church, "a child is born; unto us a son is given" (Isaiah 9:6). Thus, in the public administration of the covenant of grace, is made to all the hearers of the gospel a most gracious offer of Christ and of His righteousness and salvation, with an authoritative call to them to receive and rest on Him and on His righteousness for the whole of their salvation. The covenant itself is exhibited in gracious offers of it so that by faith they may take hold of it with gracious calls to them to do so. In this respect it is, as to God's engagement in it, a covenant made with them, and is to take effect upon them through their cordial application of the offer and the promises offered, and that in dependence on the righteousness fulfilled and presented to them in the same offer.

Now the faith of the gospel is a cordial belief of this infinitely free and full offer, with application to one's self. It is a man's believing with the heart that it is an offer made or directed to him in particular. But how few, alas, are there who thus believe it? Indeed, none will believe it to purpose till the Spirit of Christ opens up the meaning of it to their understanding, and enables them to discern in it the authority and the truth of Jehovah who cannot lie. Then they will discern in that inestimable grant the greatest reality and the highest value. Then they will be persuaded that it is directed and presented to them; and they will accept it cordially, each for his own special benefit. Multitudes of secure sinners hear that the offer of the gospel is directed to them, and seem to discern in it either the grace or the authority or the sincerity of the Lord Jesus. They hear it not as the word of Christ Himself, and His word addressed to them, but only as the word of man. Hence it has no due authority upon their conscience, no persuasive influence upon their heart. They see in it no warrant firmly to believe that the unspeakable gift of God is worthy of all acceptation, and that it is therein presented to each of them for his acceptance. Thus was Christ's offer of Himself treated when made by His own mouth. "In Nazareth all bare Him witness, and wondered at the gracious words that proceeded out of His mouth; but they said, Is not this Joseph's son? And in a little, they rose and thrust him out of the city" (Luke 4:22, 29). Again, when the convinced sinner discerns the voice of Christ in the offer, he is ready to conclude that it is to others, but not to him. The unbelief and pride of his heart dispose him to say, "The offer of such a Savior, and of such a salvation, cannot be directed to such an unworthy, such a vile, such a great sinner, as I am; especially to a sinner so entirely destitute of every good qualification as I feel myself to be." He will not believe that such good tidings from a God of infinite holiness and justice concern him, or that such a rich and glorious offer is made to him. Thus the sinner, not believing God in the record that He gave of His Son, namely that He, with His righteousness and salvation, is offered or given in offer to him, makes Him a liar (1 John 5:10, 11).

But when the Holy Spirit is working divine faith He applies with power the offer of the gospel to the soul in particular as the word of Jehovah Himself who cannot lie; by which the man is assured that it is the voice or word of Christ, and that it is to him in particular; and thus by believing he applies it to himself. Accordingly the Apostle Paul says, "Our gospel came not unto

The Way of a Sinner's Entering Into the Covenant

you in word only, but also in power, and in the Holy Ghost, and in much assurance" (1 Thessalonians 1:5). "When ye received the word of God which ye heard of us, ye received it not as the word of men, but (as it is in truth) the word of God, which effectually worketh also in you that believe" (1 Thessalonians 2:13). This is indispensably requisite. Without it there can be no receiving of Christ, inasmuch as otherwise the man can discern no solid foundation of faith for himself; for it is manifest there can be no right receiving of an offered gift where the man does not believe that the offer of it is to him in particular. Here it is that the application peculiar to the faith of the gospel commences, an application that tends to the union of the soul with Christ.

If a man then would unite with Christ, and so enter the covenant of grace, let him stoop so low as to present himself before the Lord as a sinner under the curse of the law, and cordially believe that the offer of the gospel is made to him a condemned sinner in particular. So will it come to him as the light of the morning to one sitting in darkness, or as the offer of a pardon to one under sentence of death. Let not his heart misgive him by yielding to unbelief, but let him firmly and instantly believe that the Lord Jesus Himself makes the offer, and makes it as really to him as if there was not another sinner in the world to whom it could be made. "Incline your ear," said He, "and come unto Me; hear, and your soul shall live; and I will make an everlasting covenant with you" (Isaiah 55:3).

But here it will be necessary to obviate two or three principal objections of an awakened sinner against believing the gospel-offer with application to himself.

OBJECTION 1: "Christ is now enthroned in heaven, and I hear no voice from heaven. How then can I believe that He Himself is offering Himself to me?"

ANSWER. Although it is certain that the Lord Jesus is in heaven, yet still He speaks to us from heaven; not indeed by a voice sounding through the sky, but by a voice sounding in the gospel. "See," said an apostle, "that ye refuse not Him that speaketh . . . that speaketh from heaven" (Hebrews 12:25). And not only is His voice in the gospel, but, as the same apostle teaches (Romans 10:6-8), He Himself is, by His Spirit, in it. Hence it is that the gospel is a word of life, a quickening word, to dead souls. "The words," said Jesus, "that I speak unto you, they are spirit, and they are life" (John 6:63). It is the living, the incorruptible seed of which the new creature is formed (1 Peter 1:23). The Lord Jesus did once, by a voice sounding through the sky, speak a word of conviction (Acts 9:4-7). But even on that memorable occasion the word of His offer of Himself was remitted to the preaching of the gospel by a minister thereto appointed (Acts 9:17). The voice of Christ sounding in the word, whether written or preached, is more sure than a voice sounding through the sky (2 Peter 1:18, 19). His voice in the Word is the established ground of faith on which believers must rely for salvation. The gospel of Christ is the power of God unto salvation, to everyone who believes (Romans 1:16). Indeed, no divine faith is acted but where the gospel is received as a divine testimony, or as the very word or voice of Christ Himself (1 Thessalonians 2:13). The objector therefore must, notwithstanding the pride and prejudice of his heart, attempt to believe that the gospel and the gospel-offer are the very word of Christ Himself, and His word to him in particular.

OBJECTION 2. "Christ in the gospel does not direct the offer to me by name; and therefore I cannot believe that He offers Himself with His righteousness and fullness to me in particular."

ANSWER. Neither does He direct the command and curses of the law to you by name. How did you come to believe that you are a sinner, or a transgressor of the law? Is it not that, seeing the commands of the law are directed to all men, you conclude that, as you are one of the number of mankind, they are therefore directed to you as well as to others, and forbid you in particular to commit sin? And how did you come to believe that you in particular are under the curse of the violated law? Is it not that, since the law denounces its awful curse against every one who transgresses it (Galatians 3:10; Romans 3:19), you conclude that it curses you, seeing that you are one of the transgressors of it? Now you have as good ground to believe that the gospel-offer is made to you in particular, seeing it is made to all without distinction and without exception to whom the gospel is preached (Isaiah 55:1; Revelation 22:17). You see that it is ordered to be made to every reasonable creature under heaven (Mark 16:15); and however sinful you are, you are one of those creatures. The voice of Christ in the offer of the gospel is to men, to the sons of man (Proverbs 89:4); and be what you may, you cannot but be one of the sons or daughters of man; you cannot be less than a sinner of mankind, and cannot be more than the chief of sinners. The gracious offer therefore is assuredly to you in particular. Accordingly, the ministers of the gospel are authorized to direct the general offer to every one in particular, and every one is warranted to apply it to himself. Believe then on the Lord Jesus Christ, "and thou shalt be saved" (Acts 16:31).

OBJECTION 3. "But I fear that I do not have the qualifications that distinguish those to whom the gospel offer is particularly directed. I am afraid that I have not yet attained a true conviction or sense of my sin; and I find that Jesus Christ says expressly, 'They that be whole need not a physician, but they that are sick; I am not come to call the righteous, but sinners to repentance' (Matthew 9:12, 13). The gospel offer and call run in these terms: 'Ho, every one that thirsteth, come ye to the waters' (Isaiah 55:1). 'Come unto Me, all ye that labor and are heavy laden' (Matthew 11:28). 'Whosoever will, let him take the water of life freely' (Revelation 22:17). But alas! When I review the frame of my heart, I have reason to dread that I have not yet attained that thirst after the Savior and that willingness to receive Him that are mentioned in these passages; and that I cannot be counted one of them who truly labor and are heavy laden. How then can I warrantably believe that the Lord Jesus offers Himself to me in particular?"

ANSWER. It is unquestionable that unless you have a true sense of your sin, unless you thirst after Jesus and His righteousness, unless you are heavy laden with a real sense of the burden of sin, and unless you are willing to take Christ as He is offered in the gospel, you will never accept Him by a saving faith. Nevertheless, whatever qualifications you have or have not, yet if you are a lost sinner of Adam's family (and surely you cannot for a moment doubt that), Jesus, with His righteousness and salvation is freely, fully, and particularly offered to you (John 6:32; Proverbs 8:4; Mark 16:15). For although certain qualifications are indeed necessary to move or urge you to accept the Savior, yet there is not so much as one to enwrap, entangle, or limit the infinitely free offer. Whatever your case then may be, Christ Jesus is presently and particularly, freely and fully, offered by His Father and Himself to you. And therefore if you do not, with application to yourself, so credit the immensely free grant as to receive the offered Savior, you will assuredly be damned for your disbelief (Mark 16:16).

It cannot be denied that the less sinners are sensible of sin, they are the further from righteousness; but for that very reason

The Way of a Sinner's Entering Into the Covenant

they do the more need Christ, and are the more to be called to repentance (Revelation 3:17, 18). This is plain from the whole tenor of the Scripture, as well as from the nature of the thing itself. It therefore appears to be sinners in general, and not sensible sinners merely, who are intended in Matthew 9:12, 14. In like manner, as it is sick persons in general, including even those of them who are so delirious as to imagine and say that they are perfectly well, who need a physician, and not those only who are sensible of their disease and their danger. There is no necessity to depart from this obvious meaning of the passage. Indeed, the departing from it has often occasioned much inconvenience and embarrassment to sinners in their coming to Jesus.

Neither is that thirst mentioned in Isaiah 55:1 to be restricted to a gracious and spiritual thirst, a thirst after Jesus and His righteousness; for some at least of the thirsting ones to whom the offer is there directed are expressly said in the second verse to be spending money for that which is not bread, and their labor for that which satisfies not. But it is plain that sinners truly sensible of their sin who are thirsting spiritually after Jesus and righteousness from Him are not spending their money and their labor at that rate; but on the contrary are spending them for that which is bread and that which satisfies, namely Christ the living bread that came down from heaven, of which, if any man eats, he shall live forever (John 6:51). The thirst there intended must therefore include, yea, and principally mean, that desire after felicity and satisfaction that is natural, and therefore common, to sinners of mankind in general. Men, when they are pained with that thirst, do, in order to quench it, naturally run to the empty creation and to their own deceitful lusts; and so they spend money for that which is not bread and their labor for that which does not satisfy; finding nothing there that can satisfy their hunger or quench their thirst. Now, to sinners in this miserable condition, is the offer of the waters of life made. Jesus Christ is freely tendered to them as bread and as fatness, as that which is good, and as that which will satisfy their painful thirst which otherwise can never be allayed.

Nor is the authentic offer in Matthew 11:28 to be restricted to a certain class of persons who are endued with some commendable qualifications, expressed by the terms "laboring" and "heavy laden." These terms do indeed express the painful soul of man, laboring even to weariness, and spending in labor for that which satisfies not. Adam our father, by violating the covenant of works, left his whole family with a conscience full of guilt and with a heart full of unsatisfied desire. And seeing we naturally have, therefore, an unquiet conscience and a restless heart, our soul naturally does in the same degree labor for rest to them. It labors as those did who labored in the very fire, and wearied themselves for very vanity (Habakkuk 2:13). It labors in the barren region of the fiery law for a rest to the conscience, and in the empty creation for a rest to the heart. But after all, the conscience is still heavy laden with a burden of unsatisfied desire; so that neither the one nor the other can find true and satisfying rest. This is the uncomfortable, the deplorable condition of all the children of Adam while in their natural state. They are heavy laden with a load of unpardoned guilt, with a burden of abject servitude to sin, with a load of irregular desire, with a load of legal curses, with a burden of vindictive wrath, and, if I may so say, with a load of sinful insensibility (The original word in Matthew 11:28 properly signifies the lading of a ship which, though it cannot feel its burden, may yet under it, and because of it, sink to the bottom, and be irrecoverably lost). Now the all-compassionate Jesus invites sinners who are thus laboring and heavy laden to come to Him for rest, namely for rest to their conscience in the righteousness that He fulfilled, and for rest to their heart in the enjoyment of God that He purchased. To this exposition of the passage we are led by the phraseology of the Holy Spirit, both in the Old Testament and in the New (The reader may, in order to see this, compare the following texts: Ecclesiastes 1:8 and 10:15; Habakkuk 2:13; Isaiah 55:2 and 1:3,4; 2 Timothy 3:6,7).

Last, as to the willingness of which you fear you are destitute; undoubtedly in all other cases, He who says, "Whosoever will, let him take such a thing," will, according to the common acceptation of that phrase among men, be understood to offer that thing to all, and to exclude none from it. At the same time, such a phrase may express an intimation that is not to be forced upon any against his will. There is then no reason why that manner of expression in Revelation 22:17 should be understood to limit the offer and call of the gospel to a certain description of sinners. The offer, and especially that parting offer, is far from being clogged with exceptions. At the same time, there is a vast difference between what sinners may do in point of warrant, and what they can or will do in point of fact. All sinners may believe in Jesus; none but convinced sinners can or will believe in Him. I say "can" or "will," for if they are willing they will be able; as their inability, being moral, is almost the same as their unwillingness (Psalm 110:3; John 5:40). None but they whose hearts are pierced with arrows of conviction will relish the offer of the gospel. This, however, sets no limits to the gospel-offer and call. Neither should sinners, by seeking for qualifications in themselves, throw obstacles in their way to the Savior; but they should immediately trust in Him for all His salvation, and so hope that they will be saved by Him.

I conclude therefore that Christ places no impediment in your way to Him, nor in the way of any sinner of mankind who hears the gospel. Do not any longer lay obstructions in your own way, and then complain that you cannot get over them. For it is the record of God, an infallible truth, recorded in the volume of inspiration, that Jesus Christ is freely offered to you as a sinner of mankind. Believe it cordially; believe it with application to yourself else you will, at the peril of your soul, make God a liar (1 John 5:10).

In the third place, the faith of the gospel is the faith not only of Christ's ability and willingness to save sinners, and of the offer of Him to us indiscriminately as sinners; but it is the faith of our right hereby to receive and trust in Him for salvation to ourselves. Were any of the angels that sinned to essay to take Christ for their Savior, and to trust in Him for their salvation, it would be an act of horrible presumption. Why? Because they have no warrant, and therefore no right to trust that He will save them. Far otherwise is the case of sinners of mankind to whom the gospel has come. It is not presumption in them to receive and trust in Him but, on the contrary, a duty, a present, a principal, a necessary duty (John 6:29). When they trust in Him for all their salvation, they do nothing more than what they have a sufficient warrant, and consequently a full right to do. Jesus Christ is in the gospel offered to them, and not to fallen angels. The authentic gospel-offer, with the call and commandment to accept it, affords to them, and not to fallen angels, a complete warrant to confide cordially in the Lord Jesus for all their salvation. Sinners who hear the gospel have the Lord's own warrant, and therefore have not only a right, a perfect right, but an infinite, an immutable right to receive the Savior with His righteousness and fullness. The offer affords a warrant, and the warrant creates and confers a right. It is not their conviction of sin, nor their desire of Christ, nor their evidence of interest in Him, nor even their faith that affords them a warrant, and consequently a right to trust in Him for salvation; but it is the authentic offer of Him in the gospel with the invitation and command to accept it. These, as they are directed to every sinner who hears the gospel, afford to everyone a sufficient warrant and right to entrust Christ with His whole salvation.

When a convinced sinner then cordially believes the offer of the gospel, and that with application to himself, he believes that it affords him in particular a right to Christ, a right of access to Him; a right not to be persuaded that he already has possession of Christ, but a right to take possession; a right not to abuse, but to sue Him as his own for all the purposes of His complete salvation; a right to trust in Him not for salvation to any sin, or in any sin, but for salvation from every sin. When he believes that the Lord Jesus, with His righteousness and fullness, is divinely offered to him and presented to him in the form of a gift or grant, he believes that He is his in offer; and in proportion as he believes that Christ is his in offer he believes, and cannot but believe, that He is his in right or title to trust in Him, and by trusting to take possession of Him. He is persuaded that the authentic offer to him in particular is the foundation of his title or claim of right to place an unsuspecting confidence in Jesus Christ; or that Jehovah's giving of Christ in offer to him is the ground of his right to take and trust in Him as his own for all his salvation. When a man believes that the gospel offer to him is true, and that Christ and His benefits offered are good, he believes that in virtue of the offer they so far belong to him that he may use them warrantably and freely as his own; or that he may trust in Jesus for all salvation to himself without any ground of suspicion that in so doing he will be guilty of presumption. In agonies of conscience, he often finds it much more difficult to believe that Christ thus belongs to him than merely that He is offered to him. It is not uncommon for one in such a case to put the Savior away from him on this ground, that He does not belong to him. But when the Holy Spirit enables him to act saving faith, He makes him able and willing to believe that Jesus does belong to him; or that He is his in right to accept and confide in Him. He must not think that this is too much for him to do. If he believes only in general that Jesus is the Savior of the world, but not that He is his Savior, he believes no more than the devils do. They firmly believe that He is Jesus the Savior (Mark 1:24). If he would go beyond them, he must believe cordially, that Christ is his Savior in the sense above explained, and that in the same sense His righteousness and salvation are his. He must consider that he never can lawfully receive and trust in the Savior if He is not his in right to trust in Him. A man may unjustly take possession of an object that he does not believe to be his in right to take; but no man can honestly take possession of that which he does not believe to be, in that sense, his own. Christ Jesus must first be given in offer to the sinner, and the sinner must believe that, and believe also that he has thereby a right to trust in Him, before he can warrantably receive and trust in Him. A man can receive nothing unless it is given him from heaven (John 3:27). Giving, on the part of God, is and must be the foundation of receiving on the part of the sinner. Jehovah's granting in offer to the sinner is sufficient to render what is so granted his in right to accept or take possession of it. He therefore who exercises a saving faith believes that Christ is his Savior, that His righteousness is his, and that eternal life is his in right to take possession of them.

The Way of a Sinner's Entering Into the Covenant

Does the reader now ask, "What foundation have I, a lost sinner, a sinner by nature under the curse of the law, to believe that Christ, with His righteousness and salvation, is mine in right to trust in Him?"

I answer, you may firmly belief it on the sure ground of the authority and the testimony of Jehovah who cannot lie. What is the gospel that the apostles were sent in the name of the Lord Jesus to testify? The Apostle John furnishes the answer: "We have seen, and do testify, that the Father sent the Son to be the Savior of the world" (1 John 4:14). Jesus Christ then is, by office, the Savior of the world; and if He is so, and you are one of that world of mankind, is He not therefore by office, your Savior, yours in right to trust in Him? Why then will you not believe it? God has set the sun in the firmament to be a light to this world; and do you not therefore believe that you have a right to the light of the sun as well as any other of mankind? Do not you in consequence use it freely to read or work by it, as your own by the free gift of God? Christ the Sun of righteousness is the light of the world (John 8:12), being given for a light to the Gentiles that He may be the salvation of Jehovah unto the end of the earth (Isaiah 49:6). You are one of the world of mankind, one of the Gentiles. Therefore He is your light; He is given for a light to you; and you should, on the ground of Jehovah's gift or offer, appropriate Him and say, "The Lord is my light and my salvation" (Psalm 27:1). Will you take Christ's own word for it? He said to an assembly at Capernaum, very few of whom, it appears, had Him in actual possession, "My father giveth you the true bread from heaven" (John 6:32). If a friend or neighbor offered you bread to satisfy your hunger, you would at once believe that his gift of it to you was sufficient to make it yours in right to use it; and so would freely take and eat of it as your own. If your prince gave you a house or land of which he had an unquestionable right to dispose, you would immediately account it yours in right to it by his gift and would freely go and occupy that house, or take possession of that land, as your own. How does it come to pass then that when the eternal Father gives you His Son Christ Jesus you will not believe that He is yours in right to trust in Him, nor take possession of Him as your own? Why, the truth is, you believe your friend, you believe your neighbor, you believe your prince; but you do not believe your God speaking to you in His Word, but make Him a liar, not believing the record that He gave of His Son (1 John 5:10). But whether you believe it or not, it is a most certain truth that Christ is your Savior in point of right to trust in Him for your salvation; and if you will not believe it now, to the saving of your soul, you shall doubtless discover your dangerous mistake hereafter when perishing under the infinite fierceness of the wrath of God and the Lamb you shall be fully convinced that you perish not because you did not have a Savior, but because you would not employ Him to save you.

The righteousness that Christ as the Surety of His people fulfilled is yours also in right to receive it. It is yours by free gift, being given you with Himself in offer; and therefore it is called the gift of righteousness (Romans 5:17). It is a testamentary gift; for it is revealed and offered to you in the testament of our Lord Jesus.

Eternal life is, in the same testamentary deed, together with Christ Himself and His righteousness, offered to you; and therefore it likewise is yours in right to lay hold on it. As Christ Himself is yours in right to trust in Him, and His righteousness yours in right to trust on it, so is eternal life in Him yours in right to trust for it. You have the testimony, the record, of God Himself who cannot lie to assure you that eternal life is given you in offer. "This is the record, that God hath given to us

The Way of a Sinner's Entering Into the Covenant

eternal life; and this life is in His Son" (1 John 5:11). Now, is not the record of God a sufficient ground of faith? Dare you, on any pretense whatever, venture to disbelieve it? In the passage now cited you have that divine, that authentic record, namely that God has given (in offer) to us eternal life. Perhaps you begin to imagine that the record refers only to believers, or at most to the elect, and to offer that as an excuse for your not believing of it with application to yourself. But consider, I entreat you, that it is the warrant for all to believe on Christ, and so to lay hold on eternal life in Him, being the witness of God which He has testified of His Son (1 John 5:9), to be received by all to whom the gospel is preached; but that God has given eternal life to believers merely, or to elect sinners, can never be justly deemed a warrant for all the hearers of the gospel to believe on Him. Besides, unbelief, that greatest of all sins, consists in not believing this record; but unbelief does not consist in not believing that God has given eternal life to actual believers, or to elect sinners; for the most resolute, the most desperate sinners; for the most resolute, the most desperate unbelievers, believe that; and their belief of it adds to their torment; but it consists in a man's not believing that to sinners of mankind as such, and to himself in particular, God has given in offer eternal life. To believe this record is to believe the Father's gift or offer of Christ to sinners of mankind in common, which is recorded in it, and that with application to ourselves, saying, with the church of old, "Unto us a child is born [the original word properly signifies "presented born," as an infant used to be to its relatives who had a special interest in it]. Thus the children of Machir were presented born to Joseph and laid on his knees (Genesis 1:23), and the son of Ruth to Naomi (Ruth 4:17), unto us a son is given (Isaiah 9:6). Thus it is evident that you have the surest ground for this act of faith, namely the record of God who cannot lie. If then you would be united to Christ and instated in the covenant of grace, believe cordially that He, with His righteousness and eternal life thereby purchased, is yours in right to trust in Him. Believe that it is not your faith, but the faithfulness of God in His record offering Christ to you that affords you a warrant and a right to trust in Him for your salvation.

This is a more close and, consequently, a more comfortable application of faith than the former, and proceeds from it. It is a believing with application the efficacy and effect of the gospel-offer. If God gives Christ, and if Christ offers Himself with His righteousness and fullness to you, surely the effect of that gift or offer must be that He is indeed yours in point of right to trust in Him for eternal life. And if you believe that the divine grant is real, and that God who cannot lie is sincere in it, you cannot do less than believe that it certainly conveys to you a right to confide in the blessed Jesus for all your salvation. It is not doubted that men's deeds of gift or offers, when real, and when their sincerity in them is unquestionable, convey to the persons in whose favor they are made a right to take possession of that which is so granted. If a friend of yours, having a sum of money deposited in a neighbor's hand, should by a deed under his own hand appoint that sum a gift to you to relieve you when in a strait, you would not question but you might warrantably go and take it up; or if, having the sum in his own hand, he should offer it to you as a gift, you would not for a moment doubt but you had a right to take possession of it; in either case you would freely take and use it as your own. And shall not the Father's authentic grant, and Christ's gracious offer, be at least as efficacious? Why then do you not believe its efficacy to convey to you a right to take and to trust in Jesus for all the good of the covenant?

Indeed, the believing of this right is the very next step to a soul's uniting with Christ; and therefore it is proposed to the sinner as the nearest means of bringing him close to God in Christ. "Return unto the Lord *thy* God" (Hosea 14:1); as if the Holy Spirit had said, "He is thy God in offer; thou hast a right to come to Him; return then; come near to Him, and take possession of Him as thy own God." Accordingly, when a sinner is by faith coming to Him, he comes on this very ground: "Behold, we come unto thee; for thou art the Lord *our* God. Truly in the Lord *our* God is the salvation of Israel" (Jeremiah 3:22, 23). As the eyes of Hagar were opened to see that she had a well of water by her when she had given up her son for dead (Genesis 21:16, 19), so when the sinner, under a work of conviction, lies wounded to death by the law, the Spirit of faith does, by means of the gospel, in a work of saving illumination, so open his eyes that he sees he had, in the offer of the gospel, a Savior, a righteousness, and salvation; and then, without delay, he lays hold on the same and uses them as his own. Thus the prodigal first believed that he had yet a father, and a father's house, in which there was bread enough and to spare, and then arose and went to him (Luke 15:17, 18).

Some reader, perhaps, will now be ready to ask, "Since I have ground to believe that Jesus Christ, with His righteousness and salvation, is mine, may I not then conclude that I am already interested in Him and that my salvation is secured?"

I answer, by no means. He is indeed yours in offer, and yours in right to take possession of Him; but you can have no actual or personal interest in Him, no interest accompanying salvation, till He has become yours in possession. He is already yours in right to take possession of Him, but He is not yours in actual possession till you have so availed yourself of that right as to *take* possession. You have indeed sufficient ground to believe that you have a warrant to take possession, but no ground whatever to conclude that you *have* possession of Him and His salvation till after you have taken the same.

Suppose you saw a man at the point of perishing with hunger and, being moved with compassion, you should, from your own store, bring food to him, and having set it before him should say, "Here is some food for you; take and eat of it freely." If he should reply, "I cannot warrantably take of it for it is not my own," would you not tell him that your offer of it to him makes it so far his that he may freely, and with a good conscience, eat it as his own?

But should he then say, "Why, if it is mine, I am now secured against starving. I need not at all be at pains to take and eat of it." Would you not conclude that he was either delirious, or but jesting with you; and that he did not appear sensible of the danger he was in of perishing with hunger? Would you not say to him that to keep him from starving it is not enough that food be his in right to receive it; he must actually take and eat of it, and so use it as his own, if he would have that benefit from it? In like manner, it is not Christ's being yours merely in right to trust in Him that will save you; you must by faith take possession of Him and make use of Him as your own for salvation if you would be actually saved by Him. There is a great difference indeed between a thing's being yours merely in right to *take* possession of it and its being yours *in* possession. It is in the former way only that Christ is yours before vital union with Him; and if you do not avail yourself of that right of access to Him by trusting in Him, and so taking possession of Him, you will, notwithstanding it, eternally perish. "If ye have not been faithful in that which is another man's, who shall give you that which is your own?" (Luke 16:12). Let us therefore fear lest a promise being left us of entering into His rest any of you should seem to come short of it (Hebrews 4:1).

On the other hand, the convinced sinner will here object and say, "A divine Savior, a perfect righteousness, and eternal life are objects so exceedingly great and precious, and I am so vile, so sinful, and so unworthy, that it is very hard for me to believe that they are mine, even in right to receive and use them."

To this I would reply, here indeed it is that much of the difficulty of believing lies. When the eyes of a man's understanding are enlightened to discern the glorious excellence of Christ, the exceeding sinfulness of sin, and his own extreme unworthiness, he will find it not only difficult, but impossible for him to believe otherwise than by the almighty operation of the Holy Spirit (Ephesians 1:19). But, for your encouragement, consider that they are yours by an infinitely free gift of them to you, which is so far from supposing or requiring any worthiness in the creature that it excludes, even in an infinite degree, all regard thereto. Jesus Christ Himself is the gift of the Father to you (John 4:10 and 6:32). His righteousness also is a gift, a divinely free gift (Romans 5:17); and so is eternal life, considered as in Him (1 John 5:11). Now what can be freer than a gift, than an immensely free gift. And then, though these blessings are indeed a gift infinitely beyond what you could ever have expected, yet they are not too great for a God of infinite grace to give. In making that glorious gift He acted, not according to the quality of the party in whose favor it was made, but according to His own infinite majesty and munificence. He consulted the honor of His own transcendent greatness and boundless grace. At the same time, though the unspeakable gift is infinitely above, aye, and contrary to your desert, yet it is no more than what your exigency requires. If less could have answered your necessity, there is no reason to think that the only wise God would have given His only begotten, His infinitely dear Son, to be made a curse and be crucified for you. If you do but suppose that less could have sufficed, you so far injure that matchless, that stupendous, expression of redeeming love (John 3:16). Therefore, argue with yourself after this manner: "The gift is indeed infinitely great, unspeakably transcendent; but nothing less can supply my need. If Jesus is not mine, I must inevitably perish. Since, therefore, God who cannot lie has said that He has given to me in offer, and in right of access to Him, His Son Jesus Christ; and since the infinitely glorious gift is not too much for Him to afford, and no more than my necessity requires, I must and will believe that He with His righteousness and fullness is mine in right to trust in Him, and on His righteousness, for all my salvation."

Once more, some man, it may be, will be disposed to say, "That doctrine, I fear, tends to encourage presumption, and also to lessen the motives and loosen the obligations to a holy life."

My reply to this cavil will be in few words. You may at once dismiss all your fears on that heading. That doctrine, as was above declared, is a part of the truth contained in the gospel that in all its parts is the doctrine, the only doctrine, according to godliness (1 Timothy 6:3). No man can live a holy life till he has begun to trust in the Lord Jesus for sanctification. None can warrantably trust in Him but as his own Savior. But the Savior cannot be his previous to his beginning to trust in Him except in offer affording him a warrant and a right to trust in Him. There can, therefore, be no true holiness, no acceptable obedience, without true faith as its principle; and there can be no exercise of true faith unless the sinner has a previous right to rely upon Jesus Christ for his own salvation. Now his having a right to trust in Christ, and Christ being his in right to trust in

Him, are the same. To teach hearers of the gospel therefore that Jesus with His righteousness and salvation is theirs in offer, and consequently theirs in right to rely upon Him, is necessary to their having and practicing that true holiness which has and must have unfeigned faith for its principle. As to presumption, which is an unwarrantable, and therefore a rash and unreasonable confidence in the Savior, to teach that He is freely offered to sinners in common, and that every sinner who hears the gospel is thereby warranted, or has a right to trust in Him, not indeed for a divided, but for a complete salvation, is, instead of encouraging presumptuous confidence, the only doctrine that effectually discourages it; inasmuch as it points out the only true ground of reasonable confidence in Him. To venture to trust in Christ without believing or regarding the revealed warrant to do so is, indeed, to place rash and unreasonable confidence in Him, or in other words, to presume; but to trust in Him for all my salvation on this ground, that He is previously mine in offer, and therefore mine in right so to do, is to repose warrantable confidence in Him.

In the fourth and last place, the faith of the gospel is a man's trusting in the Lord Jesus for salvation to himself in particular. When the testimony of God concerning Christ is, by the Holy Spirit, so impressed on the heart of the convinced sinner that he begins cordially to believe the ability and willingness of Christ to save, the offer that is made of Christ to him and the right that he thereby has to trust in Christ for all the good of the covenant, he accordingly places the confidence of his heart in Him for his own salvation. This he does on the ground of the authority and the faithfulness of Jehovah in His word of grace. His heart trusts in Him for salvation from sin as well as from wrath, for holiness as well as for happiness. This trust is, in Acts 15:11, expressed by an apostle in the plainest terms: We believe that, through the grace of the Lord Jesus Christ, we shall be saved. The faith of the offer, and of one's right to Christ, is a believing of God, or a believing of the Son; this trust is more; it is a believing in or on the Son; and is the same as a receiving Him (John 1:12). It is a believing or trusting in God as one who is faithful to perform what He has promised; and a believing or trusting in Christ as the one who, according to the promises, is able to save to the uttermost (Hebrews 7:25).

It is not only an assent to, but also a relying upon, the testimony of God; it is a trusting in Christ (Mr. Cross informs us in his sermon on Romans 4:2, p. 148, that Mr. [Richard] Baxter, in his book against Dr. Crisp's error, says, "I formerly believed the formal nature of faith to lie in consent; but I now recant it. I believe it lies in TRUST; this makes the right to lie in the object; for it is, I depend on Christ, as the matter or merit of my pardon, my life, my crown, my glory"), upon the testimony or witness of God, or upon the credit of that report that, in the name of God, has gone abroad concerning Him. This particular trust for salvation is the most near and the most essential act of saving faith; and it flows immediately from that belief of the truth that is, by the Holy Spirit, wrought in the heart. It is that believing in the Lord Jesus by which a sinner is vitally united to Him, and so is brought personally into the bond of the covenant of grace for salvation This is evident from the following passages of Scripture compared together: "Believe on the Lord Jesus Christ and thou shalt be saved" (Acts 16:31). "Blessed are all they that put their trust in Him" (Psalm 2:12). "He shall deliver them from the wicked, and save them because they trust in Him" (Psalm 37:40). "In Him shall the Gentiles trust" (Romans 15:12). "Whoso putteth his trust in the Lord shall be safe" (Proverbs 29:25). "Therein is the righteousness of God revealed from faith to faith" (Romans 1:17), or, "Therein is the righteousness of God by faith, revealed to faith;" revealed, in order to be believed or trusted on. "We have believed in Jesus Christ that we might be justified by the faith of Christ" (Galatians 2:16).

This trusting in Jesus Christ is a sinner's receiving and resting upon Him alone for salvation, as faith is defined in our Catechism; and, according to the use of the phrase in Scripture it is indeed a believing, and nothing more than a believing in Him.

1. It is, according to the Scriptures, a receiving and a resting upon Christ alone for salvation ("The principal acts of saving faith are accepting, receiving, and resting upon Christ alone for justification, sanctification, and eternal life, by virtue of the covenant of grace," Westminster Confession, Chapter 14: Article 2). It is, I say, a receiving of Him. "As many as received Him, to them gave He power to become the sons of God, even to them that believe on His name" (John 1:12). Here the receiving of Christ is by the Holy Spirit explained and declared to be a believing on His name. God in the gospel presents Christ as His gift, and Christ offers Himself to sinners of mankind as their Savior. The sinner in believing believes the divine grant and offer with application to himself, and hereon trusts in Christ and in Him alone for all his salvation. Is not this a receiving of Him in that character of a Savior, in which the Father gives Him? Is it not a taking, or accepting, or applying of Him to a man's self as He is offered to him in the gospel? Christ complained of the Jews (John 5:43) that although He came in His Father's name, they did not receive Him; that is, they did not receive Him in the character in which He was sent, namely in that of Messiah, the anointed Savior of sinners, and their Savior, so as to trust in Him for their salvation. This appears evidently to be His meaning from the words that immediately

follow: "If another shall come in his own name, him ye will receive." It is as if He had said, "Him ye will believe to be the Messiah and your Savior, and will accordingly trust in Him, that He will save you."

It is also, in the Scripture sense of that phrase, a resting upon Christ for salvation. "Thou wilt keep him in perfect peace whose mind is stayed on Thee, because he trusteth in Thee" (Isaiah 26:3). Indeed, one cannot conceive in what way a man can rest on a word or on a person otherwise than by trusting in or on them. We read in 2 Chronicles 32:8 that the people rested themselves upon the words of Hezekiah. How can one imagine that they did so otherwise than by trusting in them? Again, "Help us, O Lord our God, for we rest on Thee" (2 Chronicles 14:11). In what way could they rest on Him in the circumstances in which they then were but by trusting on Him for their help?

2. Trusting, according to the use of the term in Scripture, is a believing that, in entering on the subject, I endeavored to evidence from the Scripture itself. For it is a trusting in a word, namely the testimony of God, the proximate or nearest object of faith; a trusting in a person, namely Jesus Christ and God in Him, the personal object of faith (Acts 16:31); and a trusting on a thing, namely the righteousness of Christ, the ultimate object of faith (Romans 1:17)-and all this for eternal salvation. When the Apostle Peter would express his trust and that of the other apostles for their own salvation, he said, "We believe that, through the grace of the Lord Jesus Christ, we shall be saved" (Acts 15:11). And then it is nothing but a believing; for thus faith as justifying and saving is not explained away into a work, but is considered as an object quite different from a work, as it is in the Scripture contradistinguished from works.

I conclude therefore that trusting in Christ is that believing in Him by which a person is united to Him and instated in the covenant of grace. Now trusting in Jesus Christ, and on His righteousness, for salvation, includes the following particulars:

(1) It comprises a cordial renunciation of all confidence for salvation in one's self and in every other creature. In the exercise of this trust, the soul relinquishes self-confidence, creature-confidence, law confidence, and builds on ground that is entirely new. "The Gentiles," says Jeremiah, "shall come unto thee . . . and shall say, 'Surely our fathers have inherited lies, vanity, and things wherein there is no profit'" (Jeremiah 16:19). "We," says an apostle, "are the circumcision, which . . . rejoice in Christ Jesus, and have no confidence in the flesh" (Philippians 3:3). It is a trusting entirely on Christ and His righteousness for salvation, a trusting or a believing with all the heart (Proverbs 3:5; Acts 8:37). In exercising this trust the believer comes off from the works of the law to the spotless righteousness of Christ for his justification; and he comes out of himself to the Holy Spirit of Christ for his sanctification, being persuaded that no services nor sufferings of his own can ever purchase for him the pardon of the lest sin; and that no wisdom nor strength of his own can ever enable him to mortify the least member of the body of sin (Matthew 5:3; Isaiah 45:24).

(2) It includes not only a willingness, but a sincere desire to be delivered from sin as well as from wrath. In exercising this cordial trust the heart unfeignedly desires to be wholly sanctified as well as to be freely justified; to be saved as well from the power, the pollution, the practice, and the inbeing, as from the guilt of sin, according to that of the holy Apostle Paul, "Who shall deliver me from the body of this death? I thank God through Jesus Christ our Lord" (Romans 7:24, 25). It is a trusting in Jesus not for a part of His salvation, or for

deliverance only from wrath—which is all that the formalist or hypocrite cares to trust for, being by no means desirous of deliverance from some darling lust—but is a trusting in Him for the whole of his salvation, namely for salvation from wrath and salvation from sin likewise. Indeed, the heart of the true believer is chiefly set upon deliverance from sin, from all sin, and from all sin as soon as possible which, in his view, is the principal part of salvation (Matthew 1:21). Trust includes desire. A man may be said to fear that one will send him something that he desires not; but no man can properly trust in one for that which he does not desire to have. No unregenerate man, whatever his pretensions are, can sincerely trust in Jesus for salvation from all iniquity, from every idol, because, so long as he continues unregenerate, he cannot desire such a salvation. He must be born again before he can desire to be saved from all iniquity. An unregenerate man may fear that Christ will deprive him of a favorite lust; but he cannot trust that He will deliver him from it. Saving faith is a trusting or believing with the heart (Romans 10:10). The whole salvation of the Lord Jesus is that on which the heart of every regenerate man is set, and of which it willingly makes choice.

(3) This trust implies also a cordial approbation of that device of salvation according to the covenant that is manifested in the gospel. The man who believes with his heart is well pleased with that glorious plan. It appears to him to be a scheme admirably adapted, yea, infinitely suited, to the honor of the perfections and laws of Jehovah, to the case of lost sinners, and his own case in particular. And, indeed, without a cordial approbation of it no man who knows what God is, what the law is, what sin is, and what the soul is, will ever venture his eternal salvation upon it. But a man's entrusting all his salvation to Jesus Christ as his righteousness and strength shows him to be

The Way of a Sinner's Entering Into the Covenant

well pleased with Christ, as one to whom, in his estimation, a sinner may, without the least danger, entrust all the concerns of his soul. Satisfied that the everlasting covenant is well ordered in all things and sure, he sincerely approves it; and in the exercise of cordial and unsuspecting confidence he says, "This is all my salvation, and all my desire" (2 Samuel 23:5). He acquiesces for himself in that wonderful device of salvation. His heart in trusting is satisfied with it and rests in it. He cordially likes it as altogether suitable, as fully sufficient, as perfectly safe, to be trusted, being the power of God and the wisdom of God (1 Corinthians 1:24). He pronounces them safe and happy who partake of that salvation. For his own part, he desires above all things to be interested in it; for he is persuaded that he should be saved to the uttermost were it but fully in his possession. Thus the woman in the gospel-history who was diseased with an issue of blood exercised her faith. She said within herself, "If I may but touch His garment I shall be whole" (Matthew 9:21). The true believer is so well pleased with that way as to resolve to accept salvation in no other way. This is far from being the disposition of the hypocrite; if he is but saved from eternal torment he does not care how.

(4) In the exercise of this trust the sinner betakes himself to the Lord Jesus, and His righteousness alone, for all his salvation. This also is evidently included in the confidence that he places in Him. For the man, believing that Christ with His righteousness and fullness is his in offer, and in right to trust in Him, and at the same time that He is able to save him to the uttermost, accordingly trusts in Him and on His righteousness for his whole salvation; and in so doing he has recourse to Him as his only Savior; even as one who used to live upon alms, believing that, by a relative or friend, he has wealth made over to him, leaves off to beg, trusts for his maintenance to that

wealth alone, and so takes himself to it. By trusting in Jesus Christ, the man as a condemned sinner, takes himself to Him as his Savior from the guilt of sin and the curse of the law; and as a depraved and polluted sinner he takes himself to Him as his Savior from the power and the pollution of sin. Accordingly, faith is in Scripture called a coming to Christ (John 6:35), a fleeing for refuge to Him (Hebrews 6:18); and it is often expressed, as for instance in Psalm 2:12, by a word that properly signifies to retire, or take one's self for refuge to a shadow or a shelter (Judges 9:15); or to retire, as the chickens do under the wings of the hen. Thus Boaz said to Ruth, "A full reward be given thee of the Lord God of Israel, under whose wings thou art come to trust"; or, more literally, to retire for refuge (Ruth 2:12).

(5) Lastly, this trusting in Christ for salvation includes an affiance or confidence in Him that, for His righteousness, and according to His promise given us in the offer of the gospel, He will save us from sin and wrath. To trust in Jesus Christ for my salvation is humbly and cordially to trust that He saves, and will save me. It is to confide or place confidence in Him; or to commit myself and my whole salvation in confidence to Him; or with confidence to rely upon Him for my own particular salvation. The meaning of these and other similar descriptions of the exercise of faith is this: Faith is a trusting in the Lord Jesus for salvation to myself; and a trusting in Him for salvation to myself is a trusting that He saves and will save me, not in or to sin, but from sin, from all sin; or a trusting that He performs, and will continue to perform, the part not of an enemy, but of a friend; not of a destroyer, but of a Savior, even to me. That the trust of faith comprises this particular confidence in Christ, is evident:

First, from the Scriptures of truth. "Let him trust in the name of the Lord, and stay upon his God" (Isaiah 50:10). "Lo, this is our God; we have waited for Him, and He will save us" (Isaiah 25:9). "Though I walk in the midst of trouble, Thou wilt receive me; Thou wilt stretch forth Thine hand against the wrath of mine enemies, and Thy right hand shall save me. The Lord will perfect that which concerneth me" (Psalm 138:7, 8). "When I sit in darkness, the Lord will be a light unto me; He will bring me forth to the light, and I shall behold His righteousness" (Micah 7:8, 9). "Thou wilt guide me with Thy counsel, and afterwards receive me to glory" (Psalm 73:24). "We believe that, through the grace of the Lord Jesus Christ, we shall be saved" (Acts 15:11). "The Lord will deliver me from every evil work, and will preserve me unto His heavenly kingdom" (2 Timothy 4:18). "For we are made partakers of Christ, if we hold the beginning of our confidence steadfast unto the end" (Hebrews 3:14).

Second, that the trust of faith is thus particular is also evident from the nature of the thing itself. For when a man trusts in any person or thing he thereby depends upon the object of his trust as sufficient to answer the purpose of his confidence, assuring himself that if nothing unforeseen occurs to hinder it he or it will answer his expectation. Whosoever trusts in a person for anything has a persuasion of the same degree of firmness as his trust that the person will do that thing for him. As an evident sign of this, when the party trusted in fails the party who trusted in him begins to be ashamed or confounded as being disappointed in that which he trusted the other would do for him; now that he is disappointed of his expectation, he begins to be ashamed of his confidence. Since, therefore, the trust of divine faith, being placed in One who cannot fail, who cannot lie, who cannot deceive the soul that cordially confides in Him, it is never disappointed. The Scriptures assure us that "whosoever believeth on Him shall not be ashamed" (Romans 10:11), and shall not be confounded (1 Peter 2:6). This plainly implies that he who believes on Jesus for his salvation trusts or depends on Him that He will save him; otherwise, there can be no place for his being ashamed or confounded, whatever the issue of his trust may be. Accordingly, the trust of saving faith does, in proportion to its degree of firmness, fix or establish the heart. "His heart is fixed, trusting in the Lord" (Psalm 112:7). Of this we have a pertinent instance in the case of the Apostle Paul. "I am not ashamed," says he, "for I know whom I have believed," or, as in the margin, trusted (2 Timothy 1:12). Agreeably to this, faith is in Scripture called a building on Christ as on a foundation that will support all our weight (Isaiah 28:16 with 1 Peter 2:6). It is also called a staying on Him (Isaiah 26:3); a leaning upon Him (Song of Songs 8:5); a resting on Him (2 Chronicles 14:11); a relying on Him, as on one who will sustain us (2 Chronicles 16:8; a looking to Him (Isaiah 45:22), or a having our eyes upon Him, as one from whom we look for all our salvation (2 Chronicles 20:12), and in the New Testament especially, a believing on Him (1 Peter 2:6), as One by whose grace we believe or trust that we shall be saved (Acts 15:11). These figurative expressions do not each express a different act or a different degree of faith, but the true reason of the variety of these beautiful images is the variety in the declared character of Christ and in the real case of the believer. The Lord Jesus, the glorious Object of faith, is in the gospel exhibited to us under various aspects, in correspondence to each of which faith receives its denomination. As the ocean receives its various names from the different countries bordering upon it, so, according to the particular view in which the Savior is presented, faith receives its appellation.

The Way of a Sinner's Entering Into the Covenant

The man who is truly convinced of sin, relinquishing all confidence for salvation in other objects, stays himself by faith on Jesus Christ and His meritorious righteousness, trusting that, on the ground of that perfect righteousness, he shall have salvation from Him. It is true, indeed, that this particular trust is often assaulted less or more by doubts and fears; but these are things that are opposite to it and that it has in its exercise to struggle against doubt and distrust, though they are in the believer, yet are not in his faith, but are contrary to it; and therefore the weaker his faith is they prevail the more, and the stronger it is they prevail the less.

When Peter began to doubt whether Jesus would keep him from sinking in the water, and so began to sink, the Savior said to him, "O thou of little faith, wherefore didst thou doubt" (Matthew 14:31). Doubting believers there are; but a doubting faith there never was, and never can be. A doubting faith is an unbelieving faith, or, which is much the same, a believing unbelief. But each of these is a contradiction in terms. The degree of faith, indeed, is very different in different believers, and in the same believer at different times; but if all trust or confidence in the Savior for salvation to one's self is removed from faith, the very essence of it is destroyed. For in that case the convinced sinner, having no confidence for his salvation in any other object, and at the same time no confidence for it in Christ either, is left altogether unsettled. He is left to fluctuate, to waver, like a wave of the sea (James 1:6); and then, where would that leaning, that staying, that relying, that resting on Christ be by which the exercise of faith is in Scripture expressed? "Let him," says an apostle, "ask in faith, nothing wavering; for he that wavereth is like a wave of the sea, driven with the wind, and tossed; for let not that man think that he shall receive anything of the Lord" (James 1:6, 7). The man who, on the contrary, truly believes, finding his confidence in the flesh overthrown, does, in the exercise of faith, place the confidence of his heart on the Lord Jesus as his righteousness and strength, trusting that He will save him. And however much he may indeed waver in that matter, being tossed with such doubts and fears respecting his salvation as weaken his confidence and sometimes prevail so far as to cause an intermission of the exercise of it, yet, even under all that perturbation, he does not waver like a wave of the sea, which has nothing to fix it but is only like a ship at anchor. His confidence as to the principle and habit of it is never entirely rooted out; and therefore under the influences of the Holy Spirit it will again revive and exert itself. In that matter, every true believer, as a sure evidence that he has been made a partaker of Christ, holds fast the beginning of his confidence in Him, steadfast unto the end (Hebrews 3:14).

At the Reformation, and for a long time after, this trust or confidence of faith used to be called the assurance of faith. By the assurance of faith was, and by many judicious divines still is meant, not a persuasion that I am united to Christ, instated in the covenant, or already pardoned and saved, but a belief, persuasion, and confidence in Christ for all His salvation (That the fiducial reliance or trust of faith, and the assurance of faith were, by the Westminster divines, counted the same thing is evident from this their answer to the last question in the Larger Catechism: "So we by faith are emboldened . . . quietly to rely upon Him, that He will fulfill our requests." And, to testify our desire and assurance, we say, "Amen." This notion of assurance in faith is so agreeable to the nature of believing, and to the style of the Holy Scripture, that sometimes where in the original text it is read faith or believing, it is, according to the true sense of the original phrase, read, in our translation, assurance. Thus in

The Way of a Sinner's Entering Into the Covenant

Acts 17:31, "Whereof He hath given assurance," it is in the Greek, "faith," as in the margin of our Bibles. Also in Deuteronomy 28:66: "Thou shalt have none assurance of thy life." In the Hebrew it is, "Thou shalt not believe in thy life." These passages may suffice to show that to believe, in the style of the Holy Scripture, as well as in the dialect of mankind, when speaking of the common affairs of this life, is to be persuaded or assured according to the measure of one's belief. Believing is persuasion and persuasion is assurance. In proportion as a man believes the existence of an object, he does not doubt it; he is persuaded, or assured of it. To believe and to be sure are, upon the whole, synonymous phrases. Every believer has, in the exercise of his faith, a persuasion or assurance of the thing that he believes; he is sure it is that which he believes it to be; and so far as he is not sure of it he does not believe it. To believe with a divine faith is to be persuaded or assured upon the word, the covenant, the promise, and the oath of God who cannot lie. If this faith is weak, the assurance is weak; if strong, the assurance is in proportion strong. The assurance of faith then is a firm belief that Christ is able and willing to save sinners; a firm belief that He is freely offered to me a sinner, and that the gracious offer affords me a warrant to entrust my salvation to Him; and especially it is a firm trust or confidence in Him for all my salvation. Accordingly, a man may have in some measure the assurance of faith and yet not know that he has it; nay, for a season, he may obstinately deny that he has any such thing. He may have the assurance of faith that is founded on faithfulness in the Word of God without him, and yet not the assurance or sense that is founded on a feeling of the work of God within him. He may firmly trust that Jesus Christ will save him and yet not be able instantly to conclude from evidences of salvation that He has saved him. He may have the real assurance ("This faith is different in degrees, weak or strong . . . growing up in many to the attainment of a full assurance." Westminster Confession Chapter 14, Article 3). But how fan faith grow up in many to a full assurance if there is not some degree of assurance in the very nature of it? To whatever degree anything may grow, it can never, by growth, attain another nature. A plant can never become a beast nor a beast a man. In like manner, were there not some assurance in the nature of faith, it could never grow up to full assurance; and yet be far from having the full assurance of faith. To have full assurance of faith is always the believer's duty. "Let us," says an apostle, "draw near with a true heart, in full assurance of faith" (Hebrews 10:22); but it is very seldom his attainment. So full assurance of faith, as is hinted by the original word [Hesychius, that great master of Greek literature, explains the original word as a term that signifies firmness or stability]. The full assurance of understanding, of faith, and of hope, then, is a high degree of firm assent, or firm confidence, and of firm expectation, which, in a proportionate degree, establishes the heart. So as it is rendered in the passage just now cited, we are to understand a full assent or persuasion and a full confidence; or, in other words, a high degree of a firm belief of the Divine testimony, and of firm confidence in the Lord Jesus. When the believer attains full assurance of faith, like a richly laden ship whose sails are filled by a prosperous gale, wafted toward the harbor, his soul, under the irresistible influence of the Holy Spirit, is quickly carried forward to its blessed object, and to more and more of the enjoyment of Him. It is, by the propitious gales of the Sprit, carried forward to a full assent, or assurance of understanding (Colossians 2:2); to a full confidence, or assurance of faith, strictly so called (Hebrews 10:22); and to a full expectation or assurance of hope (Hebrews 6:11).

The Way of a Sinner's Entering Into the Covenant

That faith then by which persons take hold of Jehovah's covenant has in its nature a real, though not often a full assurance. Doubts and fears, in proportion to the weakness of their faith, are indeed found in true believers, but never in their faith itself. And oftentimes those doubts and fears do not immediately respect the truth of God in His Word of grace, but the truth of their own past or present experience of His grace, and so are, properly speaking, opposite more to the assurance of sense or reflection than to that of faith. If our heart sincerely disapproves, condemns, and opposes our doubting of the faithfulness of God in His offers and promises, we have a real, though not a full, assurance of faith (Psalm 41:5, 11 and 43:5 and 77:10; Matthew 14:28, 29; Galatians 5:17).

It is of unspeakable importance to the comfort and holiness of the believing soul to distinguish well between the assurance of faith and the assurance of sense. A man may have the assurance of faith without having yet attained that of sense. The assurance of faith has its foundation without the man; the assurance of sense has its immediate foundation within him. The object of the assurance of faith is Christ offered in the Word; the object of the assurance of sense is Christ formed in the soul. The ground of the former is the testimony of God without us; that of the latter is the work of God within us. By the one we embrace the promise; by the other we enjoy the promise. By the assurance of faith we receive and trust the Lord Jesus for our salvation; by that of sense we feel that He saves us. The assurance of faith, being the evidence of things not seen, can claim and cleave to a withdrawing, a hiding God. Zion said, "My Lord hath forgotten me"; and the church, "My Beloved had withdrawn Himself and was gone." So that, as holy Rutherford says, "He may be a forgetting and a withdrawing God to my feeling, and yet to my faith my God and my Lord still." But on the other hand, the assurance of sense is the evidence of things seen, of things felt. By the former the believer says, "He will bring me forth to the light." By the latter, "He hath brought me forth to it by that." One says, "Though He slays me, yet will I trust in Him; by this He shines, He smiles upon me. Therefore I trust in Him." By the one the devout Christian says, "My God will hear me." By the other, "He hath heard the voice of my supplications." By the former believers say, "He will bless us." By the latter, "He hath blessed us with all spiritual blessings."

The confounding of these two kinds of assurance, and the giving the name of the assurance of faith to the assurance of sense, which differs so much from it, have produced the most of the extravagant notions that Antinomians have imbibed. And I fear have, in the minds of many persons who mean well, perplexed and obscured not a little the Scripture doctrine of saving faith.

Suppose the reader should now object against the doctrine of a sinner's trusting in Christ for salvation to himself and say, "Since it is far from being true that all who hear the gospel shall be saved, there cannot surely be, in the case of every one of them, a ground on which that particular trust or assurance may warrantably be founded."

I would reply, every one of them has, notwithstanding, an equal and a sufficient foundation to trust on Christ and His righteousness for salvation to himself, namely the offer and call directed to every one, together with the promise of God that whosoever believes on His Son shall not perish, but have everlasting life (John 3:16). The meaning of this promise is this: Whosoever will cordially believe or trust in Christ for all his salvation shall not be disappointed, but shall certainly be saved. Here then is the faithfulness of God in His Word of grace for the foundation of that particular trust; and divine faith in the

The Way of a Sinner's Entering Into the Covenant   417

heart is always founded on divine faithfulness in the Word. It is indeed true that many to whom the gospel is preached will not in the event be saved; but still it is equally true that they who shall not eventually be saved will not cordially believe. They will not, although they have a firm foundation, a sufficient warrant for so doing, place the confidence of their heart in the almighty Savior for their salvation from all sin as well as from all misery. Now if after all they will not sincerely trust in Him for such a salvation, their destruction must be entirely of themselves; they shall perish without excuse and their unbelief will be the principal ground of their condemnation. Jesus, with His righteousness and fullness, is, by the Father's gift and His own offer, so far made theirs that every one of them may warrantably trust in Him as his Savior for his own complete salvation. If still they will not believe the infinitely free offer with application, and will not, upon the warrant of it, trust in Him, each for salvation to himself, they do, by their disbelief and distrust, make God a liar and fall most justly under His eternal wrath.

    Should it be objected that many do confidently trust in Christ that He will save them who yet continue to be either profane persons or formal hypocrites, and so are not by their faith united to Him, nor instated in His covenant of grace as all true believers are, I would answer: The Apostle Paul in speaking of faith unfeigned (1 Timothy 1:5), supposes that there is a feigned faith. And indeed this is all the faith that formalists or hypocrites have. As for that cordial trust in the Redeemer that I have attempted from the sacred records to elucidate, it is as certain that such persons have it not as it is that it purifies the heart (Acts 15:9) and sanctifies the whole man (Acts 26:18). They presume indeed to think, and even to say, that they trust in the Savior for salvation. But that unfeigned trust, that confidence of the heart in Him, they in reality do not have. For they do not trust on Him and His righteousness alone for the salvation that they pretend to desire. They do not trust in Him with all their heart, but trust partly to Him and His righteousness and partly to their own service and suffering. Between themselves and the Savior, between their own polluted performances and His spotless righteousness, their heart is divided. This is manifest especially from these words of our Lord Himself: "Blessed are the *poor in spirit*, for theirs is the kingdom of heaven" (Matthew 5:3). They do not trust in Him for the whole of their salvation; nay, deliverance from all sin, which is the chief part of His salvation, they are far from approving. The salvation, therefore, that was purchased by the Son of God, and is promised in the covenant of grace, may well be an object of their aversion and fear, but cannot be an object of their desire and trust. In a word, their confidence is not founded on the faithfulness of God in the free offer and promise of the gospel, but it is built on a foundation of sand that can bear no weight (Matthew 7:26, 27).

Thus I have in some measure shown what that faith is by which a sinner unites with the last Adam, and so enters personally into the covenant of grace. Here it will be proper briefly to observe that this confidence of the heart in Christ Jesus for the whole of His salvation is the fittest possible instrument (It would appear that the Westminster Assembly took condition and instrument to be synonymous terms. For in the Confession, Chapter 11, Article 2, they say, "That faith is the alone instrument of justification"; and in the Larger Catechism, Question 32, they assert that "God requireth faith as the condition to interest sinners in the Mediator.") of vital union between Him the infinitely glorious Object trusted in, and the soul trusting in Him; inasmuch as the soul thereby so cleaves to Him and to His consummate righteousness as from that moment wholly to stand or fall with Him as the superstructure with the foundation on which it is raised, or as that which is resting or staying with the prop on which it rests. Therefore, since the blessed Object of faith, that Rock of salvation, that foundation laid in Zion, is immovable, they who thus "trust" in Him, and thereby enter into the same covenant with Him, shall be as Mount Zion, which cannot be removed, but abides forever (Psalm 125:1). They will continue to be united to Him, and to be instated in His covenant, while eternal ages continue to revolve.

Now from what has been discoursed in this chapter it may be inferred that the first thing an unregenerate sinner should attempt to do in religion is to believe—to believe in order to repent. The unregenerate man should attempt, first of all, to believe the law with application to himself, and then the gospel. The first spiritual act of a regenerate man is an act of faith. He believes the law with application to himself, and so is convinced of his sin and misery. He believes also the gospel with application to himself, and so trusts for holiness and happiness. This he does in order to exercise evangelical repentance and to perform good works. While faith is the work of the Spirit, it is the duty of the sinner; and therefore he is to be exhorted to act it as the first of his duties.

Is true faith a cordial belief both of the law and of the gospel? In this it is distinguished from a feigned faith. A counterfeit or feigned faith is, for the most part, either a belief of the law without the gospel—and so is a turning of the law of God into an occasion of cherishing a legal spirit—or a belief of the gospel without the law, and so is a turning of the grace of God into licentiousness. A counterfeit faith makes a man either self-righteous or licentious.

The reader may also, from what has been advanced, learn that in thinking or speaking of the warrant to believe he should carefully distinguish between the Father's granting of Christ in offer to all who hear the gospel, and His giving of Him in possession to them who cordially believe in Him. It is His granting of Christ in offer, or His offering of Him to a man that affords him a warrant to trust in Him for salvation; and it is His giving of Him in possession to a man that warrants him to conclude that he has trusted in Him and has possession of Him. The former is the ground; the latter is the evidence of particular trust for salvation. Not distinguishing between the grounds of faith and the evidences of it is well known to have been a rock upon which Antinomians have split.

Hence too the reader may learn the true meaning of the appropriation of faith. To appropriate Christ with His righteousness and salvation is not to be assured upon the ground of evidences that He is mine already in possession (for this is the assurance of sense, and is not of the essence of faith); but it is a believing that He gives Himself to me in offer, and a trusting upon the warrant of the offer that He gives and will continue to give Himself to me in possession; or, it is a believing that He is mine in offer, and mine in right to entrust all my salvation to Him; and it is a trusting in Him accordingly that He will faithfully perform the part of a Savior to me. It is not an assurance that He is already mine in possession, but is a taking of Him into my possession, a taking home to my own soul in particular that Savior of the world and that common salvation (Jude verse 3) which lie before me in the offer of the gospel. The appropriation appears the same as the application of faith.

Finally, we may hence learn that, although faith is not the federal condition upon which a sinner's right to the blessings of the eternal covenant is suspended; yet it is so necessary as the means or instrument of taking possession of Christ, and taking hold of the covenant, that no man can have a saving interest in Christ and the covenant without it. Faith is, indeed, a condition of connection in the covenant; but, that it is not the condition of the covenant upon which the blessings of it are properly suspended is evident from this, that the very first of those blessings, namely regeneration, or the quickening Spirit, is bestowed previous to the first act of it. Besides, if it were the federal condition upon which the grace of the covenant was suspended, it would give the believer a federal or pactitious title to that grace; so that when he acted faith he might justly plead his faith as the ground of this title to grace, yea, and might claim grace as matter of debt to him upon that ground. But will any intelligent, any humble, any sincere Christian deliberately claim the grace of God upon the ground of his own faith? No; he knows that all the benefits of the covenant are of absolutely free grace to him; that the last of them is as much of free, of boundless grace to him as the first. Instead of pleading his faith, he by faith receives the righteousness of Jesus Christ, and pleads that alone as the foundation of his right to the good of the covenant (Philippians 3:9; Psalm 71:16; Romans 5:21). All is of absolutely free grace to the believer because his faith, although indispensably requisite as the instrument of receiving a title, yet gives him no title to the blessings of the covenant. Reader, the moment you rely on your faith as the ground of your title to the blessings of grace, you, for yourself, turn the covenant of grace into a covenant of works. Grace is no longer grace to you unless you allow it to be absolutely and altogether free. Exercise faith then in receiving all as an infinitely free gift, and do not rely on faith for a title to any blessing.

8

Evidences of One's Being Personally Instated in the Covenant of Grace

The covenant of works and the covenant of grace divide all mankind between them. Every man in the world is under one or the other of the two; and no man can, with regard to the state of his soul, be under both at the same time (Philippians 3:9; Psalm 71:16; Romans 5:21). Under the covenant of works stands a very numerous party in the first Adam, the head of that violated covenant deriving from him sin and death. Under the covenant of grace stands a select party in the second Adam, the Head of that fulfilled covenant, receiving from Him righteousness and life. These two parties will be judged, each according to the covenant under which they are. The former will be eternally punished in virtue of the curse of the covenant under which they lie; and the latter will be eternally saved in virtue of the promise of the covenant under which they stand. In the meantime there is access for sinners under the covenant of works to leave that party and that covenant and to join themselves to the party under the covenant of grace; but death, when it comes, will forever obstruct that access. It is therefore the duty and interest of the one, as well as of the other, to know which covenant they are

Evidences of Being Personally Instated 423

under. And indeed, if a man seriously considers the covenant of grace as that on which the salvation of his precious soul depends, he can scarcely refrain from putting this question to himself: "What interest have I in that covenant? I have, it is true, as other sinners who hear the gospel, a common interest therein by which, in contradistinction from fallen angels, I am warranted to into it. But this I may have and yet perish; for even children of the kingdom shall be cast out into outer darkness (Matthew 8:12). But have I a saving interest therein? Have I actually come into the bond of it? The covenant is, indeed, in the offers and ordinances of the gospel, brought to me; but am I brought into the covenant? It has been externally administered to me in common with other sinners; but have I, by faith, so taken hold of the same as to be personally interested in it?"

In order to assist the reader under the influences of the Spirit of truth to return a true and satisfying answer to this momentous question, I shall lay before him the following marks of a person's being actually and savingly instated in the covenant of grace.

1. They who are savingly interested in that sure covenant have, under a true conviction of their sinfulness and misery, fled into it for refuge from the dominion and curse of the broken covenant of works. They have fled into the covenant of the second Adam as refugees from that of the first Adam. The heirs of promise are persons who have fled for refuge to lay hold upon the hope set before them (Hebrews 6:17, 18). The time was when they dwelt secure under the dominion of the covenant of the law; but the spirit of the Lord has set fire to their habitation there so that they have found themselves unable to dwell any longer within the boundaries of that covenant. Mount Sinai has been altogether on a smoke round about them; and the trumpet of the curse of the law has waxed louder and louder till it made

them to hear it on the side of their own righteousness, and even of their best performances, where they were most deaf; and as a curse denounced against themselves in particular it caused them exceedingly to fear and quake. When the commandment came, sin revived and they died (Romans 7:9). It has chased them from every lurking place about that burning mountain; and has left no retreat within the limits of the broken covenant safe to them. Not only has it driven them out of their evil courses, but out of all confidence in their good dispositions, their pure intentions, their best performances, in order that they might escape for their life into the covenant of grace, as the manslayer did into the city of refuge. Hypocrites have been convinced of the sins of their life; but sincere believers have by the Holy Spirit been convinced not only of the iniquities of their life, but also of the sin of their nature, the deep depravity, the desperate wickedness of their heart. The former have with Simon the sorcerer wondered, or with Felix the governor trembled; but the latter have been made with the jailer so to tremble as each of them to ask, "What must I do to be saved?" Under piercing convictions of their undone condition they have begun to lay their salvation to heart as the one thing needful, as the main object of their attention and desire; and despairing of ever being able by any righteousness or strength of their own to answer the high demands of the broken law, they have betaken themselves to the covenant of grace where righteousness and eternal life are the gifts of God through Jesus Christ our Lord.

Now, reader, is this your case? Have you ever had such convictions of your utter inability to obey the precepts and to endure the penalties of the covenant of works as to be resolved to flee without delay into the covenant of grace, and to accept righteousness and life as gifts of sovereign grace? Are you, in the affair of justification, dead to the law as a covenant of works? Is

Evidences of Being Personally Instated

your hope of obtaining eternal life by your own obedience to it struck dead?

2. Those who are instated in the covenant of grace heartily approve of and acquiesce in every part of the plan of that glorious contract.

They cordially approve of it. They like it as a covenant that, in their view, is infinitely suited to the glory of Jehovah and to all the exigencies of the soul; and they are displeased with themselves for not liking it more. Regarding it as a covenant so well ordered in all things and so sure that God will not, and that man cannot break it, they are well pleased with it. In the light of the Word and Spirit of Christ, they see that everything in it is arranged in the most comely, the most convenient order. They see mercies in the covenant corresponding to all the cases and wants of every soul that is instated in it. They see, and it is a cheering sight! They see pardon in the covenant for guilt in the conscience, sanctification in the covenant for sinfulness in the soul, strength in the covenant for weakness in the creature, comfort in the covenant for sorrow in the heart, and stability in the covenant for inconstancy in the believer. They behold in the covenant all repaired, all with an infinite overplus restored that had been forfeited by the breach of the first covenant. Here they find security in danger, peace in trouble, fullness in want, and life in death. And having at the same time their heart so adapted to the Savior, and to the covenant, that less cannot satisfy and more is not desired, they say of Christ, "He is altogether lovely, and of the covenant, it is all our salvation, and all our desire" (2 Samuel 23:5). When God gives the new heart to a man, He so impresses upon it the stamp of His device of salvation in the new covenant as to render it fit to approve that glorious device. The consequence is that perceiving the way of answering the demands of law and justice and of redeeming lost sinners devised by the infinitely wise God and delineated in the covenant, he thinks it to be so good and so sure a way that he falls off in the affair of justification from the works of the law and closes with that glorious device. Now this is an inseparable concomitant of saving faith and a solid evidence of personal interest in the covenant. For whosoever duly considers the corruption of the human heart will soon perceive that the scheme of redemption laid out in the covenant of grace is entirely opposite to the discernment and the inclination of depraved human nature; so that nothing less than the infinite energy of the Spirit of grace can dispose a man cordially to approve it. The Lord Jesus, therefore, pronounces them blessed whosoever shall not be offended in Him (Matthew 11:6). Unregenerate men may indeed model the covenant in their own imagination into such a form as to render it an agreeable object to themselves. They may conceive it to be a covenant intended to make persons easy and happy, while at the same time it allows them, at least in some instances, to remain unholy; or, to be a covenant according to which they may, through Christ, obtain acceptance with God by their good works, notwithstanding their natural infirmities and evil works. But in all this they are pleased only with a creature of their own fancy and not with Jehovah's covenant of grace. Let that holy covenant be but presented to them in the light of the sacred Oracles, let them but for a moment view it in that light, and they will be sure to find fault with it. Let but the design of the covenant be plainly disclosed to them as being to exalt the sovereign grace of God upon the ruins of all dignity or excellency in man, to make Christ all and man nothing in his own salvation, and their proud heart will dislike that and turn from it with disgust. The efficacy thereof in separating forever between a soul and its beloved lusts is no sooner discovered by natural men than they flee from it as from a dangerous as well as a disgusting object. Let them be supposed seriously to think how it is adapted, both to the honor of the divine perfections and to the salvation of immortal souls, and they cannot see how that can be (1 Corinthians 2:14). To the carnal Jews it was a stumbling block, a device inconsistent with the perfections of Jehovah; to the learned Greeks, it was foolishness, a scheme of salvation unsuitable and unsafe to be trusted to. It is the eye of faith only that perceives it to be the power of God and the wisdom of God; honorable to a holy God and safe for a guilty creature.

They who are instated in the covenant likewise acquiesce in all the parts of it. Their heart rests in and is satisfied with that infinitely wise invention. While it is all their salvation, it is also all their desire. It restores whatever they have lost. It secures whatever they would desire. It is a covenant so complete as to leave nothing out that can reasonably be desired, and to admit nothing in but what is truly desirable. Here they find a full, an overflowing, fountain of life. Here, therefore, they repose their weary souls with cordial satisfaction and feed their hungry souls as with marrow and fatness so that, in the bosom of this blessed covenant, their heart is at rest and their soul dwells at ease. When the covenant is revealed to them as being made from eternity between God the Father and Christ the second Adam, with the infinite approbation of the Holy Spirit, they, in taking hold of it, satisfy themselves with heaven's draught of it so far as it is understood by them and do not attempt either to add to it or to diminish from it. They are satisfied with all that they find within the compass of the covenant without desiring any alterations to be made in their favor. They are satisfied with the conditions of the covenant as fulfilled by Christ alone as well as with the promises of it to be accomplished to themselves with the promise of sanctification as well as with that of justification or of glorification; with the laws as well as with the privileges and with the discipline as well as with the rewards of the covenant. Their heart rests with complacence in the whole, desiring nothing that is without and disrelishing nothing that is within the compass of it. Accordingly, that divine contract as exhibited in the gospel is in Isaiah 53:1, in the margin, called a hearing, that is, an object to be heard or received by faith as a sound is heard or received by the ear, according to these words, "Hear and your soul shall live" (Isaiah 55:3). The children of Adam are naturally disposed to speak rather than to hear. We are more ready to express our own will by speaking than to receive the will of God by hearing. Since the gospel is a declaration of the will of God for our salvation, only to be heard and received by faith, and therefore called the hearing of faith (Galatians 3:2), the power of divine grace is requisite to dispose our heart to hear it and to stop our mouth from making, in reference to it, proposals of our own.

Do you, reader, approve that divinely excellent, that well ordered covenant? Are you well pleased with the whole frame of it so far as you understand it, and displeased with yourself for not being better pleased with it? Do you at least see more and more reason to be well pleased with all the articles of it; and is it your habitual desire and endeavor to grow in your cordial approbation of them? Is your heart satisfied with everything that you see in that covenant? Is every article of it, in your estimation, both what it should be and where it should be? Do you wish for no amendments, no alterations, nothing added to it, nothing diminished from it? Are you content and desirous of becoming more and more content to be an everlasting debtor for all your salvation to the grace of that glorious covenant? If so, it is good evidence that you have a personal interest in it.

3. They who are actually instated in the covenant of grace sincerely love God in Christ, the Contriver and the Maker of

Evidences of Being Personally Instated

that eternal covenant. They love Him with supreme esteem, with undissembled affection, and loathe themselves in their own sight for loving Him so little. They love Him for His loveliness in Himself, and in proportion as they know Him they love all of Him. They love His holiness and His justice as well as His goodness and His truth. They also love Him for His love to them. The faith by which they take hold of His covenant works by love to Him. Great was the love of God to them, which was manifested in that covenant. The glorious contracting Parties acted therein from a principle of sovereign, unsolicited, unmerited, unbounded love. From that unmerited love to them sprang the first motion for a covenant of grace, in order that salvation might be secured for them. From that source it was that the Father determined to give His dear, His only Son for them; that the Son, with infinite willingness, resolved to die for them; and that the blessed Spirit condescended to live in them, and so to quicken, sanctify, and comfort them. It was the infinite love of God to them that gave rise to the proposal of exceedingly great and precious promises in their favor, upon terms consistent with the honor of His holiness and justice. It was the amazing love of Christ to them that induced Him to accept those terms. And when the divine contract was, by the demonstration of the Spirit, according to the gospel, opened and brought home to their souls, that love shone forth to them in such a manner that they were constrained to believe it. "We," says the Apostle John, "have known and believed the love that God hath to us. God is love" (1 John 4:16). That redeeming love of God, believed with application, kindled in their heart an ardent love to Him in return. "We love Him because He first loved us" (1 John 4:19). And therefore, although their love is not always vigorous in the same degree, but is stronger or weaker according to the strength or weakness of their faith, yet, since their faith never altogether fails, so neither does their love (1 Corinthians 13:8). It is an active principle in them, powerfully constraining them to evangelical obedience, and giving the throne in their affection to God as their covenant-God and to Christ as their covenant-Head; so that their soul says, "Whom have I in heaven but Thee? And there is none upon earth that I desire besides Thee" (Psalm 73:25). It makes it their greatest care to please Him and to be accepted of Him; and their greatest fear to offend Him, and so provoke Him to hide His face from them. It renders their duty their delight (1 John 5:3), and the remains of sin in them their heaviest burden, a burden from which they long earnestly to be delivered (Romans 7:24). They also love the Word of God in which the covenant is exhibited to them, and esteem it more than their necessary food (Job 23:12). In few words, they love the children of God, notwithstanding the sinful infirmities that cleave to them, because they bear His image. "Everyone that loveth Him that begat loveth Him also that is begotten of Him" (1 John 5:1). And again, "We know that we have passed from death unto life because we love the brethren" (1 John 3:14).

Reader, can you then say that the infinite loveliness and love of God in Christ, displayed in the covenant of grace, have been believed by you, and that they have constrained you to love Him above all other objects of your affection? To love all His perfections? All His covenant? All His words? All His people, and that with a pure heart fervently? Do you see more and more cause to esteem Him far above all creatures? And do you, in any measure, sincerely bewail the coldness of your love to Him? Is your duty your delight? Is it in all its parts matter of choice to your heart? If so, it is an evidence that you are within the bond of His covenant of grace.

4. Such as are personally interested in the everlasting covenant consent that the Lord Jesus, the Head of that covenant,

should become their Head. They have cordially accepted Him to be their federal Head, and that for all the purposes of the covenant; and they remain fixed in their determination not to alter their choice were it to be made a thousand times. Their heart willingly submits to Him, and prefers Him as a Covenant-head before everyone else. They to whom the Father in eternity chose Christ for a Covenant-head do in time approve the choice and make it over again, each for himself. They are said, accordingly, to appoint themselves one head (Hosea 1:11). As often as they renew their exercise of faith that they daily do, they upon the matter reiterate this as their choice. Being made deeply sensible of what they have lost by the transgression of Adam, their first covenant-head, the Lord Jesus is precious in their estimation as their second Covenant-head. They came in to the covenant, and they also abide in it, under the shadow of His wings entirely; expecting no benefit by it, nor from it, but only through and under Him. They have accepted Him as their Head of government as well as their Head of influence. They have surrendered themselves to Him to be ruled and disposed of, as well as to be saved and supported by Him; to be governed by His laws, and not by their own lusts, as well as to be saved by His grace, and not by their own works.

Now is this, reader, the habitual determination of your heart? Are you as willing to be ruled by the law and disposed of by the providence as to be saved by the grace of Christ? Do you prefer Him before all others, whether in heaven or upon earth, as your Head of righteousness and of life? As your Head of government, of eminence, and of influence? Do you cleave to Him, glory in Him, and grow up into Him in all things, as your Head? If you do, you are in Him and under Him within the bond of that sure covenant of which He is the glorious Head.

5. They cordially rely for all their salvation upon the conditions of the covenant performed by Him. They make that consummate righteousness of His the sole ground of their acceptance with God and of their title to all the life that is promised in the covenant. Believing on Jesus is the soul's building on Him as Jehovah our Righteousness (1 Peter 2:6). If sinners build on any other foundation they build on the sand and their confidence shall be overthrown. If, being beat off from every other foundation, they still refuse to build on this one, they must, as the chaff that the wind drives away, inevitably perish. To believe or build on the righteousness of Jesus Christ can imply no less than a man's trusting on it for all his salvation. Whether this trust is strong or weak, it must exist else faith is not relying on Christ for salvation; but the soul remains in a state of wavering, in opposition to a staying of itself by faith upon the Savior (James 1:6, 7). Now they who are within the bond of the covenant accept of the perfect righteousness of the second Adam as the sole foundation of their hope of eternal life; for the covenant exhibits not, admits not, any other (1 Corinthians 3:11). They exercise some degree of confidence for their own salvation on that ground, by which they are distinguished from the disbelieving and desponding; and the confidence that they exercise for salvation they exercise on that ground alone; by which they are distinguished from hypocritical and self-righteous formalists. Both of these things are united in the character of true believers: they rejoice in Christ Jesus, and at the same time they have no confidence in the flesh (Philippians 3:3).

Have you, reader, this evidence also of being personally instated in the everlasting covenant? Have you some measure of humble confidence, of particular trust in Christ, for the whole of your salvation? And is all thy confidence for it built on the foundation of His righteousness alone, offered to you in the

Evidences of Being Personally Instated 433

gospel? If so, you are a true believer, one of the true circumcision, one of the children of the covenant. You have covenant-security against eternal death, and a covenant-title to eternal life.

6. But, further, they are satisfied with all that is promised in the covenant. The promises of it are a satisfying portion to their hearts. The promises of sanctification please them as much as those of justification and consolation. They are indeed sensible that they have many wants, but at the same time they see as much in the promises as can abundantly supply them all. They are persuaded that there is as much water in these wells of salvation as would most effectually quench all their thirst if they could but attain the art of drawing it. It is in this respect especially that the everlasting covenant is all their desire (2 Samuel 23:5). This discovery of the covenant is not from nature, but from that grace that shows so much worth in the one pearl of great price as makes a man content to sell all that he has to obtain it (Matthew 13:46). No man will come into the covenant until he attains in some degree such a discovery; for who will deliberately connect himself with one in a marriage-covenant, or even in a contract of service, with whom he does not see how he can live? By the eye of faith elect sinners discern in the covenant not only a refuge to shelter them, but a portion to enrich them (Psalm 142:5); else they never would choose to enter into it; and none who have once attained that discovery would choose to remain out of it for a moment longer. "They," says the Psalmist, "that know Thy name will put their trust in Thee" (Psalm 9:10). As soon as the worth of the treasure, hid in the field of the gospel, is spiritually discerned, all is sold for the obtaining of it (Matthew 13:44, 45); all is counted loss for the excellence of the knowledge of it (Philippians 3:8). The men of the world really do not discern this in the covenant; and therefore it is but a mean, an empty thing in their estimation. That glorious con-

tract is in the gospel presented to them in its breadth and length, in its fullness and suitableness; but it is far from pleasing them; far, very far from being all their desire. After all, as if they saw nothing that could satisfy them, they still ask, "Who will show us any good?" (Psalm 4:6). Indeed, the heart of a sinner can never see enough in the covenant to suit and satisfy its desires till the Spirit of grace gives it a new bent, and so contracts and regulates its desires; for in the covenant no provision is made for, but against that upon which the unregenerate heart is mainly set. The true believer, on the contrary, discerns Christ and the grace of the promises to be the only satisfying good, the only enriching and ennobling portion, for an immortal soul.

Now is this, reader, in any measure your attainment? Are the promises of the covenant exceedingly great and precious in your estimation? Are they sweet to your soul, gratifying and satisfying to your heart? Are you as highly pleased with the promises of sanctification as with those of justification and consolation, with the promises of holiness as with those of happiness? Do you see emptiness everywhere else, and fullness only in the promises of the everlasting covenant? Do you now, more than formerly, see the malignity and feel the strength of the sin that dwells in you and your continual need of supplies of grace from the promises? And is it in dependence on grace in the promises, and not on grace in the heart, that you essay to perform good works? If it is thus with your soul, it is a good evidence that you are so interested in the covenant of promises as to be one of the heirs of promise.

7. They have the Spirit of the covenant dwelling and working in them. "I will," said Jehovah, "put My Spirit within you, and cause you to walk in My statutes" (Ezekiel 36:27). The Spirit who is here promised is the Spirit of Christ and the Spirit of the covenant. His saving influences were purchased by the blood of

Evidences of Being Personally Instated

the covenant, are treasured up in Christ, the Head of the covenant, and are in some measure communicated to all the people of the covenant (Romans 8:9).

Now the Spirit of Christ dwelling in His covenant-people may be known to be in them by His being a Spirit of sanctification, or holiness in general. The main design of the covenant, next to the glory of Jehovah, was that sinners of mankind might be rendered holy (Luke 1:74, 75). All the lines of the covenant meet in that as their center. Infinite wisdom and love are gloriously displayed in the making of the covenant; infinite justice in the conditions of it; infinite grace and mercy in the promises; infinite power and faithfulness in the administration of it—but infinite holiness shines with the most resplendent luster in every part of it. Hence in Scripture it is called the holy covenant (Daniel 11:30). Can it then be reasonably supposed that unholy persons, that strangers to the power of godliness, whom no bands of holiness will hold, can yet be within the bond of that holy covenant? No, doubtless they are not. They do not have the Spirit of the covenant. That Holy Spirit makes the people of the covenant holy in all manner of conversation (1 Peter 1:15). He makes a vein of holiness to run through their whole nature and their whole life, through their thoughts, their words, and their deeds, through their intercourse with God and their dealings with men. The covenant was a confederacy entered into by the Father and the Son with the approbation of the Holy Spirit in order to remove sin from the heart and life of sinners of the human race, to restore the divine image in them, and to bring them again to a perfect conformity to the holy law from which in the first Adam they fell. For this end were the conditions thereof fulfilled, the promises of it made, and the administration of it entrusted to Christ the holy One of God. For this purpose was the Son of God manifested, that He might destroy the works of the devil (1 John 3:8). All therefore who are instated in that holy covenant are partakers of the Spirit as a Spirit of holiness (Galatians 5:16, 18).

But more particularly, persons may know if the Spirit of the covenant dwells in them by his being:

First, a free and ingenuous Spirit in them. The Spirit of the covenant is a free Spirit. "Uphold me," said the holy psalmist, "with Thy free (or voluntary) Spirit" (Psalm 51:12). Some obedience to the moral law is performed by bond men under the covenant of works as well as by free men under the covenant of grace; and though a fellow-creature can discern no difference between the obedience of some of the former and that of the latter, yet the omniscient Jehovah can see not only a vast difference, but an entire opposition. Do they who are instated in the covenant pray to God? So do many who have no saving interest in it (Isaiah 58:2). Are they just and honest, candid and faithful, temperate and discreet, blameless and harmless? So are many others besides them for anything to the contrary that man can perceive (Philippians 3:6). Thus far they seem to agree. But there is a great difference between them with regard to the Spirit by which they are respectively actuated, which occasions much contrariety in the manner of their obedience. Unbelievers are actuated by a slavish or servile spirit, suitably to their state of bondage under the covenant of works (Galatians 4:24, 25). A slavish fear of hell and a servile hope of heaven are the weights that are hung upon them by that covenant, causing them to go the external round of duties. Sins are avoided and duties are performed, not from love to God and His holy law, but from love to themselves and their own safety. Believers, on the contrary, are actuated by a free and ingenuous Spirit, the Spirit of adoption, suitably to their state of adoption under the covenant of grace (Romans 8:15; Galatians 4:26). God in Christ is their gra-

Evidences of Being Personally Instated

cious Father and they serve Him not as slaves but as sons (Malachi 3:17). The Holy Spirit dwells in them and has made them partakers of a new and a divine nature (2 Peter 1:4). The consequence is that sin is hated and avoided as contrary, and duty is loved and performed as agreeable to their new nature. Christ is their elder Brother who loved them and gave Himself for them, and His love constrains them (2 Corinthians 5:14). Their belief of the love of God in Christ to them has excited in them love to Him in return as a new principle of obedience (1 Timothy 1:5). By faith they trust in the Lord Jesus for all their salvation; and this undermines in them both the slavish fear of hell and the servile hope of heaven, so that these henceforth are so far from being their sole motives to obedience that they cannot even be their prevailing motives. Nay, they cannot at all remain in them but as the enemies of their faith, love, and hope (2 Timothy 1:7; 1 John 4:18).

At the same time it ought to be remembered that it is not slavish in true believers to dread the fatherly anger of God, and thereby to be roused to their duty (Psalm 119:120; Hebrews 11:7); nor servile to persevere in performing their duty in hope of attaining more communion with Him in time (John 14:21) and the perfect enjoyment of Him in eternity, all on the sole ground of the righteousness of Christ imputed to them (1 Corinthians 15:58). Their need of these for incitements to obedience indeed argues their childish state while in this world (for there will be no need of such motives as these in heaven), but by no means a slavish state. Nor is it at all slavish in the saints to have their heart filled with a reverential dread of the infinite Jehovah when they consider the awful effects of His tremendous justice and fury upon the miserable objects of them in the place of torment, and thereby to be stirred up to obedience (Hebrews 12:28, 29). To consider what these have to endure for sin, and with fear and trembling to move away toward God in the path of duty, is entirely agreeable to the state of those who have by faith received a kingdom that cannot be moved, but are not yet exalted to the full possession of it in heaven; who are, indeed, drawn up out of the horrible abyss, but are not yet hauled up to the top of the rock, though the strong chain of the covenant is so fast about them that it will be impossible for them ever to fall down again. Nay, even in heaven, the redeemed will, on the same account, be filled with reverential fear of Jehovah, and that in a perfect degree (Isaiah 6:1-3). But it is slavish in saints to fear that they will be suffered to fall into hell for their sins, and servile to hope that they will be exalted in heaven for their duties. There is a great difference between a believer's avoiding evil from the fear of hell and his avoiding it from the fear of God, who is able to destroy both soul and body in hell. The former is a slavish dread of hell, urging the believer to cease from sin in order that he may not be damned; the latter is a reverential fear of God, disposing him to cease from sin in order that God may not be displeased nor dishonored.

Second, men may know if the Spirit of the covenant dwells in them by His being a Spirit of supplications in them. "I will," said Jehovah, "pour upon the house of David, and upon the inhabitants of Jerusalem, the Spirit of grace and of supplications" (Zechariah 12:10). The supplications here mentioned are, as the original word properly signifies, supplications for grace, or humble and acceptable prayers against the evil of sin and of misery, and for the good of the covenant of grace. Jehovah has freely promised all the good things of the covenant to His people, and has determined for the righteousness' sake of His beloved Son freely to bestow them upon them. But He has also resolved that they shall offer up humble supplications for them. His promises of them to His covenant-people are absolute prom-

Evidences of Being Personally Instated 439

ises, promises that He is resolved freely to perform to them; and yet He purposed that the benefits thus promised shall be given them as the answer of humble prayers as well as the performance of free promises. And therefore, after He had been graciously promising to His ancient people the spiritual and temporal blessings of His covenant He said, "I will yet for this be enquired of by the house of Israel to do it for them" (Ezekiel 36:37). Although He knows already all the wants of His dear children, yet He has resolved to hear of them from themselves. That, therefore, which is the matter of Jehovah's promises, must also be the matter of their supplications. By their praying for blessings promised they glorify the Giver, express their high estimation of the gifts, and acknowledge their entire dependence and put honor upon prayer as an ordinance of God. Messiah Himself must ask, and then the Father will give Him the heathen for His inheritance (Psalm 2:8); much more must they ask that they may receive.

Hence it is that the Spirit of Christ dwells as a Spirit of supplications in all the people of the covenant. He graciously instructs, inclines, and enables them, in faith and with humility, to plead in the name of Christ for the performance of the promises to them. While He is in them also as a Spirit of adoption, He enables them to cry, "Abba, Father," and acceptably to supplicate from the grace of the covenant. In consequence of this they are habitually disposed to pray, they love to pray, and they cannot but pray. As soon might one be able to live without breathing as a man, interested in the covenant of grace and under the influences of the Spirit of grace, live without praying. As one in good health and in free air does not think it a burden or a wearisome task to breathe, so a man spiritually alive and under the influence of the Spirit of supplications does not count it a burden or a weariness to pray. On the contrary, He is under a happy necessity to pour out His heart in prayer; so that it would be almost as intolerable to him to be forced to cease for a season to pray as to be forced to cease for a while to breathe.

Third, once more, men may know if the Spirit of the covenant dwells in them by His being a Spirit of sympathy in them. Persons who are in the same covenant have a common interest together, and thence a mutual sympathy or fellow-feeling with one another, regulated by the covenant that connects them together. The sympathy that the Spirit works in the confederates of heaven respects both the Head and the people of the covenant.

They have a kindly and a tender sympathy with the God and with the Head of the covenant. The essential glory of God, it is true, can never be diminished. His eternal rest in Himself can never be in the least disturbed by anything that men or angels can do or suffer; and the human nature of Christ, the Head of the covenant, is now set forever, infinitely beyond the reach of suffering. Nevertheless, His manifested glory in this world sometimes shines brightly, and at other times is under a cloud. Now, as in all their concerns, their distresses and enlargements, their griefs and joys (Isaiah 63:9; Luke 15:5), He has a sympathy with them so inexpressibly tender that he who touches them touches the apple of His eye (Zechariah 2:8), so they have a tender sympathy with Him in the great concerns of His glory, and of the glory of God in Him. They rejoice in the advancement of His kingdom (Acts 11:23); they pray for it continually (Psalm 72:15); and they habitually endeavor, in their several stations, to promote the same. They are touched with a feeling of the indignities offered to His glorious Majesty as offered to themselves (Psalm 69:9). They are mourners for the sins of others as well as for their own because of the dishonor thereby done to God and to His holy law (Psalm 119:136). They are neither opposers of

Evidences of Being Personally Instated 441

the extension of Christ's spiritual kingdom in the world, nor are they indifferent concerning it; but, according to their respective stations in society, they readily set their shoulder to the work of the Lord to help it forward. And, indeed, without some measure of such a public spirit as this, no man will be able to evidence his having the Spirit of Christ as a proof of personal interest in the new covenant (Matthew 12:30).

They have likewise a kindly sympathy with the people of the covenant. The Spirit of Christ disposes all in whom He dwells to be kind and useful to men in general, but in a peculiar manner to holy men; to do good unto all men, especially unto them who are of the household of faith (Galatians 6:10). The common bond of the covenant engages them peculiarly to love one another as, in that bond, they are not only the confederates of heaven, but the common objects of the hatred of worldly men. They bear the image of the heavenly Adam, their common Head; and that divine image, when discerned, endears all who bear it to a man who is himself within the bond of the covenant. His love therefore is love to *all* the saints (Ephesians 1:15). Hence arises that kindly sympathy that every holy man feels with all other saints, so far as they are known to him. Their joint interest in the covenant requires it for by that holy covenant the most intimate and endearing relation subsists between them. They are members one of another (Ephesians 4:25); and from their union, under the same federal Head, arises their communion, and consequently their fellow-feeling, one with another (1 Corinthians 12: 12, 26). A spirit of selfishness, therefore, that renders a man attentive only to his own private concerns and leaves him no concern for, no sympathy with, the church of Christ is an evidence that he is yet an unregenerate man. Whereas a spirit of mutual sensibility, disposing a man to feel with the people of God, or to feel, in consequence of what he knows they are feeling, is a good evidence that he is instated in the covenant of grace.

Now permit me, reader, to ask you, do you have the Holy Spirit of the covenant dwelling and working in your soul? Does He dwell in your heart as a free, as an ingenuous Spirit? Does He dispose you to be holy in all manner of conversation, and that from free choice; to perform every duty from love to God and His holy law; and to be voluntary and affectionate in your obedience? Do you habitually obey, not so much because you must as because you choose, and because you love and long after perfection of holiness? Are you more afraid of sinning against the Lord than merely of suffering for sin? Does the Spirit incline and enable you in any measure to pray in the name of Jesus Christ for all the blessings of the covenant; to plead in faith and with humility for the performance of all the promises of it to your soul? Are you habitually disposed to pray, especially in secret, and that with holy reverence and humble confidence? Do you choose to be frequent and fervent in prayer; and do you sincerely lament the wandering of your thoughts and the carnality of your heart in it? Moreover, do you have in any degree a kind sympathy with Jesus Christ the Head, and with fellow-saints, the people of the covenant? Are you habitually displeased and grieved when you see your dear Savior dishonored; and are you pleased and comforted when, either by yourself or by others He is honored, and the interests of His kingdom promoted? Are you also inclined tenderly to feel with His saints, to rejoice with those of them who rejoice and to weep with those of them who weep? If so, you have the Spirit of the covenant in you as an evidence that you yourself are within the bond of that holy covenant.

8. They have the law of the covenant written in their heart. "I," said Jehovah, "will put My law in their inward parts and

Evidences of Being Personally Instated

write it in their hearts" (Jeremiah 31:33). The law of the covenant is the moral law as a rule of righteousness in the hand of the great Mediator to all the people of the covenant. This law is, in all the parts of it, a fair transcript of the divine nature. It is, in regeneration, transcribed into the heart of everyone who takes hold of the covenant and the whole of it is written there—though every part is not written equally, nor any part perfectly clear. In proportion as the moral image of God is restored in believers, His moral law is written on their heart. Sanctification in them is already perfect in all its parts; and therefore the law in all its parts is inscribed, and that in every part or faculty of the soul, though in no part in a perfect degree. But how may person know if that holy law is written in their heart? I answer:

In the first place, no sooner is the law inscribed in the heart of any than they begin heartily to approve every precept of it so far as it is known to them. "I esteem," says the psalmist, "all Thy precepts concerning all things to be right" (Psalm 119:128). They love God, and therefore love the law as expressing the image of His holiness; and seeing there is nothing in the law but what is a transcript of His spotless holiness, they love the whole law. They are well pleased with the spirituality, the great extent, and the perfection of it. As the Head of the covenant is, in their view, altogether lovely (Song of Songs 5:16), so is the law of the covenant, which is a fair transcript of His moral image. Unbelievers do not love the holiness of Jehovah, and therefore they do not love the purity of His law (Romans 8:7); but believers, on the contrary, loving a holy God in Christ, and that because He is holy, love also His law because therein the image of His immaculate holiness and essential rectitude is expressed. They do not love it the less that it requires perfect and perpetual obedience, and that it forbids the least sinful thought or desire. On the contrary, they are cordially pleased with it for this very reason, that it is so pure, so strict, so perfect, as to forbid the least irregularity of affection or motion of sin in the soul. That holy law, they are sensible, condemns many things in them, yea, everything so far as it is not perfectly right; but so do they themselves, consenting unto the law that it is good (Romans 7:16). It condemns every sin, every lust, even the most darling idol of the depraved heart; and it is for that reason that the unrenewed soul abhors it and secretly wishes that it were forever abolished. But no sooner is the law inscribed on the heart than the man begins heartily to approve it and to condemn his own depraved inclinations and affections as contrary to its righteous precepts. "The law," says Paul, "is holy, and the commandment holy, and just, and good . . . but I am carnal" (Romans 7:12, 14).

Second, no sooner is the law inscribed in their heart than they begin to have a propensity or inclination of heart toward it, so far as they spiritually understand it. "Oh, that my ways," says holy David, "were directed to keep Thy statutes" (Psalm 119:5). The new creature that in regeneration is formed in elect sinners is, in order to show the extent of it, called the new man (Colossians 3:10). It is not a new eye, or a new ear, or a new tongue, or a new hand merely, but a new man. A fixed principle is, by the Spirit, implanted in their heart, which lies the same way as the holy law; bending away from everything that the law forbids and toward everything that it enjoins. It is true, a contrary principle still remains in them that wars against the new creature; but so do they against that contrary principle, earnestly desirous of complete victory over it and of perfect conformity to the holy law (Galatians 5:17). In regeneration, their heart receives a new bent that inclines it to exert itself not in lazy wishes for perfect conformity to the law, but in resolute, active, and persevering efforts to attain that conformity.

Third, no sooner is that the case than they begin to be habitually conformable in their practice to the whole law. The holy psalmist says, "Then shall I not be ashamed, when I have respect unto all Thy commandments" (Psalm 119:6). If the law is written in a man's heart, it will be legible in his external behavior. Sanctification in the heart will certainly issue in holiness in the life. "If thine eye be single," says our blessed Lord, "thy whole body shall be full of light" (Matthew 6:22); and the Apostle Paul said, "We are His workmanship, created in Christ Jesus unto good works, which God hath before ordained that we should walk in them" (Ephesians 2:10). What would the holy covenant avail if persons might be within the bond of it, and yet live like them who are without? Nay, but to whomever the grace of God that brings salvation has effectually appeared, it has taught them to deny ungodliness, and worldly lusts, and to live soberly, righteously, and godly in this present world (Titus 2:11, 12). If then the grace of the covenant does not teach some men to live soberly, but on the contrary leaves them enslaved to carnal affections or sensual appetites, they have no saving part in that holy covenant. If they are brought only to the duties that they owe to themselves, and yet not to those that they owe to their neighbor; if they still so neglect the duties of righteousness toward their neighbor as to dare, even in the smallest matters, to deal unjustly with him, instead of being within the bond of the covenant they are yet in the gall of bitterness and in the bond of iniquity (Acts 8:23; see also Luke 16:11). If they are brought forward to both of these and yet are not godly, are not conscientious in performing the duties of piety that they owe to God, they are still strangers to His holy covenant. Whereas they who have cordially trusted on Christ and His righteousness for all the salvation of the covenant, and have at the same time been honestly endeavoring in the faith of the promise to be more and more conformable in their practice to the whole law, although in everything they come short of the perfection required by it, thereby show that they are instated in the covenant, and ought to take the comfort of it (2 Corinthians 1:12). To have a cordial respect to all the divine commandments and a habitual purpose, as well as endeavor, in thought, word, and deed, to glorify God, is a good evidence that one is within the bond of that covenant in which the glory of His grace shines with transcendent luster. Indeed, to be a sincere lover of the whole glory of redeeming grace, of the whole doctrine of grace, and of the whole duty by which that doctrine is adorned, is a decisive mark of a personal interest in the covenant of grace.

Fourth, once more, the law of the covenant is no sooner written in their heart than their heart lies open to all that of it which they do not yet know. They are heartily willing to know all the precepts of the law, and that in all their spirituality, extent, and perfection. They sincerely desire to be taught them in order that by the grace of the covenant they may acceptably conform to them. "Give me understanding," says the psalmist, "and I shall keep Thy law." And again, "Teach me Thy statutes" (Psalm 119:34, 68). Many of the sins of true believers are hidden from them because much of the law of the covenant is yet unknown to them. Hypocrites are willingly ignorant of many things in the holy law because they have no inclination nor intention to comply with them; they do not desire to know the whole law. But sincere converts, desiring to forsake every wicked way, and to take upon them the whole yoke of Christ, abhorring all iniquity as contrary to the holy nature and will of God, and loving universal holiness as agreeable thereto do of course earnestly desire further discoveries of the sin forbidden and of the duty required in that righteous law. "He that doeth truth cometh to the light" (John 3:21); and thus he is disposed to

Evidences of Being Personally Instated

pray, "Search me, O God . . . see if there be any wicked way in me, and lead me in the way everlasting" (Psalm 139:23, 24).

Now can you, reader, say in truth that the law of the covenant is inscribed on your heart? Do you cordially approve that holy law? Are you well pleased with every precept of it? Because it is so spiritual, so extensive, so perfect, so holy, so just, so good, do you delight in it after the inward man? Are you well pleased with it because it commands the utmost perfection of every duty and forbids the least degree of every sin? Have you an inclination of heart toward the whole law, so far as you understand it? Does your heart habitually bend away from everything that the law forbids and bend toward everything that it requires? Are you habitually endeavoring through grace to be in your practice or in your thoughts, words, and actions, conformable to the whole law, and that, chiefly for the glory of God in Christ? If so, the law of the covenant is written in your heart; and this is solid evidence that you are instated in that holy covenant.

9. Moreover they dedicate or resign all that they are, and all that they have, to the service and glory of God in Christ according to the covenant. While they cordially take what the triune God is and has to themselves, they cheerfully give up what they are and have to Him. While they receive all without exception that God in Christ is and has for their portion, they give up without reserve all that by His grace they are and have for His glory. Jehovah, according to His covenant, says to them, "I am and will be your God." And they, in holy self-dedication, say to Him, "We are and will be Thy people" (Psalm 119:94, 125). The formalist receives only a part of the salvation offered in the gospel, and gives up himself only in part to God. He is a double-minded man. His heart is divided. He chooses only to receive a part and to give a part; and he resolves to give merely in order to receive. But the true Christian accepts all and returns all. He, in

some measure, receives all of Christ, all of God in Christ, and all of salvation purchased by Christ; and then he gives all back again to Christ in the exercise of spiritual graces and the performance of commanded duties. And he does not give in order to receive, but, on the contrary receives in order to give. He accepts as a free gift all the good things of the covenant; and then he devotes as a free well offering to his covenant-God all the good things that, by the grace of Christ, he has, either in his heart or in his hand. He receives Christ and God in Christ only, wholly, and forever; and thereupon he gives up himself to God as his God in covenant only, wholly, and forever (Isaiah 44:5; Psalm 116:12, 16, 17, 18). He devotes all that he is and all that he has to God, not in order that God may become his God, but because he trusts that He has already become his God. He first takes and then gives in return. Now if this is the exercise of you who read, it is an additional mark that you are within the covenant; that God in Christ is your God, and that you are one of His people.

10. Finally, they do not, strictly speaking, desire duty for comfort but, on the contrary, comfort for duty. They regard spiritual comfort properly, for the sake of the duty that they have to perform; and not duty for the sake of the comfort that they hope to enjoy. Hypocrites, as they build their comfort upon their own performances, and love duties chiefly for the comfort and the felicity that they hope thereby to procure for themselves, perform their duties not for God, but for themselves; not for the glory of God as their ultimate end, but merely for their own peace and comfort. They work from themselves as their first principle, and for themselves as their last end. They esteem the performance of duties rather for the comfort that ensues upon it than for the glory of God that is promoted by it. Whereas true believers, founding their title to spiritual comfort

Evidences of Being Personally Instated

upon the righteousness of Jesus Christ offered to them in the gospel, and not upon their own performances, desire comfort in order to duty, and duty in order thereby to glorify God who loved them and gave His only begotten Son to redeem them. They are commanded in the law, and constrained by the love revealed in the gospel, to be of good comfort (2 Corinthians 13:11), and to serve the Lord with gladness (Psalm 100:2). They, therefore, trust and pray for spiritual consolation not so much that they themselves may enjoy the sweetness of it, as that they may thereby be the more inclined and strengthened acceptably to perform every duty to the glory of their God and Savior. Although they desire spiritual comfort for itself as a part of that eternal life purchased for them and promised to them in the covenant, yet they desire it rather that by it they may serve Him cheerfully, and so by recommending religion to all around them may glorify Him as the God of all consolation. In a word, they desire to have their heart comforted that they may rejoice and work righteousness (Isaiah 64:5). They hope to have it enlarged that they may run the way of God's commandments (Psalm 119:32).

Now is it chiefly for such a purpose as this that you, reader, desire consolation of spirit? Do you trust and pray for sensible communion with God in Christ as your God chiefly that you may become more holy, and that the glory of your God and Savior may be the more illustriously displayed by your cheerful obedience? If it is thus with you it is a good evidence that you are personally interested in that august covenant in which the glory of Jehovah, as the God of all comfort, shines with transcendent luster.

Before I conclude this chapter, it may be useful briefly to remark that the Apostle Paul suggests a method of a man's attaining the knowledge of his personal interest in the covenant of grace that is as sure as it is simple. In 1 Timothy 1:5 he says, "Now, the end of the commandment is charity, out of a pure heart, and of a good conscience, and of faith unfeigned." Here the apostle teaches that the obedience of the law must flow from love, and love from a pure heart, and a pure heart from a good conscience, and a good conscience from faith unfeigned. This he makes the only right channel of good works (practical use of saving knowledge is the third requisite to evidence true faith). Here is a clue, which under the witnessing of the Holy Spirit, may serve to lead a man who believes in Christ to some degree of assurance that he is in a state of grace. If he examines himself according to this infallible rule of direction he cannot safely consider his obedience to the law as a mark of his being in a state of grace until he traces it up to his faith embracing Christ. Once he becomes conscious that, with regard to the matter of external duty, he attempts obedience to every commandment of the law as his rule of life, he is to proceed to inquire if this obedience of his flows from love—supreme love to God in Christ and love to his neighbor. If he finds that it does, he is next to inquire if his love is sincere or, in other words, if it proceeds from a pure, a holy heart; a heart abhorring all that is evil, and cleaving to all that is good, so far as the one and the other are known to him. If he finds that it does, he is further to inquire if this pure heart arises from a good, that is, from a pure and a pacified conscience; a conscience purified by the grace of God and purged from dead works by the blood of Christ; or, in other words, if his holiness of heart or his longing after perfect holiness, issue from an apprehension in his conscience of the pardon of his sins. If he finds that it does, he is still further to examine if his good conscience flows from faith; that is, from a belief of the record with application to himself, and a confidence in Christ for complete salvation to himself. If he is con-

Evidences of Being Personally Instated

scious that it does, he is, last, to make inquiry if his faith is unfeigned; that is, is not hypocritical, but sincere; or, if he cordially believes the record, and cordially trusts on Christ and His righteousness alone for all the salvation promised in the covenant. If under the witnessing of the Spirit he finds that his faith is sincere, he may warrantably conclude that his obedience to the law is genuine, and that it is a true and decisive mark of his personal interest in the covenant. Or thus: if he finds out that his faith has made him a good conscience; and his good conscience, a pure heart; and his pure heart produced love; and his love, sincere obedience to the holy commandment—in that case his sincere obedience is a true evidence of the reality and sincerity of his faith;, whence he ought to conclude that he is united to Christ and instated in the covenant.

Let us suppose now that two men conduct, according to this method, a trial of their state before the Lord; and that they pitch upon their external performances, as to the matter of them, though as yet they do not know whether those performances are sincere or counterfeit. The one finds that his external duties have not proceeded from love to God and to his neighbor; or, if they have, that yet this love has not arisen from a pure heart; or, if it has, that yet this pure heart has not proceeded from a good conscience; or, if it has proceeded from it, that yet this good conscience, such as it is, has not arisen from unfeigned faith. In all or any of these cases, it is evident that the external performances that he pitched upon can be no true marks from which he may warrantably conclude that he is in a state of grace. The other, on the contrary, finds that his external performances have flowed from love to God in Christ and to his neighbor; and that his love has flowed from a pure heart; and his pure heart from a good conscience; and his good conscience from faith unfeigned; from faith embracing and cordially trusting in Christ Jesus alone for all His salvation. Thus, under the witnessing of the Holy Spirit, he is assured that his faith is unfeigned, and that he himself is personally instated in the eternal covenant.

And now, my dear reader, have you any of those evidences of vital union with Christ and of personal interest in the everlasting covenant that have been explained? If, by the witnessing of the Holy Spirit, you are satisfied that you have all or even but some of them, you may warrantably conclude that you are instated in the covenant of grace, that you now stand on new covenant-ground, and have a covenant-right to all the sure mercies of David, to all the blessings of grace, and all the riches of glory. Jehovah has made with you an everlasting covenant, ordered in all things and sure; an everlasting covenant that He will not turn away from you to do you good, and that He will put His fear in your heart so that you shall not depart from Him. What a well-ordered covenant is this! How inestimable are your privileges, now that you are instated in it! How inviolable is your security, that you shall be kept from falling and never perish, but have everlasting life! The God and Father of our Lord Jesus Christ is your God forever and ever. He will be your guide even unto death. United to Christ as your Covenant-head you are a joint heir with Him, of God as your covenant-God, and of eternal life, as your sure, your unfading inheritance. Having taken hold of Jehovah's eternal covenant, you have begun to lay hold on eternal life; for this is the promise that He has promised you, even eternal life; and He is faithful who has promised.

But if you have none of those evidences, you are not within the bond of the covenant of grace; and if you are not instated in that gracious covenant, you are still under the broken covenant of works. You lie under an obligation to present perfect obedience to the law of this covenant on pain of death in all its direful extent; and you are, at the same time, under a firm obligation to suffer the full execution of its tremendous penalty for having already transgressed it. Ah! You, as a breaker of this covenant in the first Adam, and, times without number, in your own person, are at this moment under the dreadful curse of it, the execution of which divine justice cannot but ensure: for it is written, "Cursed is every one that continueth not in all things which are written in the book of the law to do them." You are under the dominion of the law of works, and therefore are not only under the guilt of all our sins, but under the dominion of sin; for the strength of sin is the law. The condemning sentence of the violated law chains you down under the strength of sin as a part of spiritual death, and bars out all gracious, all sanctifying, influence from your sinful soul. Deplorable, dreadful condition! You are a sinner against the infinite Majesty of heaven, an undone, a lost, an unbelieving sinner. You are therefore condemned already, and the wrath of God abides on you. It may be you do not believe this; but that does not render it the less certain, nor your condition the less miserable. How can you do anything either to pacify or to please God while you continue under His almighty frown, His overwhelming curse? Continuing under the broken covenant of works, and consequently under the dominion of unbelief, you have no saving faith; and without faith it is impossible to please Him. How then can your works please Him or recommend you to His favor? Whatsoever is not of faith is sin. But how can that which is sin, and which deserves eternal death, entitle you at the same time to eternal life, or even to the smallest favor from the hand of God? Be assured that by the deeds of the law no flesh shall be justified in His sight; for by the law is the knowledge of sin. O sinner, be convinced that your innumerable transgressions have exposed you to eternal death, and that you have no righteousness either to secure you from eternal death or to entitle you to eternal life.

The soul that sins shall die, and the unrighteous shall not inherit the kingdom of God. Besides, under the covenant of works, it will be impossible for you to be holy, and without holiness no man shall see the Lord. Ah, how sinful, how miserable are you! How inexpressibly dreadful is your condition! How imminent is your danger! How direful, how overwhelming your prospect! You are under the condemning sentence of the violated law in its federal form; and you know not but this very day or hour the tremendous sentence may begin to be eternally executed upon you; and then the smoke of your torment will ascend up forever and ever, and you shall have no rest day nor night.

Oh, then, my dear reader, flee from the wrath to come. Escape for your life that you may not be hurt by the second death. Do not remain an hour longer under the covenant of works. Come to the compassionate Savior, and by believing in Him enter the bond of the covenant of grace. Come as a sinner, an unworthy sinner to Him, and do not delay it till you see that you possess good qualifications to render you welcome. You cannot have so much as one commendable quality in you till you come to Him for it. Come as you are to Him; come with all your guiltiness, all your sinfulness, all your emptiness, all your unworthiness, and He will in nowise cast you out. Hear His own gracious invitation, "Let him that is athirst come; and whosoever will let him take the water of life freely." It is lawful and warrantable for sinners of mankind in common, and for you in particular, to believe in the Lord Jesus. The offers, invitations, and absolute promises of the gospel, together with the great commandment of the law to believe in His name, are all directed to you; and they form, for you in particular, a divine, an ample warrant, to trust in Christ for all His great salvation, and so to become united to Him and instated in His everlasting covenant.

Oh, be persuaded that you cannot otherwise escape from the covenant of works than by coming into the covenant of grace; and this you cannot do but by faith. Oh, believe then; only believe; and the moment you begin to believe in Christ the second Adam, the Head of righteousness and of life, you shall begin to have eternal life, to pass from death unto life. Trust in the Lord Jesus with all your heart, and that for all His salvation. Rely only on His consummate righteousness for a title to His whole salvation. Then you will be justified by faith. Then your faith will work by love, will purify your heart, will overcome the world; and these will be so many evidences to your mind that you are united to Christ and instated in the covenant of grace. They will, indeed, form no part of your warrant to renew your exercise of trusting in Him; but they will be so many fruits and evidences of your having already trusted in Him for His whole salvation. Consider that the Lord Jesus, with His righteousness and salvation, is wholly, freely, and particularly offered to you; and that faith, the only instrument of receiving them, is also freely promised, and offered to you. When you then at any time find that you cannot believe in Him, instead of allowing this to deter you from attempting the exercise of faith, apply, and trust, and plead these absolute promises: "Even to Him shall men come. In His name shall the Gentiles trust. I will also leave in the midst of thee an afflicted and poor people, and they shall trust in the name of the Lord."

Looking to the compassionate Savior Himself for the performance of them to your soul, attempt trusting cordially in Him and on His righteousness for His whole salvation; and according to your faith it will be unto you.

9

The Seals of the Covenant of Grace

It pleased Jehovah, in the riches of His unsearchable wisdom, and in the kindness of His redeeming love, to append seals to His covenant of grace. Those under the old dispensation of it were circumcision and the Passover; and those under the new are baptism and the Lord's Supper. The former were the ordinary seals of the covenant under the Old Testament or Jewish dispensation; the latter are the seals of it under the New Testament or Christian dispensation. While appended thereto they served, and still do serve in the hand of the Spirit of Christ, not only as signs to signify, but as seals to confirm the covenant with many (Daniel 9:27). It is only as signs and seals of the covenant that I propose in this chapter to consider those ordinances.

The uses of seals or signets in ancient times were various. They served, among other purposes, to ratify a commission (John 6:27), to denote consent or approbation (John 3:33), and especially to confirm a contract, a bond or deed. According to this last use of a seal, baptism and the Lord's Supper under the New Testament seal the eternal covenant to all who are within the bond of it; that is to say, by the blessing of Christ and the working of His Spirit they confirm that divine contract to them; they serve to attest, to settle, to ratify, or by new evidence, to put

The Seals of the Covenant of Grace

it past doubt to them. They confirm to believers the conditions of it, namely the righteousness of faith (Romans 4:11). They likewise confirm to them the promises, and consequently the blessings promised. By confirming both the conditions and the promises of the covenant they ratify or confirm the whole of the covenant; and by confirming, or making sure, or putting past doubt to them, the whole of the covenant as an object of faith those ordinances do, for that reason, confirm their faith in Him who is given for a covenant of the people. The more sure the object of their faith appears to be to believers, the firmer or stronger their faith in that object becomes (1 John 4:14). They also confirm the dedication of believers as His people to God in Christ, according to the covenant; and last they confirm their personal interest in the covenant. Thus they seal or confirm the covenant to all who are within it. Since in these ordinances there are sensible signs, or such visible confirmations of the covenant as strike the external senses, they are admirably adapted, in the hand of the Spirit of grace, to strengthen the faith and thereby the other graces of believers (Hebrews 6:17, 18). What we only hear concerning an object at a distance, if the report appears well founded, we indeed believe; but of what we see, handle, or taste we are still more assured.

As circumcision and the Passover sealed the covenant to all who, under the old dispensation, were within the bond of it, and as baptism and the Lord's Supper seal it to all who, under the new dispensation, are instated in it, so they sealed it to Christ the Head with whom it was made, as well as to believers the members of His body mystical. He as the Head and Representative of His elect was primarily within the covenant; and it is only in and under Him that they come to be personally within it. Those ordinances, accordingly, sealed the covenant of grace primarily to Christ Himself as Mediator and man, and secondarily to believers, considered as united to Him their Covenant-head. I shall therefore briefly consider them as seals of the covenant, first, to Christ Himself, and, second, to true believers in Him.

SECTION 1. The Sacraments as Seals of the Covenant of Grace to Christ

In the first place, I am briefly to consider these ordinances as seals of the covenant to Christ Himself. As the seals of the covenant of works sealed that covenant to the first Adam, so the sealing ordinances of the covenant of grace sealed that eternal covenant primarily, though not exclusively, to the second Adam. And although they could not so confirm His faith as to render it stronger than it was already, yet they appear to have been appointed means of supporting His faith as man and Mediator. For though His faith in the promises of the covenant made to Him was, during His state of humiliation, in the highest possible degree perfect, yet still it was the faith of a man, although not of a mere man; and therefore it was capable of being, by such means, supported and encouraged in its exercise (See Witsius' *Economy of the Covenants*, Book II, Chapter 10:8, 20). Besides, He received, in the sight of the church, those sacraments as seals of His own promise to the Father that He would, as the Surety of His elect, faithfully perform His part of the covenant. This will more clearly appear if we consider each of those ordinances separately.

1. The ordinance of circumcision was to Christ, as man and Mediator, a seal of the covenant of grace made with Him. We read that on the eighth day, He was circumcised, and that His name was called Jesus (Luke 2:21). His circumcision signified and sealed to Him, first, the promises that are recorded in Genesis 17:4-8; and especially that He was acknowledged by the Fa-

ther as the Head of that one people embodied with Him in the covenant, for whom He received the promises (Genesis 17:10 compared with Genesis 34:15, 16, 22), and as the seed of Abraham in whom all the nations of the earth were to be blessed. Second, it signified and sealed to Him that His being to be cut off out of the land of the living (Isaiah 53:8) should purchase for His whole mystical body eternal life; as the cutting off of the foreskin among the Israelites was a means of preserving the whole person from being cut off from that people (Genesis 17:14). Third, that from Him as their Covenant-head should be derived to His spiritual Israel, according to the covenant, the circumcision made without hands, consisting in putting off the body of the sins of the flesh (Colossians 2:11), which was to commence in regeneration to be promoted in sanctification, and to be perfected in glorification.

The circumcision of Christ was also a seal or confirmation of His promise to the Father that as the Surety of elect sinners He would, according to the covenant, fulfill the whole law. By that sign He proclaimed these gracious words, "Lo, I come . . . I delight to do Thy will, O My God; yea, Thy law is within My heart" (Psalm 40:7, 8). By the pain that He endured, and by the blood that, in His circumcision, He so early shed, He declared that He was ready to endure all the pains that would be requisite to satisfy the justice of Jehovah; and that, now being made flesh of their flesh and bone of their bone, He willingly offered Himself to be in due time cut off out of the land of the living for the salvation of His mystical body (Ephesians 5:33).

2. Baptism also was, to the man Christ Jesus, a seal of the covenant of grace. In the baptism of Christ, on the one hand, the Father openly declared, first, that He was His beloved Son in whose person and office He had the highest complacence. Second, as Mediator and man He would be so filled with the

Holy Spirit as not only to be, in the highest possible degree, qualified to fulfill all the righteousness of the law as the Surety of His people, but to supply, from His overflowing fullness, all their wants. This was signified and sealed to Him both by the water of baptism (Ezekiel 36:25, 27) and by the likeness of a dove, descending and lighting upon Him (Matthew 3:16). Third, as the baptized person came up from the water, so Jesus Christ should in due time emerge, by a joyful resurrection, from the deep waters of tribulation, anguish, and death (Psalm 40:3 and 110:7). Fourth, on the other hand, Christ thereby declared that, in fulfilling all righteousness, He was ready, in the faith and hope of emerging from them, to sink in the deepest floods of suffering and of death.

3. The ordinance of the Passover too was a seal of the covenant to Christ as man and Mediator. Thereby it was signified and sealed to Him, first, that He was acknowledged by the Father to be to Him a Lamb without blemish and without spot (1 Peter 1:19); and, second, that by His own blood He would certainly obtain for His people freedom from eternal destruction as the Israelites in Egypt were, by the blood of the paschal lamb, secured from the sword of the destroying angel. On the other hand, the blessed Jesus thereby professed that He was ready most willingly to undergo, for His elect seed, the bitterest sufferings foreshown by the bitter herbs of the Passover; that He was ready to be sacrificed, to be roasted, as it were, in the fire of divine wrath; and, as the Antitype of the paschal lamb which was wholly to be consumed, to give Himself wholly up to divine justice in their stead. In a word, as the manner of killing and roasting the paschal lamb exhibited a striking resemblance of death by crucifixion, Christ Jesus, by receiving the Passover, promised that, in the room of His people, He would continue obedient unto death, even the death of the cross.

The Seals of the Covenant of Grace

4. Last, the sacrament of the Supper was, to Christ Himself, a seal of the covenant of grace. I am well aware that in this part of my subject I stand on delicate ground. Many eminent divines differ in their opinions as to the fact whether our Lord partook Himself of this ordinance or not. I shall not trouble the reader with bringing forward the passages of Scripture that are adduced in support of both sides of the argument. Although I candidly confess that I am rather disposed to agree with those who are of opinion that He partook with His disciples of the ordinance of the Supper, which He Himself had just instituted, yet I am far from asserting that He actually did. But on the supposition that He did partake, the following things, by this holy Ordinance, were sealed to Him: First, that the perfection and efficacy of His meritorious righteousness as the Surety of His people should be celebrated by them until He would come again. Second, His broken body and shed blood would be most delicious food to the souls of His redeemed, and would nourish them up to everlasting life. Third, He Himself, together with His saints, would, in the holy place on high, sit down to a feast that would never end; and that through all eternity He would participate with them of the most exquisite delights. On the other hand, Christ thereby solemnly declared that His body would be broken and His blood be shed for the redemption of His elect seed.

Thus the Sacraments, both of the Old and of the New Testament, sealed the everlasting covenant primarily to the man Christ Himself as last Adam, the Covenant-head of a redeemed world.

SECTION 2. The Sacraments as Seals of the Covenant of Grace to Believers

It was proposed to consider these ordinances as seals of the covenant to believers united to Christ the second Adam, and under Him instated in that covenant. They were by divine appointment appended to the covenant of grace; and therefore they cannot be applied to any but such as are within that covenant. It is only they who are within the covenant by a true faith, that have a right to them before the Lord, and only they who are within it by a credible profession of that faith that have a right to them before the church. It is by these seals that Jehovah solemnly confirms the covenant with believers and, at the same time, their faith in the grace of that covenant By believing they come into the covenant; and by the sacraments Jehovah makes it firm, or solemnly declares it to be sure to them as one does a contract by subscribing and sealing the same. It is true indeed, those seals cannot render that everlasting covenant firmer in itself than it is already; but in the hands of the Spirit of truth they serve to confirm, or make it firmer, in the eye of faith; and thus they also serve to strengthen the faith and the other graces of believers, and to confirm their obligations to the obedience of faith, or to that new obedience which it becomes persons in covenant with God to perform. This will more evidently appear if we take particular view of each of them.

CIRCUMCISION. Circumcision was, to believers under the Old Testament, a sign of the covenant of grace. While it was a sign of the covenant (Genesis 17:11), it was also, to believers under the old dispensation, a seal, especially of the righteousness of faith (Romans 4:11). That it was a sign or token of the covenant with Abraham, it expressly declared in the institution of it (Genesis 17:9-14). But the covenant made with Abraham was in substance the same covenant of grace that is now made with and sealed to believers; for, as the Apostle Paul informs us, the circumcision of Abraham was a seal of that righteousness of faith that the Gentiles stand in need of as well as Jews, and for which only all who in every age believe are, in the sight of God, completely justified. Circumcision, then, was to Abraham, and to all true believers, under the Jewish economy, the initiating seal of the covenant of grace. While it signified in general the removal of their natural corruption by the blood and the Spirit of Messiah, in virtue of His resurrection on the eighth day, it sealed to them, first, that the blood of Messiah, that blessed Seed of Abraham, was to be shed for the expiation of their sins; and that His sufferings for that purpose were to begin even in His infancy. Second, after He had taken part of that flesh and blood of which they were partakers (Hebrews 2:14), He would, for the salvation of His mystical body, be cut off out of the land of the living (Isaiah 53:8), as in the circumcision of the flesh a part of the body was cut off in order that the whole man might not be cut off from His people. Third, He would give to them the circumcision of the heart, that is, the putting off the body of the sins of the flesh by that regeneration or sanctification of the Spirit which is perfected in glorification (Colossians 2:11, 12). The ancient Jewish Rabbis, accordingly, used to say that, "from the time in which a man becomes a proselyte of righteousness, he is like a new-born infant."

This initiating ordinance did, at the same time, seal to them their high obligations, first, to attain by the grace of Messiah true holiness in the inward man (Romans 2:28, 29); second, to mortify through the Spirit the members of the body of sin or to renounce all the lusts of the flesh and of the mind, however pleasant or profitable they might formerly appear to have been; third, to have no more friendship with this world that lies in wickedness, as Abraham, Isaac, and Jacob, with their posterity, were by circumcision set apart from the other inhabitants of the earth, and were despisers of their friendship (Genesis 34:14, 15; Acts 10:28); fourth, to submit cheerfully, at the command and for the glory of God, to everything in His service, however difficult or painful in itself, or however foolish or ridiculous in the view of worldly men, it might be.

PASSOVER. The ordinance of the Passover too was to believers under the Old Testament a sign and seal of the covenant of grace. In the hand of the Spirit of truth, it eminently served, first, to confirm their faith in the adorable Person of Messiah. The paschal lamb served not only to typify Messiah, the Lamb of God, but sacramentally to represent or signify Him to believers. It represented Him in His humility and meekness, in His simplicity and patience (John 1:29, 36; Matthew 11:29; Isaiah 53:7), and in His suitableness and usefulness, as supplying His people with spiritual food and clothing (Galatians 3:27). The paschal lamb was taken out of the flock, and therein represented Messiah who, in the human nature, was to be raised up from the midst of His brethren (Deuteronomy 18:15); and who, by taking part of flesh and blood, was in all things, sin only excepted, to be made like unto them (Hebrews 2:14, 17). As it was to be without blemish, and of the first year, it signified Christ, who was to be a lamb without spot and blemish, and who was, through the eternal Spirit, to offer Himself without spot to God (Hebrews 9:14).

Second, it was to confirm their faith in the sufferings of Messiah. The paschal lamb was to be killed by the whole congregation of Israel, which represented that Christ, the spotless Lamb of God, was to be slain at the desire of the whole multitude of the Jews (Luke 23:18). The blood of the lamb was shed for the people, which signified that the blood of Jesus Christ was to be shed for the remission of the sins of many. The former was not spilled upon the ground, but received into a basin, to signify that the latter was to be preserved as the precious and perpetual treasure of the church, and was to be eternally presented to the Father. The lamb of the Passover was roasted with fire to represent that Messiah was so to endure the fire of divine wrath due to us for sin as to utter this doleful complaint: "My heart is like wax, it is melted in the midst of my bowels. My strength is dried up like a potsherd; and my tongue cleaveth to my jaws" (Psalm 22:14, 15). And if, as Justin Martyr informs us in his dialogue with Trypho the Jew, the lamb, in order to be roasted, was put on a wooden spit, thrust through, from the lower or hinder part of it to its head, with its two forefeet stretched out on a cross split in the form a human body suspended on a cross; it prefigured in a lively manner Messiah the Lamb of God, tormented by the fire of divine wrath, when on the cross as our Passover sacrificed for us (1 Corinthians 5:7). In few words, the paschal lamb was killed on the fourteenth day of the month Abib, at the time of full moon, between the two evenings, that is, between the ninth and the eleventh hour, in order to foreshow that Christ the Lamb of God was, in the same month, day, and hour of the day, to be slain as a sacrifice for the sins of all who would believe in Him (Matthew 27:46, 50).

Third, it served to confirm their faith in the infinite sufficiency of the sacrifice of Christ to take away sin. The paschal lamb was to be a male of the first year to represent that Messiah was to offer Himself a sacrifice, not in His infancy, but in the prime of His life, and that His sacrifice of Himself was to be a complete atonement for their sins. It was to be killed instead of them and their first-born in order to represent that as certainly as the death of it was to be the life of their first-born, so was the death of Messiah to be the life of them who trusted in Him, and so were heirs together with Him of the grace of life. In the night in which it was killed and eaten the Israelites were delivered from their Egyptian bondage, which represented to believers among them that Christ was by His blood so to redeem them from their bondage to sin, Satan, and the world (Hebrews 2:14,

15) as to secure for them the glorious liberty of the children of God.

Fourth, it was to confirm their faith in this momentous doctrine that their salvation from eternal death was owing to the blood of sprinkling. Before they ate in Egypt the flesh of the lamb, they were to sprinkle with a bunch of hyssop the blood of it upon the lintels and two side-posts of their doors in order to distinguish their houses from those of the Egyptians, and thus to secure their first-born from the sword of the destroying angel. This represented to them that the blood of the Lamb of God applied to or sprinkled upon their consciences by faith would protect them from the curse of the law and the sword of avenging justice, and that under the covert of that blood they would be preserved from the sting and often from the stroke of divine judgments. In a word, it signified and sealed to them that the sword of divine justice would spare all of them whose consciences were sprinkled with the blood of Christ (Isaiah 52:15).

Fifth, it also served to confirm their belief of the necessity not only of having their consciences sprinkled with the blood of Messiah, but of their feeding spiritually upon Him. In order to the safety of their first-born, it was not enough that they sprinkled the lintels and side-posts of their doors with the blood of the lamb; they must also eat of its flesh. They must eat the whole of it. They must eat it with unleavened bread and bitter herbs, and must eat it presently. Now all this was to confirm their belief that in order to their eternal salvation it was not enough to have their hearts sprinkled from an evil conscience; they must also feed for their spiritual nourishment on the flesh of the Lamb of God (John 6:53); that it was not enough merely to sprinkle their hearts by applying to them in the exercise of faith the blood or righteousness of Messiah; they must likewise apply Messiah Himself, with all His promises of grace and glory for the nourishment of spiritual life in their souls; and that they must trust in Him for the whole of His salvation; must trust presently in Him and exercise evangelical repentance as well as faith.

Sixth, and last, it served to confirm their belief that there is no communion with Messiah but in His church, and in the observance of the ordinances of divine appointment. The flesh of a lamb was to be eaten in one house only; and it was unlawful for any to stir out of their houses in Egypt until the morning. If any Israelite during that night presumed to go out at the door of his house, he, that moment, went from under the protection of the blood that had been sprinkled, and so exposed himself to the sword of the destroying angel. Now this represented to them that as it was in the church only that they could be under the protection of the blood of sprinkling and have spiritual communion with Christ and with one another in the ordinances of divine appointment; so out of the church they could have no ground to expect fellowship with Him in His great salvation (Hebrews 6:4-6 and 10:39).

The ordinance of the Passover, in the hand of the Holy Spirit, confirmed not only the faith of believers under the old dispensation of the covenant but, at the same time, their obligations to holiness of heart and of life. For...

In the first place, it was the means of confirming their obligations to make an open profession of their faith and of their obedience to Messiah. The blood of the paschal lamb was to be sprinkled upon the lintels and side-posts of their doors in Egypt in order to show them that they should make an open and avowed profession of their faith in the blood of sprinkling, and of that holy obedience which is the obedience of faith. It signified to them that they should never be ashamed to own their dependence upon Messiah and their resolution to love and obey Him.

Second, it confirmed their obligations to continue in their holy profession, and never, by apostasy from it, to count the blood of the covenant an unholy thing. The blood of the lamb, although sprinkled on the lintels and side-posts, was not to be sprinkled on the thresholds of their doors, to be trampled on. This represented to them their firm obligations never to trample underfoot the Son of God, nor count the blood of the covenant, wherewith He was sanctified, an unholy thing (Hebrews 10:29). This blood is inestimably precious, and was to be precious in their sight as well as in ours.

Third, it served to confirm their obligations daily to feed upon Christ and upon the whole of Christ. The paschal lamb was killed, not to be looked on merely, but to be fed or feasted upon. The Israelites were enjoined to feed upon it and to let nothing of it remain until the morning. The whole flesh of it was to be eaten by them. This signified and sealed their obligations to feed upon Christ their Passover, who was thereby typically sacrificed for them; to meditate upon, and by faith to apply the whole of Christ to themselves, and so to feed and even feast upon Him for their spiritual nourishment and growth in grace.

Fourth, it likewise confirmed their obligations to abound in the exercise of godly sorrow for sin. The flesh of the lamb was to be eaten with bitter herbs, and that not only in remembrance of the bitterness of their servitude in Egypt, but also in token of the obligations under which they lay to exercise, in the faith of pardon, through the atoning blood of the Lamb of God, bitter contrition of heart for their sin. This would give them a true relish for the paschal lamb. Christ the Lamb of God also would be sweet to their taste in proportion as sin was bitter. Besides, their eating of bitter herbs, with the flesh of the lamb, confirmed their obligation willingly to endure the bitterest sufferings for the sake of Christ (Philippians 3:10).

Fifth, it was the means of confirming their obligations to purge out the leaven of sin that remained in them. During the seven days of unleavened bread they were to have no leaven in their houses. Leaven is, in the Scripture, a symbol of the corruption of human nature, and especially of hypocrisy, pride, and contention. Their putting away of the leaven, therefore, out of their houses on that occasion represented to them their firm obligations to purge out of their heart and life the old leaven of corruption in general, and especially the leaven of hypocrisy, pride, and contention that renders persons very unfit for communion with Christ in His ordinances (1 Corinthians 5:7, 8).

Sixth, and finally, it sealed or confirmed their obligations to rejoice in Christ Jesus (Philippians 3:3). Having eaten the Passover, they were immediately after to keep the feast of unleavened bread and to keep it seven days; on the first and last of which there was to be a holy convocation and no servile work to be done. The feast of unleavened bread was typical of the Christian life (1 Corinthians 5:8), which ought to be always a life of rejoicing in God through our Lord Jesus Christ, after having received the atonement (Romans 5:11). Their keeping then by divine appointment the feast of unleavened bread immediately after the Passover confirmed or strengthened their obligations continually to delight themselves in Messiah, and in His infinite atonement, and never to admit any earthly care, prejudicial to or inconsistent with that holy joy. If true believers, even under that darker dispensation, had not after the Passover a continual fast it was their own fault.

Thus the ordinance of the Passover was to believers under the former dispensation a sign and seal of the covenant of grace. It served, in the hand of the Spirit of Christ, to confirm their faith in the promises and blessings of that eternal covenant. And though they could not steadfastly look to the end of the comparatively obscure dispensation under which they lived (2 Corinthians 3:13), yet that ordinance served in a high degree to make the covenant appear firm and sure in the eye of their faith, and so to confirm their faith in the promises and provisions of it. It likewise confirmed their obligations to perform all the duties of the covenant. It showed them, and that in a striking point of view, how firm those obligations were.

BAPTISM. The ordinance of baptism under the present dispensation is to believers a sign and seal of the same covenant of grace. It is the initiating seal of that covenant, instituted in the room of circumcision (Acts 2:38, 39); Colossians 2:11, 12). It was in the ministry of John the Baptist that it began to be a seal of the covenant. His baptism included the substance of all that baptism afterwards, as administered by the apostles of Christ, comprehended, though it did not so clearly exhibit the Trinity of Persons in the eternal Godhead, or the actual incarnation of the eternal Son. Nor is there the least evidence that any who had been baptized by John were ever baptized again by the disciples of Jesus. Our blessed Lord Himself, and perhaps most of His apostles, had no other external baptism than that of John.

Baptism, having been instituted by the Lord Jesus, the glorious King and Head of His church, to be a sign and seal of His gracious covenant, accordingly signifies and seals to believers, first, their engraftment into Christ Himself, the true Vine, by spiritual and vital union with Him and, consequently, the imputation of His righteousness to them, according to the covenant. It serves, in the hand of the Spirit, to seal to them their engraftment into Christ by spiritual union with Him (John 15:5). In Romans 6:3, 5, the Apostle Paul informs us that believers are baptized *into* Christ, and that they who are so baptized, are planted together, or jointly engrafted into Him, as a young shoot is into a stock, in order to a participation of such virtue from Him as will make them conformable to His death by separating between their souls and sin. It likewise seals to them the gift and the imputation of His righteousness to them for their justification. For, says the same apostle, "As many of you as have been baptized into Christ have put on Christ" (Galatians 3:27). Baptism, as circumcision was, is a seal of the righteousness of the faith (Romans 4:11), and is to true believers a seal of its being imputed to them. Thus it is a means employed by the Holy Spirit to confirm the faith of their union with Christ the second Adam, and also of their communion with Him in His blood and righteousness.

Second, it signifies and seals to believers their partaking, through the blood and the Spirit of Christ, of the benefits of the covenant of grace—particularly of justification, adoption, regeneration, and of a resurrection to life eternal. The water in baptism, when set apart for that sacred purpose, signifies the blood and the Spirit of Jesus Christ. The sprinkling of that water upon the body signifies the sprinkling, or the application of the blood and of the Spirit of Christ to the heart for cleansing from the guilt and the pollution as well as for delivering from the power of sin. The washing with water, then, in the name of the Father, and of the Son, and of the Holy Ghost, signifies and seals to believers their justification, which includes remission of sins by the blood of Jesus (Hebrews 8:10, 12; Acts 2:38 and 22:16), their adoption into the family of God, and their relation to Him as their God (Galatians 3:26, 27; 2 Corinthians 6:18; Acts 2:38, 39), their regeneration and sanctification by the Spirit of Christ (John 3:3, 5; Titus 3:5, 6; Romans 6:3-5), and the resurrection of their bodies by the same Spirit to life eternal (Romans 6:4, 5;

and 8:11; 1 Corinthians 15:29). These inestimable blessings, resulting from vital union with Christ and communion with Him in His righteousness are by baptism sealed not only to the party to whom it is administered, if within the bond of the covenant, but to every believer who, in the exercise of faith, witnesses the administration of the same.

Third, it also signifies and seals to them their public and solemn admission into the family of God as members of the mystical body of Christ for, said the Apostle Paul to the believers at Corinth, "By one Spirit we are all baptized into one body" (1 Corinthians 12:13). By their baptism they are supposed, and publicly declared, to have been church-members before, and so they have their membership thereby solemnly sealed to them. Baptism, then, signifies and seals to them their having been already members of the church, the mystical body of Christ. Those true Christians who are present acknowledge them to be their brethren; and they, by their baptism, solemnly profess themselves to be incorporated with the former, and with all who truly believe, as a society separated to the enjoyment and service of their God and Savior (Acts 2:41).

Fourth, baptism seals to them who believe their engagement to be the Lord's. In this holy ordinance they solemnly profess their faith in the declarations of the gospel, relative to the Father, the Son, and the Holy Ghost, with their interest in these adorable Persons; and at the same time they openly and solemnly dedicate themselves and all that they have to be, according to the covenant, employed by them for the purposes of their glory (1 Corinthians 6:19, 20; Romans 6:4, 6; Ephesians 4:1, 5). Thus, by their baptism, their high obligations to be wholly, only, and eternally the Lord's are represented and confirmed to believers and their seed.

The Seals of the Covenant of Grace

Fifth, and last, it signifies and seals to them who believe their engagement to cultivate holy fellowship with the church of the living God (1 Corinthians 12:13, 14). Baptism confirms their obligation according to the covenant to have and to hold fellowship with the church as it is the visible body of Christ; their obligation to be one body not only with the invisible, but with the visible church, and that visibly, or in visible communion with the same.

THE LORD'S SUPPER. The Lord's Supper also is to believers under the present dispensation a sign and seal of the covenant of grace. It was, by the Lord Jesus Christ, appointed to be a visible sign and seal thereof under the New Testament dispensation, and that to all adult persons who are or shall be within the bond of it. "This cup," said the dying Savior, "is the new testament in My blood" (1 Corinthians 11:25). The Lord Jesus has received by covenant, and has bequeathed by His testament to His spiritual seed, all things necessary for the life that now is, and for that which is to come; and the word of His testament is of itself sufficient security for their being put in full possession of all. But they are slow of heart to believe. Guilt in the conscience is a source of innumerable doubts and fears. That the grace of the covenant, therefore, might, in the eye of their faith, appear to be more sure, He appended thereto this visible sign and seal which, by making every benefit of that well ordered covenant appear in the view of faith more certain and firm, is, in the hand of the Spirit of truth, admirably fitted to confirm their faith.

But more particularly, first, this holy ordinance is to believers a sign and seal of the making of the covenant and of the wonderful incarnation, according to that covenant, of the only begotten Son of the Father. The taking of the bread that, after it is set apart, signifies the body or human nature of Christ represents, in the liveliest manner, the Father's taking of Him to be the Representative and Surety of His elect and at the same time Christ's taking of the human nature into union with the divine nature in His adorable Person (Hebrews 10:5-10 and 2:14). The taking of the cup that, after it is set apart to this holy use, signifies the blood of Jesus and the new testament in His blood represents the Father's taking of His righteousness of blood in the room of His elect as abundantly sufficient to merit for them all the grace and glory promised in the covenant (Isaiah 42:21; Romans 3:25). It is not only a sign, but a seal of the making of the covenant, and of the incarnation of Christ The believing communicant may thus, within himself, say, "As certainly as I see the minister taking the bread, that sign of the body of Christ, so certain is it that the Father, in making the covenant with Him, took, or admitted Him, to be the Representative and Surety of all who would believe in Him; and that Christ Himself, in order to obey and suffer for them, took the human nature into a personal union with the divine; and as certainly as I now behold the minister taking the cup of wine, so certain may I be that the eternal Father took and held the righteousness of Jesus Christ as fully sufficient to merit for me all the grace and glory bequeathed in His testament." By this means these glorious doctrines are, in the view of faith, confirmed or put beyond doubt.

Second, the ordinance of the Supper is to believers a seal of the mediation and covenant-headship of the Lord Jesus. They may warrantably conclude that as certainly as they hear the bread and wine set apart. To be the symbols of His body and blood, by the reading of the words of institution, and by the blessing or giving of thanks over them, so certain is it that Christ in the human nature is that blessed Seed of Abraham in whom God blesses them with all spiritual blessings (Ephesians

1:3). They may thence take occasion to assure themselves that the eternal Son of God was, in the covenant, set apart to the offices of a Mediator; and that it is His office to bless them with every covenant-blessing, whether spiritual or temporal; that while it is their duty to be free receivers, it is His office to be a gracious Giver of all the blessings of the covenant.

Third, it is a sign and seal of that righteousness of faith that is the fulfillment of the conditions of the covenant. The breaking of the bread signifies the breaking of the body of Christ in His crucifixion and death by which the union between His soul and body was dissolved, and His body, as it were, broken away for a time from His soul. The pouring out of the wine signifies the shedding of His blood, especially on the cross, or the pouring out of His soul unto death (Isaiah 53:12); and that as the finishing part of His righteousness by which the new testament was ratified and the legacies of it purchased for the legatees. It is not only a sign but a seal of that righteousness of faith. For the believing communicant may within himself say, "As certainly as I now see the bread broken and the wine poured out, the body of the Lord Jesus was broken and His blood was shed for the remission of my sins. I may now be certain that it pleased the Lord to bruise Him, to put Him to grief, and so to make His soul an offering for sin (Isaiah 53:10). I may, from what I now see, be fully assured that the surety-righteousness of the second Adam is completely fulfilled, and that all the benefits of the new covenant are thereby merited for me, and for many I may henceforth be confident that by the shedding of His blood His new testament is ratified, that all the legacies bequeathed in it are purchased, and therefore that they are sure, the sure mercies of David (Isaiah 55:3)."

Fourth, it is a sign and seal also of the promises and promised grace of the covenant. The wine in the cup being a sign and seal not only of the blood of Christ, but also of the new testament in His blood, is for that reason a sign and seal of those promises of the covenant that were to be performed to His elect seed upon condition of the shedding of His blood, and which He Himself as last Adam did, in the prospect of dying, turn into the form of a testament in their favor. The promises of saving grace are promises in the covenant of grace; and they are no otherwise given or performed to sinners of mankind than according to the tenor of that gracious covenant. The ordinance of the Supper, therefore, by being a seal of the covenant, is a seal of the promises. So that the believing communicant may within himself reason thus: "As certainly as I now behold the wine in the cup, signifying the new testament in the blood of Jesus Christ, so certain may I be of the precious promises and of the inestimable blessings promised in the covenant. Now I may well believe that the promises are sure, and that the mercies promised are, to all the spiritual seed of Christ, sure mercies. Now, in taking the sacramental cup I may freely take the promises as my security for all the mercies of the covenant; and my faith in them may rise to full assurance. They are not only spoken, and written, and sworn, and witnessed, and ratified, but they are sealed, and that to me. Here I have all the grace and glory that were purchased and promised by my incarnate Redeemer, secured to me under His own seal."

Fifth, the ordinance of the Supper is likewise a sign and seal of Christ's administration of the covenant to sinners who believe. The giving of the bread and the cup to believers at the communion-table is the sign that Christ, with His righteousness and fullness, is given them in offer as sinners, and that He is given them in possession as believers. The giving of those sacred symbols to each of them in particular, accompanied with an invitation or commend to all of them to take and eat of the bread

The Seals of the Covenant of Grace

and to drink of the cup, represents the offer and call of the gospel directed to each of them as His present and particular warrant to trust in Christ and on His righteousness for all His fullness. It is a sensible sign that the Person of Christ is given him to be trusted in, the righteousness of Christ to be trusted on, and the fullness or the benefits of Christ to be trusted for. The giving of the external signs, which affords a warrant to receive them, represents the giving of Christ with His benefits in offer, as that which affords a warrant so to confide in Him for one's own salvation as to receive spiritual nourishment or increase of grace from Him. While this action serves to signify, it serves at the same time to seal the administration of the covenant to believing communicants. For each of them may warrantably say, "As certainly as these outward signs are now given to me, the body and blood of my incarnate Redeemer, with all the benefits of redemption, are given to me in offer as a sinner in myself, and are given to me in possession as a believer in Him. The giving of the bread and wine, which are the consecrated signs of them, to me is the sure token that they are all exhibited, all offered to me, and that the authentic offer and call afford me a right to trust in the Lord Jesus for the possession of them all (Mark 14:22-24)."

Sixth, it is a sign and seal of their union and communion with Christ in grace and glory. Their taking of the bread and of the cup signifies their taking or accepting of Christ, who was made perfect through sufferings. Their eating of the bread and drinking of the cup signify their trusting on Him and His righteousness for all their salvation and, at the same time, their vital union and intimate communion with Him. As the bread and wine, by being taken by the mouth into the body, become so closely united to the body as to be incorporated with it, or converted into the substance of it, so the body and blood of Christ, received by faith into the heart, become so intimately united to the believing communicant as to be one with Him. "He that is joined unto the Lord is one spirit" (1 Corinthians 6:17). To the same purpose are these words of the Lord Jesus Himself: "That they may be one, even as we are one; I in them, and thou in Me, that they may be made perfect in one" (John 17:22, 23). And as by eating of the bread and drinking of the wine the communicants derive nourishment from them to their bodies, so by the exercise of affectionate meditation and of humble confidence in Christ for all the grace of the covenant, they derive from His body and blood, signified thereby, nourishment to the spiritual life in their souls. And as the bread and wine, when one hungers and thirsts, are sweet, as well as nourishing to the body, so to the souls of them who hunger and thirst after righteousness, and who taste that the Lord is gracious (1 Peter 2:3), the body and blood of Jesus are inexpressibly sweet. These are sweet without anything else; but nothing is sweet without them. As the Lord Jesus, by His appointment, gives, and they receive the bread and the cup, so in that ordinance there is real intercourse or communion between Him and them. He on the one hand communicates His favor and love, His blood and benefits to them; and they, on the other, communicate or return their love, gratitude, and thanksgiving to Him. This holy ordinance is a seal as well as a sign of their union and communion with Jesus Christ. The believing and devout communicant may, at the Table of the Lord, say in his heart, "As certainly as I eat of this bread and drink of this cup, I by faith partake of the body and blood of Christ Jesus my Lord, with His inestimable benefits. As sure as I cordially attempt to believe that He is offered to me, and heartily essay to trust in Him for all His salvation, so is it, and so will it be, to me according to my faith (Matthew 9:29). As certainly as the bread and wine are converted into the substance of my body, so is Christ by His Spirit in me, and I by faith in Him. As sure as my body derives nourishment from the bread and wine received into it, so does my soul derive spiritual nourishment from the body, blood, and fullness of my incarnate Redeemer, in whom my heart trusts (Psalm 28:7). As certainly as the bread that I have eaten and the wine that I have drunk are now mine in possession, the body and blood and benefits of Jesus Christ, now that my heart has trusted in Him, are in like manner mine. As sure as my dear Savior has now admitted me to eat of that broken bread that is the communion of His body, and to drink of that cup of blessing that is the communion of His blood (1 Corinthians 10:16), and has enabled me in some degree to trust in Him for all the blessings purchased by His precious blood, so certain may I be that He admits me, according to the covenant, to communion with Himself in His Person, righteousness, and fullness. Truly my fellowship is with the Father, and with His Son Jesus Christ (1 John 1:3). I shall say of Him, "Surely, in the Lord have I righteousness and strength' (Isaiah 45:24). My soul shall be satisfied as with marrow and fatness (Psalm 63:5).

Seventh, it is also a public token and seal of their union and communion with Christ mystical. This holy ordinance is, to believers, a public testimony or token of their union and communion with all the other members of Christ's mystical body. For, says the Apostle Paul, "We being many are one bread, and one body; for we are all partakers of that one bread" (1 Corinthians 10:17). It is as if he had said, "As the bread taken and eaten in that ordinance is of one kind of substance, broken for us all, and is made up of many grains of corn, ground and molded into one lump, so we, who are many individual believers, are hereby represented as, and hereby avouch ourselves to be, by faith and love, united together into one holy mass or lump, and into one mystical body, of which Christ is the Head; for we are all partakers of that one loaf or substance that signifies Christ the bread of life (John 6:51); and so, in having communion with Him, we have union and fellowship one with another." Here then, believers eat of the same bread and drink of the same cup as a public token or sign that they derive their spiritual nourishment from one common source; that they are actuated by the same Spirit; and that they have as near an interest in, and as tender an affection for one another as members of the same body have. They hereby solemnly declare that they are all intimately united one to another, and that, considered as united, they constitute the body of Christ (1 Corinthians 12:27). They receive the bread and the cup as the sign or badge of their being members of that holy society who are redeemed from a world that lies in wickedness.

It is a seal also of their union and communion with all other saints. Their union and fellowship with all the other members of Christ's body mystical are thereby ascertained or confirmed to them. For each of them may, in communicating, thus say of himself, "As certainly as I, in faith, eat of the same sacramental bread, and drink of the same sacramental cup, I have, in union with Christ my Covenant-head, union with all the other members of His mystical body; and I have, in communion with Him, in His body and blood, fellowship with them who are all partakers of that one bread and that one cup that signify His body and blood and the blessings thereby purchased. This, in the hand of the Spirit of truth, assures me that while I am an heir of God and a joint heir with Christ, I am also a fellow-heir with saints, and of the same body. It confirms me in the faith that I share with them in all the merit of the blood of Jesus Christ, and in all the legacies of His testament, ratified by His death; that I and they are one body and have one Spirit, even as we are called in one hope of our calling; one Lord, one faith, one baptism, one God and Father of all, who is above all, and through all, and in us all (Ephesians 4:4-6).

Eighth, and finally, the ordinance of the supper is to believers a seal of their dedication of themselves to God and of their obligation to obey in faith and love all the commandments of His law in the hand of Christ, the great Mediator of the covenant. It confirms or strengthens their dedication of themselves to God in Christ as His covenant-people, and the high obligation that redeeming love especially has laid upon them to love Christ and to keep His commandments. While, by receiving the holy sacrament of the Supper, they solemnly declare that they are infinitely obliged to their dear Redeemer for His unparalleled love in becoming obedient unto death for them, this ordinance, in the hand of the Holy Spirit, serves to confirm the high obligation, that is, to assure them of it and to show them how firm it is. The love of Christ manifested in this ordinance constrains them not to live henceforth to themselves, but unto Him who died for them and rose again (2 Corinthians 5:14, 15). By their partaking of the sacramental bread broken, and of the sacramental wine poured out, they practically declare that they would deserve to have their own body broken in pieces no less than that bread, and their own blood poured out no less than that wine, if they should ever prove unfaithful to their solemn engagement to serve their God and Redeemer.

From what has been advanced in this chapter, the true Christian may learn for his comfort that his interest in the eternal covenant, and his begun possession of Christ, are so confirmed that he shall never fall out of that covenant. Believer, your saving interest in the covenant, and your begun possession of Christ with His righteousness and salvation are, by baptism and the Lord's Supper, sealed to you. By these ordinances He has sealed His covenant with you and made all sure. It is not you who has sealed the covenant with Him, but He who has sealed it with you. And therefore, although you may be permitted to fall under the displeasure of your heavenly Father, yet you shall not fall out of His covenant; although you may sin away your comfortable frames and the sense of your interest, yet you cannot be suffered to lose your interest itself (Isaiah 54:8-10; Jeremiah 32:39, 40). All the promises, and those especially of your perseverance in grace, are made and sealed to you; and therefore, though the Lord will chasten you for your transgressions, yet His loving kindness He will not utterly take from you, nor suffer His faithfulness to fail (Psalm 89:32, 33). He has sealed, and will keep His covenant with you; and as long as He will keep the covenant, the covenant will keep you. Look upon every promise, and every blessing of the covenant, then, as confirmed and sure to you. Derive all your comfort daily from that sure covenant and, in the diligent use of the means of grace, cleave fast to the Lord Jesus, your Covenant-head.

Hence we may also learn how solemn the ordinances of baptism and the Lord's Supper are. They are sealing ordinances. If a man's taking entitlement or possession even of an earthly estate is counted a solemn deed, how much more august and solemn must these ordinances be in which Jehovah meets with His saints, and by which He makes all the unsearchable riches of Christ sure to them! Oh, with what profound reverence, with what holy awe, should ministers dispense and saints receive, these holy mysteries!

Hence see how inexcusable it is in the believer if, instead of giving all diligence to attain the full assurance of faith and hope, he yields to distrust and despondence. The offers and promises, the grace and glory, of the eternal covenant, believer, are by Jehovah made over and sealed to you. They are all confirmed, all put beyond doubt to you. How does it come then that doubts and fears still prevail in your soul? How unreasonable, how sinful is it in you not to give the fullest credit to offers and promises, the truth of which are so amply confirmed; not to rely with unsuspecting confidence on righteousness and grace, so divinely attested! In such circumstances, to cast away your confidence in Christ Jesus for all His salvation must be your greatest sin. Are not Christ, and all the blessings of the new covenant by those sacraments, made over and irrevocably sealed to you? They are, and still you presume to doubt and despond. The mercies of the covenant are sure mercies, and yet you are not assured of them. Oh, that the Holy Spirit would now come and convince you of sin because you do not believe as you ought in your faithful Redeemer. How criminal is it when you at any time witness the administration of baptism not to avail yourself of such a precious opportunity so to exercise particular trust for salvation as to become strong in faith! Every time you see baptism rightly dispensed you should regard it as a seal of the covenant not only to the infant baptized, but to yourself, and should exercise your faith and other graces accordingly. And when you wait on your Lord in the ordinance of the Supper, do not count it enough to act faith while you yourself are communicating; exercise it also while you look on and see others partaking. Embrace eagerly every such opportunity of exercising your faith; and in believing you yourself shall be more and more sealed with the Holy Spirit of promise.

10

The Properties of the Covenant of Grace

It is of great importance, in order to having a clear and comfortable knowledge of this covenant, that persons carefully attend to those properties or peculiar qualities of it that are revealed in the Oracles of God. Of those, I shall here consider only the following:

1. It is a divine covenant. It was made between the Father and the Son, with the approbation of the Holy Spirit. I said with the approbation of the Holy Spirit for with many a good word the Spirit in the Scripture speaks of it. It is a covenant of Jehovah's making and not of ours. That glorious contract was drawn up and entered into before the world began and, consequently, before we could know anything of the matter. The eternal Father, before the foundation of the world was laid, made it with the eternal Son, and established with Him as the Representative of His elect all the articles of it. The eternal Spirit causes the elect, in the day of the Redeemer's power, to approve and take hold of that covenant, each of them for himself. Having been made by one Divine Person with another, it was made, in a divine, an infinitely excellent manner. Hence Jehovah glories in it and calls it *His* covenant: "I will establish My covenant between Me and thee, and thy seed after thee" (Genesis 17:7). "Every one

The Properties of the Covenant of Grace

that taketh hold of My covenant; even them will I bring to My holy mountain," etc. (Isaiah 56:6, 7). My covenant will I not break, nor alter the thing that is gone out of My lips" (Psalm 89:34). That covenant, then, seeing it was projected and proposed by the first Divine Person, accepted and fulfilled by the second, and applied as well as approved by the third is a divine one. And because it is wholly divine, it is inviolable, equally incapable of being either made or unmade by man. A man may take hold of God's covenant, but he can neither, strictly speaking, make it nor make it void.

2. It is a covenant of redemption. It was established between the Father and Son in order that lost sinners of mankind might be redeemed from sin and misery to holiness and felicity. In that wonderful contract the only begotten Son, upon His consenting to become, in the fullness of time, their near Kinsman, to whom the right of redeeming them should belong, was constituted the Redeemer of God's elect. As it was in the relation of a kinsman to them that the right of redeeming them could belong to Him, so it was in the same near relation that He could be capable of serving and suffering for them so as to redeem them. In that divine covenant He accordingly engaged to the Father to redeem them who, in common with others, were to be under the law as a covenant of works (Galatians 4:5), from the dominion of that broken covenant; to redeem them from the curse of the law in all its dreadful obligation and effects (Galatians 3:13); to redeem them from all iniquity (Titus 2:14) as well as from this present evil world (Galatians 1:4); and to redeem them to God (Revelation 5:9), to a state of perfect conformity to Him, and of intimate and everlasting communion with Him. Those, therefore, of the children of men who are saved are called the redeemed of the Lord (Isaiah 62:12); and the blessedness provided in the covenant through Jesus Christ for the elect is in Scripture set

forth under the general character of redemption (Hebrews 9:12).

3. It is a covenant of grace, of redeeming grace, a covenant in which all is free, infinitely free, to sinners of mankind. It was indeed, strictly speaking, a covenant of works to the adorable Surety; but it is a covenant of immensely free grace to the unworthy sinner. It was sovereign, unmerited favor to lost sinners that moved the Father to plan and propose that covenant to the Son, and that engaged the Son to accept the high proposal. What was it but infinitely free favor to the most unworthy that determined God the Father to give to the Son, and God the Son to receive from the Father elect sinners to be redeemed and so to enter in to a covenant with each other for that gracious purpose? What was it but sovereign, overflowing grace in the heart of the dear Redeemer that engaged Him, with infinite willingness, to fulfill the arduous conditions and to dispense the blessings of the covenant to persons who, instead of having done anything to deserve such kindness from Him, did everything they could to merit the fierceness of His indignation (Psalm 40:6-8)? Could it be anything else than unmerited favor, than stupendous love, to the most unworthy, the most unlovely, that engaged the adorable Spirit to apply the righteousness and fullness of the covenant to them, and to enable them so to believe as to come into the bond of that covenant? How excellent, how transcendently glorious, is this grace of the Father, the Son, and the Holy Spirit? It infinitely surpasses the loftiest conceptions of men and of angels. All that is in the covenant is freely given to sinners. Christ the Head of the covenant is the unspeakable gift of God to them (Isaiah 49:8; John 4:10). The justifying righteousness of the covenant is also His gift to them (Romans 5:17).

Eternal life, the promise of the covenant, is likewise an absolutely free gift. The gift of God is eternal life through Jesus Christ our Lord (Romans 6:23). Faith that receives all is not of themselves; it is the gift of God (Ephesians 2:8). Are the people of the covenant saved? It is by sovereign grace. "By grace," says our apostle, "are ye saved through faith" (Ephesians 2:8). And again, "Who hath saved us, not according to our works, but according to His own purpose and grace" (2 Timothy 1:9). Are they justified before God? It is by free grace. They are justified freely by His grace, through the redemption that is in Jesus Christ (Romans 3:24). Are they sanctified? It is by the operation of the Holy Spirit, as a Spirit of grace. "By which will we are sanctified" (Hebrews 10:10); "through sanctification of the Spirit unto obedience" (1 Peter 1:2). Are they glorified? It is by absolute unmerited grace. "Be sober," says the Apostle Peter, "and hope to the end, for the grace that is to be brought unto you at the revelation of Jesus Christ" (1 Peter 1:13). In the covenant God gives all, and faith receives all as His free gift. All that is required from sinners is therein given, and all that is given is given freely.

Faith only receives a right to the blessings of the covenant; it gives none. It receives the righteousness of Jesus Christ that gives a full right to all the benefits of the covenant; but in itself, or as the sinner's act, it gives no right. The self-righteous formalist is always for giving in order to take; but the true believer is for taking in order to give. He sees that, in a covenant that is wholly of grace, he has nothing to give for what he is to receive; but on the contrary, everything to receive in order that he may afford to give. He knows that he is not to do that he may live, but to live that he may do. He sees that all is freely offered to sinners who hear the gospel, and that all is freely bestowed on such as believe.

4. It is a covenant of peace. "I," said Jehovah, "will make with them a covenant of peace" (Ezekiel 34:25). And again, "My kindness shall not depart from thee, neither shall the covenant

of My peace be removed, saith the Lord that hath mercy on thee" (Isaiah 54:10). By the blood of that covenant, the offended Majesty of heaven has become a God of peace (Hebrews 13:20); and believing sinners, who were enemies, are reconciled to Him (Romans 5:10; Colossians 1:20, 21). It was by the blood of it that reconciliation was made for iniquity (Daniel 9:24), and that "God was in Christ, reconciling the world unto Himself, not imputing their trespasses unto them" (2 Corinthians 5:19). To come into the bond of the covenant is the same as to enter upon a state of reconciliation with God. It is only they who are brought into the covenant that are received again into favor with the Lord, and that begin to enjoy communion with Him as their almighty Friend. It is also by the blood of the covenant, applied to the conscience, that believers attain peace of conscience, and that the peace of God that surpasses all understanding keeps their hearts and minds through Christ Jesus (Philippians 4:7). It was likewise by the same blood that believing Jews and Gentiles were reconciled to each other. For, says the Apostle Paul, "He is our peace, who hath made both one" (Ephesians 2:14-16).

5. That divine contract is also a covenant of promise. The Apostle Paul informed the believers at Ephesus that when they were in their natural state they were strangers from the covenants of promise (Ephesians 2:12). And in his epistle to the Hebrews he declares that Christ is the Mediator of a better covenant that was established upon better promises (Hebrews 8:6). It is by this apostle called the covenants of promise because, under every dispensation of it, it has been administered to sinners in full and free promises, which are all in Christ the mercy promised to the fathers, and in Him are presented to sinners in the offers of the gospel and performed to them who believer.

6. It is an unparalleled covenant. It has no parallel, no

The Properties of the Covenant of Grace 489

equal, among all the other covenants that ever were made. The covenant of works made with Adam as the representative of his natural seed is indeed by the Apostle Paul compared with it (Romans 5:12-19; 1 Corinthians 15:21, 22, 45-49). But it is in some particulars only that he represents that covenant as parallel to it. And if we speak of other covenants, such as those that Jehovah made with Noah, Abraham, Moses, Phinehas, David, and others, they, so far as they were peculiar to those persons, deserve never to be mentioned in comparison of that eternal contract. None of those patriarchs was or could be a public representative in such an eminent sense as the second Adam is. They were, indeed, if I may so say, each of them the natural root of a peculiar party; but they were not, in such a manner, the federal representatives of those parties that the latter, in respect of their eternal interests, were to stand or fall with the former; any more than Christian parents now are who have the promise directed to them and to their children (Acts 2:39).

7. It is a righteous, an equitable covenant. By it no wrong was or ever will be done to any of the parties concerned. No injury was done to God. On the contrary, it was therein provided that a perfect and meritorious obedience should be performed to His law, and in infinite satisfaction be given to His justice; yea, that much more obedience should be yielded to the righteous precepts, and far more satisfaction be given to the awful penalties of his law, than if the elect had, in their own persons, obeyed or suffered through all eternity (Isaiah 42:21). In forgiving, therefore, the sins of them to whom the obedience and sufferings of the divine Surety are imputed, the essential righteousness of God is most gloriously displayed (Romans 3:25, 26). By the substitution of Christ, the only begotten of the Father, as their Surety, in the room of His elect, and the imputation of His consummate righteousness to them, an opportunity for the

brightest possible display of the infinite rectitude of the divine nature and government is afforded. No injury was thereby done to Christ the blessed Mediator. He had power to lay down His life and power to take it again (John 10:18). He had in Himself an original power and right both to deposit His life as a ransom and a sacrifice, and, after satisfaction made, to resume it. And as He delighted, according to the covenant, to do the will of his Father, He voluntarily laid it down as His own free act or deed. Besides, the life that He was to lay down was in all respects His own; it was entirely at His own disposal, and was not the life of His divine, but of His human nature, which He willingly assumed and assumed for that very purpose. Add to this that He was so far from having any injury done to Him that, according to the covenant, He was for the suffering of death in the human nature, crowned in the same nature with glory and honor (Hebrews 2:9; Philippians 2:8-10). No injustice could thereby be done to the Holy Spirit; for it was with His infinite consent and approbation that the covenant was made. Nor was any wrong thereby done to the spiritual seed of Christ. For, although Jehovah's having executed the sentence of condemnation upon them in their own persons as sinners would have been strictly just, yet His not executing of it upon themselves, but upon a responsible Surety in their stead, is far from being an act of injustice done them. It is an act of grace in their favor, but not of injustice. Although eternal death was due to them for their sin, yet everlasting life, including complete deliverance from eternal death, is no less due to them for the righteousness of Christ now imputed to them and received by faith. While therefore life eternal is, in one respect, unmerited grace to them, in another it is of strict justice.

8. It is at the same time a holy covenant. In raising up a horn of salvation for us in the house of His servant David,

The Properties of the Covenant of Grace

Jehovah is said to have remembered His holy covenant (Luke 1:72). This covenant was made by the Father with His chosen, His holy One, in order that the transcendent glory of His infinite holiness might be displayed, and that sinners of mankind might recover that holiness of heart and of life which they had lost in the first Adam. The main design of the covenant, next to the glory of God and of Christ, was that sinners might be rendered holy. By fulfilling all righteousness as Surety of the covenant, Christ the second Adam has merited for elect sinners those supplies of the Spirit that are necessary to make them holy. According to that inviolable covenant, He obeyed the moral law as a covenant of works for them that they might obey the same holy law as a rule of life. He yielded to it as a covenant perfect obedience that they might be enabled to perform to it as a rule, sincere obedience in time, and perfect obedience through eternity. The great promise of the covenant is a promise of that eternal life that comprehends holiness as its main and most essential part. Evangelical holiness is the very essence of true happiness. Moreover, the grace of the covenant that reigns through the righteousness of Jesus Christ unto eternal life has a moral influence upon their becoming holy. "The grace of God that bringeth salvation hath appeared to all men; teaching us that denying ungodliness and worldly lusts, we should live soberly, righteously, and godly in this present world" (Titus 2:11, 12). The grace of God, says the apostle, that brings salvation, finished by the Son of God and free for the chief of sinners, has appeared; this grace, being revealed in the gospel, and beheld by the eye of faith and thus appearing in its luster and with power to all sorts of men, teaches us to deny ungodliness and worldly lusts and to live soberly, righteously, and godly. It teaches us to deny or to renounce all ungodliness; to renounce not only all external abominations, but all worldly lusts; every depraved inclination, every irregular desire. It also teaches us to live soberly with regard to ourselves, righteously in reference to our neighbor, and godly with respect to our God. The apostle does not say that this grace prescribes by way of rule or enjoins by way of authority, but that it teaches by way of instruction; showing in the most affecting manner the only acceptable method of obeying the precepts of the law as a rule. The grace of God when, according to the covenant, it is savingly manifested to the understanding and cordially apprehended by the will renders every duty of the holy law both practicable and pleasant; it furnishes believers with a heart and a hand for all the duties of holiness. The people of the covenant therefore are, and cannot but be, a holy people.

9. It is a new covenant. "Behold, the days come, saith the Lord, when I will make a new covenant with the house of Israel, and with the house of Judah" (Hebrews 8:8). This covenant, in comparison of the covenant of works, is in Scripture called the second and the new covenant. But it is not so called with regard either to the period or to the order in which it was made. In both these respects it is the first and the old covenant; it was made in eternity before the world began, whereas the other was made only in time. But, seeing there was no place for its being revealed until after the covenant of works was broken, it is, with respect to the manifestation and administration of it, called the second and the new covenant. According to our limited mode of conceiving objects, we are necessitated to consider the covenant of grace as a covenant made of old, as made from eternity past, infinitely long before the beginning of time. But in the view of the divine Parties between whom it was established, it is always present, always new. To them, nothing that exists can be either part or future. When this covenant was first revealed to man, the performance of its proper conditions was to him a

The Properties of the Covenant of Grace 493

matter of futurity, an object that was not to exist until four thousand years after. On the contrary, to Jehovah it was always present so that, in saving His elect under the Old Testament, He proceeded upon them as conditions already fulfilled. And though it was a future object to Christ as man, until He finished it on the cross and in the grave, yet to Him as God-man it was always a present object. Concerning Himself as God-man He said to the Jews, "Before Abraham was, I am" (John 8:58). He did not say "I was," but "I am." All that is past, as well as all that is future to us, being necessarily present to Him, the eternal covenant must, to Him, be always present, and therefore always new.

This divine contract is not only new in respect of manifestation to man, and in the view of God, but is also a new covenant or testament, first, in regard to the second or new dispensation of it under the gospel. The present form of dispensing it, as distinguished from that legal form in which it was dispensed before the coming of Christ, is new. And, second, it is a new covenant because it can never decay, nor wax old, nor lose its efficacy on the faith, holiness, and comfort of believers.

10. It is also a full covenant. All things are in it—grace and glory, pardon and peace, holiness and happiness, things present and things to come; yea, Christ Himself, who is ALL IN ALL. No sooner is a man vitally united to Christ, the Head of the covenant, than he begins to be blessed with all spiritual blessings in Him (Ephesians 1:3). That blessed Immanuel in whom dwells all the fullness of the Godhead bodily, and in whom it has pleased the Father that all fullness should dwell, is given for a covenant of the people. The Apostle Paul, therefore, says to the believers at Corinth, "All things are yours" (1 Corinthians 3:21-23). And the Lord Jesus Himself says, "He that overcometh shall inherit all things" (Revelation 21:7). There are no spiritual or

temporal blessings, no gracious qualities or acceptable performances, but what flow from the covenant. It comprehends all the promises made to Christ and to the elect in Him, some of which are constitutive of the covenant, such as those between the Father and Son concerning a spiritual seed; others are executive, relating to the execution or accomplishment of the covenant (Hebrews 10:12, 13); some are principal and relate to the end, eternal life; others are subordinate, and refer to the means, whether these are internal, as a living faith, or external, as instituted ordinances; all are comprised in the covenant. The innumerable wants of all who ever have believed have been supplied from this divine covenant; and yet, instead of being hereby diminished, the grace of it is as abundant as overflowing as ever. Would you, who think you see and feel more emptiness in your hearts now than ever you saw and felt before, desire to have all your need supplied? Rely on, and plead the rich promises of this gracious covenant, and your souls shall be satisfied as with marrow and fatness (Psalm 63:5); or, as an apostle expresses it, you shall be filled with all the fullness of God (Ephesians 3:19).

11. It is a covenant well ordered in all things. "He hath made with me," says David, "an everlasting covenant, ordered in all things" (2 Samuel 23:5); or, as it is in the original, "in all." It is ordered by infinite wisdom and love and therefore is well, infinitely well, ordered in all. It was planned according to the infinitely wise and gracious counsel of God, and settled by His eternal and immutable purpose. By infinite wisdom and unbounded goodness, it was adjusted with regard to all the parties concerned, to all the work of the glorious Mediator, and to all the persons who were to be justified and saved in Him as their Covenant-head. It is well ordered likewise in all things. All the measures that were to be taken in order to purchase and to apply the benefits of it on the one hand, and all the means that

The Properties of the Covenant of Grace

were to be employed in order to receive and to enjoy them on the other, were ordered with the most exquisite skill. Every minute circumstance was so adjusted and settled as in the fittest time possible to bring to pass the glorious designs of redeeming grace. All the operations of nature, all the employments of celestial hosts, all the machinations of infernal spirits, and all the actions of mankind are so disposed, limited, and overruled as to concur, according to the eternal purpose of Jehovah, in bringing about the great designs of the covenant. It is the constant concern of the gracious Redeemer and the unwearied care of the blessed Spirit, that all things do work together for good to them that love God, to them who are the called according to His purpose (Romans 8:18). Oh, what a wonderful, what a magnificent, covenant is this! All hands in heaven, on earth, and in hell are at work, incessantly at work, to promote either directly or indirectly the good of the elect and the accomplishment of the covenant in their salvation. "Oh, the depth of the riches, both of the wisdom and knowledge of God! How unsearchable are His judgments, and His ways past finding out" (Romans 11:33). However much that amazing scheme may now seem to be, in some things, irregular, and contrary to the methods that, by a finite understanding, would be thought most eligible, yet all will appear in the issue to have been in an infinite degree well and wisely ordered. All will, in the light of glory, appear to have been so well ordered as to have, in the best manner and in the highest degree possible, advanced the glory of Jehovah, the honor of Christ, and the holiness as well as happiness of the redeemed. Herein especially is the covenant well ordered, that it entrusts the salvation of the saints not to their own custody, but to the care of an infinitely merciful and faithful Redeemer; and that whatever is required from them is promised to them. Duty performed and privilege enjoyed are according to it inseparable, as well as exactly proportionate the one to the other.

12. But further, it is a sure covenant. "He hath made with me," says David, "an everlasting covenant, ordered in all and sure," or, as the word in the original properly signifies, "kept or guarded" (2 Samuel 23:5). This covenant is kept with infinite care, and therefore must in all things be sure. The high contracting Parties sufficiently secure it. On the one hand, the eternal Father, with all His grace, faithfulness, and power; and on the other, not a mere man, not a holy angel, for such could and did fail; but the eternal Son, who is able, as the Head and Representative of His people, to save them to the uttermost; these render it infinitely sure. It is secured also by the oath of Jehovah the Father to His only begotten Son. "The Lord hath sworn, and will not repent, Thou art a Priest forever" (Psalm 110:4). "Once," said He, "have I sworn by my holiness, that I will not lie unto David" (Psalm 89:35). Thus He has sworn that the contract drawn up and concluded between Himself and the Son, these two unchangeable Parties, whose will and power are essentially the same, shall forever stand. It is confirmed by two immutable things, in which it is impossible for God to lie; namely by the oath and the word of that Jehovah who is declared to be the faithful God who keeps covenant (Deuteronomy 7:9). And, as if that were not enough, it is also sealed. "The foundation of God standeth sure, having this seal, The Lord knoweth them that are His. And, let everyone that nameth the name of Christ depart from iniquity" (2 Timothy 2:19). The foundation of God here is principally His covenant of grace. This is the foundation of His dealings with us, and of our hope toward Him. This foundation stands sure, for it has a seal, the seal of His unchanging love to His elect. It is secured likewise by the resurrection and ascension of the Lord Jesus, by the sanctifying influences of the Holy Spirit on the hearts of believers, and by the immortal seed of experi-

The Properties of the Covenant of Grace 497

mental religion. Moreover, the Parties of the covenant are not strictly speaking God and man, but God and Christ; and the believer is not otherwise a party than as he is in Christ. Here then is a ground of strong consolation to believers: Christ Jesus and they, united to Him, are within the same unchangeable covenant; and as long as the covenant stands fast with Him, it stands sure to them (Psalm 89:28; Isaiah 54:10). The promises of it in Him are yea, and in Him Amen, and so are sure to all the seed. The blessings promised in it are sure to all the seed. The blessings promised in it are the sure mercies of David. They who are within the bond of it are kept by the power of God through faith unto salvation (1 Peter 1:5). He makes an everlasting covenant with them, that He will not turn away from them, to do them good (Jeremiah 32:40). Oh, how stable, how firm, how unfailing, believer, is that divine covenant in which you are instated! And how strong are the obligations under which it lays you to be steadfast, unmovable, always abounding in the work of the Lord (1 Corinthians 15:58)!

13. It is a glorious, an honorable covenant. It was devised and made chiefly for the manifestation of the glory of Jehovah, Father, Son, and Holy Spirit. Hence it is according to it, that in the work of man's redemption the glory of every divine perfection is, with the most resplendent luster, displayed. It is in subservience to the designs of it that in creation and providence the glory of the wisdom, power, and goodness of God is eminently conspicuous. That illustrious covenant is so planned and established as to afford a continued opportunity for the most transcendent displays of the glory of the perfections, and especially of the grace of God (Ephesians 1:6). There, the excellence, the amiableness, of His nature and character shine forth with the most surpassing, the most amazing effulgence. Moreover, each Person of the adorable Godhead was to obtain for Himself pe-

culiar glory by performing a distinct office in the economy of the covenant. The Father was to glorify the justice, truth, and holiness of the Godhead by demanding and receiving perfect obedience to His law, and complete satisfaction for sin; the Son covenanted to glorify the wisdom and love, as well as the holiness and justice of the Godhead, by fully answering both these demands; and the Holy Spirit was to glorify the grace, power, and faithfulness of the Godhead by raising the dead in sins to spiritual life, and by enabling them to walk in newness of life until they should, in the mansions of glory, attain the perfection of life eternal.

Add to this that it is a most honorable contract. It confers the truest honor. The Parties contracting are infinitely honorable. The Father is the Father of glory, the fountain of honor; the Son is the Lord of glory and to them who believe is an honor (1 Peter 2:7), honoring them, and honored by them; and the Holy Spirit is the Spirit of glory, honoring them with His inhabitation and influence. They who are interested in that covenant are precious in the sight of the Lord and honorable (Isaiah 43:4). The glorious Redeemer administers the covenant to them in the most honorable manner. It is by taking sinners into near union with Himself that He admits them into the covenant; and it is by advancing believers to intimate communion with Himself, the fountain of honor, that He accomplishes the covenant to them. And does it seem a light thing to you, believers, to be confederated with Him who is the only begotten of the Father, the brightness of the Father's glory, and the Prince of the kings of the earth?

14. Finally, it is an eternal covenant. Frequently, in the sacred records, it is called an everlasting covenant. The glorious Parties between whom it was made, being each of them eternal, entered into it not in time but in eternity. The making of it

therefore is, properly speaking, eternal; it is from everlasting to everlasting; and as it never had a beginning, so it can never have an end. It never began to be made, and can never begin to be annulled. *That* is a covenant suited to you, believer! Oh, how admirably fitted are the provisions of it, to the vast capacities, to the boundless desires, of your immortal soul! The righteousness of it is an everlasting righteousness (Daniel 9:24). The comprehensive promise of it is a promise of eternal life (1 John 2:25). It was a leading condition of it that the second Adam should, through the eternal Spirit, offer Himself without spot to God; and it was stipulated that by one offering He would perfect forever them who are sanctified (Hebrews 10:14). His infinitely precious blood therefore is called the blood of the everlasting covenant (Hebrews 13:20). Upon His having covenanted to shed His blood as the finishing act of His obedience, the eternal Father promised that His mercy would be kept for Him forevermore; that His seed should be made to endure forever, and His throne as the days of heaven; and that it should be established forever as the moon, and as a faithful witness in heaven (Psalm 89:28, 29, 37). "The earth shall be removed like a cottage, and the heavens shall be rolled together as a scroll; all the things of time shall come to an end, and time itself shall be no more; but the covenant of my peace, saith Jehovah, shall never be removed" (Isaiah 54:10). It is everlasting, and must remain as long as the Father continues to be holy and just, and the Son to be faithful and true. The settlements of it are eternal, and therefore are infinitely unalterable. Oh, what a matchless, what a wonderful, covenant is this! The moment the reader by faith takes hold of it, he is delivered from eternal death and begins to have eternal life. "He that believeth on the Son *hath* everlasting life" (John 3:36).

11

The Points of Difference Between the Covenant of Grace and the Covenant of Works

As our self-righteous disposition inclines us in our intercourse with God frequently to confound or blend together these two covenants; and as it is of unspeakable importance to the holiness and comfort of true Christians that they be able clearly to distinguish between them; I shall, in this chapter, briefly point out to the reader those distinguishing characters of them that may for the most part be collected from what has been discoursed above. Though these two covenants agree in reference to their Author, to their promise, and to their ultimate end, yet they differ and are carefully to be distinguished from one another.

1. They are to be distinguished in their nature. The covenant of works was a contract of friendship, and it supposed God and man to be in perfect amity; but the covenant of grace is a covenant of reconciliation, and it supposes man to have been at variance with God. In the first covenant God and man, though infinitely distant from each other as Creator and creature, were notwithstanding most intimate friends; but in the second, God as an avenging Judge had legal enmity against man, and man as

an offending criminal had natural enmity against God. On the one hand God is represented as being angry with the wicked every day; and on the other, the carnal mind is declared to be enmity against God (Romans 8:7). And therefore it is according not to the first, but to the second covenant, that God is in Christ reconciling the world unto Himself (2 Corinthians 5:19).

2. These covenants differ in relation to the parties contracting. In the covenant of works the parties were God and the first Adam, representing all his natural posterity; but in the covenant of grace, the parties were God the Father and Christ the second Adam, representing all His spiritual seed (Psalm 89:3, 4). The first covenant was made with a mere man, a fallible creature; the second was established with God-man, the Lord from heaven, who changes not. The former depended on a righteous creature; the latter on a righteous, an almighty Redeemer. The one was made with man in his best state, and yet he did not keep it; the other was made with God-man, our blessed Immanuel, who neither could nor would fail in fulfilling it. In that the triune God is to be considered as the supreme Lawgiver and the Fountain of uncreated goodness, delighting in communicating happiness to an upright creature, in this He is to be viewed as infinitely merciful and gracious, rejoicing to give, in a manner suited to the glory of all His perfections, eternal life to an elect sinner believing in Jesus. According to the covenant of works, God could deal with man and man with God immediately; but according to the covenant of grace, He cannot deal with man, nor man with Him, but through a Mediator. With the blessed Mediator it was that He dealt primarily and immediately, and with man only in and through Him.

3. The covenant of works, by being violated, introduced death into the world of mankind (Romans 8:2); but the covenant of grace, instead of introducing death, found it already in

the world; and it was settled in this well-ordered covenant that the last Adam should make of that old enemy death a new servant, both to Himself and to His spiritual seed; that to them especially He should remove it from its place in the curse of that first covenant and convert it into a blessing (a blessing in disguise) of the second covenant (1 Corinthians 3:21, 22). By the former the first Adam had life, but instead of retaining that life for himself and his natural posterity he brought in and conveyed death to them (Romans 5:12); by the latter, the second Adam, through death, brought in life and graciously communicates it to His spiritual seed. According to the one death was, by the first man, conveyed to all his posterity; according to the other, death, having found its way from the spiritual offspring of the second man to Himself, life, as was observed above, is in its turn communicated by Him to them. For so it is written, the first man Adam was made a living soul, the last Adam, a quickening Spirit (1 Corinthians 15:45).

4. These two covenants differ in their peculiar properties. The covenant of works, as standing with the first man Adam, was but of short continuance; but the covenant of grace, as standing fast with the second man, the Lord from heaven, is an everlasting covenant. The former denounces nothing but curses against the transgressor; whereas the latter is full of blessings promised to the believer in Jesus (Ephesians 1:3). That covenant was but to make way and, if I may so say, to make work for this one. As in consequence of the breach of the covenant of works, the covenant of grace became needful; so the failing of the one serves to set off the stability of the other.

5. They are distinguished from each other by their conditions. The condition of the first covenant was the perfect obedience of Adam, a mere man; which, in no degree whatever, was adequate to the promised reward; but the condition of the se-

cond covenant was the infinitely perfect righteousness of God-man, which is completely proportionate, yea, much more than proportionate, to the life promised (Jeremiah 23:6). The perfect obedience of Adam was to have given to him and his descendants only a pactional title to life; but the consummate righteousness of Jesus Christ gives to His spiritual seed not only a pactional, but a meritorious title to life. In the covenant of works the condition of perfect obedience was to have been performed by man himself; but in the covenant of grace the same condition is performed by a divine Surety substituted in his place. The condition, therefore, of the former was personal perfect obedience; the condition of the latter is imputed perfect righteousness, and by faith received; that promises life to us if we have perfectly obeyed in our own persons; this, if we have perfectly obeyed and suffered in the person of our divine Surety.

6. They differ likewise in their respective promises. The promise of the covenant of works was conditional to man; whereas the promises of the covenant of grace are, with regard to sinners of mankind, absolutely free (Jeremiah 31:33, 34). They are all gratuitous and are all naturally and necessarily redoubled to absolute promises. In the first covenant a man was to be considered as working for life, and in that view as one to whom the reward should, in virtue of that contract, be reckoned not of grace but of debt (Romans 4:4). He could claim the life promised to perfect obedience as a debt, according to agreement, due for that obedience as soon as it was performed; whereas in the second covenant a man is regarded not as working for life, but as believing on Him who justifies those who in themselves were ungodly (Romans 4:5), and in that respect as one to whom the reward of eternal life is reckoned not of debt but of grace. Such a man receives the promise of life that was strictly conditional to Christ, but is absolutely free to himself;

and he expects eternal life only as the gift of God through Jesus Christ our Lord. By the covenant or law of works, then, boasting is not excluded; whereas by the covenant of grace or law of faith it is forever shut out of doors. "Where is boasting then? It is excluded. By what law? Of works? Nay; but by the law of faith" (Romans 3:27).

7. These covenants differ in reference to the blessings promised in them. In the first only life was promised, as that was the only blessing that Adam needed; but in the second, salvation from sin and death is promised, as well as the eternal fruition of life, together with all that is requisite to the completion of both.

8. There is also a difference between them in relation to the matter of each. The law is the matter of the covenant of works; the promise is the matter of the covenant of grace. The law is the matter of the former; and it has a promise annexed only in subservience to itself, in order that the promise might promote obedience to the precept; the promise, on the other hand, is the matter of the latter; and the law is introduced only in subservience to the promise, and in order to advance the gracious designs of God therein manifested. In the one God requires all from man and promises life only upon man's perfect obedience; in the other, He promises all, and binds man to the duties of holiness only in virtue of what he previously promised.

9. They are distinguished, the one from the other, with respect to the manner of their administration. The covenant of works was administered by the triune God, considered as an absolute God; but the covenant of grace is administered by the great Mediator who is Himself the ALL in ALL of this glorious covenant (Isaiah 49:8, 9).

10. These covenants differ likewise in the order of obedience peculiar to each. In the covenant of works, obedience was the foundation of privilege. Divine acceptance began at the

work and went on the person, provided that the work was perfectly done. In the covenant of grace, on the contrary, privilege is the foundation of duty; and gracious acceptance begins at the person, and then goes on to the work because it flows from the principle of union with Christ by faith (Genesis 4:4; Hebrews 11:4).

11. They differ in their effects on mankind. The covenant of works, by condemning the guilty criminal to eternal death, alarms and terrifies his awakened conscience; whereas the covenant of grace quiets and comforts the troubled spirit (Isaiah 42:3 and 61:1-3). The first shuts up the sinner to hell and wrath; the second opens for him a door of hope, by which he may escape from the wrath of God and return to friendship and fellowship with Him, as well as to holiness and happiness in conformity to Him.

The former, by fixing the sinner under spiritual death and binding him over to death eternal, genders to bondage; the latter, on the contrary, restores him to liberty. That can condemn, but being weak through the flesh it cannot justify, the guilty sinner; this can justify, but cannot condemn the sinner who believes in Jesus. The one drives transgressors farther from God, seeing that by it there is now no way of access to Him; the other, by representing him as in Christ, and as seated on a throne of grace, encourages sinners to draw near to Him (Hebrews 4:16 and 10:21, 22).

12. Finally, they differ from each other in their ends or designs. The subordinate design of the covenant of works was to show men what they were to do for God; but the subordinate end of the covenant of grace is to teach men who believe what God in Christ is to do for them and in them in order to qualify them for serving and enjoying Him. "Lord," said the Israelitish

church, "Thou wilt ordain peace *for* us; for Thou also hast wrought all our works *in* us" (Isaiah 26:12).

These are the leading distinctions between the covenant of works and the covenant of grace which, in the hand of the Spirit of truth, will I hope be useful to direct the exercise of the devout reader and to guard him against yielding to the motions of that self-righteous spirit that remains in him. Christian reader, would you desire to attain, under the enlightening influences of the Spirit of Christ, clear, distinct, and comfortable views of the covenant of grace? Study well, and familiarize to your mind those points of difference between it and the covenant of works that have now been mentioned. This will be a special means of guarding you, in your exercise against the dangerous extremes of legality on the one hand, and of licentiousness on the other. To have just, clear, and discriminating conceptions of that wonderful contract will also promote, more than you can imagine, the establishment of your heart in spiritual comfort and evangelical holiness.

12

The Conclusion

Having attempted at considerable length to elucidate the doctrine of the covenant of grace, I shall now conclude the whole by pointing out the duty incumbent upon all who are within the bond of that holy covenant. It was remarked above that the moral law, as a rule of life, is given to believers in the hand of Christ the blessed Mediator. In *His* hand it is the law of the covenant, the rule of duty, to all who are in and under Him as their Covenant-head. According to the covenant, the Father, having invested Him as Mediator, with all the sovereign authority of the glorious Godhead (Exodus 23:21), gave Him for a Commander to the people (Isaiah 55:4). In this character the glorious Mediator has received the law, that immutable rule of duty; and He, according to the covenant, gives it to believers as the standing law or instrument of government in His spiritual kingdom. Having Himself performed perfect obedience to it as a covenant of works for them He, in administering the covenant of grace, gives it to them as the unalterable rule of their obedience to Him, and to God in Him, and thereupon issues this high command: "Be ye perfect, even as your Father which is in heaven is perfect" (Matthew 5:48). All true believers, therefore, though they are delivered from the law as a covenant of works, yet are, and cannot but be, under it as a rule of life. The Apostle Paul did not consider himself as one who was without law to God by his being under the law to Christ (1 Corinthians 9:21), or under the law as a rule in the hand of Christ; for the name, or high authority of God was, and still is, in Christ as Mediator, and in that infinite name He issues out the law to His people.

When the moral law was first given to man, the divine Lawgiver and he were on such friendly terms together that man could receive that law immediately without any danger to himself, or any stain on the honor of the sovereign Lawgiver. But no sooner had man become a sinner than his bountiful Creator was necessitated to assume the character of an offended and avenging Judge; and man, by being a criminal, became the object of His infinite wrath. The law or covenant also, which was formerly the tie of friendship, did thereby become the instrument of vengeance; so that the guilty sinner could not regard either God or His law but as a consuming fire. Hence it was requisite, in order to reconciliation, that Christ as Mediator should fully answer the demands of law and justice, and so procure for the sinner new access both to God and to His law. Accordingly, uniting sinners to Himself, and hereby interesting them in His righteousness, the Lord Jesus, by His Holy Spirit, writes the law in their heart and erects a new sovereignty over them, according to which the law is again made the measure and the rule of their duty. God indeed still rules His people by issuing His commands and accepting their obedience, but this is only in and by His beloved Son the Mediator, without whom He cannot, consistently with the honor of His infinite holiness, have intercourse anymore with creatures who have sinned against Him. This appears to be one reason why the law is given

The Conclusion

to them from God, not immediately, but in and by the Mediator, and why it is called the law of Christ (Galatians 6:2).

The moral law as an unalterable rule of duty to mankind was, in its obligation, antecedent to any covenant that could be made with man; and therefore that obligation could not be affected by any. As it requires conformity to the nature and obedience to the will of God it was binding on Adam before the covenant of works was made with him, and will continue to be obligatory on him and his posterity even through eternity. The spiritual seed of Christ not only remain under their original obligation to keep that law but, by coming into the covenant of grace, they come under a new, an additional, and a peculiar obligation to obey it, an obligation that is to be discharged in the strength of Christ, their Covenant-head; so that, strictly speaking, there is more obedience to the moral law in the covenant of grace than there was in the covenant of works. Believers are bound not merely as others are to obey the law considered as creatures, formed and preserved by the almighty Creator, but they are brought under new and peculiar obligations to obey it, considered as new, as redeemed creatures. The infinite, immutable, and eternal grace of the new covenant lays them under new, infinite, immutable, and eternal obligations to yield even perfect obedience to that law as a rule. Their deliverance in their justification from the covenant of the law lays them under the strongest possible obligations to obey the commandment of the law. Righteousness imputed obliges as well as constrains them to the love and practice of righteousness inherent. The gift of eternal life to them binds them in an infinite degree to work from life, and to live in obedience. They are under the firmest possible ties to obey the law not only because it is the law of Jehovah, the self-existent, the supreme Majesty of heaven and earth, but because it is the law of their own God, and at the same time the law of Christ who loved them, and by His blood redeemed them to God. When they were under the bondage of the covenant of works they were, by the rigor thereof, withheld from serving the Lord in newness of Spirit (Romans 7:6). But now that they are delivered from that bondage and are brought into the covenant of grace they are free; and as they are capacitated, so they are obliged to run in the way of His commandments. If the reader is delivered from the first covenant and received into the second, instead of saying "I am now exempted from all obligation to keep the commands of the law as a rule," he will on the contrary say, "I dare not but keep them. I must out of duty, I will out of gratitude [One of the ancients says, "He finds the benefits that iron finds." This beautiful sentiment might almost serve as a comment on the tender declaration of Jehovah by his prophet Hosea: "I drew them to obedience with cords of a man, with bands of love," chapter 11:4. He who intimately knows our frame knew that these motives would be the most powerful in operation on the hearts of creatures capable of love and susceptible of gratitude. He therefore calls them the cords of a man]; and from the bent of my renewed nature, I cannot but perform obedience to them" (Titus 3:8; Psalm 116:12; Acts 4:20).

The duty then in general of those who are within the covenant of grace is, in dependence on the grace of Christ, to perform sincere, universal, unremitting, and even perfect obedience to the moral law in the hand of the glorious Mediator as the rule and measure of their duty. But more particularly...

1. It is their duty at all times to trust in the Lord Jesus as their righteousness and strength for the grace and comfort that are promised in the covenant, to apply the promises, and in every case to trust that Christ will perform these to them, and that in so doing He will, by His Holy Spirit, work in them both to will and to do. It is the bound duty of each of them, in the exer-

The Conclusion

cise of unsuspecting confidence in Him, to say, "Though I walk in the midst of trouble, Thou wilt revive me; Thou wilt stretch forth Thine hand against the wrath of mine enemies, and Thy right hand will save me. The Lord will perfect that which concerneth me" (Psalm 138:7, 8). The way to perform good works acceptably is humbly to trust that Jesus Christ gives us His Spirit to work in us all the good pleasure of His goodness, and so to attempt the performance of them in the confidence that, according to His promise, He will put his Spirit within us and so cause us to walk in His statutes, to keep His judgments and do them (Ezekiel 36:27). Suppose it were in a man's power to perform good works without trusting in Christ for continual supplies of grace; yet he could not, without doing this, perform one of the least of them so as to please God. Without faith it is impossible to please Him (Hebrews 11:6). If obedience is not performed in the faith of new supplies of spiritual strength from the promise of the covenant, it may be obedience, but it cannot be new obedience. Consider, Christian, that it is your present duty, your first work, to live upon the promises; to trust firmly that the grace of them will in all conditions be sufficient for you. Account them the capital stock, the inexhaustible fund, that you have to trust in, and rely on them with settled, with unshaken confidence (Psalm 119:162). However little you may have in hand, you have in reserve a full covenant of promises, that are heaven's bonds and securities and that, in the estimation of faith, make a good stock. Thus reckon that, although in yourself you have nothing, yet in Christ, and in the promises, you possess all things (2 Corinthians 6:10; Colossians 2:10). Does the number or the greatness of your sins dampen the exercise of your confidence in the Savior for the grace of the promise? Consider that it is contrary to the tenor of the covenant of grace to think that the number or greatness of your transgressions should hinder, or even for a moment retard, your coming to Jesus for pardon and purification. To think so arises from a self-righteous spirit, from a rooted adherence to merit in the creature, as requisite to procure the favor of God. In opposition to this, the covenant, well-ordered in all things, authorizes you to come as an unworthy sinner to the overflowing fullness of Christ for salvation from the guilt and from the prevalence of sin. Remember too that it is no less contrary to the covenant of grace and the freeness of salvation to suppose that you must not lay hold on promised mercy till you have first purposed or done something to give you a right to apprehend it. The only effectual method of alluring and reconciling the heart to spiritual obedience, as well as of breaking the power of sin, is, upon the warrant of the gospel-offer and call, to come as a sinner and trust in Jesus for pardoning mercy and sanctifying grace. Nothing will so effectually retard your progress in holiness and obstruct your comfort, as your yielding to distrust and despondence. Believe then in the Lord your God, so shall you be established. Believe His prophets, and so shall you prosper (2 Chronicles 20:20).

2. It is also their duty frequently to renew, according to the covenant, their unreserved dedication of themselves to God in Christ. To take hold of God's covenant of grace, or of God in Christ with all that He is and has, and thereupon to dedicate one's self with all that he is and has to Him, to be for Him and not for another, seem jointly to be what our forefathers used to call "personal covenanting with God." And indeed when Jehovah, in the boundless riches of His grace, gives Himself with all that He is and has to them, and enables them to accept Him as their God, they are doubtless under infinite obligations in return to resign themselves and all that they are and have as His peculiar people to Him. When He, according to the covenant, bestows Himself on them to be theirs wholly and perpetually,

they are bound by every possible tie cordially to give up in return themselves to Him, to be His wholly and forever. The great promise of the covenant is, "I will be to them a God, and they shall be to Me a people" (Hebrews 8:10). Consenting, then, according to the promise, to have God for their God, they cannot at the same time but consent to be His people, and as such to love, to serve, to glorify, and to enjoy Him forevermore. As it is your inestimable privilege, O believer, to have Jehovah for your covenant-God, so it is your bound duty heartily to surrender yourself to Him as one of His redeemed people; to resign yourself as by nature a lost and helpless sinner to Him, your almighty Deliverer; as a poor and empty creature to Him, your infinitely rich and benevolent Friend, your sure and satisfying portion; and, as an difficult and unprofitable servant to Him, your all-wise and gracious Lord who will form you for Himself to show forth His praise (Isaiah 43:21). O love nothing, desire nothing, possess nothing, delight in nothing besides Him, but for him; enjoy nothing but in him, and devote most willingly, all that thou art and hast, to him, to be wholly disposed of for the purposes of his glory.

3. It is their duty so to obey all His commands that their obedience shall always run in the channel of the covenant. All their obedience must be the obedience of faith. Their duty is first to trust that the Lord Jesus is their Covenant-head, and that God in Him is their covenant-God, in order to all their other acts of obedience; or first to believe and then to do. To place obedience before faith, or as the foundation of faith, is opposite to the manner of the covenant. All the obedience of His people must be presented to the Lord as their own God in covenant. It is only by obeying in this manner that they fear this glorious and fearful name, "The Lord Their God" (Deuteronomy 28:58). Their obedience is not to be performed for a justifying right-

eousness, but for a testimony of their gratitude to the Lord their righteousness; not in their own strength, but in that of the Lord their almighty Redeemer; not from a slavish fear of hell, nor a servile hope of heaven, but from fervent love to Him who, by His righteousness, has redeemed them from hell and entitled them to heaven; not that it may be accepted for its own worth, but for the infinite merit of the divine Savior. In all that they do, they ought to act under the influence of the covenant of grace and not under that of the covenant of works. The covenant into which they have come is a covenant of boundless grace. Let therefore the grace of this covenant, believer, be your grand motive to holy obedience (2 Corinthians 5:14). Let all your obedience be free, voluntary, and disinterested.

4. It is likewise their duty to diligently keep all the ordinances that the Lord Jesus, in His administration of the covenant, has appointed to be observed. These are, "prayer and thanksgiving in the name of Christ; the reading, preaching, and hearing of the Word; the administration and receiving of the sacraments; church government and discipline; the ministry and maintenance thereof; religious fasting; swearing by the name of God, and vowing to Him" (Larger Catechism Question 108). Now it is the duty of His redeemed, in daily dependence on the grace of the covenant, to receive these ordinances, to observe them, and to keep them pure and entire. It is their duty to receive them, that is, to approve and embrace them as devised and appointed by Christ, the King of Zion (Psalm 84:1, 2 and 26:8). They are also bound to observe those ordinances, that is, to regard them attentively, to keep them religiously, and to practice them diligently (Psalm 55:17 and 119:164). They ought likewise to keep them pure, which is to endeavor as much as possible to preserve them from all mixtures of human invention (Deuteronomy 12:32; Revelation 22:18). It is no less incumbent on

them to keep them entire or, in other words, to keep them unbroken, undivided, and to attend on each of them in its proper season. It is recorded to the honor of the grace of God in Zacharias and Elisabeth that they both walked in all the commandments and ordinances of the Lord blameless (Luke 1:6). Those ordinances are appointed means by which the Lord Jesus communicates the grace of the covenant to His people; and therefore He has commanded them diligently and constantly to use them for that important purpose.

5. It is also the duty of Christ's spiritual seed cordially to espouse any interests and invariably to pursue the designs of the covenant. Having been graciously received into the bond of the covenant, they are bound heartily to espouse the interests of it and frequently to offer up this prayer: "Thy kingdom come. Thy will be done on earth as it is in heaven." Their own interest is in the covenant, wrapped up with that of the kingdom and glory of Christ; and therefore they should make the interests of His kingdom in the world their own and so war the good warfare against the devil, the world, and the flesh, those enemies of the covenant, and of all who are within it. They ought to treat the friends of their Covenant-God as their friends, and His enemies as their enemies.

They are likewise obliged constantly to pursue the designs of the covenant. These are the mortification of the body of sin in themselves and others, and the acceptable service of their God and Savior. For this purpose the Son of God was manifested, that, according to the covenant, He might destroy the works of the devil (1 John 3:8). Now this great design of the covenant they are bound, in union and communion with Him, constantly to pursue. Study, O Christian, in dependence on the grace of Christ, daily to mortify the members of the body of sin in yourself; and endeavor, as often as you have opportunity, to weaken the power of sin in others around you. Serve the Lord your God without slavish fear, in holiness and righteousness before Him. Serve Him with gladness (1 John 3:8), and with holy diligence, in all the acts of spiritual worship and in all the duties of Christian morality. And thus, as the holy Apostle Paul did, follow after, if that you may apprehend that for which also you are apprehended of by Christ Jesus. Forgetting those things that are behind, and reaching forth unto those things that are before, press toward the marks for the prize of the high calling of God in Christ Jesus (Philippians 3:12-14). Seeing that holiness, next to the glory of God, is the great end of the covenant, long earnestly and pray fervently for the increase and even the perfection of holiness in your soul.

6. It is incumbent on believers, at all times, to walk worthy of the covenant. To do so is to have their behavior such as it becomes the gospel of Christ, in which that holy covenant is exhibited to men. The principles and the practice of all who have been received into the covenant ought in everything to be suitable to the covenant. The duty of such is to walk worthy of the Parties contracting in the covenant, to walk worthy of the Lord unto all pleasing (Colossians 1:10), and to be followers of God as dear children (Ephesians 5:1). It is their duty and ought to be their delight to imitate God, their covenant-God and Father, in all His imitable perfections, striving to advance daily, in conformity to His holy nature and will, and at the same time to be conformed more and more to the image of Christ His Son (Romans 8:29; 1 John 2:6). They ought also to be heavenly in their mind and behavior (Philippians 3:20) because God, who made the covenant, and Christ, with whom it was made, are in heaven. The stupendous love of the Father, of the Son, and of the Holy Spirit, should constrain them to seek and to set their affection on the things that are above, where Christ sits on the

The Conclusion

right hand of God (Colossians 3:1, 2). They ought to walk suitably to the conditions of the covenant. While all their hope of eternal life is built on the perfect righteousness of Jesus Christ, they are infinitely bound, in dependence on His grace, daily to present to the law as a rule increasing conformity of nature and of life, and to have their old man so crucified in conformity to Him as more and more to die to sin.

They are likewise obliged to walk suitably to the promises of the covenant. They ought constantly to believe them, and that with application to themselves. They should attempt to perform no duty, to endure no affliction, to resist no temptation, but in the faith of the promises, and of grace promised. It is the believing of the promises that brings in comfort from the covenant, when other sources of consolation fail. Moreover, it is the duty of believers to behave suitably to the administration of the covenant. This they are to do by coming to the Lord Jesus for all that they need; by having respect to all His commandments as their Lord and King (Psalm 119:6); by submitting willingly to the discipline of the covenant as administered by Him; and by believing that all His dispensations to them are infinitely well-ordered for their good.

7. The people of God are, according to the covenant, bound to watch against backsliding; or against falling off to those lusts that they served when they were strangers to the covenant. As obedient children they ought not to fashion themselves according to the former lusts in their ignorance (1 Peter 1:14). The people of the first covenant are dead in their sins because, under that covenant, death reigns, and living lusts prey on their souls as worms do on a dead body in the grave; whereas under the second covenant life reigns, and believing sinners, being restored to spiritual life, put off the old man, which is corrupt according to the deceitful lusts (Ephesians 4:22). Guard then, O

believer, guard incessantly, against backsliding, either in principle or in practice. How terrible is this threatening: "The backslider in heart shall be filled with his own ways" (Proverbs 14:14). Trust daily, and trust with all your heart, that your almighty Savior will preserve you from backsliding. Believe that He will, and pray that He may, perform this promise to you: "The just by his faith shall live" (Habakkuk 2:4). Beware of yielding to the motions of that legal spirit that remains in you; for this would be a turning back to the broken covenant of works, where spiritual death reigns, and would be a provoking of the Lord to hide His face from you, and to leave you for a season under the dreadful prevalence of spiritual declension and deadness.

8. The covenant in which the saints are instated obliges them to beware of being conformed to this world (Romans 12:2). As a separate company, under a new covenant and a new Head, they are bound by the firmest ties not to choose the company, nor to conform to the way, of worldly men. Why would the believer choose their company? They are not going his way. By his having taken hold of the covenant, he has declared himself to be of a different, nay, of a contrary society. Why then would he desire to be as they are or to do as they do? Why would he be again molded into the depraved habits and tempers, the evil courses and manners, of worldly and wicked men? Why would he who is an heir of glory, an expectant of celestial blessedness, choose to imitate the evil practices, the depraved customs, of them who walk according to the course of this world and mind earthly things.

9. The people of the covenant are indispensably bound to glorify God in their body and in their spirit, which are His. The Apostle Paul, writing to the believers at Corinth, says, "Ye are not your own; for ye are bought with a price; therefore glorify

God in your body, and in your spirit, which are God's" (1 Corinthians 6:19, 20). The saints are no longer their own, but are by covenant the Lord's. God has offered His holy covenant to them; and they, by taking hold thereof, have come into the bond of it. Hence they are Christ's, and Christ is God's. Let this then, O believer, be your answer to every temptation with which you may be assailed: "I am not now at my own disposal; for I am Christ's, and Christ, with me united to Him, is God's." Say, as Jephthah said to his daughter, "I have opened my mouth unto the Lord, and I cannot go back" (Judges 11:35). If the men of the first covenant say, "Our lips are our own; who is lord over us?" (Psalm 12:4) you cannot say so; for, by having taken hold of His covenant you have said, "I am the Lord's" (Isaiah 44:5). Are you bought with a price? Are you redeemed for the service and enjoyment of the infinitely blessed God, and that with the precious blood of His only begotten, His incarnate Son? Is your body, according to the covenant, the temple of the Holy Spirit, and are you a habitation of God through the Spirit? Oh, let it then be your constant care, your diligent endeavor, in the faith of promised grace, to yield your soul and all its faculties, your body and all its members, as instruments of righteousness to your gracious God that they may be always employed for the glory of His holy name.

10. Finally, it is no less their duty earnestly to long and diligently to prepare for the endless blessedness promised in the covenant. Laying hold on eternal life by embracing the promise of it, long, O believer, long ardently, long incessantly, for that perfect vision and fruition of God and the Lamb; for that perfect conformity to the adored Immanuel, and for that ineffable and endless joy in the blissful presence of Jehovah, Father, Son and Holy Spirit, of which you have received the promise and the pledge. Let your hope of the completion of eternal life be more

lively and the exercise of it more frequent; for the more firmly you expect the blessedness of heaven, the more ardently will you desire it. "Looking for that blessed hope, and the glorious appearing of the great God, even our Savior Jesus Christ" (Titus 2:13). Gird up, dear Christian, the loins of your mind; be sober and hope to the end for the grace that is to be brought unto you at the revelation of Jesus Christ (1 Peter 1:13). Be diligent also in preparing for the felicity promised in the covenant. Study to be actually as well as habitually prepared. Let every duty be conscientiously and seasonably performed; and see that it is performed spiritually, or in the lively exercise of the graces of the Spirit in you. Do not be slothful, but be a follower of them who, through faith and patience, inherit the promises (Hebrews 6:12). "Grieve not the Holy Spirit of God, whereby thou art sealed unto the day of redemption" (Ephesians 4:30); but, on the contrary, invite and cherish His gracious influences on your soul; and so grow in grace, and in the knowledge of our Lord and Savior Jesus Christ. "To Him be glory both now and forever. Amen." (2 Peter 3:18)